Auxiliaries are one of the most complex areas of English syntax. Disagreement over both the principles and details of their grammar has been substantial. Anthony Warner here offers a new and detailed account of both their synchronic and diachronic properties. He first argues that lexical properties are central to their grammar, which is relatively nonabstract. He then traces in detail the history of processes of grammaticalization in their development, and claims most notably that we can identify a group of auxiliaries in English from an early period on formal, not just semantic, grounds.

This book meets the dual challenge of accounting for both the grammar and the history of the English auxiliary. It will be essential reading for all those interested in English syntax and its history.

CAMBRIDGE STUDIES IN LINGUISTICS

English auxiliaries

In this series

40 KENNETH J. SAFIR: *Syntactic chains*
41 J. MILLER: *Semantics and syntax*
42 H. C. BUNT: *Mass terms and model theoretic semantics*
43 HEINZ J. GIEGERICH: *Metrical phonology and phonological structure*
44 JOHN HAIMAN: *Natural syntax*
45 BARBARA M. HORVATH: *Variation in Australian English: the sociolects of Sydney*
46 GRANT GOODALL: *Parallel structures in syntax; coordination, causatives, and restructuring*
47 JOHN M. ANDERSON and COLIN J. EWEN: *Principles of dependency phonology*
48 BARBARA A. FOX: *Discourse structure and anaphora*
49 LAUREL J. BRINTON: *The development of English aspectual systems*
50 DONNA JO NAPOLI: *Predication theory*
51 NOEL BURTON-ROBERTS: *The limits to debate: a revised theory of semantic presupposition*
52 MICHAEL S. ROCHEMONT and PETER W. CULICOVER: *English focus constructions and the theory of grammar*
53 PHILIP CARR: *Linguistic realities: an autonomist metatheory for the generative enterprise*
54 EVE SWEETSER: *From etymology to pragmatics: metaphorical and cultural aspects of semantic structure*
55 REGINA BLASS: *Relevance relations in discourse: a study with special reference to Sissala*
56 ANDREW CHESTERMAN: *On definiteness: a study with special reference to English and Finnish*
57 ALESSANDRA GIORGI and GIUSEPPE LONGOBARDI: *The syntax of Noun Phrases: configuration, parameters and empty categories*
58 MONIK CHARETTE: *Conditions on phonological government*
59 M. H. KLAIMAN: *Grammatical voice*
60 SARAH M. B. FAGAN: *The syntax and semantics of middle constructions: a study with special reference to German*
61 ANJUM P. SALEEMI: *Universal Grammar and language learnability*
62 STEPHEN R. ANDERSON: *A-Morphous Morphology*
63 LESLEY STIRLING: *Switch reference and discourse representation*
64 HENK J. VERKUYL: *A theory of aspectuality: the interaction between temporal and atemporal structure*
65 EVE V. CLARK: *The lexicon in acquisition*
66 ANTHONY R. WARNER: *English auxiliaries: structure and history*

Supplementary volumes

RUDOLF P. BOTHA: *Form and meaning in word formation: a study of Afrikaans reduplication*
AYHAN AKSU-KOC: *The acquisition of aspect and modality: the case of past reference in Turkish*
MICHEAL O SIADHAIL: *Modern Irish: grammatical structure and dialectal variation*
ANNICK DE HOUWER: *The acquisition of two languages from birth: a case study*
LILIANE HAEGEMAN: *Theory and description in generative syntax: a case study in West Flemish*

Earlier issues not listed are also available

ENGLISH AUXILIARIES

Structure and history

ANTHONY R. WARNER

Lecturer in English Language and Linguistics,
Department of Language and Linguistic Science,
University of York

CAMBRIDGE UNIVERSITY PRESS
Cambridge, New York, Melbourne, Madrid, Cape Town, Singapore, São Paulo, Delhi

Cambridge University Press
The Edinburgh Building, Cambridge CB2 8RU, UK

Published in the United States of America by Cambridge University Press, New York

www.cambridge.org
Information on this title: www.cambridge.org/9780521103213

First published 1993
Reprinted 1995
This digitally printed version 2009

A catalogue record for this publication is available from the British Library

Library of Congress Cataloguing in Publication data

Warner, Anthony.
English auxiliaries: structure and history / Anthony R. Warner.
p. cm. – (Cambridge studies in linguistics; 66)
Includes bibliographical references and index.
ISBN 0-521-30284-6
1. English language – Auxiliary verbs. 2. English language – Syntax. I. Title.
II. Series
PE1315.A8W37 1993
425–dc20 92-41068 CIP

ISBN 978-0-521-30284-5 hardback
ISBN 978-0-521-10321-3 paperback

Contents

For Trish, Kate, David and Philip

Preface

Auxiliaries (words such as *must, shall, is*) are central to English grammar. They are also puzzlingly complex in their behaviour. So much so that disagreement about their nature has been radical, and they remain a major area of difficulty. The interest of this area is compounded by the possibility of working out its history in some detail, given the abundant data available for earlier periods of English. It is clear that the area was much less well defined in earlier times; indeed it has even been claimed that modals were not to be distinguished grammatically from straightforward verbs at the earliest periods for which we have substantial records. Thus change has apparently been considerable. This means that the process of change will itself be important and interesting, and that we may achieve some insights into the nature of the modern category from an understanding of its development. So there is a major twofold challenge: to provide an appropriate synchronic account of English auxiliaries, and to show how this area of grammar developed historically. These are the twin challenges taken up in this book.

First, then, I have established a new account of the working of the modern auxiliary system. Its distinctive claim is that although auxiliaries carry apparently verbal categories such as 'finite' or 'infinitive' these are not inflectional in auxiliaries but are lexically specified, so that forms such as *should* or *been* behave in some respects like independent items. This leads to a simple, new and nonabstract account of a range of the properties of auxiliaries in terms of their distinctness from verbs, and to a fundamentally 'lexical' account of major properties of this 'grammatical' area. Secondly, I have investigated the historical development of this system. This has meant both justifying appropriate analyses for earlier stages of the language, and providing a historical interpretation. So I give a detailed review (and reinterpretation) of relevant data in the history of auxiliaries, and add to that some more speculative comments on changes in their categoriality and the rationale for such changes. My most striking historical claim is that we can identify a group of 'auxiliaries' in English from an early period on formal (not just semantic) grounds. So I disagree with Lightfoot's (1979) seminal claim that the category of modals was established *de novo* rather suddenly in the sixteenth century, while finding more evidence for a shift in the nature of their categoryhood at this period. My account reconciles two puzzling aspects of the development of this class: that it is apparently a gradual, long-term matter, but that there is a clustering of changes focussed on the sixteenth century. And *en route* there is something to say on such matters as the development of 'periphrastic' *do* and of the double-*ing* constraint.

I am grateful to those who have helped to improve the book: to David Lightfoot and Frank Palmer, who read the whole book and gave me very useful comments; to Roger Lass, who gave me some specific and valuable advice; to Bob Borsley, Gerald Gazdar, Carl Pollard for their very helpful comments on particular sections of the book; to my colleagues Patrick Griffiths and Steve Harlow for a variety of discussions over the years; and to Robert E. Lewis, editor-in-chief of the *Middle English Dictionary*, for kindly supplying me with information from the *MED*'s files. Needless to say I have not taken all the advice offered me, and whatever you think is cranky, muddle-headed or plain wrong is my fault.

I am grateful to my colleagues at York for teaching-free terms in 1986 (Chapters 5 and much of 6), 1989 (Chapters 2 and much of 9) and 1991 (when I finally finished the first draft of the whole). Thank you also to Suzie Roberts (who typed Chapter 7), to Elizabeth McKeown, who helped with the tedious task of transferring the manuscript from one word-processing system to another, and to David Newton for preparing the indexes. Much of Chapter 5 appeared in print as Warner (1992a): I am grateful to John Donald of Edinburgh for permission to republish this material. Finally, thank you to Cambridge University Press for their willingness to tolerate an author who took so much longer than he said he would. I can only plead the novelist's commonplace, that the characters are prone to highjack the plot. The modals, *be* and *have* were simply intolerant of my initial attempts at a swiftly written history. They insisted on having things their way, and our developing relationship took time.

This book is for Trish, who shares my life, which has included more auxiliaries than one human should ask of another, and for Kate, David and Philip, who have allowed me to steal time that should really have been theirs, and who have tolerated an abstracted dad who seemed to care more about *can't* and *won't* than about building a tree house. But the tree house was, after all, completed before the book.

Abbreviations and references to primary texts

General abbreviations

ASW	Akmajian, Steele and Wasow (1979)
BT	*An Anglo-Saxon Dictionary Based on the Manuscript Collections of the Late Joseph Bosworth*, edited and enlarged by T. Northcote Toller. London: Oxford University Press. 1898
BTS	*An Anglo-Saxon Dictionary Based on the Manuscript Collections of the Late Joseph Bosworth. Supplement,* edited by T. Northcote Toller. London: Oxford University Press. 1921, and *Enlarged Addenda and Corrigenda to the Supplement*, edited by A. Campbell, Oxford: Clarendon Press. 1972
e	early (as in eME: early Middle English)
EDD	*The English Dialect Dictionary* edited by Joseph Wright. 6 vols. Oxford University Press, 1896–1905
EETS (OS)	Publications of the Early English Texts Society, Ordinary Series
EETS ES	Publications of the Early English Texts Society, Extra Series
EETS SS	Publications of the Early English Texts Society, Supplementary Series
GB	Government–Binding
GPS	Gazdar, Pullum and Sag (1982)
GPSG	Generalized Phrase Structure Grammar
HPSG	Head-driven Phrase Structure Grammar
l	late (as in lME: late Middle English)
M§234	Mitchell (1985: §234)
ME	Middle English (twelfth to fifteenth century)
MED	*Middle English Dictionary*, ed. by Hans Kurath, Sherman M. Kuhn, Robert E. Lewis and John Reidy. Ann Arbor: University of Michigan Press (1954–)
ModE	Modern English (sixteenth century to the present)
NE	New English = Modern English (sixteenth century to the present)

OE	Old English (records mainly from the ninth to eleventh century)
OED	*The Oxford English Dictionary*, ed. by J. A. H. Murray, H. Bradley, W. A. Craigie, and C. T. Onions. Oxford: Clarendon Press. 1933
PE	Present-day English
V§345	Visser (1963–73: §345)

References to primary texts

I have often used abbreviations in references to Old English texts: for the major prose texts those of Mitchell (1985 vol. I: xxxiv ff., vol. II: xliv ff.); for minor prose texts those of Healey and Venezky (1980). These are expanded below, as are abbreviated references to the poetry. Citations from later texts are preceded by their date. For Middle English texts I give the dates assigned by the *Middle English Dictionary*. This gives the date of the manuscript without parentheses or the date of composition in parentheses or both. If the presumed or conjectured date of composition is at least twenty-five years earlier than the date of the manuscript, then (for the dictionary's preferred manuscripts) the date of the manuscript is followed in parentheses by the date of composition. But where the date of composition is well established and is less than twenty-five years earlier than the date of the manuscript, only the date of composition is given (in parentheses). Citations from Chaucer and Shakespeare are from the following editions:

The Works of Geoffrey Chaucer, ed. F. N. Robinson, 2nd edn, London: Oxford University Press. 1957

William Shakespeare: the Complete Works, ed. Peter Alexander, London and Glasgow: Collins. 1951

For other citations I have given bibliographical information, or have referred the reader to a source such as Visser (1963–73) or *The Oxford English Dictionary*, which contains the citation.

Abbreviations of Old English texts

ÆAdmon 1	Admonitio ad filium spiritualem. *The Anglo-Saxon Version of the Hexameron of St. Basil ...* , ed. H. W. Norman, London 1848, 32–56
ÆCHom i	*The Sermones Catholici* or *Homilies of Ælfric*, vol I, ed. B. Thorpe, London: Ælfric Society. 1844

ÆCHom ii	*Ælfric's Catholic Homilies: the Second Series*, ed. M. Godden, EETS SS 5, London 1979
ÆColl	*Ælfric's Colloquy*, ed. G. N. Garmonsway (Methuen Old English Library) 2nd edn. London: Methuen. 1947
ÆGram	*Ælfrics Grammatik und Glossar*, ed. J. Zupitza (Sammlung englischer Denkmäler I) Berlin 1880
ÆLS	*Ælfric's Lives of Saints*, ed. W. W. Skeat, EETS 76, 82, 94, 114, London 1881–1900
ÆTemp	*Ælfric's De Temporibus Anni*, ed. H. Henel, EETS 213, London 1942
ASPR I	*The Junius Manuscript* (The Anglo-Saxon Poetic Records I), ed. G. P. Krapp, New York: Columbia University Press. 1931
ASPR III	*The Exeter Book* (The Anglo-Saxon Poetic Records III), ed. G. P. Krapp and E. V. K. Dobbie, New York: Columbia University Press. 1936
ASPR IV	*Beowulf and Judith* (The Anglo-Saxon Poetic Records IV), ed. E. V. K. Dobbie, New York: Columbia University Press. 1953
ASPR V	*The Paris Psalter and The Meters of Boethius* (The Anglo-Saxon Poetic Records V), ed. G. P. Krapp, New York: Columbia University Press. 1932
ASPR VI	*The Anglo-Saxon Minor Poems* (The Anglo-Saxon Poetic Records VI), ed. E. V. K. Dobbie, New York: Columbia University Press. 1942
Bede	*The Old English Version of Bede's Ecclesiastical History of the English People*, ed. T. Miller, EETS 95, 96, 110, 111. London 1890–8
BlHom	*The Blickling Homilies*, ed R. Morris, EETS 58, 63, 73. London 1874–80
Bo	*King Ælfred's Old English Version of Boethius' De Consolatione Philosophiae*, ed. W. J. Sedgefield, Oxford 1899
ChronA	*Two of the Saxon Chronicles Parallel*, ed. C. Plummer, Oxford, Clarendon Press 1892–9. The Parker MS: Corpus Christi College, Cambridge 173
ChronE	*Two of the Saxon Chronicles Parallel*, ed. C. Plummer, Oxford, Clarendon Press 1892–9. The Laud MS: Bodley Laud Misc. 636

CP	*King Ælfred's West-Saxon Version of Gregory's Pastoral Care*, ed. H. Sweet, EETS 45, 50, London 1871
GD	*Bischof Waeferths von Worcester Uebersetzung der Dialoge Gregors des Grossen* (Bibliothek der angelsächsischen Prosa 5), ed. H. Hecht, Leipzig and Hamburg 1900–7
HomS 34 (Peterson VercHom 19)	Sermon for Monday in Rogationtide. The Unpublished Homilies of the Vercelli Book, ed. P. W. Peterson, New York dissertation 1951, 43–51
LawGer	*Die Gesetze der Angelsachsen*, ed. F. Liebermann, Halle. 1903–16, 453–5
LawICn	*Die Gesetze der Angelsachsen*, ed. F. Liebermann, Halle. 1903–16, 278–306
Or	*King Ælfred's Orosius*, ed. H. Sweet, EETS 79. London 1883
WHom	*The Homilies of Wulfstan*, ed. D. Bethurum, Oxford: Clarendon Press. 1957

1 *Basic properties of English auxiliaries*

1.1 Introduction

This book aims to give an account of the grammar and history of English auxiliaries, that is of words like those italicized here:

(1) *Could* John *have* written it if Mary *didn't*? – No, it *wasn't* written by a man.

Since this group includes words associated with modality, aspect, tense and voice (as in *could, have, didn't, wasn't*) they have often been labelled 'auxiliary' or 'helping' verbs, where an auxiliary is 'a verb used to form the tenses, moods, voices, etc. of other verbs' (*OED* Auxiliary, *a.* and *sb.* B *sb.* 3). This terminology encodes the traditional view that such properties are fundamentally those of verbs, as they are (for example) in the Latin one-word forms *cantabo, cantarem, cantabatur* in contrast with the corresponding English (*I*) *shall sing*, (*I*) *might sing*, (*it*) *was being sung*.

The problems of the present-day analysis and the historical development of this group of words have been a major area for discussion and disagreement in recent years. In this book I will present and justify new analyses in both structure and history. In the first half of the book I will argue that the most appropriate characterization of some of the major idiosyncrasies of the English auxiliary system follows directly from the nature of the categorial relationship between auxiliary and full verb. Auxiliaries do not share morphosyntactic generalizations appropriate to full verbs. Instead we need a fundamentally lexical account of the interrelationships between their categories. This insight leads to a fresh and illuminating account of ordering restrictions on English auxiliaries, of restrictions on the availability of their morphosyntactic categories, of their distribution in ellipsis and of some other individual properties. It also supplies a freshly argued and more detailed answer to the perennial question of whether auxiliaries are like (main) verbs and essentially just a subclass of verb.

The second half of the book will examine the history of English auxiliaries from the earliest times. It is clear that they developed from full verbs, but there is dispute as to whether this happened rather suddenly in the sixteenth century or more gradually. I will show clearly that there was already a subordinate 'auxiliary' word class in Old English with distinctive formal characteristics, not just a group of verbs which happened to have uses which were 'auxiliary' in some loosely semantic or functional way. Then I will discuss and interpret the formal and semantic history of this group in early English and the rapid sharpening of its properties at the beginning of Modern English. The rise of periphrastic *do* will also be shown to fit coherently with the more general history of auxiliaries. This all requires the development of a more structured view of word classes. I will suggest an account which is related to work in psychology and 'cognitive grammar', and in which the lexicon is appropriately seen as a point of contact between principles of generative grammar and more general principles of cognitive organization. I will also develop a coherent view of the nature of processes of grammaticalization within this area, and discuss the relevance of possible universal characteristics of a class 'auxiliary'. But I would not claim to have given a complete account of the history. Instead, I have focussed on a coherent area of study which has proved very illuminating and which will form part of a more complete account.

The general assumptions of the argument are those of a relatively nonabstract lexically based syntax. My basic reason for choosing this type of framework is that I have come to think that a major series of generalizations about the auxiliary system of Present-day English essentially involves the lexicon and word-class structure. So the framework is simply the one which most closely reflects the essential properties of the data as I see it. For most of the book the argument is conducted without formalism, but a brief formal account of the present-day system will be given within Head-driven Phrase Structure Grammar in Chapter 3. This belongs to the general class of unification-based approaches to grammar (represented also, for example, by Generalized Phrase Structure Grammar and Lexical Functional Grammar). It has the advantage that unification formalism is coherent, and offers rather simple, general and insightful accounts. The major current alternative is Government–Binding. What I have to say is, however, largely independent of current preoccupations in that area, though I believe my conclusions are (and should be seen as) relevant. But whatever view is taken of the relative merits of these theoretical approaches, it is important to maintain a healthy pluralism despite (or perhaps because of) the recent rapid development of analyses of clause and auxiliary systems, in particular following Pollock (1989).

The central focus of this book is on the grammar of English, and not on the development of any particular linguistic theory. It is partial in that it focusses on the properties of words: the reader will not find here a compositional semantics of auxiliary structures, or an account of the progressive. I have found Head-driven Phrase Structure Grammar most centrally relevant because it supplies an appropriate account for the data as I interpret it. But the general argument is not particular to this framework, and it will be relevant to work within other theories in two kinds of way. First, as complementary. It must surely be common ground within any modular approach that there is a considerable place for lexical and lexical class properties within grammar. What I have done should therefore be more or less directly complementary to other types of account. And secondly, I give distinctive rationales for some of the properties of auxiliaries in Present-day English and for their historical development. These offer distinct ways of thinking about some of these grammatical properties.

1.2 Traditional criteria for auxiliaries

The first half of this book is devoted to the grammar of auxiliaries in Present-day English. Chapter 2 argues in detail for a particular type of lexical account, and Chapter 3 provides a short formal account. In this chapter I first review the traditional criteria which distinguish English auxiliaries and discuss the semantic identity of this group. Then I briefly discuss the basic assumptions of my analysis and provide a rapid review of previous work within the generative tradition.

The English auxiliaries are rather sharply defined as a group by distinctive formal properties. The group includes both modal auxiliaries (principally *can*, *could*; *may*, *might*; *must*; *shall*, *should*; *will*, *would*) and non-modal auxiliaries (*be*, *have* and *do*); a full list is given below. Here I will briefly review the traditional formal criteria for auxiliaryhood. This is well-trodden territory, and will be familiar to many readers; see especially Palmer (1988: 14ff.), Huddleston (1980) and Quirk *et al.* (1985: §3.21ff.). Notice that the most important criteria largely apply to the finite auxiliary which is often referred to as the 'operator'.

Criteria distinguishing auxiliaries from full verbs[1]

(a) *Negation.* The operator typically has a form with contracted *-n't*: *can't*, *couldn't*, *won't*, *needn't*, *isn't*, *hadn't*, *don't*, etc. unlike full verbs: **prefern't*, **stopn't*, etc. Some dialects lack *mayn't* or have it with only a restricted distribution, for example in tag questions; others (especially American) lack *mightn't*, or *shan't*, though *shall* may itself be uncommon or virtually absent (see Quirk *et al.* 1985: §3.39 note [d], §11.8 note [c]). In Standard English *am* lacks such a form, except in inversion: *aren't I?* But dialects in England normally have an *-n't* form for *am*: *aren't, amn't* or *ain't* (Hughes and Trudgill 1987: 14). Only a proportion of *-n't* forms is phonologically predictable as the addition of a cliticized *-n't* to the positive, and they are open to analysis as a series of negative forms (as traditionally in e.g. Marchand 1938), or, more recently, as carrying a negative inflection (Zwicky and Pullum 1983). Palmer (1988: 240) observes 'there is indeed a good case for talking about "a negative conjugation"'. Note that imperative *don't* occurs, but that there is no imperative *ben't* or *haven't*.

The *not* of 'sentence negation' follows the operator but not a 'full' verb. Hence the contrasts of (2). 'Periphrastic' *do* is used with the *not* of 'sentence negation' in cases where there is no other auxiliary, as in (2.c). 'Sentence negation' here is a syntactic concept, essentially equivalent to Klima's 'strong sentence negation', and a rather sharp distinction between auxiliaries and full verbs can be constructed using Klima's tests to separate instances like (3.a), which lacks 'strong sentence negation', despite its semantic closeness to (b) (Klima 1964: 270, Stockwell, Schachter and Partee 1973: 232ff.).

(2) a. She will not hurt him; you need not laugh; she was not happy; they have not the courage to proceed. (some British English)
b. *She hurt not him; *he left not; *he stopped not the exam; *when he sings he stops not.
c. She did not hurt him; he did not leave; he did not stop the exam; when he sings he does not stop.

(3) a. The baby appears not to be awake.
b. The baby doesn't appear to be awake.
(examples from Quirk *et al.* 1985: §14.36)

We must also distinguish the restricted usage of *I know not*, and the negative proform *not* (corresponding to positive *so*) of *I think not*, etc. which is not 'sentence negation'.

(4) a. I know not. *I know not whether they are coming.
b. I think not. He said not. They hope not. *I think not that they are coming.

(b) *Inversion.* Inversion of subject and finite operator is typical of a range of largely grammaticized contexts: it occurs in main clause interrogatives, in tag questions, after a fronted negative with scope over the auxiliary, in *and neither* and *and so* tags, and restrictedly in conditionals and comparatives (Quirk *et al.* 1985: §§18.24, 15.36). Tag questions may also involve ellipsis (Huddleston 1970).

(5) a. Will she hurt him? Will she not hurt him? Won't she hurt him?
b. *Goes he? *Hurts she him?
c. Does he go? Does he not go? Doesn't he go?

(6) a. You saw what was intended, didn't you?
b. At no point could I see what was intended.
c. I could see what was intended, and so could Harry.
d. Could I but have anticipated his next move, things would have been very different. (also with *had, might, should, were*)

With nonauxiliary verbs such inversions are very restricted, and there is no general pattern like that above. *How goes it?* is formulaic; the type *and so said Mary* is strictly limited in range (thus not **and neither said Mary*).

Here we must distinguish inversions of subject and verb which occur (particularly in narratives) with a range of pragmatic functions. These have a distinct pattern of distribution, and may involve the 'verbal group' as in (7.c).[2] See Quirk *et al.* (1985: §§18.23), Green (1980, 1985) for surveys.

(7) a. Round the corner came the little red engine.
b. Into the room pranced Morris.
c. By 'strategy' is meant the basic planning of the whole operation. (Quirk *et al.* 1985: §§18.23)

(c) *Ellipsis*. Auxiliaries both finite and nonfinite may appear in elliptical constructions without their normal complement, where the sense of the complement is to be retrieved from the linguistic context of utterance.

(8) a. John may come on Tuesday, but I don't think Paul will [sc. come on Tuesday].
b. – John may come on Tuesday.
– Well, I don't think Paul will [sc. come on Tuesday].
c. Paul has written to his grandmother, and I suppose Robert may have too, even if Charlie hasn't [sc. written to his grandmother].
d. – Mary is happy to eat meat or fish.
– Is she? Well Paul never has been, and John certainly won't be [sc. happy to eat meat or fish].
e. Paul will bring Mary because he should [sc. bring Mary].

I will refer to this construction as 'post-auxiliary ellipsis', not 'Verb Phrase Deletion'. The analysis this term implies is unsatisfactory for several reasons. First, there is no general ellipsis of verb phrases in English (contrary to what Akmajian, Steele and Wasow 1979 among others imply); rather ellipsis is dependent on the presence of a particular item (here an auxiliary). Secondly, *be* and *have* equally occur in this construction when the retrieved complement is a predicate phrase or noun phrase. Thirdly, since this retrieval may cross discourse, syntactic deletion was always an inappropriate analysis (Napoli 1985).

Here I accept the arguments of Hankamer and Sag (1976) and Sag (1979) that we need to distinguish elliptical constructions which require a linguistic antecedent from those which do not, and that post-auxiliary ellipsis belongs to the first class (for further detail and distinctions see also Quirk *et al.* 1985: §§12.31ff.). There is a good general distinction here, and auxiliaries form a subgroup among items permitting ellipses which require a linguistic antecedent.

But there is also another elliptical construction which gives us a more particular test for auxiliaryhood. In it an auxiliary precedes a partial ellipsis and some of the complementation of the missing head is retained. This construction is discussed by Levin (1978, 1980), who calls it 'pseudogapping'. The examples of (9.a–d) are attested utterances cited from Levin (1980: 76-7).

(9) a. Probably drives him crazy to have her call him all the time. It would — me —.
b. If you don't believe me, you will — the weatherman!
c. – I just hope it will make you happy.
– Hasn't it — you — ?
d. I'm going to call him back on Monday, as I am — several other people —.
e. John will eat the bananas, even if he won't — the apples.
f. Mary gave money to the orphanage partly because she hadn't — to the church.

It seems clear that pseudogapping should be generalized with post-auxiliary ellipsis, so that essentially one account should be given for both constructions (hopefully within a more general account of ellipsis). Pseudogapping indeed shows an overt similarity to gapping, but its distribution implies that it is more closely related to post-auxiliary ellipsis. The two constructions share the context of a preceding auxiliary (which is *do* in default of another form), and both have the freedom to occur within a range of structures; see (8) and (9).[3] Gapped constructions, by contrast, lack their highest auxiliary, and are virtually restricted to coordinate structures in Present-day English; see (10) and Quirk *et al.* (1985: §13.92).[4]

(10) a. Paul will drink tea, and his wife, coffee.
b. *If Paul will drink tea, (then) his wife, coffee.
c. *Paul will drink tea, partly because his wife, coffee.
d. *– Paul will drink tea.
– His wife, coffee.

Thus pseudogapping gives us another and more particular test for auxiliaryhood.

(d) *Emphasis*. There is a straightforward contrast between the sentences of (11). In the first the tonic (or sentence stress) is on *do*, and what is emphasized is apparently the polarity of the sentence. This is not necessarily contrastive, but may simply be an affirmation of a proposition open to doubt. In the second the tonic (or sentence stress) is on *eat*, and here the scope of the emphasis lies within the verb phrase, centrally involving the verb itself.

(11) a. I *do* eat chocolates (in case you thought otherwise).
b. I *eat* chocolates (I don't stuff them in my ears).

Although this may provide a useful test for auxiliaryhood especially in the case of *do*, perfect *have*, and *be*, it is not to be stated as a property peculiar to auxiliaries, but rather follows from the principle that emphasis involves paradigmatic contrast within a relevant semantic field. Thus in *My leg* ***hurts*** a tonic on *hurts* would customarily imply contrast with not hurting or with tickling, rather than with being hairy or with stamping. In the case of auxiliaries the point is that the relevant contrasts may be extremely impoverished, so that contextually there may be focus on polarity. But modality and tense/aspect may surely also be included in what is emphasized, as in the following, and indeed quite generally.

(12) a. – They're on the floor.
– But they *can't* be on the floor.
b. They're on the floor. They *must* be on the floor.
c. If you arrive early enough, there *should* still be some food.
d. Please go. You simply *must* leave.
e. *If* they arrive; my dear fellow, they *have* arrived.

I do not then see this as a independent property of auxiliaries so much as a consequence of the structuring of the semantic fields to which they belong.

(e) *Clitic forms*. Some operators have clitic forms which are available after pronouns, or (in the case of *'s*) more generally. Some are represented orthographically, as in (13.a). But not all are; Palmer (1988: 243) additionally lists weak nonsyllabic forms for the items in (13.b).

(13) a. 's (has, is), 'm (am), 'd (would, had), 've (have), 'll (will, ?shall), 're (are)
b. can, could, must, shall, should, do, does, did, was, were

Here we must distinguish reduced forms with vowel, like [əv] in *They will have eaten*. In *They have eaten, They've eaten* this is a possible pronunciation, but so is a further reduction to [v]. The clitic in question is the full nonsyllabic reduction. In the case of *'re* in nonrhotic dialects the full reduction is to a brief glide, or even to complete absorption into the preceding form in the case of *they're, you're, we're*.

(f) *Adverb position.* Some adverbs, in particular epistemic adverbs like *probably, certainly, maybe* and adverbs of frequency like *often, always, never, hardly* may occur after an auxiliary operator, but do not generally occur after V within VP with the relevant wide scope (unless they form a separate tone group). See Chapter 2 note 10 for some sceptical comments on this criterion.

(14) a. They will probably have eaten by six o'clock.
b. They will hardly have eaten by six o'clock.
c. ?They intend probably to eat by six o'clock.
d. They intend never to eat by six o'clock. (narrow scope)
e. *They ate probably their dinner by six o'clock.
f. *They ate hardly their dinner by six o'clock.

(g) *Non-occurrence after periphrastic* do. Auxiliary *do* does not occur with a following nonfinite auxiliary except in imperative sentences. I shall distinguish 'periphrastic' and 'imperative' *do* because of their distributional differences. Thus (nonimperative) periphrastic *do* never occurs in construction with *be* and perfect *have*, and it differentiates auxiliary/nonauxiliary constructions with other items. (But see Palmer 1988: 159f. for an exception to this statement.)

(15) *They didn't have left. *They do be naughty. They don't need *(to) leave yet.

These criteria apply generally to the group of auxiliaries. Modals have some further distinctive properties.

(h) Modals lack nonfinites in Standard English (though not all do in all dialects).

(16) *They will can come. *They have could come. *For Paul to may go.

The fact that modals may not occur in sequence, or after an initial auxiliary, is taken here to follow from their lack of nonfinites, and not to be a separate property (see Chapter 2).

(i) Modals lack the third person singular present indicative inflection of full verbs. *He will* contrasts with *he wills. Dare* allows *if he dares go*, but this is probably better seen as an exception to the next criterion.

(j) Modals are followed by a plain infinitive, and so is *do*. Only *help* among full verbs has this possibility, though some verbs take a plain infinitive with preceding NP, for example *make, see. Ought* and *used* occur with the *to*-infinitive. *Dare* and *need* only do so when they are not characterized as modals.

(k) 'Tense' relationships in modals are not parallel to those of verbs. Some lack preterites (*must, need*). Where 'preterites' are found, as in the 'secondary' modals *could, might, should* and *would*, they are distributed very differently from those of verbs. They may appear in a range of hypothetical, tentative or polite expressions where contextual support is not always required. But reference to past time is uncommon and typically restricted.[5] The preterites of verbs in contrast are freely used of past time, but typically restricted in their hypothetical, tentative and polite uses. It seems rather doubtful that the secondary modals should be identified as containing the same morpheme 'tense' as is found in verbs, despite the common identification of the 'unreal', 'tentative', or 'remote' past tense (or wider category of which tense is one manifestation) as a component of all these hypothetical senses.[6] If it is the same, this raises the problem why its use to refer to past time is so limited in modals, and why its use for the present (with little or no reflex of the supposed force of the preterite, at least with *might* and *should*) is so free.[7] *Could, might, should* and *would* with their final dentals could indeed all be interpreted as members of a morphological schema for the preterite (Bybee and Slobin 1982). But *could, should* and *would* could also show an interrelated modal subgroup in *-ould*, as is perhaps argued by the historical transfer of *could* into the group. Thus it makes equal sense to suggest that secondary modals do not carry the tense morpheme of verbs but show a distinction proper to modals which may occasionally realize tense.

1.3 Auxiliaries as a word class

Given the substantial coincidence between these properties, it is no surprise that most analysts have agreed in isolating a class or subclass consisting of auxiliaries, or consisting of modals where there is some further relationship to *do, have* and *be*. Some such conclusion seems unavoidable. I will first outline my assumptions about the nature of word classes, then discuss the structuring of the class of auxiliaries.

1.3.1 Word classes

Within a lexical model of syntax which avoids the postulation of highly abstract structures (and of movement) a rather surfacey and traditional set of assumptions about the word-class structure of a language is appropriate. Let me first say what these assumptions are, then add something in further justification. The first two statements here simply apply the basic methods of structuralism to the properties by which categories are discriminated.

(i) Classification is grouping by relevant similarities and differences. A word class exists in opposition to other classes, so that a group of properties typical of one class stands in opposition to the group of properties typical of another. Consequently, within the class properties (and groups of properties) tend to correlate with each other, or be mutually predictive.

(ii) Formal and distributional properties (which in practice are largely syntactic and morphological) are of central importance for word-class membership and structure. Purely semantic properties have no special place in establishing the membership of classes. (Indeed they may be secondary; see Maratsos and Chalkley 1980, and traditional structuralist practice, e.g. Harris 1951.) Thus the semantic near equivalence of *fond* and *love* does not prevent them from belonging to different classes.

(iii) To this basic position we may add the commonly made observation that a class need not be homogeneous, but normally has some internal differentiation whereby a 'nuclear' or 'prototypical' set of members shows more of the properties of the class than other less fully characterized members. A class may also not show sharply definable boundaries.

(iv) Finally, the typical semantics of a class has a separate importance for the cross-linguistic identification of classes, and this point will be taken up below.

How should we take these assumptions? On one view they might be seen as a pretheoretical descriptive statement about word classes, bearing no interesting relationship to an appropriate theory of the area. But equally we might suppose that linguistic categorization is essentially like other areas of human categorization. On this view 'Parts of speech are much more like biological species than has generally been recognized' (McCawley 1986: 12). This is an economical and plausible hypothesis; indeed it is the 'null hypothesis'. This general approach is adopted in work in psychology by Rosch (1978, 1988) and her associates, or in linguistics by Lakoff (1987) and others. The assumptions above can be theoretically based in Rosch's work, and what is distinctive about the application to 'parts of speech' is (ii), the predominance of the formal properties of words over their semantic properties, and (iv) the consequent status of semantics in identification. There are many questions here (e.g. about the interpretation of (iii)), some of which will be taken up when this is considered in more detail in Chapter 4. A general issue is clearly that of the extent to which cognitive principles and autonomous linguistic principles are brought into play in establishing word classes, and the nature of their mutual interaction. Note that an account like that given above is compatible with a substantial degree of innatism in the determination of word classes and word-class structure, so that its adoption does not deny the possibility that autonomous linguistic principles of a detailed and structured kind are involved.

1.3.2 The structuring of the group of auxiliaries

The membership of the group defined by the criteria listed above is surprisingly sharp. It is correlated sets of criteria which are important (see (i) above): the absence of *mayn't*, or the limited possibility of ellipsis represented by *Come if you want*, do not affect the general patterning, though there are relatively few cases where individual criteria differ or are vague in application. The criteria listed above were formal, not semantic, as is appropriate given my (ii) above. To a large extent their cooccurrence is therefore apparently arbitrary, not independently motivated, and we need a class account of it.[8] The degree of mutual predictiveness between properties is striking. It is also worth noting the extent to which this mutual predictiveness holds between properties drawn from different linguistic levels. For a detailed statement of the application of a similar (but more extensive) set of criteria see Huddleston (1980).

The group is structured as in A and B below:

A. First the group of operators, or finite auxiliaries. These are distinct from full verbs on all or virtually all of criteria (a)–(f):

(i) The modal auxiliaries are further distinguished by (h)–(k):
can, could; *may, might*; *must*; *shall, should*; *will, would.*
Plus: *had* (*better*); *had* (*rather*); *would* (*rather*).
In some dialects BE, DO, also have criterion (i), a distinctive uninflected third person singular.

(ii) Non-modal auxiliaries:
is (all uses, including 'modal' *is* (*to*), finites of copula BE, 'progressive' BE, 'passive' BE, BE with ~ *going to*, ~ *about to*, etc.);
'perfect' *have*; *have* (*got*) (in British English);
periphrastic *do*;
imperative *do/don't.*[9]

(iii) Instances of less clear or overlapping membership:
uses of *dare, need, ought, used*;
instances of stative 'possessive' *have*, and of *have* (*to*).

B. Second the group of non-operators, whose membership is less clear:
imperatives of BE and HAVE;
the infinitive marker *to*;
nonfinites of BE and HAVE.

C. Full verbs are distinguished from the auxiliaries of A (both the modals of (i) and the other auxiliaries which are listed under (ii)) on a wide range of criteria. Aspectual catenatives such as *begin* and 'raising' verbs like *seem* are both distinct, as are the first person imperative *let us*, *let's*; the *go* of *go see*; the *get* of *get killed*; and other items which have sometimes been referred to as auxiliaries or as sharing in the semantics of auxiliaries.

The modal auxiliaries of (i) form the most coherent and best-distinguished group. It is clear that they are the prototypical members of the class.[10] On the face of it the nonmodals of (ii) do not differ from (i) in a sufficiently coherent way to form a separate subgroup: *do* and *is to* are like (i) in lacking nonfinites, *do* in taking a following plain infinitive. Notice too that there is no immediate basis for distinguishing copula *be* from (say) 'progressive' *be*: although what follows them differs, they share the distinguishing auxiliary properties. In the case of (iii) each item behaves differently, and there is also variation between dialects. In particular, stative 'possessive' *have*, and *have* (*to*) occur as auxiliaries in British rather than American English. *Dare* and *need* are also restricted to nonassertive contexts (Quirk *et al.* 1985: §2.53). But the general picture is very clear, and as far as operators are concerned 'there is no dispute (how could there be?) over the distinction between [operators and catenatives]' (Huddleston 1984: 143).

The status of nonfinites is not, however, so clear. Most of the criteria above do not apply, and the core modals of (i) lack such forms. The only properties which are relevant here are occurrence in ellipsis (including pseudogapping), and (for infinitives) failure after (nonimperative) periphrastic *do*; for some speakers also the positioning of adverbs.[11] These tests do, however, distinguish the forms of B from full verbs. But in some American English *being* and *having* do not precede post-auxiliary ellipsis. Here they might be classified as auxiliaries on the evidence of adverb position, and because the forms of a lexeme generally belong to the same word class and *is* is auxiliary (but see §2.2.3(iii)). For the status of *to* as an auxiliary see Pullum (1982). Note the peculiarity that imperative *do/don't* is an operator, but that imperative *be* and *have* are not. I append some examples of pseudogapping with imperatives and nonfinites including *to*, since this is a fresh criterion for their status. In assessing these examples, note that stress conditions affect acceptability.

(17)
a. I want to take orders from a hero; I don't want to — from a wimp [sc. take orders].
b. I processed everyone's [cheque], but I must not've — yours [sc. processed]. (Levin 1980: 76–7)
c. Which was more surprising: Paul's being angry with Mary or John's being — with Christine [sc. angry with]?
d. Which was more surprising: for Paul to be angry with Mary or for John to be — with Christine [sc. angry with]?
e. I hope you are patient with father. And please be — with mother [sc. patient].
f. What! Not made peace with either of your parents yet! Please have — with at least one of them before I return [sc. made peace]!

It is very clear from this mutual predictiveness of properties which are apparently essentially independent that auxiliaries form a distinct 'class' of some type. But the interesting questions remain. In particular nothing has so far been said about the semantics of the class, nor about the relationship between this class and the class of full verbs. Other questions involve interrelationships within the class, and what universal properties sustain and constrain the language-particular class. I will turn directly to the first of these, which is also relevant to the question of universals.

1.4 The semantics of modals

In discussing the interrelationship between formal and semantic criteria for classes of expressions, Lyons notes that 'in all languages that have been investigated and reported upon, there is a correlation between the grammatical and the semantic classification of expressions' (1977: 449) and he claims that the traditional semantic criteria for the major 'parts of speech' hold for 'nuclear' members of these classes across languages (when they are distinguished; 1966, 1977: Ch. 11). Indeed this is how we may justify the assignment of labels such as 'noun' in different languages (though Lyons also envisages universal syntactic criteria). Thus a word class in some language can be thought of as established in the first instance by reference to criteria which are largely formal and distributional (and indeed arbitrary or potentially so). Then the question of the class's identity can be dealt with cross-linguistically. The answer depends on the semantics of its most typical, basic or central members. So in English there is a class of words with these characteristics: they may occur after *the*; they have a form with suffixed [-s, -z, -ɪz]; their forms show agreement patterns with *these/those*, and with *entrap/entraps*, etc. This major class has words which denote discrete concrete ('first-order') entities among its central membership, and other languages also have such a major class. They can therefore be identified and labelled 'noun'.

Lyons' discussion is based on major classes. But in view of the widespread occurrence across languages of items labelled 'auxiliary' it is reasonable to try extending this type of account to such items. What distinguishes prototypical auxiliaries from prototypical verbs in English then is likely to be relevant to a more general characterization of the distinction between these classes. I therefore turn to a brief review of the semantics of modals.

1.4.1 Parameters of modality in the present-day modals

The major types of modality

I want to distinguish three major basic types of modality in the English modals: epistemic, deontic and dynamic; compare the distinction laid out in Palmer (1979: 36–7). *Epistemic* modality typically involves a statement of the speaker's attitude towards the status of the truth of a proposition: that the proposition is necessarily true, probably true, predicted to be true, etc. An assessment based on logical inference from evidence (commonly unstated) may be involved, and a paraphrase in such terms or in terms of the speaker's confidence in the truth of the proposition is often reasonable, as in (18).[12]

(18) a. Have sent off my diary a couple of days ago – you should get it soon.
'I think it's probable that ...'
b. [*Speaker has lost keys*] I may have put them down on the table – they're not in the door.
'It's possible that I put them down ...'

Since they involve the speaker, such instances are usually called *subjective* to distinguish them from *objective* epistemic modality which deals with necessity and possibility within a logical system divorced from the speaker's evaluation. Epistemic modality is normally subjective; truly objective instances are infrequent and restricted in occurrence (Coates 1983: 247, Palmer 1986: 102), but examples do occur:

(19) The simple truth is that if you're going to boil eggs communally they must be hard ...

The term 'root' is sometimes used for nonepistemic modals in general. But I shall distinguish 'deontic' and 'dynamic' modality, both of which are concerned with the occurrence of events, or the existence of states of affairs.

Deontic modality involves permission and obligation, or what is possible and what is necessary with respect to some authority, or to a set of moral values.

(20) a. 'You must play this ten times over', Miss Jarrova would say, pointing with relentless fingers to a jumble of crotchets and quavers.
b. If you want to recall the doctor you may do so.
'You are allowed to do so.' Deontic source = legal rules.
c. May I read your message? – Yes.
'Do you allow me ...?' Deontic source = addressee.

In declaratives (like (20.a)) the source of obligation or permission may be the speaker's authority, in interrogatives (like (20.c)) the hearer's. I shall follow Lyons (1977: 792–3) in using the term *subjective* for such modality (another recent term is Palmer's 1979 'discourse oriented'). Nonsubjective deontics, then, are those in which the source of obligation or permission is not the speaker (in declaratives). This source is normally unspecified: it may be some other person, be some general social, moral or legal system, or even be left vague. Finally, *dynamic* modality evaluates the occurrence of events or the existence of states of affairs as necessary, important, advisable, possible, desirable, etc. within a circumstantial frame of reference (commonly not stated). This may include reference to the abilities or volition of the subject (for which see below). There is no subject selection, however, in cases of *neutral* dynamic modality. Here are included examples like the following:

(21) a. Clay pots must have some protection from severe weather.
b. I must have an immigrant's visa; otherwise they're likely to kick me out, you see.
c. I've spotted ... a solecism, but it can easily be rubbed out.

This may be difficult to distinguish from other root modalities (deontic or subject-selecting dynamic). In fact Coates (1983: 21) argues that root modality forms essentially one semantic field, and Palmer takes neutral (dynamic) modality not to be wholly distinct, so that 'neutral *can* shades into' the subject-selecting *can* of ability and 'neutral *must* into deontic *must*' (1988: 103).

Subjectivity

The essentially subjective nature of many of the uses of modals is very striking. It is the speaker's attitude or evaluation which is essentially concerned. On the face of it, this distinguishes modals sharply from verbs (see the discussion of Chapter 2). To the categories discussed above we may add that many instances of 'future' *will* may be interpreted as epistemic, hence as subjective (see Coates 1983: 169ff., esp. 181f.), and that uses of the secondary modals *could*, *might*, *should* and *would* appear in unreal or counterfactual statements (with or without an expressed condition) and in tentative or polite expressions (Coates 1983: esp. Ch. 8). Such instances also contain a substantial subjective element.

(22) I should ask him if there are any seminars you ought to go to.
(Suppressed condition = 'if I were you'. Polite version of 'Ask him if there are any seminars you ought to go to'.)

Modals and subject selection

In most of their functions, modals are most straightforwardly analysed semantically as modifying the clause they occur in as a whole, not as mediating selectional relationships with their subject and complement. An epistemic clearly imposes no selectional restrictions on its subject or complement: the equivalence of active and passive is not disturbed by the intervening modal, nor is the relationship between existential *there* and the narrow range of complements it permits (*be* and a few intransitive verbs). The same line of argument may be followed for deontic modals. Thus examples which show voice-neutrality and failure to select for subject lead to the conclusion drawn by (among others) Huddleston (1974), that deontic modals, along with many instances of what I term dynamic modals, are basic one-place predicates.

(23) a. Paul may finish the biscuits.
'I permit Paul's finishing of the biscuits.'
b. The biscuits may be finished by Paul.
'I permit Paul's finishing of the biscuits.'
c. There may be singing but no dancing on my premises.
'I permit singing but not dancing on my premises.'

It has, however, been suggested that deontic modals are not one-place predicates at a more abstract level, but that they should be assigned a deep syntactic structure (or a semantic analysis) containing an argument position for the deontic source, and perhaps also for the addressee who is obligated or permitted. A consequence of this might be to draw a more abstract distinction between 'intransitive' epistemic structures (with clausal subject) and 'transitive' deontic structures (with clausal complement) (as in Ross 1969). But Lyons (1977: 841ff.) points out that such an account is really based on an unequal comparison between objective epistemic and subjective deontic instances, and that a 'transitive' account of subjective epistemic meanings is equally plausible, so that there is no semantic justification for the distinction. Moreover, the existence of subjective interpretations for deontic modals which lack subject selection as in (23.b, c) above implies that we should adopt a one-place (semantic) analysis for both epistemic and deontic modals in which they are analysed as not imposing any selectional restrictions on their subject or complement. Thus there is no need to suppose that deontic modals assign an (adjunct) theta role to their subject.

Among dynamic uses of modals, however, there are apparent instances of selection of subject (and complement). The most straightforward cases are *dare* and the *will* that characterises its subject's willingness, intention (and perhaps power), or typical (and even persistent) behaviour, the last especially when stressed. Here existential *there* cannot be subject, and voice-equivalence fails, as here.

(24) a. Mothers *will* smack their babies. ≠ b in 'typical behaviour' interpretation.
b. Babies *will* be smacked by their mothers.

(25) a. Mothers daren't smack their babies.
b. *Babies daren't be smacked by their mothers.

The *can* of ability or capacity is also often analysed as showing subject selection (e.g. by Palmer 1979, 1988, though Huddleston 1974: 222 disagrees), and parallel uses are even found with *must* (Palmer 1979: 106). Thus though the extent of such uses is debated, their existence is hardly disputable. But the semantic properties of word classes are not absolute and definitional: though lacking subject selection is a prototypical property of modals, there may be less central instances which do select their subject. Lack of subject selection does however distinguish prototypical modals from prototypical nonauxiliary verbs, and the importance of the distinction is shown by its occasional extension to *dare* in attested instances like the following in which subject selection clearly fails. (For other examples see Jespersen 1909–49: V, §20.1$_1$; Pullum and Wilson 1977: 785.)

(26) These two aspects of death cannot be successfully separated, but they dare not be confused or identified.
(Ehrman 1966: 71)

Semantic parameters of modality

The notion of modality is potentially a very wide one, as are its possible realizations. This second point is made very clearly by Perkins (1983) who surveys the range of devices which may express modality in English, for example (among epistemics) adverbs (*perhaps*), parentheticals (*I think*), performative expressions (*I suggest that*), other embeddings (*it is likely that*), etc. But here we are concerned with the semantic characterization of a word class which opposes other word classes, particularly that of nuclear verb. The most striking general semantic characteristics which identify prototypical modals seem to me to be the following. These are not of course definitional in the sense that all modals show them or that no uses of verbs do.

(i) The fact that modals typically qualify the event or proposition as a whole, and do not generally select their subjects. This makes them sharply distinct from nuclear verbs. This is pointed up by the behaviour of *dare*, as was noted above. I will refer below to items with this characteristic as 'sentence modifiers'.

(ii) Subjectivity. A striking characteristic of modals which distinguishes them sharply from other (indicative) verbs as a group is their typical use in utterances which give expression to a speaker's judgements and will. The notions which Lyons takes to be basic to modality are precisely such subjective judgements and the issuing of mands (Lyons 1977: esp. 845–6); and note Palmer's view that 'Modality could ... be defined as the grammaticalization of speakers' (subjective) attitudes and opinions' (1986: 16).

Thus the subject-selecting, objective dynamic uses are those most like nonauxiliary verbs. Indeed they are not categorized as modal by all linguists. Most centrally modal are the subjective epistemic and subjective deontic areas which lack subject-selecting instances.

(iii) There may be a further candidate in the interlinked system of semantic notions central to modals: necessity, probability, possibility; obligation and permission; futurity, volition and intention. These concepts are found expressed by auxiliaries in other languages, and the use of one expression for both necessity and obligation as for possibility and permission is also paralleled (Palmer 1986: 121ff.). The central concepts of necessity and possibility are basic logical operators, central to other semantic interrelations (and themselves interrelated by negation); they are also reasonably taken to underlie the concepts of obligation and permission. This part of the semantics of modals in particular is open to analysis as a tightly organized system (e.g. by Leech 1969, Anderson 1971). It is possible that concepts of necessity and possibility are themselves basic to modality (see Palmer 1979: 8), or that the focus might be on the domains over which it may range, say Sweetser's (1982) 'sociophysical and epistemic worlds', or sets of laws (Perkins 1983). But the highly abstract and general nature of the concepts involved and the fact that these notions in themselves can also be expressed within the class of verbs makes me wonder whether these notions (and their structuring) are themselves central to modality or whether they are involved because of their conceptual centrality and their poor correspondence to the nuclear verb prototype.

Other auxiliaries

Is this sufficient to cope with the less central auxiliaries? *Ought* is well analysed as lacking subject selection, and it has subjective uses (Coates 1983: 69ff.). Modal *need* also lacks subject selection, and *dare* sometimes shows such uses. Perfect *have*, periphrastic *do* and most uses of *be* do not select their subjects and can be interpreted as 'sentential modifiers' in the relevant sense. Periphrastic *do* also realizes tense, which is centrally subjective in that it places other times in relationship to the speaker's now (and which has uses interinvolved with modality, Lyons 1977: §17.3, Quirk *et al.* 1985: §4.16). But the presence of these items in the category auxiliary is justified from a semantic point of view not so much by their possession of prototypical properties as by the fact that they are even more remote from the verbal prototype, which denotes an action or event (Hopper and Thompson 1984). Compare the opinion of Lyons (1977: 437) 'there is no convincing syntactic or semantic reason for classifying "be" in English as a verb'. Possessive *have* too is far from the verbal prototype, perhaps simply denoting a relationship between entities of which its various 'senses' are contextual interpretations (Bendix 1966). These are all 'secondary' auxiliaries in that they are at various distances from the semantic prototype, though this need not make them any less 'auxiliaries' with respect to other properties: the question of prototypical structuring of word-class semantics is distinct from that of 'degrees of membership' in general.

1.4.2 Conclusion: auxiliaries as a word class

The basic notions of structuralism lead us to expect classes distinguished by correlations between opposing criteria. English auxiliaries clearly form such a class. The modals *can, may, must, will, shall, could, might, should, would* are its prototypical members. They are distinguished by several striking semantic properties, in particular their subjectivity and their lack of subject selection, which may be more general properties capable of distinguishing auxiliaries from verbs cross-linguistically. *Be*, and perfect *have* (sometimes possessive *have*) with their nonfinite forms also belong to the class, as does periphrastic *do*. This is to be understood not in terms of their having semantic and other properties which are in themselves especially close to those of modality and the modals, but in terms of their being assigned to the most appropriate class given their opposition to the class of full verbs alongside a measure of similarity to modals.

1.5 Problems and historical context of analysis

The analysis of English auxiliaries gives rise to a range of problems, which have attracted a wide range of different answers. The principle questions which focus particularly on auxiliaries within the generative tradition over the last three decades have been the following:

1. Do they constitute a (word) class?
2. How are they related to the class of verbs?
3. What constituent structures do they occur in?
4. What is the relationship between an auxiliary and the verb it is in construction with? Is the auxiliary a specifier, or a head, or what?
5. Why are auxiliaries restricted to a particular order?
6. Why are modals finite only?
7. How should we account for the curious distribution of periphrastic *do*, which looks as if it supplies a suppletive form of tense where an auxiliary is required, but is otherwise absent?

These all of course relate to the language-general question of the appropriate characterization of auxiliaries both structurally and as a class.

The first part of this chapter has been partly devoted to a preliminary consideration of the first of these questions. I turn now principally to questions of constituent structure (3 and 4), and to a preliminary discussion of 2, the nature of the relationship between auxiliaries and full verbs.

1.5.1 Structure and class

Structure

I shall assume without discussion that constituent-structure analysis is appropriate in syntax and that it is well represented by labelled trees, in accordance with the mainstream generativist tradition. Given this, it is clear that both operators and nonfinite auxiliaries are best analysed as occurring in structures like (27) in basic, 'kernel' sentences.

(27)

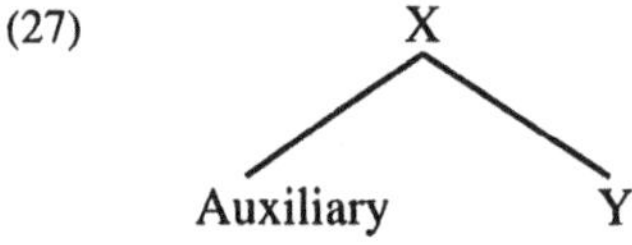

The justification for this is that the sequence auxiliary + full verb + complement behaves like a constituent both in coordinations and in 'Right Node Raising' constructions, as does the sequence full verb + complement. The same points hold recursively for auxiliary + auxiliary + full verb + complement. This is true for modals, 'aspectual' *be* and *have*, 'passive' *be*, copula *be*, and possessive *have* (see Akmajian, Steele and Wasow 1979: 44; and esp. Gazdar, Pullum and Sag 1982: 617f., 621ff.; hereafter abbreviated as ASW and GPS).

(28) a. On Tuesday, Mary [will finish writing her first essay] and [may even begin the second].
b. On Tuesday, Mary will [finish writing her first essay] and [begin the second].
c. By Tuesday, Mary will have [finished writing her first essay] and [begun the second].
d. By Tuesday, Mary will [have finished writing her first essay] and [have begun the second].
e. By Tuesday, Mary [will have finished writing her first essay] and [may even have begun the second].

(29) a. Paul pretended to be, but George actually was, enjoying Nielsen's Inextinguishable.
b. Paul may pretend to, but George actually will, be enjoying Nielsen's Inextinguishable.
c. I was told that George, but I can't imagine that Paul, was enjoying Nielsen's Inextinguishable.
d. Today George, tomorrow perhaps the whole world, will enjoy Nielsen's Inextinguishable.

Strictly, neither of these tests is sufficient to demonstrate the constituency structure assigned above, since there are instances of coordination and 'Right Node Raising' constructions which contain apparent nonconstituents; see Abbott (1976) for 'Right Node Raising', Dowty (1988) for a recent discussion and analysis of nonconstituent coordination. But the simplest assumption in my framework for the examples above (and others like them) is that they do indeed involve constituents, and good evidence for an alternative constituency is lacking. It is best, then, to adopt the constituent-structure configuration given above, in the spirit of Chomsky's remark that 'the possibility of conjunction offers one of the best criteria for the initial determination of phrase structure' (1957: 36). This also derives weak support from the facts of post-auxiliary ellipsis, which may also be interpreted as involving a constituent.

Headedness

In two recent papers Zwicky (1985) and Hudson (1987) debated the importance of a series of criteria for establishing the head of a construction on the basis of six English constructions. Warner (1989a) briefly reviewed this discussion and (dissenting only marginally from Hudson) listed the following five criteria as central in determining headedness (1989a: 182).

1. A lexical head is typically a semantic functor.
2. A head is typically a 'morphosyntactic locus'.
3. A lexical head is typically the item which subcategorizes for any complements.

4. A head is typically distributionally equivalent to its phrase as a whole.
5. A head is typically obligatory outside elliptical constructions.

The relevance of these criteria to auxiliaries is swiftly summarized. We are able to apply the criteria to auxiliaries simply as occurring within S alongside a nonauxiliary verb, or within VP alongside a nonauxiliary verb, without relying on the structure given above. This works out as follows.

1. Those auxiliaries which function as 'sentential modifiers' are well interpreted as semantic functors on S or on a VP or predicative complement. Others, possessive *have* with its object, or auxiliaries with subject selection, parallel full verbs and may equally well be taken as functors.
2. A syntactic operator is very clearly the 'morphosyntactic locus' which carries information relevant to the identity and distribution of the clause within which it occurs. Within VP both finite and nonfinite auxiliaries similarly bear information which morphosyntactically identifies their VP. The nonauxiliary verb of a clause does not meet this criterion if an auxiliary is present.
3. The categorial and morphosyntactic properties which an auxiliary 'imposes' on the verb (or auxiliary) in construction with it are parallel to other cases of subcategorization (in most cases there is indeed an exact parallel).[13] Thus taking the auxiliary to be the item which subcategorizes for its sister would be entirely appropriate. If the auxiliary is not the head some special mechanism must control this relationship. This criterion in particular implies support for the constituent analysis of (27).
4. In post-auxiliary ellipsis the auxiliary is distributionally equivalent to the sequence auxiliary + full verb + complement; within VP it is distributionally equivalent to its phrase as a whole. This criterion also implies support for the constituent analysis of (27).
5. Auxiliaries are not, however, typically obligatory, either in S or VP. But they are obligatory in the nonbasic constructions discussed above.

Here the best decision is plainly that the operator (within S), or the auxiliary (within VP) is the head. In sentences or VPs which contain an auxiliary, the nonauxiliary verb is not even a serious candidate for head on these criteria. So these considerations support the constituent analysis given above.[14]

More on structure

In this discussion I shall make a series of assumptions about the analysis of English which are familiar from work in Generalized Phrase Structure Grammar and Head-driven Phrase Structure Grammar. They include the interpretation of V as the head of S (which is V^2), and the general possibility of VP as verbal complement. These assumptions impose certain views about the categorial nature of auxiliaries; they must be recognized but they are not harmful to the major points I wish to make here or in the next two chapters. Given this framework of analysis, if we make the orthodox assumption that there is (normally) some categorial identity between head and the (phrasal) node which immediately dominates it (its 'mother'), and if we suppose that we should generalize across finite and nonfinite auxiliaries (as is implied by the evidence of (28) and (29) above) it is clear that the best analysis is one in which in basic, 'kernel' sentences, auxiliaries occur as head in this structure:

(30)

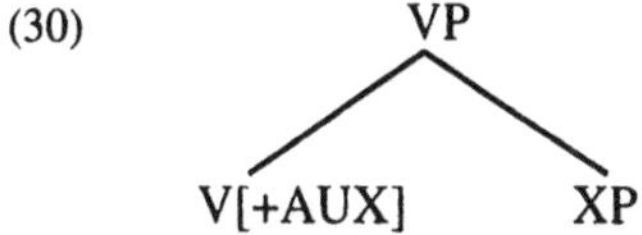

This is essentially the analysis proposed by GPS. Like any head the auxiliary is subcategorized for its complement. XP will be a bare infinitive VP in the case of modals, a past participial VP after perfect *have*, a predicative phrase after copula *be*, etc., and the fact that the grammar imposes virtual identity of feature values between mother and head will ensure this information holds of the lexical 'daughter'. I shall assume that it is reasonable to identify the auxiliary as V[+AUX], its mother as VP. The tree assigned to *must have been climbing trees* is given in (31).

(31)

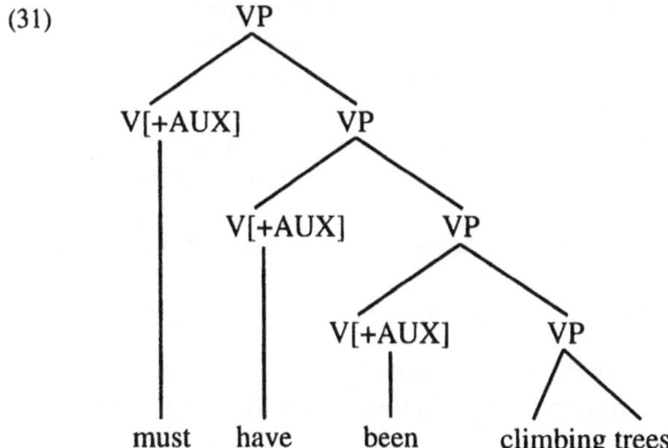

The analysis of be

An important subtopic here is the analysis of *be.* This is sometimes subdivided. 'Progressive' *be*, 'passive' *be* and copula *be* have distinct subcategorizations in ASW, and are generated in distinct positions in structure. But there is a reasonable case that at least 'progressive' *be*, 'passive' *be*, and *be* with attributive and locative complements should be treated as a single item, which just happens to occur with complements of distinct form and semantics (though 'identifying' *be* may be different). The evidence for this is twofold. In the first place, the complements of *be* have an independent distribution and semantics. This is argued in Chapter 2 for progressives. Passive phrases also occur independently, and see the phrasal analysis of the passive proposed in Bach (1979–80), Keenan (1980). Predicative phrases also show a limited independence.

(32) a. What, Thatcher known to be a crypto communist!
b. Anyone thought to be an Iraqi by the Home Secretary was interned.
c. What, Dana advisor to the committee!

Secondly, these different categories may be conjoined after *be*, and this argues for at least a measure of categorial identity. This is not an unavoidable conclusion, but it stems from well-established methodological principle, and it leads to a strikingly simple account in a framework where the complement of predicative *be* is underspecified so that it is compatible with a wide range of complements, which may be coordinated (Sag *et al.* 1985 give such an account). Falk (1984) also argues for a unitary account of *be.* Since the coordinated phrases after *be* in such instances behave as a constituent, there is no justification for an analysis with an empty V in (only) the second conjunct (see (34); cf. Peterson 1981).

(33) a. He is very angry indeed and throwing furniture about the room.
b. Paul is already in the car and waiting for you.
c. I'm still expecting to go and very keen about the prospect.
d. Paul was taunted by his classmates and very angry as a consequence.
e. Paul is horribly misshapen, a creature of darkness, and thought to practice witchcraft. Please don't ask him round again.
f. The contraband was inside the wheel arch and thought to be safely hidden.
g. John was put into a state of turmoil by the decision and hoping for its reversal.
h. He was trying to follow the dictates of his conscience but known to be unhappy about what he was doing.

(34) She said she would have it prepared, and on the table and ready to eat it was.

It may be that instances of the *to*-infinitive after 'modal' *is* should be similarly analysed, though it is not fully clear whether examples like the following are zeugmatic or not, since many other similar examples are rejected. Note, as before, that *to* VP in the required sense has an independent distribution, and the range of meaning of *is to* ('futurity with varied connotations of "compulsion", "plan", "destiny", etc. according to context'; Quirk *et al.* 1985: §3.46) is included in that found with *to* in other contexts (e.g. when postnominal).

(35) a. He was new to the school and to be debagged the following day.
b. The old man is an idiot and to be pitied.
c. You are under military discipline and to take orders only from me.
d. You are a mere private and not to enter this mess without permission.
e. He was an intelligent boy and soon to eclipse his fellows.

The relationship between auxiliaries and verbs

This, the second question of the list which began this section, will be dealt with in the next chapter. But it is appropriate to give it a preliminary airing here since in what precedes auxiliaries were labelled V[+AUX], distinct from full verbs V[–AUX]. This polarizes a subtle issue, as does the debating question 'Are auxiliaries main verbs?' which has underlain some discussion. We need to ask not whether auxiliaries are verbs or main verbs but rather what the nature of the category space which contains auxiliaries and verbs is, and how they are related to one another. Let us review verblike properties of auxiliaries in this spirit.

1. *Auxiliaries may head 'VP'.* The phrasal constituent containing (headed by) a nonfinite auxiliary is on the face of it to be identified as (some kind of) VP since it behaves so substantially like VP in coordination and subcategorization.

2. *Tense and agreement.* It has been suggested that auxiliaries are like verbs in showing tense and (in nonmodals) agreement. Modal *could, might, should, would* are indeed available as preterites, though only restrictedly (in the case of *might* and *should* only in indirect speech; see §1.2). But this is not an argument for any very close identity, especially given the diachronic perspective of steadily diminishing past-tense uses of these forms and the fact that cross-linguistically tense may be an independent particle as well as appearing on verbs. Agreement, too, is cross-linguistically not only a feature of verbs, and some English dialects show the effects of historical loss here too in *be*, and in auxiliary *have* and *do* (in contrast with nonauxiliary *have* and *do*).

3. *Modals carry finiteness.* In particular they show the finite properties of requiring a subject, and requiring that it be nominative. In this they parallel finite verbs, and contrast with the particle *to* and with nonfinite verbs (see Evers and Scholten 1980: 96).

4. *Gapping.* It has been claimed there is evidence that auxiliaries and verbs form a single class in that both are involved in gapping constructions. In the simplest cases gapping constructions contain clausal conjuncts which lack a finite verb or auxiliary whose sense is to be supplied from a preceding conjunct, as in these examples.[15]

(36) a. John likes sausages and Paul — beefburgers.
b. Mary drinks beer, Harry — lime juice and Pauline — tonic water.
c. John must eat his supper and Paul — finish his homework.

It has often been suggested that the apparent ellipsis must involve at least a verb, most recently by van Oirsouw, who uses the term 'verb site' for the medial ellipsis of gapping, which 'always involves deletion of at least a verb' (1987: 123). In line with this general tradition of analysis Pullum and Wilson (1977: 744) followed by Schachter (1983: 148) see in the ellipsis of both full verbs and auxiliaries in this construction straightforward support for the claim that they belong to a wider category 'verb' or [+V].[16]

But 'small clause' constructions and exclamative constructions also apparently show gapping as in (37).[17] Here, however, no verb or auxiliary is involved: what is 'gapped' is a noun or an adjective. And, just as nonconstituent strings which include 'at least a verb' or auxiliary may be gapped, as in (38), so too there are cases which show the 'gapping' of strings which include a noun, adjective or preposition (39).

(37) a. I consider the courts arbiters of law and theologians — of morals.
b. What, the courts arbiters of ethics and theologians — of law!
c. I thought John happy with his present and Mary — with hers.
d. What, John happy with his present and Mary — with hers!

(38) a. John will try to come on Wednesday, and Paul — on Thursday. (will try to come)
b. Harry told this story to his mother, and Tom — to his father. (told this story; from Kuno 1976: 306)

(39) a. I consider Claudius the foul murderer of his brother and Hamlet — of his uncle. (the foul murderer)
b. What, Caesar an instigator of factionalism among patricians, and Spartacus — among slaves! (an instigator of factionalism)
c. I thought John happy to be superintended by a man, and Mary — by a woman. (happy to be superintended)
d. What, John in a temper with Elizabeth and Paul — with Mary! (in a temper)

The gapping of verbs and auxiliaries is restricted to coordinate constructions (see (40)), and to cases where the gap is 'high' in the conjunct (see (41)). But just the same restrictions hold of these cases of putative gapping (see (42) and

(43)). Thus there seems to be no good reason to reject their straightforward pretheoretical classification as gapping. But then it is not the case that gapping 'always involves deletion of at least a verb'. Rather it may involve ellipsis of a wide range of strings, and it seems unlikely that any essentially categorial restriction on what is crucially included in gapping will be appropriate. Hence there is no direct argument that auxiliaries are verbs here.

(40) a. *John likes bacon. Paul — eggs.
b. *John likes bacon, although Paul — eggs.
c. *If John likes bacon, then Paul — eggs.
d. *If John must eat his supper, then Paul — finish his homework.

(41) a. *John likes bacon and I know (that) Paul — eggs.
b. *John must eat his supper, and your mother says (that) Paul — finish his homework.

(42) a. *I consider the courts arbiters of law, though theologians — of morals.
cf. *The courts are arbiters of law, though theologians — of morals.
b. *I consider Claudius the foul murderer of his brother if Hamlet — of his uncle.
c. *What, John pleased with Mary because Paul — with Elizabeth!

(43) a. *The courts are arbiters of law, and I consider theologians — of morals.
b. *What, John pleased with Mary and you say Paul — with Elizabeth!

But there clearly are restrictions on what may be gapped. Note that in each of the cases above the gapped string is part of a larger constituent and it includes the highest head (or the highest semantic functor) appropriate to that larger constituent. If the ellipsis in gapping can be characterized as including such a head we have here a further line of argument to support the view that auxiliaries are heads, rather than a direct argument for their categorial status. See Warner (1989b) for a more detailed discussion of the gapping data and its significance.

5. The fact that classes 'auxiliary' and 'full verb' would have some overlapping membership has been taken to imply some sharing of identity. Most relevant here is *dare*, which for many blurs some of the definitional criteria discussed above. *Ought* is perhaps similar. But the blending of properties from more than one class is not so unusual. Less impressive are claims based on *need*, possessive *have* and *have* (*to*). Here it is rather the case that the word is a member of both classes, generally keeping their properties discrete. But membership of a form in more than one class is typical of English word classes. There does not seem here to be much support for any important level of identity.

6. *Conclusion.* Auxiliaries seem to have relatively little in common with full verbs. The fact that they may both head VP and that auxiliaries sometimes

realize categories of finiteness, tense and agreement found on verbs may justify the feature representation V[+AUX], V[–AUX]. But these are rather well distinguished classes. The claim that auxiliaries are a subclass of verb is somewhat misleading, as is the older claim that they are main verbs, if these claims are taken to imply that auxiliaries share essentially the set of properties of verbs, to which they add their own peculiarities.

1.5.2 Other analyses of auxiliaries

In the generative tradition over the last three decades there have been two broad types of analysis of auxiliaries. One has stressed their distinctness from full verbs, and has assigned them a special position in structure. The other while generally recognizing their distinctness from full verbs, has stressed their constructional similarity to verbs, sometimes under the slogan 'auxiliaries are main verbs'. The analysis argued for here is essentially that of GPS in many major respects. It is a variant of the 'main verb' position in the structures it assigns, see (31) above. This structure does not, however, follow from a claim that 'auxiliaries are (like) main verbs', but simply reflects the head-plus-complement structure of English. Thus the structure can be divorced from particular claims about relationships between word classes.

Auxiliaries in AUX and INFL

The alternative tradition of analysis has stressed the categorial and positional distinctness of auxiliaries. But in the preceding arguments for structure and headedness we have justification for rejecting the major 'classical' variants of the AUX analysis of auxiliaries: for detailed discussion of previous views see GPS in particular.

(i) *Auxiliaries in AUX.* In Chomsky (1957) a special position in syntactic structure is assigned to modals, perfect *have*, 'progressive' *be* (and 'passive' *be*) as a group. These form a constituent AUX which is sister to the lexical verb, essentially as in (44). Thus the 'verbal group' consisting of auxiliaries plus full verb is here analysed as a constituent. The 'verbal group' is also a constituent in the analysis of Huddleston (1984: 6), which differs essentially in lacking the intermediate node AUX and in assigning individual auxiliaries to the major class verb. Huddleston's position (which is in this respect like Palmer's (1988 and elsewhere)) represents a syntactic interpretation of the traditional position that *will have taken* (etc.) forms part of the paradigm of TAKE. Thus these analyses reflect major earlier traditions. Chomsky develops structuralist analyses (see Fries 1952); Huddleston and Palmer continue a type of analysis favoured by traditional grammarians. Later generative analyses which retained this constituent AUX tended to promote it up the tree, so that it became first the sister of VP, then also the daughter of S.

(44)

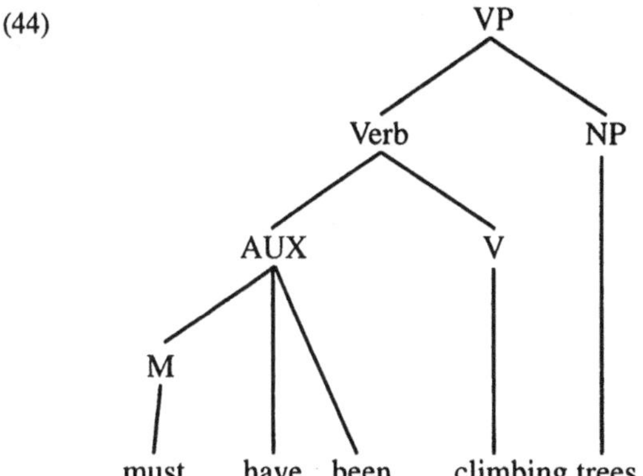

Sufficient reasons for rejecting these analyses are given above. They do not accord with the distributional data, and they treat auxiliaries as nonheads: in early analyses headedness was not an issue, but more recently Huddleston explicitly refers to auxiliaries as 'dependents' in VP structure. Moreover, there is no distributional basis to support the constituency of the verbal group or of AUX (though there is some psycholinguistic evidence for the verbal group; Griffiths 1987). Two distinctive features of this type of transformational analysis are, however, worth noting. First, it permits a very straightforward statement of the ordering of auxiliaries. This is simply given in the phrase-structure rule for AUX. Second, it contained an ingenious characterization of the distribution of periphrastic *do*, which was inserted whenever the rule realizing a tense morpheme on the verb (or auxiliary) which followed it was blocked by an intervening element: the subject in inversions, *not* in negatives, or an emphasis morpheme in the case of emphatic *do*.

(ii) *Auxiliaries in AUX, daughter of S.* A second major series of analyses assigned a distinctive position and category to the finite operator. This was labelled AUX, and generated as an immediate daughter of S. Part of the justification for this was that the availability of a unique constituent for the operator simplified the statement of the mapping relations between basic structures and the negations and inversions derived from them by transformation. In ASW's account, AUX initially contained a modal, or the tense morpheme and *do* (which was analysed as a modal). *Have* and *be* were generated within VP (which has bar levels up to V^3 in ASW's analysis given in (45)).[18] In finite clauses a transformation moved these morphemes into AUX when the modal position was empty or contained only *do*, thus accounting for their behaviour as syntactic operators. This type of analysis incorporated a rather sharp distinction between modals and *do*, which are necessarily operators and require a plain infinitive, and *be* and *have*, which also have nonfinites and occur in construction with a wider range of phrase types. Basic features of this type of analysis are attributed to class lectures at MIT given by Klima; printed exemplars of this general type of analysis include Jackendoff (1972, 1977), Akmajian and Wasow (1975), Emonds (1976) and, in a nontransformational framework, Falk (1984).

(45)

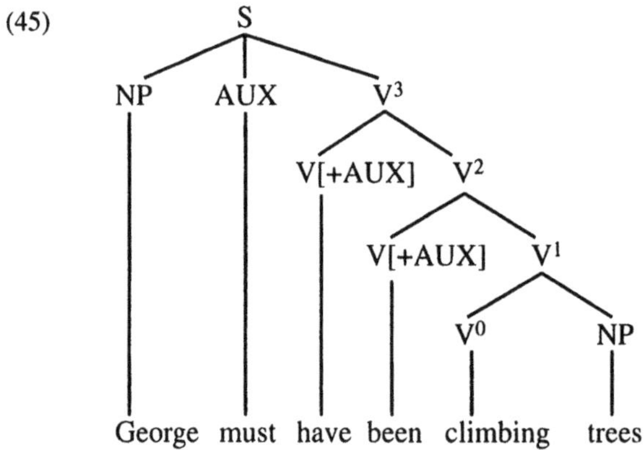

This type of analysis is largely consistent with the distributional data given above in the case of nonfinites (but see GPS 621–2 for a problem for ASW). The constituent-structure position of AUX, however, is hardly defensible (see the discussion of problems in GPS: 614f.). The distribution of *do* is not dealt with in an attractively unitary manner,[19] and there are difficulties for the ordering of *have* and *be* (which will be discussed in the next chapter).

(iii) *Auxiliaries in INFL or I.* Finally, an important recent line of analysis resolves the somewhat mysterious status of AUX as the constituent of tense and modality by interpreting its successor, INFL or I, as the head of S, with the subject as its specifier and VP or an intermediate category as its complement. This integrates the category within X-bar theory, and other similarly integrated 'functional categories' such as C(omplementizer), T(ense), Agr(eement) Asp(ect) have been postulated. One major proposal in this area, Pollock (1989), assigns the initial structure of (46) to the English verbal group.[20] Modals are generated in T, periphrastic *do* in Agr, *have* and *be* within VP, though Pollock does not discuss whether they originate as heads or specifiers. He suggests that English Agr is morphologically too weak for a verb moved into it to assign 'thematic roles' (or 'theta roles': agent, patient, etc.) to its arguments, so that raising of V is blocked by the 'theta criterion' (which requires the assignment to each argument of one and only one theta role). Consequently the only verbs which can be raised to T are *be* and *have* (which do not assign theta roles) and *do* which is pro-verbal *do* and therefore copies the theta grid of the main verb by a distinct mechanism. Thus Pollock apparently gives a motivated characterization of auxiliaries, but he needs somewhat arbitrary assumptions to separate raising verbs like *tend* and *seem* (which are taken to assign theta roles to their predicates) from subject-selecting modals which are not, but which are taken to assign 'adjunct' theta roles (like those assigned by adverbs such as *deliberately*) to their subjects. Moreover *be* and *have* are only integrated by virtue of being given a complex representation in their 'lexical' senses. More importantly, it is not clear that there is a good justification for the 'short movement' of *be* and *have* from within VP to Agr in terms of which Pollock characterizes the distribution within infinitives of adverbs and *not.* Iatridou (1990) gives an attractive account of Pollock's essential data (for English) in which *be* and *have* occupy independent verbal projections and there is no Agr. Ouhalla (1990) goes further in suggesting that *be* and *have* form a category distinct from V and generated outside VP. Such lines of analysis have clear points of contact with the position that I outline in the next chapter. But I shall not be adopting either of these analyses (or a related analysis) for the more general reasons discussed at the beginning of this chapter: that unification grammar provides a simple and coherent framework, and one which is better suited to the nature of the data that I wish to discuss.

(46)

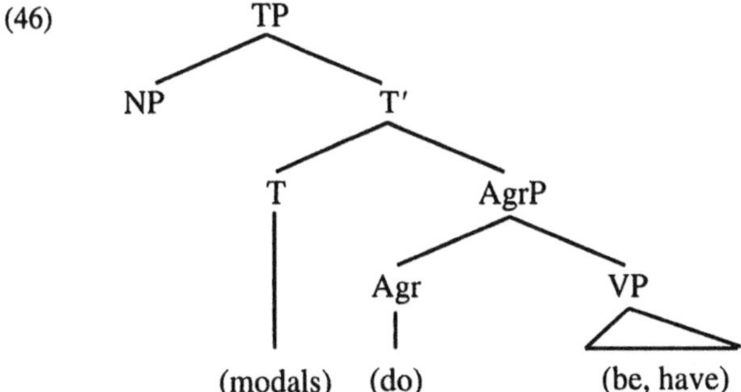

1.5.3 Conclusion

The most satisfactory account then is that sketched at the end of §1.5.1, in which each auxiliary heads a VP and is subcategorized for the morphosyntactic identity of its complement. This answers (for the moment at least) two of the questions from my list earlier in the chapter (p. 20):

3. What constituent structures do auxiliaries occur in?
4. What is the relationship between an auxiliary and the verb it is in construction with? Is the auxiliary a specifier, or a head, or what?

A preliminary answer has also been given to the question of word class.

In the next chapter I will consider two interrelated problems. First, the question of how this class is organized, and how it is related to the class of verbs. Secondly, the problem of the ordering of auxiliaries and of the restricted availability of their morphosyntactic categories.

2 *The morphosyntactic independence of auxiliaries*

This chapter will consider two interrelated problems: how the class of auxiliaries is related to the class of verbs; and what principles underlie the ordering of auxiliaries and the restricted availability of their morphosyntactic categories (questions 2, 5, 6 of my §1.5). Here English auxiliaries show two special properties: they occur in a fixed order; and they do not show all the morphosyntactic categories typical of verbs. I want to propose a new account of these properties, based in a fresh interpretation of the word-class status of auxiliaries.

2.1 Ordering and categorial availability

2.1.1 Some restrictions on auxiliaries

The fixed order is that shown in (1). Thus modals and periphrastic *do* are always first in their verbal group in Standard English, and perfect *have*, 'progressive' *be* and 'passive' *be* do not iterate and only occur in the order of (1.b). So the examples in (2) and (3) are not possible.

(1) a. The morning would have been being enjoyed.
    b. modal – perfect *have* – 'progressive' *be* – 'passive' *be* – main verb

(2) a. *John will must leave tomorrow.
    b. *John has could make some headway.
    c. *Mary will do laugh at this example.
    d. *Mary has done laugh at this example.

(3) a. *John has had finished. perfect + perfect
    b. *Mary is having left. progressive + perfect
    c. *Paul was being singing. progressive + progressive

Ordering clearly interlocks with the availability of morphosyntactic categories. If modals and periphrastic *do* only have finite categories, they cannot occur after other auxiliaries in their verbal group as in (2). Here it is apparently the restriction to finite which is primary, since modals and periphrastic *do* are not available in other nonfinite positions.

(4) a. *(For John) to must leave tomorrow ... (cf. to have to ...)
b. *John's musting leave tomorrow ... (cf. having to ...)
c. *(For John) to do laugh at this example ...
d. *Mary's doing leave early is a shame.

The same restriction affects *is to*, which is also only finite:

(5) a. *It is a shame for John to be to leave tomorrow.
b. *I don't like our being to leave tomorrow.

In the case of perfect *have* and 'progressive' *be* the ordering restrictions of (3) can also be interpreted as restrictions on the availability of categories (provided we can make the relevant distinctions). Thus the failure of the perfect to iterate as in (3.a) might depend on the fact that perfect *have* lacks a past participle, and the absence of the orders in (3.b, c) might follow from the lack of progressive participles of *be* and of perfect *have*. Here either ordering or the availability of categories might apparently be taken as prior. Restrictions on the passive may be different; arguably there cannot be a passive of perfect *have* and 'progressive' (and copula) *be* because they are not transitive, but the absence of a passive of possessive (auxiliary) *have* could depend on its lack of a passive participle.

The basic question then is: What is a coherent and adequate account of these facts of ordering and availability of categories?

2.1.2 Previous accounts

Approaches to this question have been both formal and semantically based, with ordering imposed as a consequence of restriction of categories to special syntactic positions, or by virtue of the incompatibility of the sense of particular combinations. But no adequate account of these facts has yet been offered.

Within the 'auxiliaries are distinct' tradition, ordering was initially imposed syntactically within AUX, as for example in Chomsky (1957), in a type of structure rejected in the last chapter. More recently, modals and periphrastic *do* have been seen as restricted to initial and finite because they are generated in finite AUX or I (though this actually presupposes a finite/nonfinite distinction since I occurs nonfinite, dominating *to*, as in Pollock 1989: 375). Various accounts have been given of restrictions on the ordering of perfect *have* and 'progressive' *be*, but none is convincing. ASW's ordering of perfect, progressive and passive depends on their postulation of three distinct bar levels within VP (see (45) in §1.5.2), but their attempt to justify this is undercut by Lapointe (1980b), who shows that their supposedly syntactic generalizations are better dealt with by a semantic account; see GPS: 628f. for a further objection. Within the 'auxiliaries as main verbs' tradition, GPS impose finiteness on modals in the phrase-structure rule which introduces them, and rule out present participles *having* and *being*, and a perfect participle *had*, by barring the relevant combinations of features. Hence the ordering facts exemplified in (3) above are imposed. But this is essentially stipulative and is ultimately unconvincing because it offers no explanatory rationale or justification for setting up the analysis as it does.[1] These major syntactic accounts have not been successful.

Within the 'auxiliaries as main verbs' tradition it has often been claimed that modals are defective, and this is typically seen as a morphological property; sometimes it is also seen as supported by their irregularity: what needs to be listed may have a gap instead of an entry (McCawley 1971, 1975, and very forthrightly, Pullum and Wilson 1977: §3.4). The problem here is that of understanding why the gap is preserved, why what is systematic for full verbs cannot be extended to modals, and (even more remarkably) why the full paradigm of other uses of *be* and *do* is not extended to *is to*, and to periphrastic *do*. Baker (1981: 315) suggested the principle that 'partially filled paradigms in which the attested forms show a high degree of irregularity are exempted from the effects of general morphological redundancy rules'. On his account, since modals lack the third person singular *-s*, they are exempted from rules forming nonfinites. But Baker does not really show that his principle is appropriate or sufficient. He refers in support to the absence of a past participle of *stride* (following Pullum and Wilson 1977): 'Given that the existing forms suffice to identify this verb as irregular, the paradigm is immune to being completed by the regular rule' (1981: 316). But here it is easy to believe that the problem is essentially morphological, since there are only seven verbs in the relevant subgroup (Quirk *et al.* 1985: §3.16) and alternative analogies are available (*broke – broken*). It may indeed be that speakers have an insufficient basis here to predict a particular form. But there would be no morphological problem predicting the base form of *can* or *will*. Baker also suggests that perfect *have* lacks a past participle, thus accounting for the absence of (3.a). Here he appeals to a second principle: 'paradigms for radically different senses of the same word (possibly radically different subcategorizations) must be stated independently of one another' (Baker 1981: 316). This would also be directly relevant to periphrastic *do*. But this principle seems implausible because it contradicts the position on the morpheme convincingly argued for by Aronoff (1976) that formal interrelationships may be independent of meaning, hence *stand–stood* : *understand–understood*. This would imply that Baker's principle should read 'paradigms ... *may* be stated independently of one another' and this would be insufficient.

Semantic principles have often been appealed to in attempts to account for the ordering of 'aspectual' *have* and *be*. For example the lack of a progressive perfect **is having* has been referred to the general absence of progressive statives, or to the general impossibility of using a perfective complement after a 'verb of temporal aspect' (McCawley 1971, Emonds 1976: 209–10, Pullum and Wilson 1977: 774f.). But ASW (18–20) show that the classification of *be* and *have* as 'verbs of temporal aspect' on which some of these accounts depended is flawed. Falk (1984) attempts to give a more general semantically based account, but it is undermotivated; see Warner (1985: 73) for a critique. Mittwoch (1988) also gives an account of the absence of the perfect progressive, but it should permit iterative interpretations with appropriate adverbials, and her account of their absence is not convincing. But ASW raise a more essential problem for semantic (and pragmatic) accounts, that the constraints on auxiliary ordering are fully grammaticalized and inviolable, whereas violations of semantic (and pragmatic) constraints are sometimes comparatively acceptable (see ASW: 18–20, GPS: 618–19). This makes it seem unlikely that accounts based on incompatibilities of meaning will in fact be sufficient to cope with the facts of auxiliary order.[2]

Thus there is not yet any coherent account of the ordering of English auxiliaries. And the sharpness of these restrictions leads one to suspect that a semantic account will not be appropriate.

2.1.3 A new lexical account

I will argue (i) that the absence of particular morphosyntactic categories in auxiliaries is basic to their order, and (ii) that these absences follow from the fact that the word class 'auxiliary' is distinct in its internal morphosyntactic relationships from the class of full verbs. The occurrence of particular categories is not therefore to be automatically predicted; they must be listed. Thus individual categories (mainly nonfinites) may be absent. Moreover, such individually specified categories may have distinct properties. In particular, they may differ in the morphosyntax they require of a following category. I shall assume that auxiliaries are heads of their phrases, and are subcategorized for their complements as argued in Chapter 1. Then the lexicon will include the information given in (6). In (a) finite categories of modals and DO are listed. In (b) the categories of perfect HAVE are listed; note that *having* only occurs as a nonprogressive *ing*-form, and not as a progressive.[3] In (c) are listed the categories of 'predicative' BE. Here I assume that 'progressive' and 'passive' BE are identified with predicative BE for the reasons given in Chapter 1. BE is however entered as a series of morphosyntactic categories whose subcategorizations are not all the same. The restriction of *is to* to finites is dealt with by subcategorizing nonfinites for a noninfinitival predicative phrase.[4] *Being* also has a distinct subcategorization: it may not be followed by an *ing*-participle. Thus predicative, 'progressive' and 'passive' BE are unified, but BE is split along morphosyntactic lines.

(6) *Auxiliary category and subcategorization information in the lexicon*

	Category	*Subcategorized for a phrase headed by*
a.	can, could, etc. (finite)	plain inf.
	do (finite)	non-aux. plain inf.
	ought (finite)	*to* inf.
b.	has (finite)	past ptc.
	have (plain inf.)	past ptc.
	having (nonprogressive)	past ptc.
c.	is (finite)	non-inf. predicate; *to*-inf.
	be (plain inf.)	non-inf. predicate
	been	non-inf. predicate
	being (progressive and nonprogressive)	non-inf., non-*ing* predicate

This account most resembles earlier work by Baker (1981) and GPS (and Warner 1985 of which it is a development). It differs radically, however, in the nature of the underlying principles taken to control ordering and the availability of categories, and therefore in its systematicity, which is most distinctive in its treatment of BE. Notice that if this approach is correct it implies that the syntactic decomposition of the morphosyntax of auxiliaries which has figured so prominently in discussions of the auxiliary system, particularly in the case of nonfinites, may be inappropriate.

Here ordering follows from the relationships between the morphosyntactic categories listed for auxiliaries and their complements.[5] Finites show the fullest range of subcategorizations. But no nonfinite is subcategorized for an infinitive, no participle is subcategorized for a past participle, and no progressive participle is subcategorized for a progressive participle. Thus ordering possibilities are sharply constrained, as can be seen from Table 2.1.[6] It is therefore morphosyntactic categories which are most directly ordered. Ordering has typically been thought of in terms of the lexemes and classes of lexemes involved: modals, perfect *have*, 'progressive' *be*, 'passive' *be*, as in

Table 2.1 *Category and subcategorization properties relevant to the ordering of auxiliaries*

Categories of auxiliary	Finite	Inf.	Past ptc.	Progr. ptc.	Pass. ptc.
modals	+	SC			
do	+	SC			
'modal' be	+	SC			
perfect have	+	+	SC		
'progressive' be	+	+	+	SC	
'passive' be	+	+	+	+	SC
copula be	+	+	+	+	

Here 'SC' (for 'subcategorizes') indicates the morphosyntactic category an auxiliary requires on a dependent verb or auxiliary, and '+' shows which morphosyntactic categories are available.

(7.b). But (8) gives a more appropriate conceptualization.[7] With the exception of the nonprogressive *ing*-forms, this is exemplified in (9).

(7) a. The morning would have been being enjoyed.
  b. modal – perfect *have* – 'progressive' *be* – 'passive' *be* – main verb

(8) finite – infinitive – past participle – progressive participle – passive participle

(9) a. For the morning *to-have been being enjoyed ...*
  (infinitive – past participle – progressive participle – passive participle)
  b. Paul *will be being tormented.*
  (finite – infinitive – progressive participle – passive participle)
  c. Paul *has been tormented.*
  (finite – past participle – passive participle)
  d. Paul *was being tormented.*
  (finite – progressive participle – passive participle)
  e. John *would have been* miserable.
  (finite – infinitive – past participle)

If this account is correct it implies that the standard conception of auxiliary order as essentially an ordering of TMA (tense, modality, aspect) components, or in English more particularly of specified lexemes and classes of lexemes (modals, *do*, perfect *have*, 'progressive' *be*, 'passive' *be*), is misguided, at least from the point of view of formal grammar. It has been suggested that the ordering TMA is a universal, even a syntactic universal. In English, however, it corresponds to nothing in the formal grammar, but arises only as a rather indirect function of formal statements. Thus if TMA ordering is indeed universal, this must be explained in some other component than syntax (for example, as depending on the interaction of semantics and language processing).

2.2 Morphosyntactic independence of auxiliaries

In the rest of this chapter I will mount a series of arguments for the position I have just sketched. Essentially they concern:

observational adequacy;
learnability;
arguments that morphosyntactic categories of verbs do not generalize to auxiliaries;
arguments that morphosyntactic categories of auxiliaries have individual properties and are therefore given some measure of separate status in the lexicon.

2.2.1 Accounting directly for the data

Given the lexicon of (6), the ordering of auxiliary categories and their availability in nonfinite constructions are immediately dealt with. Modals are finite only, preventing double modals and the occurrence of modals in infinitives, etc. Similarly for DO and 'modal' *is to*. Perfect HAVE lacks a past participle and a progressive *ing*-form, which rules out double perfects and progressives of the perfect. Finally, *being* may not take an *ing*-form in its complement, so that double progressives are impossible. The data is fully covered in a rather non-abstract way. The account achieves a striking 100 per cent observational adequacy.

This account also gives us an immediate integration of the 'double-*ing*' constraint with auxiliaries. Note that it is not only the double progressive as in (3.c) which is unavailable, but cases like (10), where *being* is not itself progressive.[8]

(10) a. *Paul's being talking ... (cf. the fact that Paul was talking)
b. *Paul walked along, being humming as he went.
c. *The choir being singing the national anthem was cheered by the crowd. (Cf. The choir which was singing ...)

Thus accounts which rule out only the double progressive, like Schachter's (1983) semantic account, or the syntactic accounts of GPS and ASW, miss a generalization; see Warner (1985: 7 n. 4) for discussion of this topic in GPS and ASW. It looks very much as if the required statement is a syntactic or morphosyntactic one preventing contiguous *ing*-forms within the verbal group, as has often been suggested. It is apparently fully grammaticized and is therefore distinct from the stylistic restriction found with other (e.g. aspectual) verbs, which is frequently violated (at least in British English). The straightforward statement that *being* is not subcategorized for an *ing*-form has already been adopted to prevent double progressives. It generalizes directly to the more general 'double-*ing* constraint', which is simply another fact of the same type, fitting within the general scheme suggested here.

2.2.2 Learnability

A central problem for any account of the ordering of auxiliaries is its learnability. Why should learners restrict the ordering in the appropriate way? Under the assumptions made here it is easy to sketch an idealized account of acquisition. Learners do not generalize the availability of auxiliary categories on the model of verbs. Instead they treat the forms as individual items, and make only more cautious generalizations. Note in support of this that children do not generalize verb properties to modals, but refrain from developing inflected third person singulars, infinitives, complements with the *to*-infinitive, and so forth. Now, if at whatever is the appropriate stage of development, the separate forms of HAVE and BE are treated as items which may have distinct properties, and are assigned properties on the basis of primary data, then there will be no progressive *having*, or past participle *had* for there will be no evidence for these categories. Similarly, *be* will be permitted with *ing*-complements, but *being* will not. So no 'double-*ing* constraint' is added to the grammar: the effect follows directly as a failure to generalize beyond the primary data. Thus this account provides a trivial but real answer to Baker's (1981) 'learnability problem' for auxiliary order and for the failure of morphosyntactic categories to generalize.

Interestingly, this also gives us the basis for an account of the development of the 'double-*ing* constraint', which was not a characteristic of earlier English, but seems to follow rapidly on the appearance of progressive *being* in the early nineteenth century. This is discussed below in §2.5.

2.2.3 Indications that the morphosyntax of verbs does not automatically apply to auxiliaries

The formal specification of any word class must include an account of its regular morphosyntactic categories, and their methods of formation. These two topics must be at least partially distinct, since suppletive and irregular formations may occur without special syntactic or semantic properties. Here I shall argue that at neither of these levels does what holds for 'full' verbs automatically carry over to auxiliaries.

(i) In support of this, note first that regular verbal morphology is weak or absent in auxiliaries. In the case of modals the indicative third person singular is endingless and the 'preterites' are irregular both morphologically and semantically. Finites of BE are irregular, and add distinctions to those found in full verbs (*am* : *are*; *was* : *were*; subjunctive *were*). Moreover the forms *does*, *did*, *has*, *had* must be listed, because of their irregular stems. Forms with *-n't* must presumably also be listed, as must clitics, and the unstressed forms which show idiosyncratic reductions, such as [bɪn] 'been', [əd] 'had', [dz] 'does' (Palmer 1988: 242ff.). Listedness does not, of course, mean that there is no regularity. But there is a very high degree of listedness involved here. The only fully regular forms are *being* and *having*, and I argue below that they might well be analysed as nonauxiliary forms. *Been* shows a nonproductive regularity, and should perhaps be seen as listed (Quirk *et al.* 1985: §3.16, Class 4B). Thus, if we look at auxiliaries as a separate group what is striking is how remarkably little regularity there is (particularly if we examine phonology rather than spelling). The most defensible account is indeed one in which the productive morphosyntax of full verbs is irrelevant: no productive rule defines either a category, or its particular form. Such rules are defined for V[–AUX]. In the case of [+AUX], there are remnants within irregular words: the *-d* of *could*, the *-es* of *does*, etc., and there may indeed be structuring: be_{AUX} – en_{PTC}, do_{AUX} – es_{3SG}, but the forms are not interrelated by systematic rule. It seems best to interpret such categories as synchronically 'dead' items. This reflects the distinction drawn by, among others, Aronoff (1976) between lexical structure which results from productive rules of word formation yielding regular and semantically transparent formations, and the structure (of varying degrees of completeness) which is listed as a property of individual lexical items which depart in some way from the full regularity of such rules. Aronoff noted that words once formed tend to develop idiosyncratic properties, and become no longer fully predictable by rule. I suggest that the status of the morphosyntactic categories of auxiliaries is in this sense akin to that of distinct words, retaining elements of structure but having 'drifted off' from a motivating rule.

Two further points to reduce the importance of the partial regularities shown by auxiliary DO and HAVE. First, note that these are supported by their identity to full verb paradigms in Standard English, where they are partly motivated by rule: $do_V - es_{3SG}$. Secondly, note that in some dialects they have become distinct from verbal inflection, as in parts of the west of England: *He does his best, do he? He has a sister, have he?* (Cheshire 1982: 32ff., Hughes and Trudgill 1987: 17).

(ii) *Need* and *dare* provide some further striking evidence. Both are found as modals and as full verbs. In the case of *need* these sets of properties contrast sharply (see *OED Need, v.*[2] 8., Quirk *et al.* 1985: §3.42). What is striking is the absence of a past tense *needed* with the modal. The regular rule of verbal morphology fails: indeed the form is rejected. Modals certainly may have past-tense uses (*could* in particular), and speakers use the form *need* as a past in restricted contexts (Jespersen 1909–49: IV, §1.7; Visser 1963–73: §§796, 1348–9; hereafter simply referred to as 'V§796', etc.).[9] This is a revealing gap. It is as if the relevant generalization is 'A modal may have a distinctive form with (some) past-tense uses, but it may not be formed according to the regular morphology of full verbs.'

(11) *You needed not go. *You neededn't go. *Needed you go?

(12) a. there was nobody who need be guarded from anyone else. (V§1349; example for 1956)
b. she was wondering whether she dare ask him to come to dinner. (V§1363; example for 1900)

Dare shows a much less clear partitioning of modal and full verb constructions, and the plain infinitive is found with *dares* and nonfinites of *dare* as well as with the regular past *dared* (see V§1355ff., *OED Dare, v.*[1], Quirk *et al.* 1985: §3.42). But the uninflected *dare* is also used for the past (V§§796, 1363, *OED Dare, v.*[1] A.1.), and in dialect the two normal negative preterites are formations of the types *durstn't* and *daren't*; while the type *daredn't* is uncommon (Nelson Francis 1968). This bears out the generalization offered above.

(iii) *Being* and *having*, the forms in which verbal morphosyntax most obviously does generalize, show the weakest evidence of auxiliary behaviour, and are open to analysis as nonauxiliaries. For nonfinites in *ing*, as we saw in the last chapter, the major test of auxiliary status is provided by ellipsis.[10] In American English, however, *being* and *having* fail this test; see the judgements of this ellipsis reported in Akmajian and Wasow (1975), Iwakura (1977, 1983), GPS, and elsewhere.

(13) a. *Kim is being noisy and Sandy is being, too.
b. *Kim was being watched by the FBI, and Chris was being, too.

c. *Kim's having resigned was surprising, but Lee's having came as no surprise.
(examples and judgements from GPS: 607)

The simplest account of such data is that ellipsis 'is blocked if an *ing*-form immediately precedes the deletion target' (GPS: 624, and see Sag 1977). This generalization will be captured if the grammar does not generate auxiliary *ing*-forms with post-auxiliary ellipsis. But now we can see a motivation for the puzzling failure of post-auxiliary ellipsis to generalize across auxiliaries. The transparency of formation of *being* and *having*, together with the productive nature of *ing*-forms with nonauxiliary verbs, leads to an analysis of *being* and *having* as V[–AUX].[11] Hence their lack of post-auxiliary ellipsis, which is restricted to [+AUX]. This is supported by a further consideration. ASW and GPS both discuss restrictions on the 'fronting' of the complements of auxiliaries. The paradigm ASW report is one (to put it in my terms) in which a nonfinite VP headed by a nonauxiliary verb or by *being* may be fronted, but one headed by *be* or *been* may not. The main facts are recapitulated in (14.a–j), which are taken from GPS (604), with the addition of (k–m), which are not explicitly discussed by ASW or GPS.[12]

(14) a. *... and went he.
b. ... and go he will.
c. ... and going he is.
d. ... and gone he has.
e. ... and taken by Sandy he was.
f. *... and to go he is.
g. *... and to go he wants.
h. *... and be going he will.
i. *... and have gone he will.
j. ... and being evasive he was.
k. ?*... and be happy/tortured he will.
l. *... and been good/tortured he has.
m. ... and being tortured he was.

If *being* is [–AUX], then there is a straightforward generalization here: a nonfinite VP may be fronted provided it is not headed by an auxiliary. If *being* is [+AUX], however, there is no obvious generalization. Thus these two exceptional aspects of the behaviour of *being* follow straightforwardly from its analysis as [–AUX], and their acquisition and maintenance are accounted for as motivated by morphological transparency. Notice that this gives a direct and unitary account of the two most important pieces of evidence cited by ASW (25f.) in favour of their rule restructuring *be* from V^1 into V^2.[13] It also compares well with the more recent treatment of fronting data in Roberts

(1990). He is forced to assign exceptional status to passive and copula BE, which 'induce AUX Reanalysis at DS, and occupy the same V-projection as the main verb throughout the derivation. Therefore they are required to undergo [fronting] with the main verb' (1990: 395). But as presented the analysis does not cover the facts, since it apparently treats (14.l) as grammatical, and it fails to generate the impeccable ... *and tortured he has been.*[14]

British English is not so neatly dealt with. Here, post-auxiliary ellipsis does not fail with *being*, though for many speakers it does with *having* (GPS: 607): the type of (13.a, b) is generally acceptable, and (c) is for some. But the fronting of VP headed by *being* is grammatical as in American English. The most straightforward analysis treats *being* and *having* as [–AUX], but allows that they may occur with ellipsis, which is after all not only conditioned by auxiliaries but also by individual nonauxiliary verbs. It is, however, worth noting that there is a basis for an account of the double-*ing* constraint with such verbs as *begin, finish*, etc. if the rejection of *ing*-complements after *being* is reinterpreted as a property of the affix. The fact that this more general constraint is apparently stronger in American English than in British English may show that British English has not so fully accepted the implications of the transparent analysis, something also implied by the ellipsis facts; perhaps then British English *being* would be better analysed as unspecified for [AUX].

2.2.4 Special properties of auxiliary forms which imply that they are individually specified

In addition to this evidence that verbal morphosyntax does not run for auxiliaries, there is additional evidence that auxiliary forms have independent properties, as required by the account of §2.1.3. This is supported both by some direct evidence of idiosyncratic properties and by a tendency for finites and nonfinites to have distinct subcategorizations.

(i) The *of*-infinitive of perfect HAVE. The use of a form [ɒv] for the perfect infinitive *have* is common in nonstandard dialects and the language of children. It clearly represents a restressing of the [əv] which originated as a reduced form of *have*, but the result is homophonous with (and spelled like) the preposition *of*. This usage is recorded in *OED* since 1837 (Supplement III 1982, *Of*), and is found both after modals and *to*, and (in my experience) before ellipsis.

(15) a. I wouldn't of tried to muscle in on it.
b. I'm certainly glad to of made your acquaintance.
(*OED* Supplement III 1982, *Of*)

It is as if those who have little contact with the written form at first suppose that perfect HAVE is suppletive or that a separate lexeme (perhaps a branch of OF) is in question. Older children reanalyse the form as belonging to HAVE presumably after sufficient contact with the written form. What is interesting here is not the nature of a proper analysis of this form, but the fact that such a 'misidentification' should be prevalent. It seems that the formal identity of perfect HAVE is not prized by learners and nonliterates, but is maintained by the written standard language. This argues that the normal rule for English verbs that the base infinitive and the uninflected present indicative are identical does not hold with any force for perfect HAVE, and that the identity is not so much systematic as accidental.

(ii) *Been to.* There is a curious use of the past participle *been.* In construction with a phrase implying motion or purpose it can mean (roughly) 'gone' (see *OED Be*, *v*. B.6).

(16) a. I have not yet been to Helsinki, though I should like to go.
b. Nor have I been over the Golden Gate bridge.

This sense is not available for other forms of BE (although it was in earlier English). Again this implies that the generalization of lexical sense and subcategorization normal across verb forms within a lexeme (past participle, indicative, infinitive, present participle) does not automatically hold for BE. This could be straightforwardly stated within an account in which the morphosyntactic categories of BE were individually listed in the lexicon and permitted to have distinct properties.

(iii) The idiosyncrasies of imperative *do* and *don't* imply that these should be analysed as separate items. Briefly: (a) they differ from periphrastic *do* in that they may occur in construction with auxiliary *be* (and *have*); (b) *do* is unlike *don't* in not permitting a following subject; (c) *do* and *don't* are unlike imperative *be* and *have* in their occurrence with *not* and *-n't*.

(17) a. Don't be a nuisance. Do be quiet.
b. Don't you talk to me like that! *Do you come and see me!
c. *Be not a nuisance. *Ben't a nuisance.

Thus special statements are required for each of these forms, and this is consistent with the account developed here.

(iv) *is to* VP. The restriction of 'modal' BE to finite is also in accordance with the general scheme adopted here, under which the subcategorization of finites and nonfinites may differ. If it was clear that 'modal' BE and 'predicative' BE were the same item, this would be quite a strong line of argument. Unfortunately the evidence of coordination (though unclear) is if anything against a shared subcategorization. Here, too, then we have a relatively weak supportive argument, but a suggestive one.

(v) *Have got to*. In British English *have got* may be the perfect of *get* (corresponding to American English *have gotten*), but it also occurs as a simple equivalent to *have*, and that is the usage discussed here. It never occurs after *do* and is always the auxiliary. It may always be a nonimperative finite. Other categories, however, are not freely available. In the case of *have got to*, Quirk *et al.* (1985: §3.45) and Huddleston (1980) claim that all nonfinites are missing, and imperatives are also surely unavailable.[15] Some of this absence may be semantically motivated, granted the fact that *have got to* is unlike *have to* in that it 'tends not to have habitual meaning' (Quirk *et al.* 1985: §3.48, and see Coates 1983: 54). But the absence of the infinitive and nonprogressive *ing* looks like a formal restriction, as does that of the past participle which is totally impossible (this can hardly follow from analysis of the construction as a perfect, which is not plausible), and this should probably be generalized so that only nonimperative finite forms of HAVE are available in this construction.

(18) a. This contrast will surely have to be attributed to some other aspect of stativity.
b. *This contrast will surely have got to be attributed to some other aspect of stativity.

In the case of *have got* with an object, imperatives and progressives are absent, but this may follow from the construction's stativity. Infinitives and nonprogressive *ing*-forms vary in acceptability, and there can be much individual uncertainty in judgements (see Jespersen 1909–49: IV, §4.3). Thus there may be some restriction here but the matter is unclear.

(vi) When *have* is subcategorized for NP or *to* VP it may show either nonauxiliary properties or auxiliary properties (especially in British English, Quirk *et al.* 1985: §§3.34, 3.48). Is it possible that auxiliary properties are restricted, say to finite categories? This is difficult to maintain since occurrence with ellipsis, which is our major test for nonfinite auxiliaryhood, is also found with some verbs, including nonauxiliary (dynamic) *have*. None the less, ellipsis is sometimes restricted in a suggestive way, as in these two cases.

(a) The type of American English reported by Akmajian and Wasow (1975, 1977) distinguishes finite and nonfinite possessive *have*. Ellipsis is permitted after finites (which are presumably auxiliary) but not after nonfinites. (In their terms, *have*-shift is blocked unless AUX contains nothing but tense).[16]

(19) a. John has had a temperature whenever Mary has (*had).
b. You might have an opinion, but I won't (*have).
c. We have volunteers, but we don't want to (*have).
(examples and judgements from Akmajian and Wasow 1975, 1977)

(b) For some speakers of British English the *have* of *have to* rejects ellipsis when it is nonfinite, as in (20).[17]

(20) a. Have you to go? – Yes I'm afraid I have.
b. *No, but I soon will have.
c. *No, but in the past I have had.
d. *No, but he's having.
e. *Mary's having to leave was unexpected, but I was really surprised at Paul's having.

These two sets of facts would be accounted for if *have* with NP or *to* VP had auxiliary properties only when finite, so that [+AUX] was nonimperative finite only, and [–AUX] allowed a full range of morphosyntactic categories. It is attractive to have an essentially single account both of the difficult data noted by Akmajian and Wasow, and of a British parallel. Clearly, there is only an indirect supportive argument here, and variability obscures the data. But it is highly suggestive none the less.

(vii) The past *had* occurs with a following infinitive *have*, apparently with the construction of a modal (being perhaps historically related to *would*). This is common in spoken and nonstandard British English. For examples, see V§2157.

(21) If you hadn't have come, God, it would have been terrible.

2.2.5 *Plausibility*[18]

Finally let me support the plausibility of this account by briefly discussing English personal pronouns. The status of these words has been argued. They seem to belong in a more general class which includes nouns and determiners, though it is less clear which (if either) of these they are more closely associated with. Huddleston (1984: 96, 229) classes them with nouns. Postal (1966) associated them more closely with determiners (see also discussions in Sommerstein 1972, Hudson 1984: 90f.; 1987: 121ff.). This would also follow if determiners head noun phrases as Hudson (1987) argues. A similar line is pursued in some recent work in GB (see Abney 1987, Stowell 1989 *inter alia*). Whichever view is taken here, there are several points of contact between the relationship 'personal pronoun : noun' and 'auxiliary : full verb'. In both cases we have a grammatical category which shares some of the subcategory distinctions of the full class category, and which may head a phrase which contains the full class category (perhaps within a further phrase). But now note these two points about English personal pronouns.

(a) Their categories do not simply reflect those of nouns (and noun phrases containing nouns), though they are related.

Thus personal pronouns show number and definiteness, like other noun phrases. But they also encode gender, as 'full' noun phrases do not, and they have a different system of case. Case in noun phrases is common : genitive, where the *s*-genitive belongs to noun phrases not to nouns. In pronouns case is subjective : oblique : genitive, where genitive shows the further distinction determiner (*my*) or nominal (*mine*).[19]

(b) The members of their paradigms have rather distinct properties, which are not interconnected by regular morphological or morphosyntactic relationships as in the case of paradigms of the major parts of speech.

None of the regular morphosyntactic relationships of the noun and noun phrase obtain, except arguably *it – its* (though note fossilized *s*-genitives in the nominal genitives *hers*, *ours*, *yours*, *theirs*, which might be better regarded as a subregularity of personal pronouns). Moreover, members of the 'paradigm' (e.g. *I*, *me*, *my*, *mine*; *we*, *us*, *our*, *ours*) are liable to have different properties. For example, *my*, *our* are determiners, *we* either may be one or has a subcategorization additional to *I*.

(22) *I Britisher, *you (sg.) Britisher *(acceptable as a direct address)*, *he Britisher, we British, you British, *they British

Here a grammatical category related to the major category shows a similar but far from identical set of categories, the morphology of these categories differs, and members of the paradigm may show properties unrelated to those of other members.[20] There are interesting parallels here with my proposed account of auxiliaries. These have a partly distinct set of categories from full verbs (adding negative forms, agreement in BE, subjunctive *were*), and the categories appropriate to full verbs do not simply carry over to auxiliaries but need individual specification. The morphology of these categories is different (in the modal third person singular) or is typically opaque, not the result of the application of regular rules of formation. Finally, members of the paradigm may have distinct properties, though this is shown in subcategorization rather than in subclass membership.

I would not want to press the parallel just discussed too far. Auxiliaries seem 'closer' to verbs than personal pronouns do to nouns, and the interrelationships may differ in a variety of ways. But given the limited nature of parallels possible in English, the case of personal pronouns bears some major resemblances to that of auxiliaries, and it enhances the plausibility of the analysis proposed above.

2.3 Inflected auxiliaries as 'anaphoric islands'

In this section I will develop a further argument that the morphosyntactic categories of BE and HAVE are not related to each other in the same way as such categories are in verbs, but show a more independent, 'word-like' status. This depends on the fact that inflected auxiliaries and inflected nonauxiliary verbs behave differently in elliptical constructions.

Postal (1969) noted that the parts of words, unlike parts of phrases, do not enter into anaphoric relations. Hence there are contrasts like the following (using some of Postal's examples):

(23) a. Max's parents are dead and he deeply misses them [sc. his parents]. (= Postal's (3))
b. *Max is an orphan and he deeply misses them [sc. his parents].
(where an *orphan* is someone (immature) whose parents are dead, so that 'the meaning of *orphan* involves reference to the parents of an indiviual'; 1969: 206)

(24) a. The girl with long legs wants to insure them [sc. her legs]. (= Postal's (45))
b. *The long-legged girl wants to insure them [sc. her legs].

(25) a. Max's parents are dead but mine are alive [sc. my parents]. (= Postal's (21))
b. *Max is an orphan but mine are alive [sc. my parents].

(26) a. Max wanted to fasten the boards together with glue but Pete wanted to do so with tape [sc. fasten the boards together]. (= Postal's (35))
b. *Max wanted to glue the boards together but Pete wanted to do so with tape [sc. fasten the boards together].

Postal looked at coreference (as in (23)), identity of sense anaphora (as in (25)), and *do so* anaphora (as in (26)) both with morphologically transparent antecedents like *long-legged*, and with morphologically opaque monomorphemic antecedents like *orphan*. His general conclusion was that the three types of anaphora he considered are denied access to the internal composition of both derivatives and monomorphemic items (1969: 217).[21] In Postal's terminology 'words' are 'Anaphoric Islands'. But (as Postal notes) inflection does not block such access, so that it will be necessary 'to appeal to something like the traditional inflection–derivation distinction' (1969: 227). Though Postal does not put it this way, it is the lexeme or the inflectional stem which forms an anaphoric island, rather than the surface word form.[22]

(27) a. John's book is making him rich [sc. John]. (= Postal's (103))
b. Paul has written two books, Mary only one [sc. book].
c. Harry killed himself but I won't do so [sc. kill myself]. (= Postal's (104))

This has a direct application to post-auxiliary ellipsis, which involves retrieval of the sense of an appropriate antecedent (with some systematic substitution of reference, as in the case of *do so* in (27.c) above) (see Hankamer and Sag 1976, Sag 1979).[23] Like the other 'identity of sense' anaphoras discussed by Postal, post-auxiliary ellipsis is apparently subject to his constraint on anaphoric islands: all his *do so* examples can be paralleled with instances of post-auxiliary ellipsis and others can readily be constructed.[24]

(28) a. Max wanted to fasten the boards together with glue but Pete wanted to with tape [sc. fasten the boards together].
b. *Max wanted to glue the boards together but Pete wanted to with tape [sc. fasten the boards together].

(29) a. People who jog really shouldn't [sc. jog].
b. *Joggers really shouldn't [sc. jog].

Now, crucially for my argument, when post-auxiliary ellipsis involves a VP headed by a nonauxiliary verb, it is like the other 'identity of sense' anaphoras discussed by Postal in not requiring inflections on the head verb of the antecedent VP and on that 'required' at the site of ellipsis to match. Thus in cases of inflectional mismatch it is apparently the sense of the head lexeme or uninflected stem which is retrieved. Pullum and Wilson cite (30.a–d) to establish the irrelevance of participial affixes to post-auxiliary ellipsis (1977: 766 example 47); Sag gives (30.e):

(30) a. I haven't done it yet, but I will [sc. do it]. past ptc. – inf.
b. Harry will probably tell Sarah – in fact he probably already has [sc. told Sarah]. inf. – past ptc.
c. Max is selling hot dogs for a living, and soon all of us will have to [sc. sell hot dogs for a living]. pres. ptc. – inf.
d. I'm hoping that not all of my gerbils will die, but the weak ones already are [sc. dying]. inf. – pres. ptc.

e. John said he would never take money on the side, but I knew he was [sc. taking money on the side]. inf. – pres. ptc. (Sag 1977: 51)

See V§1756ff. for further instances. Other related examples support and generalize the point. There are instances of lowered acceptability but it seems reasonable to attribute these to processing difficulties and conclude that there is no general requirement of inflectional identity; see Warner (1985: 58f.) for some discussion. The only exception is that a passive participle may not normally be supplied from a preceding active form or vice versa. But more than straightforward inflection is involved here.

(31) a. Harry told Sarah. At least I think he did [sc. tell Sarah]. indic. – inf.
b. Harry told Sarah. At least I'm pretty sure he has [sc. told Sarah]. indic. – past ptc.
c. I hope that not all of my gerbils die, but the weak ones already are [sc. dying]. indic. – pres. ptc.
d. If Harry isn't telling Sarah right now it's because he already has [sc. told Sarah]. pres. ptc. – past ptc.
e. If Harry hasn't told Sarah yet, I'll bet he is right now [sc. telling Sarah]. past ptc. – pres. ptc.

(32) a. *John has loved but hasn't himself been [sc. loved].
b. *John has never been loved, though he often himself has [sc. loved].

So, if we leave aside the passive, we can conclude that inflection of the antecedent is transparent in the post-auxiliary ellipsis of phrases headed by verbs, but the 'word without inflection' is an anaphoric island.[25]

The conditions under which phrases headed by auxiliaries undergo ellipsis are, however, quite different, though there is no reason to suppose that a distinct process is involved.[26] This difference is very striking when the antecedent is an indicative form of BE. Ellipsis is quite impossible and the contrast with nonauxiliary verbs is very sharp. Compare (33.a) with (33.b), (34.a) with (34.b). In the first the infinitive phrase *grow tomatoes* can be retrieved from the indicative *grows tomatoes*. But the nonfinite *be happy* cannot be retrieved from indicative *is happy*. A common reaction to this type of example is incomprehension, and a failure to recognize that the retrieval of a BE-phrase is in question.[27] Notice that the properties of the antecedent are crucial here, witness the difference between (b) and (c). It is, of course, examples which show ellipsis of both BE and its predicate which are involved, and not instances which like (d) show only ellipsis of the predicate.

(33) a. John grows tomatoes, and Mary soon will [sc. grow tomatoes]. indic. – inf.
b. *John is happy, and Mary soon will [sc. be happy]. indic. – inf.
c. John will be happy, and Mary may too [sc. be happy]. inf. – inf.
d. John is happy, and Mary soon will be [sc. happy]. pred. – pred.

(34) a. John seems happy today, and he often has in the past [sc. seemed happy]. indic. – past ptc.
b. *John is happy today, and he often has in the past [sc. been happy]. indic. – past ptc.
c. John has been happy today, and he often has in the past too [sc. been happy]. past ptc. – past ptc.
d. John is happy today, and he often has been in the past [sc. happy]. pred. – pred.

There is a parallel situation when the antecedent form of BE is nonfinite. But here there are two problems: firstly, there is a good deal of interpersonal variation in judgements of acceptability; secondly, it seems that several cross-cutting factors (which I discuss briefly below) are likely to be relevant. But at least some speakers of British English judge that the ellipsis of a phrase headed by a nonfinite form of BE is only normally acceptable when there is morphological identity between this form and its antecedent. This judgement is recorded by Huddleston, who finds examples without identity 'not acceptable (or only marginally so)' (1978: 57). I share it, and it is well supported in the results of a questionnaire intended to provide a securer data base which I administered at York in 1985 to nineteen undergraduates who were native speakers of British English.[28] This questionnaire included over sixty sentences in which the ellipsis of a verb phrase was to be retrieved from a preceding nonfinite verb phrase whose head was of a differing morphosyntactic category, as in the following.

(35) a. John was stealing small amounts, and I'm afraid Mary has once or twice too [sc. stolen small amounts].
b. *John was being dishonest, and I'm afraid Mary has once or twice too [sc. been dishonest].

Sentences containing BE were (as here) typically paired with parallel sentences of similar sense containing V, but the order of presentation was otherwise random. Informants were asked to rate the acceptability of sentences on the scale: ✓, ?, ??, ?*, *. The results were rather striking, and are most easily summarized in terms of three groups (of six, six and seven informants respectively).

(i) In the first group the great majority of judgements (84 per cent) showed ellipses with BE less acceptable than ellipses with V. Overall, over half of the judgements were of a sharp contrast in which ellipses with BE were marked * or ?*, those with V were marked ✓ or ?. Rather few pairs (12 per cent) were accorded equal status.

(ii) In the second group two-thirds of the judgements rated ellipses with BE worse than the corresponding ellipses with V, but the distinction was often narrower than in the first group. About one-third of the judgements rated ellipses with BE and with V equally acceptable.

(iii) Finally, in the third group, nearly two-thirds of the instances of ellipsis with BE were judged to be as acceptable as the corresponding ellipsis with V, and the majority of these were rated fully acceptable (✓). But about one-third were still rated worse than a corresponding ellipsis with V.

These results are strikingly clear. For some there was a sharp distinction between ellipses headed by BE and V involving retrieval from a morphologically distinct nonfinite form. For others it was less sharp. But it remained a factor even for those who most often found no difference.[29] Thus there is a clear distinction here between nonauxiliary verbs and BE. Once again it is the properties of the antecedent that are involved, since, with some restrictions, such ellipses seem generally acceptable with an identical antecedent in British English (see Halliday and Hasan 1976: 174). Some examples of the types of (36) with a morphologically identical antecedent were included in the questionnaire, and they were rated fully acceptable (✓) by the great majority of the respondents, with a small proportion of rejections.

Ellipsis of *be* etc. with identical antecedent

(36) a. John will always be a brute, and I expect his son will too [sc. be a brute].
b. The children have been very good here. Do you think they would have at home [sc. been very good]?
c. If John was being awkward yesterday, no doubt he is again today [sc. being awkward].

Here follow examples of ellipsis of BE-phrases and of V-phrases which are drawn from those used in the questionnaire. I have indicated my own judgements which normally distinguish sharply between sentences with ellipsis of BE and with ellipsis of V: * versus ✓. But for some readers the difference will sometimes or typically be narrower (say ?* versus ??) or it may be absent. My claim does not depend on absolute judgements here, but on the existence of a contrast between sets of judgements for some speakers of English.

Ellipsis of *be* with antecedent *been*.

(37) a. *The children have been very good here. I wish they would at home [sc. be very good].
b. The children have eaten all their food here. I wish they would at home.

Ellipsis of *be* with antecedent *being*.

(38) a. *Paula was being really wilful this evening. I do wish she wouldn't [sc. be wilful].
b. Paula was making snide remarks all afternoon. I do wish she wouldn't.

Ellipsis of *been* with antecedent infinitive *be*.

(39) a. *Paula may be late this evening. She already has once this week [sc. been late].
b. Paula may arrive late this evening. She already has once this week.

Ellipsis of *been* with antecedent *being*.

(40) a. *John was being naughty when I arrived, and they told me Paul had earlier in the morning [sc. been naughty].
b. John was throwing a tantrum when I arrived, and they told me Paul had earlier in the morning.

Ellipsis of *being* with antecedent infinitive *be*.

(41) a. *He can be really bloody-minded. Indeed, it's likely enough that he is at this very moment [sc. being really bloody-minded].
b. ?He can make a real nuisance of himself. Indeed, it's likely enough that he is at this very moment.

Ellipsis of *being* with antecedent *been*.

(42) a. *John has already been unkind to Ruth for most of the afternoon, so at this very moment he probably still is [sc. being unkind to Ruth].
b. ?John has already teased Ruth for most of the afternoon, so at this very moment he probably still is.

HAVE also has nonfinite forms. When it is the perfect auxiliary it seems to behave like nonfinite forms of BE, in that there is a range of responses to its ellipsis. Some individuals apparently have quite strong judgements favouring morphosyntactic identity between ellipsis site and antecedent and rejecting examples which lack it, though for others the judgements involved are not so clear, or so consistent. A similar rejection of a non-identical antecedent also seems to hold for instances of possessive HAVE following a HAVE which shows auxiliary behaviour. A striking point of contrast with BE is that the retrieval of nonfinite from indicative HAVE was not strongly rejected by virtually all informants: both for perfect and possessive HAVE one-third of judgements found such ellipses acceptable or merely questionable (✓ or ?).[30]

(43) a. *The lower floors haven't caught fire, so the upper floors can't yet either [sc. have caught fire]. indic. – inf.

b. The lower floors can't have caught fire, so the upper floors can't yet either. inf. – inf.

(44) ?*You haven't seen one yet? You should by now if they're really there [sc. have seen one]. indic. – inf.

(45) a. ?*If John hasn't any money, then Bill won't [sc. have any money] either. indic. – inf.

b. John may still have the money you gave him, but Bill won't [sc. have the money you gave him]. (But the antecedent need not be the auxiliary.)

The implication is that the requirement of morphological identity under discussion holds not merely for BE but also for auxiliary HAVE, that is, for those auxiliary verbs which have nonfinite forms.[31]

This is a complex and murky area, in which a variety of factors apparently influences acceptability. Some of these are:

(i) To some extent in British English, but particularly in American English, forms of BE and HAVE which are identical to their antecedents may resist, or prefer, ellipsis in particular circumstances (see Levin 1980, 1981, 1986, Steele *et al.* 1981 Appendix A). Levin investigates the ellipsis of infinitive *be* with an infinitive as its antecedent in American English in some detail, and concludes that it is normally acceptable after a modal and unacceptable after *to*, but that acceptability after *to* 'improves slightly if the state of affairs described in *be*'s complement is one which is under (the) immediate control of the subject' (1980: 153; 1986: 183). The effects of this weaker 'semantic/pragmatic' factor can also be seen after modals. It seems that in British English too ellipsis of BE, though more generally acceptable than in American English, is easier with an agentive than with a stative interpretation. My questionnaire focussed on examples after modals rather than after *to*, and (outside passives) on agentive examples rather than stative ones, in order to reduce the involvement of these factors and highlight the contribution of the morphosyntactic identity.

(ii) Intonation and information structure are relevant (Local and Wells 1983, and cf. Zwicky and Levin 1980, Zwicky 1980). In particular, the givenness of the auxiliary preceding the site of ellipsis plays a role in some instances, for example stranded *being* is less acceptable when it is given, but *ought* prefers to be given (Huddleston 1980: 70–1).[32]

Now the element of variability in the data and the range of factors which apparently control acceptability both make for uncertainty. But the series of contrasts established above has some striking features:

(i) the exceptionlessness of the contrast when an indicative form of BE is antecedent;
(ii) the firmness with which the contrast holds for some speakers for HAVE and nonfinite BE;
(iii) the fact that the contrast remains for other speakers though it is weaker.

This points to the reliability of the following generalization: in cases of ellipsis of a VP after an auxiliary, if the head of the VP in ellipsis is an auxiliary verb, it must belong to the same morphosyntactic category as its discourse antecedent, if it is a nonauxiliary verb it may differ from its discourse antecedent in morphosyntactic category, provided it does not differ in voice.[33]

Where the antecedent is an indicative form of BE this apparently holds without exception in standard dialects.[34] But where it is a form of HAVE or a nonfinite form of BE the statement does not hold equally for all speakers. For some it is a tendency rather than a (virtually) exceptionless statement.

This generalization is clearly consistent with the assignment of a separate status to the morphosyntactic categories of English auxiliaries: they are anaphoric islands because they are uninflected. But it is possible to go beyond this, because they can be divided into those which are monomorphemic and those which have some morphological transparency. This gives us an account of the odd skewing of the data, whereby (i) indicative forms of BE are exceptionlessly anaphoric islands; (ii) both indicatives and nonfinites of HAVE are classed with nonfinites of BE as variably anaphoric islands. One obvious property which distinguishes these groups is that indicative forms of BE are fully opaque in morphology, whereas forms of HAVE and nonfinites of BE, though largely irregular, retain some degree of morphological transparency. When Postal discussed anaphoric islands he divided them into two categories: 'monomorphemic lexical items' and 'derivatives', where the second were largely transparent in morphology. He starred all violations equally. But Lakoff and Ross (1972) pointed out that the two categories in fact differ. Where there is no morphological relationship, there is clear unacceptability. But derivatives with some structural transparency lead to weaker judgements of unacceptability, or may even be accepted, though this is subject to variation between speakers. Thus there are contrasts like the following (where the *flutist/flautist* examples are given by Lakoff and Ross to show the surfacey nature of the transparency involved, which they dub 'surface phonetic analyzability'):

(46) a. *There is a chiropodist round the corner. Why don't you let him look at yours [sc. your feet]?

b. ?*There is a foot-doctor round the corner. Why don't you let him look at yours?

c. There is a man who doctors feet round the corner. Why don't you let him look at yours?

(47) a. *Flautists are a strange breed: it [sc. the flute] appears not to sound shrill to them.

b. ?Flutists are a strange breed: it appears not to sound shrill to them.

Lakoff and Ross were discussing pronominal coreference. But if their results hold for anaphoric islands more generally, then clearly *is* and *been* etc. may be interpreted as a monomorphemic item and as a derivative respectively. Then we have the following typology.

(i) Morphosyntactic categories of nonauxiliary verbs: inflectional – transparent to anaphoric retrieval.

(ii) Morphosyntactic categories of auxiliaries: not inflectional.
(a) with some degree of 'surface phonetic analyzability' or of structural transparency: forms of HAVE, nonfinites of BE – variable transparency to anaphoric retrieval.
(b) without 'surface phonetic analyzability' or structural transparency: indicatives of BE – no transparency to anaphoric retrieval.

This typology fits the facts rather convincingly. Let me make two immediate points about it. First, the restriction on indicatives of BE is very striking. All speakers of Standard English seem to agree that the type is impossible. This must, moreover, be due to a property of BE and not one of indicative auxiliaries, since (in some British English at least) the ellipsis of a HAVE-phrase with an indicative antecedent is quite different, being sometimes relatively acceptable. So the status of examples like (33.b) cannot be due to a structural property of indicative auxiliaries in general, or to their being a separate word class distinct from nonfinites, though either suggestion might otherwise seem plausible (see Steele *et al.* 1981 Appendix A).

Second, the restriction on indicatives of BE cannot simply be attributed to the fact that these forms are suppletive. There is more to it than just this. This is clear both from the fact that the restriction was absent in earlier English, when indicatives of BE were already suppletive, and from the fact that speakers typically seem to find ellipsis involving retrieval from suppletive instances natural, though reactions can vary. Thus Sag (1977) cited (49) as grammatical without comment despite the retrieval of *go* from suppletive *went.*

(48) 'If you were never particularly struck by her manners before,' said she 'I think you will [sc. be struck by her manners] to-day.'

1816 Jane Austen, *Emma* (ed. by R.W. Chapman, Oxford University Press, 1923) 194

(49) Although John went to the store, Betsy didn't [sc. go to the store]. (Sag 1977: 8, example 1.2.9a)

It is worth noting too that mere 'lexical listedness' cannot be what distinguishes nonfinites of BE either, since retrieval with nonauxiliary verbs is unrestricted in the case of irregular morphology of the type that would presumably be listed in the lexicon even under weak versions of the lexicalist hypothesis, for example *taught, kept.*

(50) a. John kept smiling, and Mary did too [sc. keep smiling].
b. John taught syntax and morphology together, but you don't have to [sc. teach syntax and morphology together].

Thus whatever controls the transparency and opacity of these morphosyntactic categories it does not depend on the regularity of their (affixal) morphology.

I conclude that the contrast between the behaviour of auxiliaries and nonauxiliary verbs as antecedents to ellipsis points to a distinct status for the morphosyntactic categories of auxiliaries, and supports the position argued for earlier in the chapter that they do not share verbal inflection. Their forms do not behave as if they were inflected, but like monomorphemic or derived items. This account has the particular virtue that it straightforwardly predicts the rather peculiar distinction between indicative forms of BE and other auxiliary forms.

2.4 Implications for modals of this account

The rationale for the independent status of indicative forms of BE and HAVE in elliptical constructions within the account I am developing is clear: they are members of the class auxiliary, and this class is not subject to the morphosyntactic generalizations which run for verbs. Thus apparently 'inflected' combinations of BE and HAVE with tense or mood are in fact unanalysable, and this renders them opaque to the retrieval of distinct categories. (The status of agreement is doubtful; note that the acceptability of ellipses of auxiliary HAVE does not depend on whether an antecedent finite shows agreement or not: *have/has* vs. *had.*) Now, this rationale must surely extend also to modals. These will therefore be analysed as having either tense, mood, or both, incorporated in a way which is not morphosyntactically factorizable. After all, if they could be factored, learners would have some basis for a generalization including auxiliaries which might permit retrieval of *be* from *is* in anaphora.

But if they cannot be factored, we can interpret the opacity of *is* not as idiosyncratic but as based in a more general fact about auxiliaries. This is important since it will account for the failure of learners to generalize the anaphora properties of verbs.

Regrettably the most straightforward evidence for this is not available in Standard English, for although modals are not retrievable in post-auxiliary ellipsis, this might follow from the absence of nonfinites.[35] More generally, however, this view seems rather plausible: the idiosyncrasy of 'preterite' modals has often been noted, and modals are arguably opaque also to mood.

Opacity of tense

In §1.2(k) I pointed out that the 'preterite' of modals had a distribution very unlike that of the preterite of verbs: they are much more widely available in generally hypothetical and conditional uses and with present reference, much less available as past tenses. Indeed reference to the past seems to be virtually restricted to indirect (or virtual indirect) speech and to cases involving dynamic modality with subject selection (see Palmer 1979: §§2.3.4, 5.3.3, 7.4.3). It is far from clear that *might* contains the same morpheme 'past' as verbs; if it does then the modal itself constitutes a context which often renders this opaque.[36] If it does not, then we may have a form–meaning correlation special to modals, say 'conditional' versus 'non-conditional' manifested with a range of implications such as hypothetical, formal, polite, etc. (see e.g. Perkins 1983: 50ff. – though he later identifies this with tense). But the correlation holds for only a handful of items, and there are exceptions (*must*, *need*, etc.). Under either of these types of analysis it is plausible to interpret the preterites of modals not as incorporating an inflectional rule, but as stated in the lexicon as noncompositional items corresponding at best to a minor lexical redundancy rule.[37]

Opacity of mood

Here by 'mood' I mean oppositions relevant to clause meaning and distribution which are encoded in the form of the verb: indicative, imperative, infinitive. There seems to be no justification for suggesting a special mood category of the clause distinguishing modals; they largely occur in clauses with the distribution of straightforward indicative clauses. Presumably therefore they are themselves at least generally indicative.[38] When they are subjective, however, they interact with mood differently from full verbs. Non-auxiliary verbs occur within the scope of the indicative, which underlies the force of an assertion. But subjective modals can be seen as specifying or modifying the force of the indicative. Thus the subjective deontic *You will go to bed!* is a command (whether or not it also remains a statement). The subjective epistemic *They may be happy* is 'I say with some doubt that they are happy' rather than (the objective) 'I say that it is possible that they are happy'. Thus the modal conveys an aspect of the speaker's subjective commitment to the utterance. It seems reasonable to suppose that semantics must give some account of oppositions of mood, probably a rather minimalist one for the reasons advanced in Levinson (1983: 274ff.). An example is Huntley's (1984) account of the indicative : imperative/infinitive opposition. In this the indicative merely 'locates states of affairs in a way that makes essential reference to *this world* (i.e. the actual world)' (p. 120). Modals are potentially in opposition to such an indicative (as indeed in Huntley's sketch), and may essentially belong to the semantic mood system on such an account. This might be captured within a linguistic account by treating modals as syntactic indicatives which do not necessarily carry the semantics (or the conventional pragmatics) of the indicative (though indeed they may do so); thus they are not 'objective', but may be subjective.

This is a frankly speculative account, which places the subjectivity of modals centre stage. The importance of this characteristic is clear from the fact that it is normally present with epistemics (Lyons 1977: 791ff., Palmer 1986: 16), and is at the 'core' of both epistemic and 'root' modality (Coates 1983: 13). The typical subjectivity of modals also clearly accounts (historically at least) for their predisposition to interpretations in present time, and for their disregard of the opposition of tense; note that the instances of past time reference reported above (dynamics and instances in indirect speech) are not subjective. It has sometimes been suggested that epistemic modality is necessarily finite, but this does not seem to be correct. It does not hold for Icelandic (Thráinsson 1986), Dutch (Cremers 1983), nor for Present-day English, as is shown by uses of *have to* as in (51). Thus the general connection with finiteness may rather be one established through subjectivity.

(51) ... whereas old Dot was seriously trying to create an effect. Well, hardly that, perhaps, at her time of life, in front of this mob; though the present carry-on would have had to be descended from the beginning of her career of piss-artistry, when she could still pretend she got sloshed out of not knowing about alcohol.
Kingsley Amis, *The Old Devils* (London: Hutchinson, 1986) 228

We should not, however, be surprised at the occurrence of instances (dynamics, objective deontics and objective epistemics) in which the indicative seems to retain its normal force. Since the account is a lexical one, it can tolerate some exceptionality. Many lexical combinations have opaque interpretations while also retaining transparent interpretations. This is one of the recurrent observations of word formation (see e.g. Aronoff 1976: 38ff. on *variety*, *curiosity*, etc.).

Imperative do

There is a further instance in English grammar to support the notion of this type of opacity, namely imperative *do* and *don't*. I suggest that these might be analysed as formal indicatives which are opaque to mood and mean virtually the same as the imperative. In support of this, note first that these forms are thoroughly idiosyncratic in their distribution (§2.2.4(iii) above, Quirk *et al.* 1985: §11.24ff.). *Do* may not have a subject; *don't* may, but it must follow *don't*. They do not generalize with either imperatives or with periphrastic *do*. But if a separate statement has to be made for *do* and *don't* the best will be one which accounts for their behaviour with negation, for they are like nonimperative finite auxiliaries in that they may precede *not*, and in the occurrence of *-n't*. Imperative *be* and *have* do not have these properties in Present-day English. Thus *do* and *don't* are plausibly taken as indicatives whose mood is opaque, in line with the analysis suggested above for modals (see §3.4.3 for some further discussion and justification).

So there is some plausibility to an analysis in which modals are 'lexical packages': they are syntactic finite indicatives, but they are not put together out of modal + indicative/tense either morphosyntactically or from a semantic or semantic–pragmatic point of view; in particular they may lack the 'objectivity' of the indicative and the time reference of the preterite. The availability of *perhaps* ... V shows that there is no need for a lexical account of such a subjective combination, as does the more verbal behaviour of modal equivalents in other Germanic languages, and other types of account can readily be envisaged.[39] But my speculative account here has three advantages which may recommend it.

(i) It is of a piece with the 'opacity' of auxiliaries argued for in the rest of this chapter, and if my argument from the learnability of restrictions on retrieval from *is* in anaphora holds, the opacity of modals follows from these restrictions.

(ii) It gives an account of the restriction of modals to finite in terms of their subjectivity, in line with a suggestion made by Palmer (1983) (though our accounts of the mechanism differ).[40]

(iii) There is historical warrant for treating this as a potentially lexical

> restriction: as we shall see below, some modals are restricted to finites before this becomes a general property of the class and this looks initially like a property of individual words; it also seems to go with subjective uses, and it is possible that opacity of mood is involved from an early date.

This points to an account of grammaticalization via lexicalization: the indicative mood of an individual lexeme is given a special interpretation. Thus the gap between the morphosyntactic oppositions of mood and the richer set of subjective modalities is bridged by the fact that modals are noncompositional lexemes which have the syntax but not the semantics (or conventional pragmatics) of the indicative.

So far in this chapter I have argued that auxiliaries form a word class which is distinct from verbs in lacking their morphosyntactic properties (with the partial exception of *being*, *having*). Evidence for this has included the grammaticalized ordering of auxiliaries and its learnability, a wide range of idiosyncratic properties of individual forms, and a striking series of restrictions on anaphora. A natural generalization of this position suggests that modals are best analysed as 'lexical packages' which are formally indicative, and which include mood and tense (if indeed this is present) in a way which is not open to morphosyntactic or semantic–pragmatic factoring. If this is reasonable then the finiteness restriction in modals follows from the fact that modals are uninflected lexical items which incorporate mood. This has a dual motivation. Modals are not subject to the morphosyntactic generalizations which underlie inflection in verbs; and modals typically involve a subjective modification of the force of mood within the lexeme. Three more of the seven questions raised at the beginning of §1.5 have now been discussed (nos. 2, 5 and 6), and the final question (no. 7), the status of periphrastic *do*, will be discussed in the next chapter, where I will provide a more formal account of the grammar of auxiliaries. But before that I want to discuss the history of auxiliaries over the last two centuries because it provides some support for the analyses of BE and HAVE that I have suggested here.

2.5 Recent history

This account of auxiliaries provides a good framework for the interpretation of a series of changes in late Modern English. The fact that the changes make coherent sense within this framework supports it. Moreover it seems possible that these changes signal the development of the present-day relationship between auxiliaries and full verbs, which apparently goes back at least to the late eighteenth century. The changes are as follows.

1. The progressive *is being* appears at the end of the eighteenth century. It is found first in passives. Mossé's (1938) first example is (52.a); earlier progressive passives had the form of (b), without *being*. Thus it seems possible that the increasing frequency of the progressive (Dennis 1940) led to the need for a more explicit form of progressive passive. It is later generalized to constructions with predicative adjectives and noun phrases. In my interpretation this is the introduction into English of the progressive participle *being* which is absent in early Modern English (see §9.3.3).

(52) a. a fellow whose uttermost upper grinder is being torn out by the roots by a mutton-fisted barber.
1795 Robert Southey, *Life and Correspondance*, Vol. I: 249 (Mossé 1938, II: §263)

b. At the very time that this dispute was maintaining by the centinel and the drummer, was the same point debating betwix't a trumpeter and a trumpeter's wife.
1759–67 Laurence Sterne, *Tristram Shandy*, 179 (V§1879)

It is rather striking that earlier English does not show the 'double-*ing* constraint' with BE, and we find examples like (53), though they are never common.[41] But shortly after the first appearance of progressive *being* we find the last relevant instances of *being* + *ing*. These occur in Jane Austen, who lacks progressive *being* (see V§1834, Phillipps 1970: 115, Denison 1985b):

(53) One day being discoursing with her upon the extremities they suffered ...
1719 Daniel Defoe, *Robinson Crusoe*, Vol. II: 218 (V§1834n.)

(54) and exclaimed quite as much as was necessary, (or, being acting a part, perhaps rather more,) ...
1816 Jane Austen, *Emma* (ed. R. W. Chapman, Oxford University Press, 1923) 145

Now under the interpretation advanced above we can see these events as interconnected in the following way. Double progressives conveyed a very specialized meaning; they probably therefore failed to occur in the learners' primary data. This absence was learned as a subcategorization restriction on progressive *being*, and it was generalized to nonprogressive *being*, presumably because this was acquired later. This gives us an attractive account both of the puzzling development of the double-*ing* constraint and of its temporal coincidence with the rise of the progressive passive. But this account requires *being* to have independent subcategorizational properties, and this argues that the modern system was effectively in existence by this period.

2. Two other restrictions on the subcategorization of particular forms of BE seem to arise at or after this period. Firstly, the restriction of directional phrases (and purpose infinitives) as complement to *been* is after 1760, which is *OED*'s last date for occurrence with a finite (*Be*, *v.* 6).

3. The restriction of 'modal' *is to* to finite forms belongs to the late nineteenth and early twentieth century. Earlier, nonfinites are also found (V§1378, Jespersen 1909–49: V, §15.6_1). The rise of these two restrictions also implies the relative independence of particular forms of BE.

(55) You will be to visit me in prison with a basket of provisions; ...
1814 Jane Austen, *Mansfield Park* (ed. J. Lucas, Oxford University Press, 1970) 122

4. There are two other nineteenth-century developments which may imply the relative independence of particular forms. It is only with this century that there is convincing evidence that the infinitival marker *to* occurs with ellipsis. Visser gives plentiful examples from the mid nineteenth century (§1000). But most of his earlier examples, especially for the modern period, are open to some other interpretation (generally with prepositional *to*, or with *too*).

(56) If I should do That which the Satyr did advise me to
1647 Sir R. Fanshaw, translation of Guarini's *Il Pastor Fido* 4.7.150 (V§1000)
Advise so. *to* sth. = *OED Advise*, *v.* 9.b. (obs)

There is at least a major burgeoning of this use of *to*, perhaps its development. But this use is the best piece of evidence that *to* is an auxiliary. The development might therefore show the reanalysis of a syncategorematic item as an auxiliary. And this in turn might reasonably require the relative independence of auxiliary forms (and perhaps their distance from full verbs) given that *to* is elsewhere a preposition.

5. The second development is parallel. The form *of* for the perfect infinitive *have* is first recorded in *OED* in 1837 (*Of*, Supplement 1933; *of*, Supplement III, 1982). This need not reflect an identification with *of* as present-day pronunciation implies, but it may do, and it may well indicate that it is not identified with *have*. This would square with the relative independence of nonfinites of HAVE by the first half of the nineteenth century. But its appearance in writing might have been considerably delayed by normative considerations.

(57) Soposing seven hundred and sixty [servants] to of advertised and the same number to not of advertised
1837 W. Tayler, *Diary* (*OED* Supplement III, 1982)

6. Finally, a more complex and striking piece of data. It was argued above that the failure of post-auxiliary ellipsis when an indicative of BE was the antecedent showed that *is*, *are*, etc. have a relatively independent status. In earlier English, however, indicatives (and subjunctives) of BE were transparent to retrieval. Examples like (58.a) with ellipsis after a modal can be found throughout Middle English, and for Modern English until the end of the eighteenth century (see V§§1752ff.). The last author to use such constructions that I know of is Jane Austen (see Phillipps 1970). The type of (59) with ellipsis after *have* is less common but also appears.[42]

(58) a. Þe Niȝtingale sat & siȝte,
& hohful was, & ful wel miȝte
'The nightingale sat and sighed, and was anxious, and full well might [be]'
*c*1250 *The Owl and the Nightingale* (ed. E. G. Stanley, London: Nelson, 1960) 1292–3

b. That bettre loved is noon, ne never schal
'So that no one is better loved, or ever shall [be]'
*a*1500 (*c*1370) Chaucer, *A Complaint to his Lady*, 80

c. I think, added he, all the Charges attending it, and the Trouble you had, were defray'd by my Attorney: I order'd that they should [sc. be defrayed]. They were, Sir, said he; and Ten Thousand Thanks to you for this Goodness
1740–1 Samuel Richardson, *Pamela*, 3rd edn. London, 1741, Vol II: 129

d. 'I wish our opinions were the same. But in time they will.' (sc. be the same)
1816 Jane Austen, *Emma* (ed. R.W. Chapman, Oxford University Press, 1923) 471

e. 'And Lady Middleton, is *she* angry?'
'I cannot suppose it possible that she should.'
1811 Jane Austen, *Sense and Sensibility* (ed. C. Lamont, Oxford University Press, 1970) 237

(59) And therfore it appereth well, that the manner of spekyng was nat lyke. For, if it had [sc. been like], then wolde nat the olde exposytours haue vsed suche so far vnlike fashyon in the expounyng of them.
1533 Thomas More, *Works* (London 1557) 836 D17; *The Complete Works of St. Thomas More*, Vol. 7 (ed. Frank Manley, G. Marc'hadour, R. Marius and C. Miller, New Haven: Yale University Press, 1990) 240.21

This must reflect a change in English structure: it cannot be attributed to the effects of grammatical prescription. Prescription would not provide adequate motivation for the clear ungrammaticality of the construction in Present-day English, and I know of no evidence that the construction ever was the specific focus of grammatical prescription (it is not mentioned in Leonard's 1962 survey; see especially VI.4). In terms of the account given above the change is one from a system in which *is*, *are*, etc. behave like suppletive items within a system of verbal morphosyntactic categories, to one in which they have a relatively independent status. And this should probably be referred to the eighteenth century. Visser notes that the type of (58) 'seems to have fallen into disuse in the seventeenth century' (§1752), but there are eighteenth-century instances, and Phillipps (1970: 142f.) cites half a dozen from Jane Austen's writings.[43]

It is particularly interesting that this period coincides with that of the loss of two clearly verbal properties shared by auxiliaries and full verbs: agreement, and occurrence in inverted structures; and the virtual loss of a third: occurrence in negated structures.

(i) Loss of shared constructions (see Ellegård 1953, Tieken 1987). In early Modern English either a full verb or auxiliary *do* could appear in inversion (in interrogatives and other contexts) or before *not* where a full verb is no longer permitted. With individual lexical items full verb inversion can occur throughout the eighteenth century. But inversion without *do* is infrequent in some texts even from the first half of the century, and seems largely to be restricted to a handful of recurrent items, such as *mean*, *say* and *think*. Loss of postverbal *not* is rather later. Examples are not uncommon throughout the eighteenth century (and even into the nineteenth), though again, from the second half of the eighteenth century it seems to be a few recurrent items which are mainly involved.

The loss of these constructions with full verbs clearly removes important properties shared by auxiliaries and nonauxiliary verbs (see §9.5 for a possible analysis). A grammar of English written before 1700 would have to identify finites as the locus of negation and inversion. By 1850 finite auxiliaries alone were involved.

(ii) Loss of agreement inflection dependent on the loss of *thou*. Before the loss of *thou*, modals retained some subject–verb agreement. They carried the normal verbal agreement inflection for *thou* in the preterite and some present forms (see the examples of (60)), and they had some special forms in the present (found also with BE) (see (b)).

(60) a. may(e)st, might(e)st, would(e)st; speak(e)st, spok(e)st; (wast).
b. shalt, wilt, art, wert.

The loss of *thou* in standard colloquial English, used between intimates, to children, to servants and inferiors, or to show contempt, seems to belong to the second half of the eighteenth century. It is common in appropriate circumstances in Richardson's *Pamela* of 1740–1, and it appears in plays later in the century (see Bock 1938). But nineteenth-century occurrences are very infrequent, and belong to dialect or the language of prayer or heightened discourse. With this loss, modals reach their present inflectional state.

Thus the arguments mounted above that auxiliaries as a group can be interpreted as lacking the properties of full verbs, and most particularly as lacking their morphosyntactic category specification, would not be convincing if mounted for English *c*1700 (though I shall argue below that modals show opacity of tense and mood by this date, and see §9.3.3 for a further comment on agreement). But it seems clear that an essentially modern situation obtained by 1850. The evidence for this largely depends on BE, and it seems that there is a reinterpretation or restructuring of BE and perhaps HAVE *vis à vis* full verbs at this period and that this is when they develop their full modern distinctness from verbs.[44] We might interpret this as follows. In the eighteenth century the last major formal properties Standard English auxiliaries shared with verbs were lost or radically weakened. Modals had previously been opaque to tense and mood; now auxiliaries as a group were reanalysed as a class for which none of the morphosyntactic categories of full verbs automatically held, and which did not show regular verbal inflection. In consequence, indicatives of BE became opaque to anaphora, nonfinites tended to develop idiosyncratic properties, the development of the explicit progressive passive led to the double-*ing* constraint and *to* could be integrated as an auxiliary. There is a little further suggestive evidence of such a shift in the development of British English *have got* and nonauxiliary possessive *have*, if these are interpreted as developments whose effect is to take possessive *have* out of the auxiliary category after a widening of the gap between full verbs and auxiliaries. The timing of these developments jibes well. *Have got* as a simple equivalent to *have* (rather than perfect of *get)* in Standard British English seems to develop in the eighteenth century, probably in its second half. Charleston's detailed investigation of texts in the period 1710–60 found no unambiguous instances (1941: §3.3_2), though Visser and *OED* imply earlier development (V§2011ff., *OED Get, v.* 24). *Do* + possessive *have* is not found until the nineteenth century (V§§1466–76); *have got to* and *do have to* are also nineteenth century (V§§2012, 1467).

I conclude that the account of auxiliaries given in this chapter gives us a coherent general interpretation of a series of developments since 1700. This further supports the postulated framework of analysis. Moreover it includes an account of the rise of the 'double-*ing* constraint' with auxiliaries, and of the failure of anaphora with indicative BE. This implies a sharper justification, because these are mysterious but systematic differences between two closely related historical dialects of English. Any truly convincing account of these phenomena in today's English must be supported by a plausible account of the relationship with those earlier dialects which permitted the constructions.

3 *A formal interlude: the grammar of English auxiliaries*

So far I have suggested in Chapter 1 that auxiliaries show the prototypicality structuring typical of word classes, and in Chapter 2 I have argued that their grammatical behaviour reflects their lack of verbal morphosyntax. The argument was informal, and the claim is presumably compatible with a range of linguistic theories, at least in the sense that they do not preclude such an analysis. In this chapter I will underpin my argument by showing that there is a simple and coherent account of the type of lexical structuring of auxiliaries which I have posited, in which relevant generalizations are captured, within the formal framework of Head-driven Phrase Structure Grammar (HPSG). This includes an account of the distribution of periphrastic *do*, which I shall suggest is found when tense cannot be realized as an affix because it has some characteristic which is properly that of a word, thus providing an answer to question 7 of the list at the beginning of my §1.5. The discussion will necessarily be somewhat technical, and some readers may prefer to take the demonstration of this chapter for granted, and proceed directly to Chapter 4; I have recapped the small amount of discussion that is relevant to succeeding chapters so that the book coheres if it is read in this way.

In adopting HPSG I do not, of course, wish to suggest that it provides the only possible formalization of the account of Chapter 2. But, apart from the general virtues of theoretical parsimony and generality which characterize the framework, it has the quite specific virtues that it takes the lexicon seriously and that its account of the inheritance of information within the lexicon allows us to capture the prototypicality structuring of the class of auxiliaries. So it has a particular appropriacy for the topic in hand.

3.1 Head-driven Phrase Structure Grammar

Head-driven Phrase Structure Grammar (HPSG) is a member of the class of 'unification grammars' which include Generalized Phrase Structure Grammar,

Lexical Functional Grammar (the functional level), and Functional Unification Grammar. These are distinguished (among other things) by possessing a formal theory of categories and features, and a set of principles (including or based on the notion 'unification') which determine how categorial information may be combined in syntax. Unification simply involves the merging of information contained in two or more category structures without loss, increment or modification (when possible: categories do not always have a unification). This interrelationship is therefore 'monotonic', in that information is always preserved, and from a theoretical viewpoint this is a very simple and restrictive position. See Shieber (1986) and Uszkoreit (1986b) for general accounts of this type of formalism, Pollard and Sag (1987, forthcoming) in particular for HPSG.

In HPSG categories are described by 'attribute-value matrices'. These consist of an array of feature names ('attributes') with their values, which may be atomic or which may be described in terms of other attribute-value matrices. Semantic and phonological information is presented within the same framework. Thus the basic information structure of the theory is the sign. It is not merely a theory of syntax but is in principle an integrated account of linguistic information, though Pollard and Sag (1987) only discuss syntax and selected aspects of semantics in any detail. In syntax a central idea is that the grammar will be simpler and more general if lexical heads carry information about the categories they combine with and this is used to 'project' syntactic structures. Since the verb is analysed as the head of its clause it carries information about both its subject and its complements. In Pollard and Sag (1987) this information is encoded within a single feature SUBCAT, whose value is a list of categories, but here I will follow Borsley (1987, 1993) and distinguish valency information about subjects (given as the value of a feature SUBJ), from valency information about complements (given as the value of the feature SUBCAT). Thus the sign for *likes* includes the information [SUBJ <NP>, SUBCAT <NP>].[1] When combination with an appropriate set of complements or a subject takes place there is a process of 'cancellation' (reminiscent of Categorial Grammar) and the mother lacks the specification for that combination. So *likes* [SUBJ <NP>, SUBCAT <NP>] combines with NP *fruit* in the phrase *likes fruit*; the phrase *likes fruit* is itself [SUBJ <NP>, SUBCAT < >], and by a further application of the same principle the clause *Eve likes fruit* is [SUBJ < >, SUBCAT < >], that is, it has empty SUBJ and SUBCAT lists, which are said to be 'saturated'. This is spelled out in the 'Subcategorization Principle' given below.

There is a second central principle involved in the relationship between phrases and their heads: the Head Feature Principle. This ensures that a mother and its head daughter carry the same value for the attribute HEAD (which includes information about major category and morphosyntax). The appropriate 'projection' of categorial information between lexical and phrasal categories follows. The adoption of these principles has some interesting consequences. Firstly, with information about subjects and complements lexically encoded, syntactic rules defining dominance can be few and schematic. Secondly, given a feature LEX which distinguishes the lexical level (as [+LEX]) from other levels, there is no need for the concept 'bar-level' or for a feature BAR to define projections of phrase structure: the opposition between saturated and nonsaturated SUBJ and SUBCAT is sufficient.[2] The projection of syntactic structure from the lexicon is also subject to compliance with very general rule schemata, which are intended to belong to a small universal set. Since the word-class category of the mother and head is not restricted in these rules (though they must agree in HEAD features to satisfy the Head Feature Principle), and the head's sisters are specified not in the rule but by SUBCAT or SUBJ features on items in the lexicon, these rules are sufficient to generate many of the structures of English. Rule 1 corresponds to the more traditional S → NP, VP; rule 2 to rules introducing a lexical head V with its complements. Here I give informal (and abbreviated) versions of these rules, and Borsley's informal version of the 'Subcategorization Principle'.[3] These rules specify immediate dominance, not linear order, which is the province of separate principles of Linear Precedence.

(1)
a. *Rule 1*
   [SUBJ < >] → H[–LEX, SUBCAT < >, SUBJ <C>], C
b. *Rule 2*
   [SUBCAT < >] → H[+LEX, SUBCAT <C*>], C*
   In these rules H stands for 'head', C for 'complement (or subject)' and C* for any number of complements (including none). The attribute LEX distinguishes lexical items [+LEX] from phrasal categories [–LEX].
c. *'Subcategorization Principle'*
   'A category that is on the SUBCAT list of a head and not on the SUBCAT list of its mother or on the SUBJ list of a head and not on the SUBJ list of its mother must be matched by a sister of the head.' (Borsley 1987: 6)[4]

Thus the example of (2.a) has the analysis shown in the tree of (2.c), where *reveals* has a lexical entry which includes the information of (2.b).[5]

(2)
a. Tom reveals his hairy chest to Martha.
b. reveals: V[+LEX, +FIN, –PAST, SUBJ <NP[3sg.]>, SUBCAT <PP[to], NP>]

c.

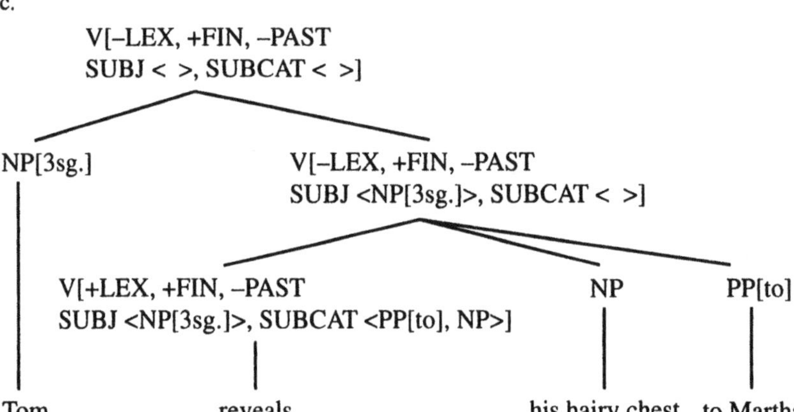

There has been a good deal of disagreement about the status of subjects, and their relationship to other aspects of verbal valency. In HPSG Pollard and Sag did not originally see any need to assign subjects a distinctive status, though they admitted that such an account was broadly consistent with their position (1987: 118). But more recently they have admitted the persuasiveness of the position that subjects and complements should be encoded in different attributes as above (forthcoming: Ch. 9). Earlier they had argued for the subcategorization of the subject by its verb as one of the values of SUBCAT. But the weakness of their argument from English-based data contrasted strikingly with the strength of the argument from languages where the verb could case-mark its subject (as e.g. in Icelandic) (1987: 129ff.), and this may imply that there are differences in the employment of SUBJ in different languages as I shall suggest below.

For Present-day English there seem to me to be several advantages to an account of verb valency which splits it between the two attributes SUBCAT and SUBJ, as proposed by Borsley, instead of dealing with it by the single attribute SUBCAT. They are as follows. The first two are discussed in Borsley (1987); see also Pollard and Sag (forthcoming: Ch. 9) for some discussion.

(i) S and VP form a natural class: V[SUBCAT < >] (within which VP has nonsaturated [SUBJ <[XP]>], S saturated [SUBJ < >]). There is no such generalization with the single attribute SUBCAT.

(ii) A natural and straightforward account of *that t* phenomena can be given. See the discussion of Chapter 9 below.

(iii) Pollard and Sag's rule 3, which generates VSO structures, including English auxiliary inversion structures, can be generalized with their rule 2 (which introduces a lexical head V in VP) as will be clear from the account below, and this removes a rule schema which resists generalization with other schemata.

(iv) If the use made of SUBJ may differ between languages, as seems not implausible, then there is a natural account of a series of differences between earlier and later English in terms of this parameter. This constitutes an effective argument for the parameter. See the discussion of Chapter 9 below.

This brief introduction to HPSG has left many topics untouched, in particular the question of linear order and the nature of interrelationships within the lexicon. These will be taken up below as the topics arise. But it is clear that HPSG has important advantages. It is a largely monotonic, information-preserving system, and this is theoretically attractive. It is based in a formalized feature system, and it is capable of capturing a large number of linguistic generalizations without resorting to transformational devices. It also has a theory of lexical structure which permits a coherent statement of interrelationships between auxiliaries, within an appropriate theoretical framework.

3.2 Morphosyntactic features

The question of an appropriate set of features for auxiliary and verbal morphosyntax is related to other choices made in the grammar. I want to adopt two conservative criteria. First, I shall assume that such logical operations as disjunction, negation and quantification are not available within categories, though disjunction at least may feature in the statements about categories made in lexical entries. This apparently reverses the position of Pollard and Sag (1987: 40ff.), but within a theory that allows the (lexical) statement of default values the type of argument put up by Karttunen (1984) for this theoretical extension does not necessarily hold, and it may be more satisfactory to do without it. Secondly, I will also assume that it is better to adopt syntactic features which correspond directly to morphological categories where this is possible. This might be defended on grounds of simplicity, or of learnability. Note that if it is necessary to characterize the complement of *being* in such a way as to bar infinitives and *ing*-forms even in a coordination of complements, then the first of these criteria is consistent with the assignment of attributes which may have negative values to carry this information. This is some defence for my adoption of Boolean valued morphosyntactic features below. It is not clear that there is a simple characterization of such a prohibition on the complement (given my first criterion) in terms of the finite/nonfinite/participial feature VFORM with the values {FIN, BSE, INF, PSP, PRP, PAS} proposed in Gazdar *et al.* (1985) or Pollard and Sag (1987).

Participles and gerunds

Let us follow the second criterion just proposed, and suppose that present participles and gerunds share a feature [+ING], and that past and passive participles, which always show the same morphology in English, share a feature [+EN]. These categories can be subdivided by the single feature PRD, which characterizes the 'predicative/nonpredicative' distinction in Pollard and Sag (1987: 64ff.). The complement of *be* is [+PRD] where it characterizes the subject, and (when a noun phrase) does not refer.

(3) a. Mary is a charlatan.
b. That was an inaccurate statement.

There are several reasons for adopting such a feature. For one thing such noun phrases are structurally distinct from other noun phrases. Thus neither of the predicate noun phrases in (4.a, b) can appear referentially.

(4) a. Dana was advisor to the committee.
b. Mary is too much of a fool to take seriously.
c. *I ran after advisor to the committee.
d. *Too much of a fool to take seriously was appointed to the committee.

[–PRD] can also distinguish those adjectives (*mere*, *outright*, *utter*, *very*, etc.) which are never predicative or postnominal, and [+PRD] can those which may be predicative or postnominal, but which cannot occur between article and noun (*ablaze*, *awake*, *ready*, etc.). Further justification comes from coordination, given that some level of categorial identity is in general a necessary condition for constituent coordination. Predicate phrases of different categories may apparently be coordinated with each other after *be* (as in other positions) (see (5)). But they may not be conjoined with 'identifying' phrases even when the phrases are overtly of the same category (see (6)). These can be distinguished as [+PRD] and [–PRD] respectively, where [+PRD] is common to the different predicate (and locative) phrases.

(5) a. Mary is unintelligent and a bit of a charlatan.
b. Your statement is inaccurate and without foundation.

(6) a. *The man/men you need is/are John but a complete fool.
b. *He's an intelligent fellow and the man I told you about.
c. *The point is a clear one and that he hates you.

But passive and progressive phrases may themselves be conjoined with predicate phrases, as with each other, so they too will be [+PRD]. Compare the examples and discussion of §1.5.1, where instances like the following are cited:

(7) a. He was a liberal and considered to have left-wing tendencies.
b. The contraband was floating in the petrol tank and thought to be safely hidden.

This is sufficient to distinguish the past participle [+EN, –PRD] from the passive participle [+EN, +PRD], and a feature PASSIVE does not seem to be necessary. Notice that this is in accord with the fact that the semantic and distributional properties of the passive belong to the participle, not to the combination *be* + participle (as noted in §1.5.1).

Progressive and nonprogressive ing-*forms*

The distinction drawn for *ing* by PRD is one between progressive and nonprogressive *ing*-phrases. We need such a distinction which is at least semantic, possibly also syntactic. My reasons for arguing this are as follows.

(i) The meaning of the progressive is a property of the *ing*-form and not of the combination *be* + *ing*-form. This is clear from the occurrence (and failure) of progressive exclamatives without *be*,[6] and from the occurrence of other instances without *be* which are progressive. Thus (8.c, d) are clearly ambiguous, and in restrictive postnominal modification a progressive interpretation is virtually obligatory with *being* itself.

(8) a. What, Major droning on again!
b. *What, Major only owning one house!
c. John's sitting down when we arrived ... ('the fact that he sat ...', 'the fact that he was sitting ...')
d. Any boy sitting when I enter the room ... ('who sits' or 'who is sitting')

(ii) Although the difference between progressive and nonprogressive *ing*-forms is often neutralized, progressive *ing*-forms have a distinct distribution: for example after *be*, in the complement of transitive verbs of physical perception (see Huddleston 1971: 169, Emonds 1972: 27ff.), and perhaps in the complement of aspectual verbs (see Boertien 1979).

(9) a. She found her father pacing up and down their apartment. (Jespersen 1909–49: IV, §14.8(1))
b. *He began knowing more than Emily.
c. He began to know more than Emily.

I conclude that we must distinguish between progressive and nonprogressive *ing*-forms, and PRD is sufficient for this.[7] But it does not seem to me to be necessary to suppose any further lexical level distinction (say between 'gerund' and 'participle') among *ing*-forms with verbal rection.[8]

The distinctions proposed so far, then, are these:

Nonprogressive *ing* [+ING, –PRD]
Progressive *ing* [+ING, +PRD]
Past participle [+EN, –PRD]
Passive participle [+EN, +PRD]

Finites and infinitives

It is natural to assume a feature FIN 'finite', and I will assume with GPS that the 'bare' infinitive (the infinitive without *to*) is distinguished by a feature BSE, both having values {+, –}. Imperatives are clearly [+FIN], despite attempts to treat them as infinitives (e.g. in Bolinger 1977a: Ch. 8, but cf. his Ch. 9; Downes 1977). In the first place they conjoin with finites, not with infinitives.

(10) a. Don't touch me or I'll scream.
b. Give me the money and I'll see what I can do for you.
c. I hate girls in trousers and don't pretend you don't know it.
d. I hate girls in trousers but try this pair on for size anyway.

They also negate like finites with *do not* or *don't*, and clitic *-n't* is otherwise found only in finites. Even though imperative *be* and *have* are unlike other finite auxiliaries in negating this way, yet the pattern *don't be* is still not a nonfinite one. What imperatives never do is negate with a preceding *not* like infinitives and other nonfinites. So in (11), (a) is unambiguously a hypothetical infinitive and (b) is not possible.

(11) a. Not wait for her? What an idea!
b. *Not wait for her! That's an order!

Finally, imperatives have a nonoblique subject (except in so far as obliques may occur in coordinated NPs as the subject of finites).

(12) a. You and he take that upstairs. Come on, hurry now.
b. Don't you and he try to get away with that trick!

Clearly imperatives are best analysed as finites, and must be somehow distinguished from other finites. It also seems desirable to capture the fact that (if we except *don't* and *do*) imperatives are always the base form of the verb, even with the highly irregular *be*, in accordance with the criterion suggested above. Hence imperatives (except *don't* and *do*, which will be discussed below) are [+FIN, +BSE].

The bare infinitive is taken to be [–FIN, +BSE]. I follow Pullum (1982) in taking *to* to be an auxiliary verb, and I will characterize it by a feature TO with values {+, –} so that *to* is itself a base form, [–FIN, +BSE, +TO].

The full set of morphosyntactic category distinctions suggested for the verb then are these:

Nonimperative finite	[+FIN, –BSE]
Imperative	[+FIN, +BSE]
Bare infinitive	[–FIN, +BSE, –TO]
To infinitive	[–FIN, +BSE, +TO]
Nonprogressive *ing*	[+ING, –PRD]
Past participle	[+EN, –PRD]
Progressive *ing*	[+ING, +PRD]
Passive participle	[+EN, +PRD]

Using these features, the lexicon for a speaker of English who has all the restrictions noted in Chapter 2 will include the information in Table 3.1.[9]

Table 3.1 *Auxiliary category and subcategorization information in the lexicon*

Form [+AUX] unless specified [–AUX]	Subcategorized for phrasal complement
can, could, etc. [+FIN, –BSE]	[–FIN, +BSE, –TO]
do [+FIN, –BSE]	[–FIN, +BSE, –TO, –AUX]
ought [+FIN, –BSE]	[–FIN, +BSE, +TO]
to [–FIN, +BSE, +TO]	[–FIN, +BSE, –TO]
is [+FIN, –BSE]	[+PRD, –BSE]; [–FIN, +BSE, +TO, –PRD]
be [+BSE]	[+PRD, –BSE]
been [+EN, –PRD]	[+PRD, –BSE]; PP[DIR]
being [–AUX, +ING]	[+PRD, –BSE, –ING]
has [+FIN, –BSE]	[+EN, –PRD]; NP; [–FIN, +BSE, +TO]; [–FIN, +BSE, +GOT]
have [+BSE]	[+EN, –PRD]
having [–AUX, +ING, –PRD]	[+EN, –PRD]

The attribute AUX is justified on the grounds that it is required to state the relevant range of partly idiosyncratic properties distinguishing auxiliaries from full verbs, and that the class has a universally based identity. Pollock's attempt to characterize this identity directly in theta-role terms seems to me too stipulative to succeed, cf. §1.5.2. In what follows I will also refer to a feature INV {+, –} which characterizes inverted clauses as [+INV]. This will be discussed in §3.4.

3.3 The lexical structuring of auxiliaries

The structuring of the class of auxiliaries in terms of a prototype, which was argued for in Chapter 1, can be readily captured within the theory of the lexicon in HPSG. This also permits lexical statements of little redundancy, though my approach (which requires separate statements for *been* and *being*, and so on) must have seemed open to the objection that it paid insufficient attention to shared properties. That neglect will here be redressed.

HPSG has a 'full entry' lexicon, and two ways of capturing relevant generalizations within it. One involves lexical redundancy rules, like those proposed by Jackendoff (1975) or Bresnan (1982), relating (for example) a passive participle to the active base of a verb. The other way in which relevant generalizations are captured is by inheritance within a structured network of information, and this also reduces redundancy of representation.[10] In Pollard and Sag (1987: Ch. 8) the organization is essentially that of the hierarchy of 'types' which defines the category structure and feature structure of the language. Flickinger (1987) presents basically the same kind of account though with a less explicit interpretation in terms of feature structuring; see also Flickinger, Pollard and Wasow (1985) where it is referred to as a frame-based inheritance system. Flickinger proposes a series of hierarchies proceeding from the most general 'class'[11] (WORD CLASS) down through 'subclasses' which state information (about category, subcategorization, etc.) of decreasing generality, until finally we reach the level at which information idiosyncratic to the individual lexical entry is given. The complete lexical entry can be retrieved by proceeding up the hierarchy merging the information in each of the classes: more technically the information is the 'unification' of the contents of the separate classes (for the role of unification, Flickinger 1987: 82; Pollard and Sag 1987: 208).

This can be illustrated by considering some of the hierarchy relevant to the lexical entry for *kisses*. Here I adapt the general account of Flickinger (1987: Chapter 2), reinterpreting it in terms of my feature system, and with other minor changes and simplifications.[12] A fully specified lexical entry for *kisses* will include much information that is shared: agreement for third person singular with the corresponding forms of other verbs, [–N, +V] with other verbs, [SUBCAT <[NP]>] with other transitives, [+LEX] with other words. Such redundant information is stated within the hierarchically organized series of classes (or types), so that *kisses* inherits this information, and its nonredundant lexical entry will contain the information given in (13) (which includes the 'addresses' of the dominating 'superclasses' from which it inherits). So from TRANSITIVE subcategorization information is inherited, and TRANSITIVE is dominated by WORD CLASS from which [+LEX] is inherited. Inheritance is typically multiple: *kisses* inherits major class features from a sequence including MAIN VERB and VERB, which is also rooted in WORD CLASS; and it inherits morphosyntactic information through the sequence 3SG., NONPAST, FINITE. Relevant parts of the hierarchy are presented in Figure 3.1.

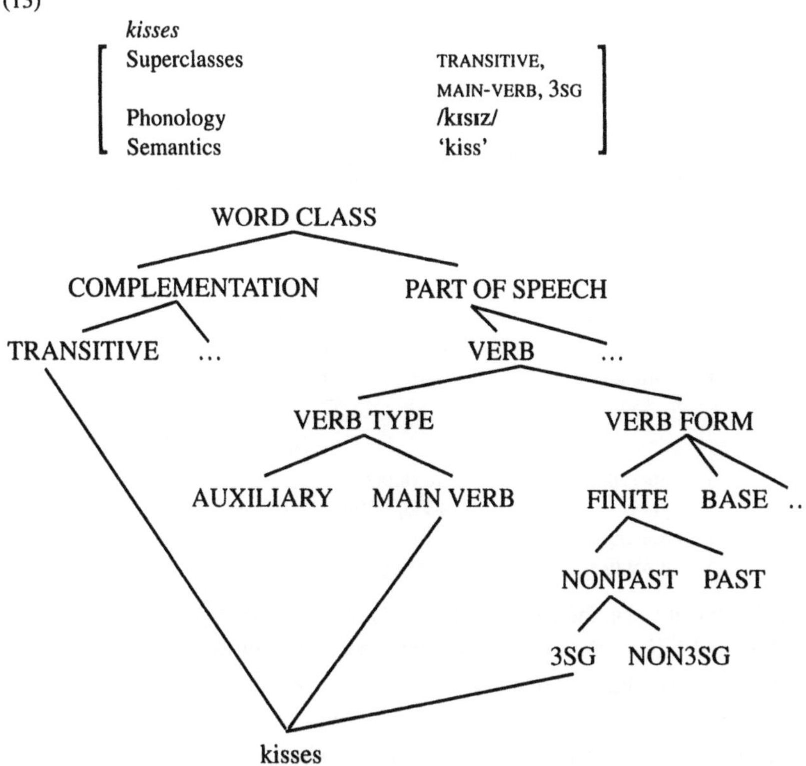
(13)

kisses

Superclasses	TRANSITIVE, MAIN-VERB, 3SG
Phonology	/kɪsɪz/
Semantics	'kiss'

Figure 3.1 Partial lexical hierarchy for *kisses*

Within such a framework it is clearly possible to capture aspects of the prototype structuring of word-class properties discussed above. A detailed account of this is given in Warner (1992b), and here I will simply sketch some of its major characteristics. The prototypical properties of auxiliaries are given in the class AUXILIARY.[13] It is 'indicative': [+FIN, –BSE, –ING, –EN], as well as being [+AUX, –INV]. It is subcategorized for the plain infinitive: SUBCAT <[+BSE, –FIN, –TO, –PRD]>.[14] [+V, –N] will be inherited from VERB-TYPE. Thus modals are central and all that needs to be specified in their non-redundant lexical entries is their form and their individual semantics (see (14.b)). A special statement will be required for any departure from this prototype. In Flickinger's system information lower in the hierarchy has precedence over the 'default' information in higher classes (see Pollard and Sag 1987: 194 n. 4).[15] Hence in the case of the infinitive marker *to* in (c), the 'default' prototypical 'indicative' [+FIN, –BSE] is superseded by [–FIN, +BSE], but the subcategorization for the plain infinitive is inherited directly.[16]

(14) a.

AUXILIARY

Superclass	VERB-TYPE
Syntax	+AUX, –INV
	+FIN, –BSE, –ING, –EN, –PRD
	SUBCAT <[+BSE, –FIN, –TO, –PRD]>

b.

would

Superclass	AUXILIARY
Phonology	[wʊd]
Semantics	'would'

c.

to

Superclass	AUXILIARY
Syntax	+TO, –FIN, +BSE, (+PRD)
Phonology	[tu]
Semantics	identity

Predicative BE can then readily be analysed as subcategorized for [+PRD, –BSE] and having the superclass AUXILIARY.[17] For BE we also need a statement of the paradigm: lexical redundancy rules cannot be appealed to here. So I will adopt a BE-FORM class (or subhierarchy) to specify the phonological shape of its morphosyntactic categories (see Pollard and Sag 1987: 214–15 for a similar disjunctive statement). This might contain a simple disjunction of forms specified for their morphosyntax, but is better stated in a more structured way, as I hope to argue elsewhere. An effect of the general hierarchy is to require a special statement to be made about the existence of any morphosyntactic category which is not [+FIN, –BSE] (in accordance with the analysis of Chapter 2). Thus (to exemplify) there will be a special statement for *being*. The nonredundant lexical entry of (15.b) will inherit through the class 'Predicative BE': its form from BE-FORM, and its syntax (and its 'raising' semantics) from the class AUXILIARY. The [–AUX] specified in (15.b) will have priority over the [+AUX] of AUXILIARY. *Being* is specified '(+PRD)', so it may inherit [–PRD], the default value given in AUXILIARY, or be specified [+PRD]. Hence *is being* will be generated. But *being singing* will not be possible because of SUBCAT <[–ING]>.

(15) a.

Predicative BE	
Superclasses	AUXILIARY, BE-FORM
Syntax	SUBCAT <[–BSE, +PRD]>
Semantics	'be'

b.

being	
Superclass	Predicative BE
Syntax	–AUX, +ING, –FIN, (+PRD) SUBCAT <[–ING]>

Warner (1992b) gives a complete hierarchy for BE and HAVE (including a HAVE-FORM class). A similar hierarchy can be constructed for periphrastic DO. There will also be statements to cope with the noncore constructions in which auxiliaries occur, such as inversion, ellipsis and negation. These will involve distinct subclasses, predictable by lexical redundancy rules which will be discussed below.

In this section I have sketched the broad outlines of a coherent statement of the prototypicality structuring of the class of auxiliaries, which requires the individual specification of non-indicative categories and which is none the less consistent with the existence of a single paradigm for BE. Thus the general structuring posited in Chapter 1 and argued for in Chapter 2 has been shown to be capable of nonredundant statement in a formal framework. The most striking formal characteristic of auxiliaries in this account is the intermixing of morphosyntactic and subcategorizational information. This distinguishes them from major classes for which categorial and subcategorizational information appear in separate hierarchies (see Figure 3.1). Both Flickinger (1987: 38f., 64ff.) and Pollard and Sag (1987: 203f.) give accounts of auxiliaries, but neither characterizes them in this way.

3.4 Auxiliary constructions

Now that the prototype structuring of the relationships within the class of auxiliaries has been dealt with, I will first discuss the lexical redundancy rules which interrelate construction types and their interaction, then I will turn to two more particular topics: the distribution of periphrastic *do* and the statement of imperative *do*.

3.4.1 The NICE Constructions

The distinctive constructions involving auxiliaries are best dealt with in the present framework by lexical redundancy rule, as interrelated subcategorizations. Here I will say something about the construction in each case, then formulate the rule.

Post-Auxiliary Ellipsis

This construction will be characterized in terms of the subcategorization of the auxiliary preceding ellipsis. This has the virtue that it should permit a generalization with pseudogapping constructions (in which the auxiliary has a real if partial complement), as was argued in Chapter 1. The complement within SUBCAT will be characterized with the *ad hoc* feature [ELLIPSIS] (cf. GPS's NULL).

> *Post-Auxiliary Ellipsis*
> [+AUX, SUBCAT <XP>] → [+AUX, SUBCAT <XP[+ELLIPSIS]>]

Negation

The distribution of *not* is unique, and it seems reasonable to introduce it within SUBCAT as a sister to a finite auxiliary and its complement. It may also be generated within [$_{VP}$ *not* VP] as is sometimes implied by coordination and scope contrasts. GPS argue for both of these possibilities, which are illustrated in (16):

(16) a. I will not permit you to escape without blame! You may not [$_{VP}$ not own up].
b. May we either [$_{VP}$ not go] or leave early? – You may not! (sc. not go or leave early)
c. Kim may have been [$_{VP}$ not drinking].

GPS tie the distinction to scope contrasts, as follows (1982: 604f.):

(17) a. Kim may – not – drink. Wide scope. 'Kim is not permitted to drink'.
b. Kim may – [$_{VP}$ not drink]. Narrow scope. 'Kim is permitted to not drink; It is possible that Kim does not drink'.

But doubt is shed on this close identification of syntactic and semantic scope by the existence of scope ambiguities where structural ambiguities are not in question, such as these:

(18) a. He may have talked to nobody. Narrow scope (possible not)
b. You may talk to nobody. Wide scope (not permitted) as well as narrow (permitted not, possible that not)

And there is a problem for GPS's account of ellipsis. They generate the elliptical $[_{VP}$ *not* e] :

(19) Kim may – $[_{VP}$ not e]. Narrow scope. 'It is possible that Kim does not [sc. drink].'

But nothing in their account prevents the occurrence of $[_{VP}$ *not* e] after nonfinite auxiliaries generally, and this represents a massive overgeneration.

(20) a. Paul has not been; The book may not be; Mary might not have.
b. ?*Paul has been not; ?*The book may be not; ?*Mary might have not.

There is a general contrast whereby finite + *not* readily allows ellipsis, but with nonfinite + *not* it is very restricted. This follows directly if *not* is generated as sister to a finite auxiliary whether the scope of negation is wide or narrow.[18]

Negation
[+AUX, +FIN, –BSE, *–n't*, SUBCAT <XP>] → [+AUX, +FIN, –BSE, *–n't*, SUBCAT <XP, *not*>]

Here *not* is identified by a feature [FORM not] (simply abbreviated *not*), and *–n't* identifies the auxiliary as not being a negative form with *n't*.

Subject–Auxiliary Inversion
I shall suppose that the structure required here is one in which S immediately dominates the finite auxiliary, the subject phrase and the complement phrase, and both subject phrase and complement phrase correspond to values of SUBCAT on the finite auxiliary (as suggested in the context of a framework containing the attribute SUBJ by Borsley 1986: 83). Both S and auxiliary will carry the feature [+INV], which is justified by the restricted distribution of inverted clauses and from the lexical uniqueness of *aren't* in *aren't I* beside **I aren't*. There are apparent difficulties for this analysis. One is that the sequence subject–complement can be coordinated (see (21)). This implies that they form a constituent. It was partly on this ground that GPS did indeed analyse the sequence subject–complement as a constituent.[19] But such non-constituent coordination is found also with ditransitive-type structures (see (c)). Since the difficulty is more general it perhaps does not have any necessary implication for structure here.

(21) a. Will Kim sing and Lee dance? (GPS (49.a) p. 612)
b. Is Kim beautiful and Lee a monster? (GPS (49.g) p. 612)
c. John gave a record to Mary and a book to Harry.

There is, moreover, a syntactic argument against the constituency of subject–complement here based on the fact that the subject survives in ellipsis. Since a clause complement of an auxiliary may undergo ellipsis, as in (22.a), it is hard to see why the possibility of ellipsis should not generalize to the sequence [subject e] (as in *Will* [*they e*]*?*) in (b) if this is also a clause complement. After all, the elliptical nature of the construction will be specified on the node dominating [*they e*] (necessarily since that is all that the introducing auxiliary's SUBCAT can refer to). But then one might expect it to be possible for the subject to be absent in (22.b). But this is not found in well-formed ellipses. Thus the survival of the subject here also implies a flat structure.

(22) a. – Would they rather Paul came on Tuesday?
– Yes, they would rather. (tonic on *would*)
b. – Will Paul and Mary put us up for the night?
– I don't know. Will they?

There is another difficulty for the suggestion that the subject phrase corresponds to a value of SUBCAT. This concerns the presence of gaps in filler–gap constructions. In HPSG such gaps are encoded in a feature SLASH which may percolate beyond the local structure. Since the complement of a lexical head may correspond to a gap, and the subject of a flat structure is here treated as a complement (being listed in SUBCAT), it too should presumably correspond to a possible gap. But this opens the unwelcome possibility of multiple analyses for uninverted sentences with a finite auxiliary. Alongside the NP – VP analysis a 'filler–gap' analysis becomes possible with NP – S[+INV], where the NP is the filler and the subject of S[+INV] is the gap (see (23), where [*may e evaporate*] is a clause structure with empty subject).

(23) The water [may e evaporate].

One solution to this problem is to introduce a further rule schema for flat structures in which the subject remains a value of SUBJ (see Pollard and Sag forthcoming: §9.6; see also 1987: 156, their rule 3).[20] But we can retain the analysis above if we suppose that the lexical rule which defines the possibility of gaps in SUBCAT (the 'Complement Extraction Lexical Rule') has a particular condition in English, where it holds only for [–INV]. The plausibility of this suggestion is borne out by the fact that it generalizes to VP complements which also may not correspond to a gap in inverted structures (see (24) below). There is a straightforward solution, then, to this problem. Given this, we do not need Pollard and Sag's special schema for flat structures in English. This avoids at least for English the unwelcome asymmetry that it introduces into the set of schemata (but this may not hold for other languages; see Borsley (1992) for the suggestion that both schemata will be necessary).

(24) a. *John said he would be honest with Mary, but be honest with Mary can he?
b. *John said he would pay me back, but pay me back will he?

Subject–Auxiliary Inversion
[+AUX, +FIN, –BSE, SUBJ <XP[1]>, SUBCAT <...>] → [+AUX, +INV, +FIN, –BSE, SUBJ <...>, SUBCAT <..., XP[1]>]

This lexical redundancy rule changes the valency requirements of finite auxiliaries in inversion. The value of SUBJ is transferred to SUBCAT. Hence the combination of auxiliary with subject takes place not by rule 1, but by rule 2, and the subject becomes a sister of the lexical head.

Emphasis
It was argued in Chapter 1 that 'emphasis' is not a distinctive auxiliary property but a straightforward reflex of the normal stress rules for English which will assign appropriate phonetics and statement of meaning, including an appropriate delimitation of the range of contrast. So there is no special syntactic or lexical statement made that is peculiar to emphatic auxiliaries.

Interaction of rules
The three rules given above feed one another as follows. The output of Ellipsis may be the input to Negation and Inversion, while the output of Negation may be the input to Inversion.[21] The resulting SUBCAT and SUBJ values are given in Table 3.2, taking *may* with third person singular subject as illustration.

Linear Precedence
Rules 1 and 2 are Immediate Dominance rules, and generalizations about the left–right order of sisters are made by Linear Precedence Constraints. Pollard and Sag give two very general ones. Linear Precedence Constraint 1 (LP1) says simply 'lexical heads in English are phrase initial' (1987: 172).

LP1 HEAD[LEX +] < [ ]

This ensures that the auxiliary is first in its VP, and that it is initial in inverted constructions.

Table 3.2 *Output of lexical redundancy rules for auxiliary* (he) may

SUBCAT	SUBJ	Lexical redundancy rules
<VP[+BSE; –FIN]>	<NP[3sg.]>	
<VP[+BSE; –FIN; +ELL]>	<NP[3sg.]>	Ellipsis
<VP[+BSE; –FIN]; *not*>	<NP[3sg.]>	Negation
<VP[+BSE; –FIN]; NP[3sg.]>	< >	Inversion
<VP[+BSE; –FIN; +ELL]; *not*>	<NP[3sg.]>	Ellipsis + Negation
<VP[+BSE; –FIN; +ELL]]; NP[3sg.]>	< >	Ellipsis + Inversion
<VP[+BSE; –FIN]]; *not*; NP[3sg.]>	< >	Negation + Inversion
<VP[+BSE; –FIN; +ELL]]; *not*; NP[3sg.]>	< >	Ellipsis + Negation + Inversion

The second Linear Precedence Constraint refers to the 'obliqueness hierarchy', which for complements is established by the order of categories within SUBCAT (and SUBJ, in our revision of Pollard and Sag's position). The subject is the least oblique complement, and the list within SUBCAT has less oblique complements to the right. So the obliqueness hierarchy from the least oblique complement to the most oblique complement is established by placing the value of SUBJ first, followed by the SUBCAT list in reverse order. Linear Precedence Constraint 2 does not simply impose this hierarchy however, since particles show a limited departure from it. The correct generalization is that 'complements must precede more oblique *phrasal* complements' (1987: 176). For inverted structures this establishes the ordering 'subject < other complement' (where the 'other complement' may be a VP, or XP[+PRD] or NP). Since *not* is subcategorized for, it seems that it too will be placed in the obliqueness hierarchy, between subjects and other complements according to its position in SUBCAT.[22] Then it too will be required to precede the 'other complement'. But since it is (presumably) [+LEX], no ordering will be established between subject and *not* in inverted structures. Hence the principles set up for English by Pollard and Sag account immediately for the variation in position of *not* found in inverted structures.[23]

(25) a. Will not this hypothesis be upheld? H[+LEX] – not – subject – VP
b. Will this hypothesis not be upheld? H[+LEX] – subject – not – VP

3.4.2 Periphrastic do

Periphrastic *do* has a distribution which is unlike that of other auxiliaries in two ways. It does not appear with a dependent auxiliary: **does be*, **did have* *eaten*, etc. It also does not appear without accent in positive clauses: *they do go* can only have the (generally) accented *do* which focusses the mood and tense of the sentence.[24]

GPS dealt with the first characteristic here by subcategorizing *do* for VP[–AUX]. This is a unique subcategorization in Present-day English, but it is striking that it picks out at phrase level the domain which at lexical level is just that of morphological mood and tense, given that auxiliaries are not subject to productive rules affecting verbs. I shall (for convenience) speak here simply of 'tense', taking for granted the potential relevance of mood (and finiteness).

The second peculiarity of distribution has generally not been covered in 'lexical' accounts, so that unaccented *they do go* has simply been generated as grammatical (Lapointe 1980a, GPS, Falk 1984: 485 n. 3). One of the impressive strengths of the analysis of Chomsky (1957) on the other hand was the integrated way in which it dealt with the distribution of periphrastic *do,* inserting it when the rules of syntax left a tense affix stranded. More recently in Pollock (1989) the conceptual framework is entirely different, and unaccented *do* is not explicitly ruled out (see p. 420 n. 49). But here too there is a direct complementarity in the expression of tense between *do* and affix, and it is controlled by syntactic conditions.

This notion of complementarity in the expression of tense between *do* and affix is supported by the fact that they are both restricted to nonauxiliary contexts, as noted above.[25] I suggest that a natural way of characterizing this complementarity is simply as one between affix and word. Tense is realized as an affix whenever the grammar of English does not assign it additional properties which identify it as a word. To put it differently, its default value is 'affix'. If we consider the categories in which *do* occurs, they can be seen to possess nonaffixal properties, as follows.

(i) With 'inflectional' *-n't*. Inflections apply to words (or stems) in English, not to affixes (or processes).[26]

(ii) With subcategorization for more than one item in inverted and negative constructions: SUBCAT<VP, NP>; SUBCAT<VP, not>; SUBCAT<VP, not, NP>. Specification for SUBJ <NP[nom]> is presumably a characteristic of tense whether realized by *do* or morphology, since tense confers nominative morphology on its subject. So too is subcategorization for V. Hence morphological tense is anyway [SUBJ <NP[nom]>, SUBCAT <V[–AUX]>]. In inversion we find subcategorization for a further phrasal element, the subject. Affixation on phrasal stems is either absent or highly marked in English: see Allen's conclusion that such apparent counter-instances as *every dayness* or *bread and buttery* involve noncompositional phrases which must be listed in the lexicon. This supports their reanalysis as nonphrasal items within word formation (see Allen 1978: 236ff., Scalise 1984: 154ff.) in conformity with the 'No Phrase Constraint' on rules of word formation. Similarly DiSciullo and Williams (1987) permit 'phrase structure' in morphologically complex structures, but only as a marked phenomenon (as reanalysis or coanalysis). Moreover, a subcategorization for more than one element would also on the face of it violate the 'Binary Branching Hypothesis' (Aronoff 1976, Scalise 1984).

(iii) With subcategorization for an item which is not realized in cases of ellipsis. Zero elements are not involved as stems in English morphology.

(iv) When it bears accent, and in some further unaccented cases.[27] Such instances typically involve a contrast of polarity, though this may be Ossleton's (1983) '*do* of implicit contrast' and not directly retrievable from context. Words can carry a tonic accent in English; prefixes and some suffixes can, but in situations of more direct contrast; it does not, however, seem possible to place such an accent on an inflectional suffix except where an essentially metalinguistic correction is involved. English tense affixes are also largely nonsyllabic, hence unavailable as the focus of a tonic. The type of accent shown by *do* is most centrally a property of words; so is the unaccented use where 'implicit contrast' is involved.

(26) a. I saw a eucalyptus on the hill. – Only one? I saw *bush*es (*bush-es*, *bush-*es*) on the hill.
b. ?I saw a bush on the hill. – No, you saw bush-*es*. (?metalinguistic)
c. The bushs [ʃs] on the hill. – No, the bush*es* on the hill. (metalinguistic)
d. A hot day? A hotter day than Tuesday? It was the *hott*-est (*hott-est*, *hott-*est*) day of the year!
e. I hope the church soon becomes *dis*established.
f. Here comes not the count but the count*ess*.

I suggest then that the distribution of *do* and morphological tense is essentially a choice between realizing tense as a word form or as an inflection. Tense is basically [SUBJ <NP[nom]>, SUBCAT <V[–AUX]>], and the 'default' value of this is the affix. But the various uses of *do* all have some further property (over and above the fact that *do* is itself a word) which identifies them as word rather than affix. This is not an absolute matter; it is identification within the structure of English, and on the assumption of a conservative theory of the interrelationship between syntax and morphology. They have an inflection (-*n't*), or subcategorizations, or a use (whether accented or involving prominence) which would be very highly marked within morphology. So *do* is used just in case English grammar requires tense to be realized as a separate word.

(See also §9.5 for some discussion of the factors involved in the earlier loss of inversion with English verbs.)

This complementarity of realization of tense need not be treated syntactically but can be stated in the lexicon, as the range of properties involved suggests. Pollard and Sag (1987) permit categories to contain such logical operations as disjunction and implication, and though I wish to avoid them in syntactic structures their use in the lexicon is appropriate. Then an inheritance hierarchy for tense can include a condition which effectively states that *do* is only possible if tense has independent word properties apart from those entailed by *do*. There is a variety of ways of formulating this.[28] As far as I can see all suffer from the apparent disadvantage that they involve an additional statement to restrict the occurrence of *do*. But this may be appropriate. Historically the decline of unaccented affirmative *do* was slow, lasting from *c*1575 until the eighteenth century or even later in specific contexts (Tieken 1987: 115ff., Sweet 1891–8: §2180). Moreover children overgeneralize unaccented *do*, and it is surely one of the few cases where frequency makes absence salient, so that an additional restriction could be learned later. The phenomenon is presumably originally at least the 'blocking' (Aronoff 1976: 43) of a form by a synonymous form, though it is virtually allomorphy in today's English. Thus taking the absence of *do* to be a marked phenomenon does not seem unreasonable.[29]

3.4.3 Imperative do *and* don't

The imperative auxiliaries *do* and *don't* share properties with other imperatives. Phrases containing them coordinate with indicatives just as other imperatives do, the subject of a *don't* imperative is nominative, and *don't* equally fails to show agreement when the subject is third person. So they are [+FIN] like other imperatives, though it is less clear that they are [+BSE] (see §3.2).

(27) a. She loves me and don't (you) try to deny it!
b. Don't you and he misbehave again!
c. Nobody (don't anybody) say a word about himself – stand on the Fifth if you have to. (a lawyer advising a group of clients before a hearing, cited from Bolinger 1977a: 153)

One striking structural peculiarity, however, is that the subject of a *don't* imperative follows *don't*. Examples with a preceding noun phrase seem rather to be peremptory declaratives, or to contain a vocative (see Quirk *et al.* 1985: §11.25 for some discussion of this distinction). This is clear from cases with *don't be*, which show a sharp contrast.

(28) a. *You don't be careless again or I'll kill you!
b. You, don't be careless again or I'll kill you! (*you* is vocative)
c. Don't you be careless again or I'll kill you!

The subordinate verb here (as in subjectless constructions after *do/don't*) is a bare infinitive, not itself an imperative, since it negates like a nonfinite. There is also no clear evidence that subject and complement VP form a constituent, while the case of the subject is if anything evidence against such constituency.

(29) Don't (you and he) not come to our party! (with 'constituent' negation)

Thus the required structure is apparently a 'flat' structure as in Subject–Auxiliary Inversion, though with a distinct set of properties. It occurs only with *don't* among auxiliary imperatives (not *do*, or *be*). And imperatives with a subject are unlike questions in not permitting ellipsis of VP. Imperative **don't you!* is impossible, question *don't you?* impeccable. The simplest and most natural analysis introduces *don't* and *do* directly under S, generating *don't* with an optional subject in a 'flat' structure, *do* without a subject. The identity in order between question and imperative structures will then follow from separately required Linear Precedence Constraints (being identical to the order found within VPs) so that this apparent parallelism between questions and imperative structures is captured by the grammar.

Don't and *do* are also distinct in a further series of respects. They are like non-imperative finite auxiliaries in occurring with *-n't* and *not*. Imperative *be* and *have* do not behave like this. This idiosyncrasy follows directly if *don't* and *do* are indicatives whose mood is opaque, as suggested above in §2.4. So they are [+FIN, –BSE] forms, hence parallel to indicatives, though none the less imperative in semantics.[30] Their properties are sufficiently distinct for there to be no worthwhile generalization with 'periphrastic' *do* (Quirk *et al.* 1985: §11.30 n. [a]; Warner 1985: 48–9; note that Pollock 1989 also treats imperative *do* as idiosyncratic, e.g. as a main verb with 'fossil' negation). Their lexical entries will include the following information.

don't V[+AUX, +FIN, –BSE, +*n't*, SUBCAT <VP[+BSE, –FIN, –TO], (NP)>, SUBJ < >]
do V[+AUX, +FIN, –BSE, SUBCAT <VP[+BSE, –FIN, –TO]>, SUBJ < >]

Given this formulation, the lexical redundancy rules of Ellipsis and Negation may both apply to *do*, but only Ellipsis may apply to *don't*, and then only when the subject is not specified within SUBCAT. Thus the contrasts between elliptical *do!, don't!, do not!* and **don't you!* and negative *don't you touch me! *do not you touch me!* follow. Imperative *don't* and *do* also fail to satisfy the input condition for the rule of Inversion, unlike indicative *do* and *don't*. Hence the contrast with the series of elliptical questions *do you?, Don't you?* and *Do you not? Be* and *have* are [+FIN, +BSE]. The only rule they are subject to, therefore, is Ellipsis. Negation does not apply. Thus we get a simple and complete account of these differences.

3.5 Conclusion

In this chapter I have underpinned the argument of my Chapter 2 by showing that within the HPSG theory of the lexicon there is a coherent way of capturing both the individual status of particular morphosyntactic categories of auxiliaries, and appropriate generalizations. Moreover, the interrelationships between the major auxiliary constructions are clearly well captured by the proposed lexical redundancy rules whose simple statements cover a wide range of data. The distribution of periphrastic *do* can be appropriately interpreted as dependent on a lexical statement, and the treatment of imperative *do* as indicative has been shown to be defensible. You can see how it all works, and I hope that makes my argument more convincing. The general plausibility of my account of auxiliaries is established.

4 *Distinguishing auxiliaries and verbs in early English*

4.1 Introduction

The first part of this book has established the essential grammatical and lexical characteristics of the modern auxiliaries. Armed with an understanding of the most recent point of their development, I want in the second part of the book to ask how the modern auxiliaries developed, and what kind of grammatical status they had in earlier English. Their Old English[1] ancestors already appeared in constructions which can sometimes be translated using modern auxiliaries, so they had at least some 'notional' points of contact with their modern congeners, if arguably often a contextual one, but their grammar was clearly much closer to that of nonauxiliary verbs. Most strikingly, periphrastic *do* did not appear in Old English, so that as in present-day French and German it was finite verbs generally which appeared in inverted interrogatives and were involved in the placement of sentential negation. The ancestors of the modern modals were also not as sharply distinctive in morphology and subcategorization as today. One view of these differences is that 'pre-modals' (and presumably other 'pre-auxiliaries' too) were simply verbs in Old English (see Allen 1975, Lightfoot 1979, Roberts 1985). In Lightfoot (1979) this leads to an account of the emergence of modals as a sudden, cataclysmic development early in the Modern English period, and to an account of syntactic change in terms of sharp discontinuities. But this account leaves the nature of earlier developments obscure; it claims that the definitional properties of 'pre-modals' developed essentially by chance, in some quite mysterious way. Critics of this account have tended to stress the continuity of developments, pointing to earlier evidence of modal properties and claiming that a class of modals emerged more gradually (see Warner 1983, Plank 1984, among others, and the recent accounts of van Kemenade 1989, Nagle 1989). But many questions are raised about the nature of these developments.

The application of the term 'auxiliary' to Old English is familiar but problematic. Traditionally the term has been used with reliance on an essentially semantic (or functional) equivalence. Thus Mitchell (1985: §594) distinguishes 'auxiliary verb' from 'verb with full meaning', where his criterion is the traditional definition (as in *OED*). This is a sensible descriptive convenience, but it cannot be the answer to a question about the history of a word class since formal criteria are centrally involved in the establishment of classes, though notional criteria have their place (see discussion in §4.4 below). For similar reasons I disagree with Brinton (1988: 105) when she suggests 'primarily on semantic and functional grounds' that 'Old English had several independent elements in AUX, certainly the passive and perfect auxiliaries, and possibly the progressive auxiliary and the modals', and I am unhappy about the primacy given to semantic criteria in Goossens' (1987) account of the 'auxiliarization' of modals in Old English. Claims about Universal Grammar have also been appealed to in setting up some some type of auxiliary category for earlier English: see Steele *et al.*'s (1981) AUX which contains tense and mood, or the framework adopted by van Kemenade (1989). But the status of 'pre-modals' and 'pre-auxiliaries' still needs detailed and independent discussion. They have clear properties which align them with verbs, and they lack most of the formal criteria which make them distinctive today. So Lightfoot (1979: 99) could argue with some initial justification that 'What we translate with modals in NE, all behave exactly like ordinary, complement-taking verbs in OE.'

In the following chapters I want to re-examine the status of auxiliaries in early English, and develop an account of their history. I shall establish that 'pre-auxiliaries' (and 'pre-modals') did indeed already have a distinctive status before the sixteenth century, not just on traditional notional grounds, but (crucially) on the basis of their formal properties. This permits a coherent understanding of developments without the need to invoke teleological mechanisms. Then I will show how this relatively fuzzily defined word class changed its status *c*1500, when it developed from a subordinate word class into a sharply defined, non-subordinate word class, and I will discuss the later consequences of this change. So I am offering a fresh account of the status of 'pre-auxiliaries' and a particular interpretation of their historical development within an extension and reinterpretation of the traditional structuralist-cum-notional theory of word classes adumbrated in Chapter 1.

In this chapter I will start with a brief summary of the situation in early English, listing the verbs involved. Then I will explain why they are indeed to be analysed as members of the class of verbs, and will briefly discuss word classes and how they can be isolated to clarify the methodology of succeeding chapters. My focus in this chapter, as in the rest of the book, will be on the 'pre-modals' since they are of central importance for the characterization of the general class. There will be no detailed discussion of the progressive, perfect or passive, but in so far as these are combinations with *be*, their development is a secondary topic, since I shall assume as for Present-day English that *be* takes predicates which may be participle phrases (which have an independent distribution) rather than that *be* is a formative specific to the perfect, passive or progressive. Regrettably there will not be space for much on *be* or *have* themselves.

I will from now on generally avoid the terms 'pre-modal' and 'pre-auxiliary' since I shall argue later that these words belong to distinct subclasses of verb which are to be identified cross-linguistically on notional grounds with more general categories 'auxiliary' and 'modal'.

4.2 The ancestors of present-day auxiliaries

The words and constructions which are relevant to us in Old English can be divided into the ancestors of modals and the ancestors of nonmodals. Since it is grammatical properties of groups of words which are important, I of course include words which do not survive today, and words which, while relevant, are not of central importance.

4.2.1 Ancestors of modals

These words have uses which often seem to correspond in translation to present-day modals, though most of them also occurred in a range of other senses and constructions noted below. They were distinguished from most other verbs by their morphology, which is 'preterite-present' (except for *wile*; see §6.2 for the term) and by the fact that an infinitive in construction with these verbs always lacked *to*. The most important verbs under this heading were the following. (I cite these in their present indicative third person singular, apart from *uton*, and give references to their descendants in *OED* in parentheses.)

cann 'know, be acquainted with, know how to, be able' (> PE *Can, v.*[1]; *Con, v.*[1])
dearr 'dare' (> PE *Dare, v.*[1])
mæg 'be strong, have power, be able, be allowed, may' (> PE *May, v.*[1])
mot 'be allowed, may; be obliged, must' (> later *Mote, v.*[1]; PE *Must, v.*[1])
sceal 'owe, shall, ought, must' (> PE *Shall*)
þearf 'need to' (> later *Tharf, thar, v.*)

uton 'let us' (> later *Ute, v.*)
wile 'intend, desire, be willing, will' (> PE *Will, v.*[1]; *Nill, v.*)

Finally one preterite-present, *agan* 'have, (ought to)' (Mitchell 1985: §§932–3, hereafter cited as 'M§§932–3', etc.) (> PE *Owe, v.*, preterite > PE *Ought, v.*) regularly takes *to* when it occurs with an infinitive.

This list differs from Mitchell's list of '"modal" auxiliaries' (§990) by the addition of *uton*, and by distinguishing *agan* as having a less integrated status (and I shall not always include it in my discussions). There are some changes in membership in Middle English which are noted in Chapter 6; in particular *mun* 'must, shall' (> PE *Mun, v.*, and see *Maun, v.*[1]) appears in northern and midland dialects. Examples of these words in contexts where a modern modal seems appropriate in translation can be found in Chapter 7.

4.2.2 Ancestors of nonmodal auxiliaries

Here belong *beon* and *wesan* which correspond to 'be', with which *weorðan* 'become, be' is often classed, *habban* 'have', and 'pro-verbal' *don* 'do'. Other uses of *don* may be relevant, as may some aspectual verbs, principally *onginnan* 'begin' (see Brinton 1988).[2] *Beon, wesan* and *weorðan* occur with a range of predicate phrases, and *habban* takes a direct object in the sense 'possess' and its generalizations. Both *beon/wesan* and later *habban* also occur with a dependent *to*-infinitive indicating obligation or futurity. More prominent are constructions in which *beon/wesan* and *weorðan* occur with participles which often seem to correspond to modern progressives, perfects and passives, though their semantics is not necessarily the same as today's.

Beon/wesan *with the first participle*

The first (or present) participle may head participial constructions in Old English and it may have verbal rection; certainly by late West Saxon it may take an accusative object in appositive use (Callaway 1901), and adjectives do not occur with the accusative. It occurs after *beon/wesan* (occasionally *weorðan*). The construction looks parallel to the modern progressive, but seems to connote duration or, less clearly, habitual action (M§687f.), and it may occur when duration is unlimited and the progressive would be impossible today (M§686, Mitchell 1976: 484ff.). Its origins involve not just *beon/wesan* + predicative participle, but also *beon/wesan* with an agentive noun of form similar to the participle, and appositive uses of the participle (Nickel 1967, M§697–701). It is reasonably common in Old English, but its frequency declines very sharply with early Middle English, then gradually increases with each century. It is not until early Modern English that its distribution begins to look recognizably like today's, and the modern construction may depend also on the *be in singing, be a-singing* type. For the general development see especially Mossé (1938, 1957), Nehls (1974), Scheffer (1975); for Old English: Nickel (1966), Mitchell (1976, 1985: §§682ff.).

(1) a. ðæs modes storm se symle bið cnyssende ðæt scip ðære heortan
'the mind's storm, which ever tosses [lit.: is battering] the ship (of) the heart' (Sweet's translation)
CP 59.4

b. se consul wæs monega gefeoht donde
'the consul was waging many battles [lit.: many battles doing]'
Or 188.19

c. We wyllað nu mid sumere scortre trahtnunge þas rædinge oferyrnan, and geopenian gif heo hwæt digeles on hyre habbende sy.
'We intend now with some short exposition to go over this reading [lit.: this reading to-go-over], and expound (it) if it has anything obscure in it [lit.: if she anything obscure (gen.) in her having is].'
ÆCHom i.388.29

Beon/wesan *(and* weorðan*) with the second participle*

Both *beon/wesan* and *weorðan* occur with the second (passive or past) participle in a construction which apparently corresponds to the modern passive (M§744ff.; see Lightfoot 1979: 252ff., 1980 for discussion of the possible implications of some distributional differences). This participle may also occur independently as the head of participial constructions (see examples in Callaway 1901). *Beon/wesan* (much less commonly *weorðan*) also occur with the second participle of certain intransitive verbs in a construction which looks like a perfect which is parallel to those of French and German (M§734ff.). For the later history of this see Traugott's summary (1972: 144ff.), Fridén (1948), and especially Rydén and Brorström (1987) and references there.

(2) a. þa earman ceasterwaran toslitene and fornumene wæron fram heora feondum
'the poor townsfolk were rent and destroyed [lit.: rent and destroyed were] by their foes' (Miller's translation)
Bede 46.24

b. geseah him fram deoflum tobrohte beon þa boc his agenra sinna
'saw to-him by devils brought (fem. acc. sg.) to-be the book (fem. acc. sg.) (of) his own sins'
'saw the book of his own sins being brought to him by devils'
Bede 24.3

c. þa he þær to gefaren wæs
'when he was arrived there'
ChronA 87.6 (894.65)

Habban *and the* 'have *perfect'*

Habban occurs with a direct object in 'possess' and related senses. It also appears in a construction parallel to the modern perfect (M§705ff.). This is apparently a reinterpretation of the construction in which *habban* occurs with a nominal object plus passive (second) participle, presumably via the development of instances in which the distinction between old and new interpretations was neutralized (as in (3.a); see M§724, *OED Have*, *v.* II). This reanalysis must have meant a new category of past (second) participle capable of taking an accusative object, and a reinterpretation of the complement of *habban* as a verbal rather than nominal construction. It must have been available early, because in early West Saxon (of the late ninth century) this perfect has already been generalized beyond verbs taking an accusative object, to verbs taking other cases and to verbs without a complement (M§§706ff., 722). An inflection indicating agreement between participle and accusative is already often absent at this period, though it continues to be found occasionally later (M§710). A result of the generalization of *habban* is that perfects formed with *beon/wesan* and with *habban* are both found with intransitives of motion and change of state.

(3) a. Læran sceal mon geongne monnan, ... oþþæt hine mon atemedne hæbbe
'One must teach [lit.: teach shall one] (a) young man until one has him tamed – until one has tamed him' (neutralized)
Maxims I (ASPR III, 156ff.) 45

b. Swiðe wel ðu min hæfst geholpen æt þære spræce
'Very well hast thou assisted me [lit.: thou me (gen.) hast helped] in this argument' (Fox's translation)
Bo 41.145.1

c. þa he þærto gefaren hæfde
'when he had arrived there'
An Anglo-Saxon Chronicle from British Museum, Cotton MS., Tiberius B. IV (ed. E. Classen and F. E. Harmer, Manchester University Press, 1926) 35.27 (894.59) (corresponds to (2.c))

4.3 Verblike characteristics

4.3.1 Verblike characteristics in Old English

In Old English all the verbs listed above shared major properties with the rest of the class of verbs, and were clearly to be identified as members of this class.[3] This situation continued in Middle English. They were like verbs in the following respects.

(i) *Formal paradigmatic contrasts.* In Old English these words showed the major formal contrasts of tense (past : nonpast), mood (indicative : subjunctive), person and number found with other verbs, though nonfinites are not recorded for all of them, and the invariable *uton* 'let's' lacked all contrasts. Note that although preterite-present verbs had an endingless form in the third person singular of the present indicative, they had a morphologically distinct plural and second person singular. The class had a potentially complete verbal paradigm for the indicative and subjunctive. This situation continued into Middle English, though the formal distinction of mood weakened for these words, and their preterite forms increasingly developed special functions.[4]

(ii) *Semantics and subcategorization.* Most of the verbs listed above as Old English ancestors of today's modals appear in senses and constructions which align them with full rather than with helping verbs. So *wile* may mean 'want', 'desire', *cann* 'know', 'recognize', *mæg* 'be strong'. There are intransitive uses (*mæg*), and transitives with one or more objects (e.g. *sceal*) or with complement clauses (e.g. *wile*). They may appear with directional prepositional phrases as complement, and in this are also like full verbs. We find instances like the following (and I do not intend here to exemplify the full range of constructions). Thus the potentially 'modal' uses of these verbs for the most part occur alongside clearly 'nonmodal' uses.

(4) a. Ðas VIIII magon wið nygon attrum
'These 9 are-powerful against nine poisons'
Metrical Charms (ASPR VI, 116ff.) 2.30

b. & gif hwa oðrum sceole borh oððe bote æt woruldlicum þingum, gelæste hit him georne
'and if someone to-another [dat.] owes (some) debt or compensation in secular affairs, (he) should-pay it to-him eagerly'
LawICn 17.3

c. þonne ne ðorfte he no maran fultomes þonne his selfes
'then he would not need [lit.: not would-need he] any [lit.: no] more help [gen.] than himself [gen.]'
Bo 26.59.30

d. he symble wyle god . and næfre nan yfel
'he [God] always desires good and never any [lit.: no] evil'
ÆLS i.1.48

e. Hu wilt þu þæt ic gelyfe ðæt Simon þis nyte
'How wilt thou that I should-believe that Simon does-not-know this, ... ?' (Morris' translation)
BlHom 179.33

Subcategorization for the plain infinitive was also less distinctive in Old English, being found more generally among verbs (but see §6.1 below). Thus examples which seem to correspond to modern modal uses occur alongside other examples, generally (but not always) less frequent, in which sense and construction seem typical of the general class of verbs. This holds also for *beon/wesan*, which retains the fuller sense 'exist' and occurs without a complement as well as with locative predicates, and for perfect *habban*, which is not always so readily distinguished from broadly possessional or relational uses as today (see above). *Uton* and *mot* are, however, exceptions to this general statement, and OE *dearr* may also be an exception. These are restricted to occurrence with the plain infinitive and to instances where the sense of an infinitive is to be supplied.[5] In Middle English 'modal' uses became more prominent, but many of the senses and constructions which are typical of full verbs survive throughout this period and into early Modern English, though others are lost. Details of this are given in Chapters 6 and 7 below.

(iii) *Syntax*. In today's English occurrence in interrogative inversion or with the *not* of sentential negation distinguishes full verbs from auxiliaries. But in earlier English full verbs appeared in inversions and with the *ne* (later *not*) of sentential negation (as noted above) so that the clear modern distinction was absent. I will argue in Chapter 9 that Old English is well analysed as having for all verbs both inverted 'flat' clause structures (lacking VP but with the verb sister to its subject and its complements) and clause structures with VP; in contrast, Present-day English restricts the inverted structure to auxiliaries. Furthermore, there are parallels in Old English between the positional syntax of constructions with a head verb and dependent infinitive phrase, and constructions where an ancestor of a modern modal occurs with an infinitive. The implication is that parallel structures are involved. Similar comments hold for *beon/wesan* and *habban* in constructions related to today's progressive and perfect. Thus there seems to be a gross similarity in potential positional syntax within the clause between the ancestors of today's auxiliaries and other verbs.

To illustrate this, consider clauses with subject (S), the ancestor of a modern auxiliary (v), verb (V) and verbal complement (C). Where the subject is initial, and where pronominal complements (with their tendency to appear early) and heavy complements (with their tendency to appear late) are not involved, the two most commonly attested orders in Old English are (5.a) and (b). A third, (c), is also common. Of these orders main clauses are generally stated to prefer (a), while (b) is most typical of subordinate clauses.[6]

(5) a. S v V C
b. S C V v
c. S v C V

Appropriate schematic structures for Old English are as follows.

(6) a. S v [$_{VP}$ V C]
Ic wille [wyrcean min setl on norðdæle]
'I will build my seat in (the) north' (Sweet's translation)
CP 111.24
b. S [$_{VP}$ C V] v
ðonne mon [ða earce beran] scolde.
'when the ark had to be carried [lit.: when one the ark carry should].'
CP 171.24
c. S v [$_{VP}$ C V]
cuæð ðæt hie scolden [leasunga witgian]
'said that they would prophesy untruth [lit.: untruth prophesy]' (Sweet's translation)
CP 91.8

This analysis recapitulates some of the essential aspects of the account of Old English 'modals' given by Allen (1975) (though differences of theoretical framework led her to permute order transformationally, and to assign these words a complement S whose subject was deleted by transformation). Allen intended her analysis to support the view that the Old English 'modals' did not constitute a separate class from verbs. Part of her evidence was the possibility of generalizations about verb position between clause types, since verbs are typically second in main clauses, like v in (a), but may occur late in subordinate and coordinate clauses, like v in (b); see Allen's rule (8) permuting SOV to SVO. These generalizations will be captured in the present framework by Linear Precedence Constraints.[7] There are clearly much more detailed questions about parallels between the ancestors of auxiliaries and other verbs to be asked here. But (as yet) what is striking (at an admittedly gross level) is the similarities between the potential positional syntax of the ancestors of the present-day auxiliaries and other members of the class of verbs in Old English.

4.3.2 The development of verblike characteristics

It is not just the case that the ancestors of today's modals show certain verblike characteristics in Old English which they retain in a less distinctive form into Middle English. There is also diachronic evidence for their status as verbs in the way they develop. This further evidence is important because it shows that their categorization as verbs was sufficient to provide a basis for historical change. Moreover, it shows that verbal status was maintained in Middle English. The evidence is as follows.

(i) *Reformed present indicative plural.* Some of these words appear in Middle English with a present indicative plural reformed on the model of full verbs, though they retain the endingless third person singular. Thus instead of *þei shulle(n)*, with the historically expected ending of preterite-presents, in some parts of the south and south-west midlands we find forms with the *-eþ* termination of full verbs, both with a dependent infinitive and in other constructions. *Shulleþ* and *conneþ* occur, as does *moueþ* (apparently less frequently). *MED* does not give such forms for *mot* or *dar.* OE *agað*, ME *oueþ* probably develop as part of this verb's more general tendency to give up preterite-present forms, and this may hold for *witeth.* A reformed plural not supported by a reformed singular is apparently also found in *unneþ.*[8]

Wile is not historically a preterite-present, and its present tense indicative plural in Old English is *willaþ.* No doubt the retention of *willeþ* in parts of the south and south-west midlands generally provides a bridge for the development of *shulleþ*, etc. But the importance of the analogy with the more general class of verbs is shown by the fact that in late Middle English manuscripts the innovating *shulleþ* is partly independent of *willeþ* in its distribution, in that the presence of *shulleþ* as a normal form in a manuscript by no means implies the presence of *willeþ.*[9]

(ii) *Additional nonfinites.* Even before the modern period nonfinites for these words are not fully evidenced in surviving documents, and some at least may have been absent from the language. Categories additional to the paradigms generally established for Old English, however, continue to appear. The infinitive of MAY is first recorded in the middle of the eleventh century, the infinitive of DARE and past participles of DARE, MAY and WILL appear in the course of Middle English. These nonfinites are not restricted to constructions with a relatively verbal type of subcategorization, but appear with a following plain infinitive or ellipsis.[10] Given the apparent absence of nonfinites with SHALL and MOT, it seems possible that some at least of these apparent additions represent real developments, and a grammatical account within which this is plausible is given in Chapter 8. Such developments give some evidence of verbal status.

There is more discussion of this topic in Chapter 6, where defectiveness is dealt with in more detail. But one case in particular, that of the infinitive of MAY, may help to convince readers of the possibility of real developments here, rather than mere accidents of the record. The infinitive of MAY is not found in classical West Saxon, and is even apparently avoided by Ælfric in his *Grammar* of *c*1000. He gives forms of *queo* '*ic mæg*', but remarks of the future participle *quiturus* that 'we know no English for it' (ÆGram p. 252) though he commonly glosses future participles with 'will or shall' plus infinitive (see pp. 246, 248, 252), and has just glossed *iturus* as '*se ðe wyle oððe sceal faran*' ('(he) who will or shall go'). The infinitive first appears in a gloss of *c*1050, and is reasonably common in Middle English (see *OED*, *MED*, V§§1684–5). This is at least suggestive that in late Old English the form was innovating or dialectal, and that a real addition to the language is involved here.

(iii) *Impersonal constructions.* Constructions in which an affected NP associated with a predicate is oblique and there is no nominative NP are found in both Old and Middle English. One of the semantic categories identified as involved in such constructions by McCawley (1976) was that of 'need, duty, obligation'. In Middle English there is some turnover of vocabulary in this syntactic and semantic category. New developments include the possibility of impersonal constructions with *ouen* 'ought' and, strikingly, with both *þarf* 'need' and *mot* 'must, ought' which appear in impersonal constructions in which they take an oblique NP and a plain infinitive.[11] (*Dar* also occurs impersonal in the sense 'need', see *MED durren* v. 2(b). But this is better taken to be because of contact with *þarf* than as a separate development.)

This development is shared by full verbs and by members of the group of ancestors of today's modals, so it provides some evidence for a shared common status. It is worth noting that *þarf* and *mot* are among the most distinctive members of this group since they lack nonfinite forms in Middle English and are only found with the plain infinitive or in ellipsis, not with other verblike subcategorization types.[12]

So the ancestors of today's modals and other auxiliaries share a range of properties with verbs throughout Old and Middle English. And though some of these properties (like the possession of a distinct subjunctive inflection) weaken, others develop. Thus there is evidence (not all unequivocal or of equal value) that these words continue to be rather closely related to verbs even in late Middle English.

4.3.3 Distinctive characteristics

There are, however, properties which show the distinctness of these words from other verbs. As in the preceding section they are conveniently divided into two groups. First come distinctive characteristics found in Old English which apparently continue into Middle English (though the Middle English evidence is sometimes less copious). Second are characteristics which show some development, so that they appear increasingly distinct with time. These properties will be discussed in Chapters 5 and 6, but I will briefly list them here. This list shows properties which occur with at least some of the verbs in question. All are present to some extent in Old English. A–C belong to my first group, D–F show considerable development and belong to my second group.

A. Occurrence in ellipses like the modern post-auxiliary ellipsis and pseudogapping.
B. Occurrence within impersonal constructions where the subordinate verb controls the case of nominal arguments.
C. Restriction of some of these words to finite forms.
D. Use of past-tense forms without past time reference, outside a motivating context.
E. Subcategorization for the plain infinitive, not for the *to*-infinitive.
F. Preterite-present morphology.

There are also three further potential characteristics. The first yields a very weak criterion for distinctness; the second is probably not satisfactory; and the third does not (as far as I can yet see) yield a distinction.[13] The first two will be briefly discussed below.

G. The availability of negative forms in *n-* in Old English.
H. Failure to occur as the antecedent to pro-verbal *do*.
I. Word order patterns involving 'verb raising'.

4.4 Word classes

The question of the development of English auxiliaries is at least in part a word-class question, and here I will outline my approach to word classes. This marries elements of traditional structural linguistics, the 'notional' approach of Lyons (1966), and work on cognitive categorization by Rosch and her associates (see 1978, 1988 for surveys). It has already been briefly discussed in Chapter 1. This approach has several advantages: first, it is grounded in a general theory of human categorization; second its generality permits a relatively neutral, descriptive approach to the linguistic data, which is important given our ignorance of the relevant parameters and their structuring; thirdly, it clarifies a methodology for determining the status of word classes in earlier English; fourthly the approach includes concepts which illuminate the status of 'pre-auxiliaries' and which enable us to interpret some of the dynamic of change.

I shall make a series of very general interlinked assumptions about the word-class structure of a language (including its subclasses), which derive partly from general linguistics and partly from the work of Rosch and her associates on cognitive categorization.

(a) The establishment of a category depends on two factors in the general case: the extent of resemblances between the members of the category, balanced against the extent of differences between the members of the category and the members of other categories. Thus there are properties common to some or all of the members of a category (or subcategory) which are typically mutually predictive in that the presence of one in a member implies also the presence of others.[14] These groupings (or correlations) of properties stand in opposition to groupings which characterize other categories.

From the perspective of general linguistics this can be seen as an implementation of the notion 'opposition' between classes in terms of oppositions between properties. It is of course to be expected that properties will differ in their importance for classification. Rosch's approach does not require that all properties should be on a par, but allows for their differential weighting (see e.g. Tversky 1977). I assume that semantic properties are less determining of the status of an individual member than formal properties (see (d) below), and I hope that some indication of the relative importance of different properties will emerge from my attempt to understand the synchronic and diachronic structuring of auxiliaries. This clearly leaves opens a line of doubt or objection which asks how the properties chosen are themselves justified. My defence is that many of them are apparently basic to a grammatical and semantic account, so they at least give us a serious starting point.

(b) Categories have internal structure in the sense that some members will share more of the relevant grouping of properties than others and so will constitute its central membership (also called its 'nuclear' or 'prototypical' membership). In Rosch's work the notion that a particular member or members should be identified as the prototype has been replaced by the view that this is established by a particular set of properties and need correspond to no particular item or items (1978: 40f.). It may also be that categories have indeterminate boundaries, and admit of degrees of membership, but these two further positions are not required by the existence of prototype structure.

In the traditional 'Aristotelian' view of categories the question of membership is simply answered 'in' or 'out'. Categories are homogeneous, they have sharp edges, and there are simple and definitive criteria for membership. This view (in its strong form) has never suited the word classes of natural language well. It has recently been subject to various challenges, most importantly for our purposes from Rosch and her associates; see also Lakoff (1987) and work cited there. This work suggests that cognitive categories need not be homogeneous; they may have indeterminate boundaries, and there need be no simple defining criteria for membership. On the face of it, this type of view suits the word classes of natural language much better, and some of the ideas here are close to traditional positions, or have been adopted by linguists who have discussed word classes (e.g. Huddleston 1984, McCawley 1986). I want to adopt this general view as being clearly the most suitable one for the word classes of natural language, and I shall also adopt some of Rosch's particular theoretical statements. But a point I want to stress is that this view and the specific assumptions I shall make leaves me with a position which is neutral to many of the issues under discussion in theories of cognitive categories. This is a complex area in which theorizing is still rather preliminary. It may indeed be that at least some categories are 'Aristotelian' at some level of representation. Rosch herself clearly takes the view that prototype effects in the general case may arise in various ways and that they constrain a model of representation rather than determining one (see e.g. 1988). Natural-language categories clearly accord with the 'non-Aristotelian' view in the first instance, so this is our best starting point, but we do not need to assume that it is the whole solution or an ultimate theoretical truth. To illustrate directly from linguistics, Maling's (1983) reconsideration of *like, near* and *worth* resulted in a discrimination between criteria in a way which established their 'relevance' and enabled her to claim a clear-cut category membership for these words, despite their initial appearance of overlapping or fuzzy adjective/preposition status.

(c) Categories are not all on the same level as one another, and categories of different levels may differ in the sharpness with which they are defined. In Rosch's work (and the work of some folk taxonomists) there is an intermediate level at which category structuring is clearest. This is Rosch's 'basic level'. At levels below this categories share more properties and oppositions between them are weaker. Thus the basic-level 'chair' is distinguished from other kinds of furniture on more criteria than the subordinate-level 'dining-room chair' is distinguished from 'kitchen chair'. The focussing of the basic level is interpreted by Rosch as a consequence of the requirements of cognitive economy: it is at the basic level that category structuring makes the best use of similarities and differences. A natural consequence of this is that subordinate categories may not only involve fewer criteria, but may also show greater indeterminacy of boundary. This will be important for us because I will suggest that auxiliaries develop first as a relatively less well-defined subordinate-level category.

These three statements about the nature of categories are general principles derived in large measure from work on cognitive classification (especially the second and third). They are relevant to a range of different aspects of human behaviour, having priority in perceptual and processing tasks, as well as developmentally (see Rosch 1978, 1988 and references there). Clearly this does not imply that Rosch's theories necessarily have any relevance to the formation of linguistic categories. One might object that her investigations involved specific aspects of behaviour interpreted for their cognitive relevance to limited areas outside the structure of language, so that arguably she has tapped quite different cognitive processes of no relevance to language. But it would seem surprising if principles of such generality did not also apply to language structure, whatever the details of their interaction with properties peculiar to linguistic classification. The null hypothesis is surely that linguistic categorization is essentially like other areas of human categorization, which typically shows the characteristics above. But the question can be interpreted as one of the 'trading relationship' between cognitive and (postulated) autonomous linguistic principles; see Chomsky's (1980) comments on the consequences of modularity for the incorporation in language of elements not developed by the language faculty. The position is compatible with a universalist, even innatist, position on category structuring, in which categories must be constructed in accordance with, or depend on a substantive selection from, Universal Grammar, or are notionally tightly structured (Anderson 1991b), or are derived from discourse function (Hopper and Thompson 1984). Rosch's ideas were, after all, developed in the domain of colour, where there is a biologically given perceptual structuring. They allow for an independent weighting of critera, and may interact with an independent structuring. Thus the question of the trading relationship between these sets of principles is open, though the general untidyness of the details of word-class structure implies that a considerable domain is subject to Roschian principles (see Maratsos and Chalkley 1980: 209). It is relevant that such principles have been claimed to hold not just for major lexical categories but more generally in the structure of language, most convincingly in morphology (Bybee and Slobin 1982, Bybee and Moder 1983). But see Lakoff (1987) and Taylor (1989) for references to other potentially relevant work. So I am confident that a word-class account broadly like this will be required within any theoretical approach.

Two further assumptions arise from work in linguistics.

(d) A classification relevant to the word-class structure of a language is characterized by the mutual predictiveness of properties from different linguistic levels. This is sharpest in the case of 'formal' or structural properties from syntax or morphology (less commonly phonology). These properties often have a semantics, and are indeed referred to as 'semantico-distributional' by Maratsos and Chalkley (1980); my use of the term 'formal' is meant to focus an aspect of these properties, not to deny the possibility of a semantic correlate. In this sense it is clear that in today's English word-class distinctions are formally based in the first instance. The near semantic equivalence of *like, fond* or of *possibly, possible, might* is overridden by their formal (including distributional) properties and they are assigned to distinct classes. It has also been claimed that it is formal rather than semantic properties which guide children's acquisition of classes: errors dependent on semantically based misclassification, say of actional adjectives as verbs (**he naughtied, *she is nicing*) are said to be rare (for this and the preceding point see esp. Maratsos and Chalkley 1980). Thus in the determination of word-class categories, the most important properties are clearly the formal ones, and not those which are essentially semantic.

(e) Classes may be identified cross-linguistically from the semantics of the class (or its prototype), and perhaps also from the nature of associated grammatical properties. But the presence of individual items in a class may be at odds with the prototypical semantics of the class. To exemplify, at this level the noun is the class whose prototypical members denote continuing entities and which may be associated with categories of number, definiteness and inherent gender. This is essentially the position of Lyons (1966, 1977) or Huddleston (1984). But nouns such as *beauty* or *phonetics* are not prototypical. This does not deny the possibility of detailed semantic interconnections like those suggested by Wierzbicka (1988) or that classes may be broadly iconic in aspects of their relationship to discourse structuring (Hopper and

Thompson 1984), but it rejects a strong version of such views and accepts that semantic criteria are generally less good predictors of class membership than formal properties.

Methodological consequences

This framework clarifies the questions we can put to our pre-Modern English data to illuminate the status of a potential group of auxiliaries (or of modals). It is clear that we must focus in the first instance on formal properties in establishing word-class categories. They are crucial to a category. Methodologically, they are also more safely identifiable than semantic properties. And finally (in the absence of a theory which will make substantial predictions about the properties of classes), it is the correlation of properties which are not inherently interconnected which will most impressively demonstrate the reality of a classification, and this must largely mean formal properties. Then, if we assume that the items concerned do indeed belong to a more general class including verbs in Old and Middle English (as was argued above for Old English) we can ask:

(i) Do these words have formal properties which distinguish them from other verbs?

(ii) If so, do such formal properties typically cooccur with each other, or with other properties which are uncommon in the general class of verbs, so that there is a measure of predictability between properties which might characterize a distinct group?

(iii) If (ii) and (iii) are given positive answers, then, is there an appropriate notional characterization of nuclear members or of the associated grammatical properties which might enable us to identify the group cross-linguistically?

In the next four chapters I will apply these three questions in due order to the verbs listed at the beginning of this chapter. In the first two of these chapters I will argue for the existence of mutually predictive formal properties which characterize these verbs in Old and Middle English, some of them as yet unrecognized or so far inadequately stated. Then in Chapter 7 I will discuss the historical semantics of what will be identified as the 'modal group'. Finally I will argue that there is a sufficient correlation of properties to identify a coherent and distinctive grouping of verbs in English, forming at least a potential subcategory, well before the fifteenth century, indeed even from Old English. I will further identify it in notional terms as 'auxiliary' and note that a 'modal group' may be further distinguished within this grouping. But this includes an important caveat about the force of the term 'auxiliary': note that it is far from the claim that this grouping was already a full-blown 'word class' or that they were in a full sense of the word notional 'auxiliaries' on a par with the modern class. Either claim would be too brutal a simplification. Finally I will discuss what we can learn about the nature of word classes and grammaticalization from this history.

5 *Identifying an 'auxiliary group' before Modern English: sentence-level syntax*

The ancestors of our modern auxiliaries before the Modern English period certainly had more verblike properties than their modern descendants, as we saw in Chapter 4. And most of the formal differences which distinguish so sharply between modern auxiliaries and full verbs had not then developed. But it is too simple to conclude that they were therefore verbs four square in all essential syntactic properties with other verbs at this period, with (say) Lightfoot (1979), for they already share striking characteristics which apparently isolate them. This chapter will be taken up with the establishment and discussion of two of the most striking of these characteristics, their behaviour in ellipsis and with impersonals. These are important because they hold at the level of sentential syntax and they look on the face of it like potential word-class properties. The conclusion which will seem most plausible for Old (and Middle) English is that there was already a formal subcategorial distinction within the class of verbs. In the next chapter this position will be reinforced, and Chapter 7 will discuss the notional identity of this grouping.

At the end of Chapter 4 three questions were isolated as methodologically central in determining word-class status. The first two were:

(i) Do these words have formal properties which distinguish them from other verbs?

(ii) If so, do such formal properties typically cooccur with each other, so that there is a measure of predictability between properties which might characterize a distinct group?

In this chapter I shall assume that the potential group of auxiliary (and modal) verbs listed in the last chapter belong to a more general class including verbs in Old and Middle English (as was argued in the last chapter), and these two questions will be put in respect of their occurrence in elliptical constructions (in §5.1), then in construction with impersonals (in §5.2). Discussion will largely be based on Old English, but Middle English will also be considered. In §5.3 there follows a discussion of the possibility of a distinctive correlation of properties (question (ii) above). Question (iii), that of a notional basis for the grouping which emerges, is postponed until Chapter 7.

5.1 Elliptical constructions

In today's English post-auxiliary ellipsis and pseudogapping provide distinctive criteria for identifying auxiliaries, and I argued in §1.2 that they are essentially different aspects of the same construction. They require a linguistic antecedent (using 'antecedent' in the familiar recent sense which subsumes cataphoric as well as anaphoric reference) in the discourse, and may occur in a range of structures. Parallel constructions with *do* are found most generally in British English, where they are possible even where 'pro-verbal' *do* is nonfinite and (presumably) nonauxiliary.[1] Examples are given in (1).

(1) a. – Is Paul bringing Mary?
– If he isn't, I'll tell him he should.
b. – That carpet reminds me of the kind of thing you see in waiting rooms.
– It doesn't me. (Levin 1980: 76–7)
c. I would like to rely on friends, and I wish I could do.
d. I feel more willing to rely on my friends, since you tell me you can do on yours.

It looks as if there is a very similar situation in Old and Middle English. It is therefore clearly worth investigating whether the availability of elliptical constructions, and more especially the occurrence of pseudogapping, is characteristic of a group of 'auxiliary' verbs at these periods.

Since the Old English situation is better investigated than the Middle English, and since similar examples can be presented for Middle English and a parallel line of argument pursued, I will concentrate in the first instance on Old English in what follows, and present a detailed case based on Old English with less full reference to Middle English.

5.1.1 Arguing for ellipsis in Old (and Middle) English

Old and Middle English contain a construction apparently parallel to today's post-auxiliary ellipsis in which the infinitive complement of a verb is absent, but may be retrieved from linguistic context. Apparent ellipses after BE and (in Middle English) after perfect HAVE are also found. Here are some Old English examples.

(2) a. forðy is betere þæt feoh þætte næfre losian ne mæg ðonne þætte mæg & sceal.
'therefore better is the property which can never perish [lit.: never perish not can] than that which can and will.'
Bo 11.25.24

b. Wenst ðu þæt se godcunda anweald ne mihte afyrran þone anweald þam unrihtwisan kasere, … gif he wolde? Gise, la, gese; ic wat þæt he mihte, gif he wolde.
'Thinkest thou that the heavenly Power could not [lit.: not could] take-away the empire (from) that unrighteous Caesar, ... if he would? Yes, O yes, I know that he could, if he would!' (Fox's translation, corrected)
Bo 16.39.30

c. & cwædon þæt hie þa burg werian wolden, gif þa wæpnedmen ne dorsten.
'and said that they [= the women] would defend the city [lit.: the city defend would (subj.)], if the men (did) not dare.'
Or 194.12

d. hi ... gearowe wæron ehtnysse to ðoligenne. and deaðe sweltan gif hi ðorfton
'they ... were prepared to undergo persecution and to suffer death [lit.: ready were persecution to suffer and death (dat.) die] if they needed'
ÆCHom ii.78.212

e. wa þam, þe godcunde heorde underfehð and naþær gehealdan ne can ne hine syfne ne þa heorde, þe he healdan scolde to godes handa; and wyrst þam, þe can and nele.
'woe to-him who undertakes spiritual custody [lit.: spiritual custody undertakes] and knows how to preserve [lit.: neither to-preserve not knows] neither him self nor the flock which he ought to guard on God's behalf [lit.: to God's hand] and worst to him, who knows (how to) and will-not.'
Wulfstan: Sammlung der ihm zugeschriebenen Homilien (ed. A. Napier, Berlin, 1883; repr. Dublin and Zurich, Wiedmann and Max Niehans, 1967) 276.14

f. deofol us wile ofslean gif he mot.
'(the) devil will kill us if he can'
ÆCHom i.270.10

(3) a. *est?* is hit swa? *est* hit is; *non?* nis hit swa? *non* hit nis.
'*est?* is it so? *est* it is; *non?* isn't it so? *non* it isn't.'
ÆGram 227.8

b. and gehwa wende þæt he þæs cyldes fæder wære. ac he næs
'and everyone thought that he was [= *wære*] that child's father, but he wasn't'
ÆCHom i.196.12

c. & gedeð hit ðonne sweotol, gif hit ær næs.
'and makes it then clear, if it previously was-not [sc. clear].'
Bo 16.38.32

d. Wære þu todæg beswuncgen? Ic næs
Fuisti hodie uerberatus? Non fui
'Were you beaten today?' – 'I wasn't'
ÆColl 280

e. *amabar* ic wæs gelufod, *amabaris* ðu wære, *amabatur* he wæs
'*amabar* I was loved, *amabaris* you (sg.) were, *amabatur* he was'
ÆGram 140.2

I will argue that at least in some cases such examples involve distinct elliptical (or pro-verbal) constructions in Old (and Middle) English which I will call 'postverbal ellipsis'. Here it is necessary to distinguish cases where a verb of motion or 'be' (perhaps also 'do') is to be supplied in translation as part of the meaning of the verb together with its construction. There is no need to suppose any syntactic ellipsis in such instances, which can be accounted for in terms of the semantics of the combination verb + adverbial/prepositional phrase or verb + complement (see M§1007 for the first of these, and note that motion may also be understood from an adverb or preposition in other contexts; see Karpf 1930: 130f. for Chaucer examples). We must also distinguish cases where an apparent gap may be related to some specific aspect of the construction, as, for example, in some instances of coordination or comparative clauses.[2] Given these distinctions we may go on to ask whether the apparent ellipses of (2) and (3) involve special constructions, or whether these might simply show intransitive uses of the verb in question (see M§§1000ff.). Consider the modern sentences below. These might seem at first sight to be elliptical, in that the sense of *eating* or *to climb the wall* is to be supplied in the second conjunct.

(4) a. Paul is eating, but Tom hasn't started.
b. Tom climbed the wall, but Paul didn't even try.

But these are unlike cases of post-auxiliary ellipsis in that *start* and *try* are not restricted to contexts with a linguistic antecedent. Both may occur without a complement where the sense is obvious from the nonlinguistic situation, as in (5). Notice that *start to* and *try to*, which would involve post-auxiliary ellipsis after *to*, are not possible without a linguistic antecedent.

(5) a. You may start (*start to).
(spoken instruction at beginning of an examination)
b. I don't see why you even try (*try to).
(lecturer commenting to student on fail-grade essay)

So we must distinguish cases of ellipsis which require a linguistic antecedent from examples where the sense can be made more complete by information derived from the general situation. This may indeed involve reference to a piece of preceding text, but it may equally be nonlinguistic in origin. *Start* and *try* fall into this second broad category.[3]

There are two pieces of evidence which point to the existence of a distinct elliptical construction type in Old English. In the first place there are several verbs which seem from BT(S) and *OED* to lack a more general intransitive or absolute use of appropriate sense of which apparently elliptical uses might be taken as a special case. *Dearr, mot* and *sceal* in particular belong here, as does *beon/wesan*. These seem (in the relevant senses) to occur either with a complement, or without one in a context of apparent ellipsis where there is a potential linguistic 'antecedent'.[4] So there are apparently 'grammatically "defective"' constructions which exhibit a 'structural "gap"', in the terminology of Quirk *et al.* (1985: §12.34).[5] We may contrast *mæg* and probably *cann*, which do have apparently relevant intransitive or absolute uses, so that parallel examples need not at first sight involve ellipsis (though there may be more finely grained semantic reasons for supposing that ellipsis is involved).

Secondly, there are instances which seem to parallel the modern 'pseudo-gapping'. Here the verb occurs with some or all of the complements of the infinitive which is to be contextually supplied (see (6)). An apparent example of this construction after *beon/wesan* is given in (7).[6]

(6)
a. We magon monnum bemiðan urne geðonc & urne willan, ac we ne magon Gode.
'We can hide from men [lit.: from-men hide] our thoughts and our desires, but we cannot [lit.: not can] from-God.'
CP 39.12

b. se ðe wille godcundne wisdom secan ne mæg he hine wiþ ofermetta.
'he who will seek heavenly wisdom [lit.: heavenly wisdom seek] may not [lit.: not may he] [sc. seek] it with arrogance.'
Bo 12.26.22

c. Be ðæm is awriten ðæt Dryhten besawe to Abele & to his lacum, & nolde to Caine ne to his lacum.
'Concerning this (it) is written that (the) Lord had-regard for Abel and for his gifts, and would-not for Cain nor for his gifts.'
CP 234.5

d. Hu mæg he bion ðonne butan gitsunge, ðonne he sceal ymb monegra monna are ðencean, gif he nolde þa þa he moste ymb his anes?
'How can he be (then) without covetousness, when he has to-think about many men's benefits, if he was-not-willing [sc. to be without covetousness], when he had to [sc. think] about his own?
CP 56.21

(7) ac hit nis nanum anum men getiohhod, ac is eallum monnum.
'but it is offered to no one man [lit.: no one man (dat.) offered], but (it) is to all men.' (Fox's translation)
Bo 37.112.27

The sentences of (6) are clearly in some sense 'elliptical', for the constructional peculiarity of pseudogapping depends on the properties of an item which is not there. Thus the dative *Gode* in (6.a) has the case of a complement of *bemiðan*, not *magon*, though *bemiðan* is not present in the final conjunct. Moreover, there is a linguistic antecedent in all the examples given in the sources cited below in §§5.1.2–5.1.3. And this cannot simply be part of coordination processes since examples are not restricted to cases of coordination, and the distribution across verbs is not general, as we will see below. So it seems reasonable to conclude that distinct elliptical constructions are probably represented in these sentences in Old English. They apparently exhibit a structural 'gap', and the missing material is recovered from the neighbouring text and not from the wider context of situation. These are two of the five criteria for elliptical constructions given by Quirk *et al.* (1985: §§12.32ff.).[7]

The situation in Middle English is parallel, in that the same two points can be made. Firstly, then, among the verbs which occur in apparently elliptical constructions like those of (2) above, there are several which seem from *MED* and *OED* to lack an appropriate intransitive or absolute use to which these may be referred. As before, we set aside cases where the sense of an infinitive (or other complement) is to be supplied from some other aspect of the construction, say from a directional phrase sister, or because of the type of coordinate structure it occurs in. Once again, the implication is that the constructions are indeed elliptical. *Dar*, *mot*, *mun*, *ouen*, *shal* and *þarf* occur here, as do *ben* and perfect *hauen*.[8]

Secondly, examples to parallel pseudogapping continue to occur, where the overt complement of the verb would be anomalous if analysed as such, but instead has the properties of the complement of a verb which is to be understood. Again, ellipsis is supported. Some Middle English examples follow. But the best example I can muster for *ben* is weakened by the presence of *so* which may be involved in the construction.

(8) a. andette his sennen him ðe ware necst him ... oððer ʒif he ware all hone, ðanne most he to godd ane.
'[if a man were suddenly upon his death, and he could have no priest,] he-ought-to-confess his sins to-him who is nearest to-him; ... or if he were alone, then he must [sc. confess] to God only.'
*a*1225 (*c*1200) *Vices and Virtues* (ed. F. Holthausen, EETS 89) 123.18

b. Iloren ich haue Iosep, ... & nou ich ssal Beniamin
[Jacob speaks] 'I have lost Joseph, ... and now I am-going-to [sc. lose] Benjamin'
?*a*1300 *Iacob and Iosep* (ed. A. S. Napier, Oxford, 1916) 462

c. [we] habbeð ou iseið twa uers. and wule nuþe þet þridde.
'We have told you two verses and will now [sc. tell you] the third.'
*a*1225 *The Lambeth Homilies* (*Old English Homilies*, 1st series, ed. R. Morris, EETS 29, 34) 77.16

(9) Ector ... & cesar ...
Heo beoþ i-glyden vt of þe reyne
so þe schef is of þe cleo.
'Hector ... and Caesar ... they are departed from the earth [lit. out of the kingdom] as the sheaf is from the hillside.' (see *MED clif* n.(1), surely preferable to *claue* n.(1) 2.(b).)
*a*1300 A Mayde Cristes (*English Lyrics of the Thirteenth Century*, ed. Carleton Brown, Oxford, Clarendon Press, 1932, item 43) 72

5.1.2 The distribution of these constructions in Old (and Middle) English

I have argued that Old English had two formal construction types, postverbal ellipsis and pseudogapping, and I have suggested that a similar line of argument will hold also for Middle English. So, referring back to the first question above, the possession of a formal property has been established, and we must now ask whether it was distinctive. What then was the distribution of these construction types?

A. Wülfing gives instances of pseudogapping for Alfredian Old English with *mæg*, *sceal* and *wile*, and both he and Antipova supply apparent examples of postverbal ellipsis for these three verbs and for *dearr*, *mot* and *þearf* ('apparent' because the possibility of an intransitive construction without real ellipsis cannot be ruled out for all items as noted above).[9] Apparent postverbal ellipsis is found elsewhere with *cann* (see (2.e) above). To these verbs we may add *uton* 'let's'. A search through the Venezky and Healey concordance (1980) yielded a couple of apparent instances of pseudogapping (less clear than those of (6) above), but only the example cited below as (10.b) to provide relatively weak or indirect evidence for postverbal ellipsis.[10]

(10) a. He us gegearwað galnesse; uton we ongean clænnesse
'He prepares wantonness for us; let us in-return purity'
HomS 34 (PetersonVercHom 19) 86

b. He winnð mid ofermodnesse; uton we ongean mid eaðmodnesse
'He fights using [lit.: with] pride: let us in-return using [lit.: with] humility'
HomS 34 (PetersonVercHom 19) 85

Dictionaries and Visser give instances of pseudogapping in Middle English with *mot*, *shal* and *wil*, less clearly with *dar*, *may* and *ouen*. Apparent postverbal ellipsis is evidenced with all of these, and with *can*, *mun* and *þarf*.[11]

B. *Beon/wesan* occur with ellipsis of a range of predicates (as exemplified in (3), possibly also with partial ellipsis parallel to pseudogapping as in (7)). The situation in Middle English is parallel (see (9) for a possible instance of pseudogapping). In neither period do I know of an example with ellipsis of a present participle after BE. Since the construction is clearly elliptical and depends on linguistic context, and since the range of predicates includes verbal predicates, it seems plain that this is at least closely related to postverbal ellipsis with the verbs of A. Neither Antipova's survey (1963) nor Brown's (1970) explicit report of *Cura Pastoralis* give any examples with *weorðan*.[12]

C. Examples with perfect HAVE do not seem to occur until Middle English, when both postverbal ellipsis and (in the second half of the fifteenth century) pseudogapping types are recorded.[13] An instance with ellipsis is cited below. Examples of possessive HAVE with a contextually supplied object occur in both Old and Middle English, but there is a more general possibility of object ellipsis, so that this is not necessarily to be classified with the other 'auxiliary' instances (M§§1570ff. and references, Mustanoja 1960: 144f. and references, V§§612ff.). OE *onginnan* and *aginnan* 'begin', which might be thought to belong with a potential auxiliary group in other respects, both have an intransitive sense 'undertake an action, proceed to an action' which occurs in potential ellipsis contexts and elsewhere, so that no distinct construction need be involved in potential ellipsis contexts. The same holds for ME *ginnen* and derivatives. In neither case have I noted examples with pseudogapping which might support the case for ellipsis. But I have not searched systematically in Venezky and Healey (1980).

(11) I shal yow nevere offende;
And if I have er this, I wol amende.
'I shall never offend you, and if I have before now, I will make amends.'
*a*1425 (*c*1385) Chaucer, *Troilus and Criseyde*, ii.245

D. Parallel constructions are also found from Old English with pro-verbal *don*. This may 'stand for' a verb phrase which is retrieved from linguistic context, as in Present-day (particularly British) English (see (12.a)), though examples outside a context within a comparative or involving *swa* are few. Sentence

(12.e) is a Middle English example. *Don* is also found with the complements of its verbal antecedent, and (less clearly) with a subset of these complements as in (12.d). I only know Old English examples of this second type in contexts which are potentially comparative in some way or follow *swa*, etc. and this weakens the evidence for that period, though (12.f) is a Middle English instance outside such a context.[14] But these constructions look like parallels to postverbal ellipsis and pseudogapping, and this suggests that these constructions with *don* are to be identified at some level with those given above in (2) and (6), so that we should add *don* to our list of verbs for Old and Middle English. Since periphrastic *don* is not found in recorded Old English (Tieken's (1988) recent defence is not convincing), or in all Middle English, a straightforward ellipsis is not involved here in the general case. For further instances see in particular V§§181ff., 580ff., *MED don* v. (1) 12, *OED Do*, *v.* 24a, c.

(12) a. Eower lareow ne gylt he gafel. þa cwæð he gyse he deð.
Magister vester non solvit didrachma? Ait: Etiam.
'Your master, doesn't he pay tribute [lit.: not pays he tribute]? Then he said: Yes, he does.'
The West-Saxon Gospels (ed. M Grünberg, Amsterdam, Scheltema and Holkema, 1967) Matthew 17.24

b. ne cepð nan hungrig man næfre his gereordes na swyðor, þonne þa sceoccan doð þære sawle.
'No hungry man ever desires his food more strongly [lit.: not desires no hungry man never his food (gen.) not more-strongly], than the devils do the soul (gen.)'
Wulfstan: Sammlung der ihm zugeschriebenen Homilien (ed. A. Napier, Berlin, 1883; repr. Dublin and Zurich, Wiedmann and Max Niehans, 1967) 249.1

c. gif þe licode his dysig & his unrihtwisnes swa wel swa his dysegum deorlingum dyde.
'if his folly and his injustice had pleased thee [lit.: if thee (dat.) pleased his folly and his injustice] as well as it did his foolish favourites [lit.: as well as his foolish favourites (dat.) did].' (Fox's translation)
Bo 27.62.12

d. Hwi nolde god him forgyldan his bearn be twyfealdum. swa swa he dyde his æhta?
'Why would not God compensate him (for) his children twice over, just as he did (for) his possessions?'
ÆCHoms ii.267.210

e. I love youre honour ... and evere have doon
'I love your honour ... and I always have done'
*c*1390 Chaucer, *Canterbury Tales*, VII.1687

f. Ne luȝe þu na monnum; ac dudest gode.
'Thou liedest not to-men, but [thou] didst to-God.'
*a*1225 *The Lambeth Homilies* (*Old English Homilies*, 1st series, ed. R. Morris, EETS 29, 34) 93.2

5.1.3 Characterizing the distribution of these constructions

It is striking that the verbs of A and B above include most of the ancestors of our modern auxiliaries, and that they have uses classified as 'auxiliary' by Mitchell (1985). *Uton* 'let's' is also clearly qualified to belong in such a group both by sense and by morphology. It is, however, worth remarking that these ellipses are not restricted to reduced 'auxiliary' senses of Mitchell's (1985) '"modal" auxiliaries' and that postverbal ellipsis is not restricted to 'periphrastic' constructions with *beon/wesan* (see (2.c), (2.e), (3.a–c), (6.c) above and other examples given by Wülfing 1894–1901, Antipova 1963, and *MED ben* v. 16(b)). The apparent absence of *weorðan*, the late appearance of perfect HAVE, and the presence of pro-verbal *don* (classified as an auxiliary by Wülfing 1894–1901) are also noteworthy.

But were these types of ellipsis potentially characterizing properties of this group of verbs (hence of a potential auxiliary group) or were they simply properties of verbs in general? We await detailed descriptions and analyses of ellipsis before Modern English, as of the possibilities for coordination and exbraciation which are very relevant to such accounts. Without such generally based accounts a question mark must hang over any proposal. But on the basis of the currently available evidence it seems to me more satisfactory to suppose that these ellipses were a potentially characteristic property of this group of verbs than that they were not. This will be justified mainly with reference to Old English, the period for which these ellipses have been better documented.

Clearly, one interim view of this period might be that since ellipses are found after a range of verbs, and verbs were also subject to gapping, examples resembling the modern post-auxiliary ellipsis and pseudogapping can be accounted for under more general processes. Any apparent restriction of distribution ('only after members of a potential auxiliary group') might then be attributed to the greater frequency of these verbs and (perhaps) their saliency to investigators.[15] But this view raises a question over the systematic status of apparent ellipsis of a subordinate verb and its complements after verbs in Old English. Real ellipsis may, indeed, be less general than might at first appear, given the distinctions drawn above for Present-day English. It is clear that throughout English other expressions (nouns, adjectives and participles as well as verbs) have been able to occur in contexts where the sense of a verbal complement is to be supplied. And some of the expressions concerned have absolute or intransitive uses, which may imply that this sense need not be retrieved from linguistic context. So, for example, beside (13.a) with retrieval from preceding text, we find the absolute instance of (13.b). Here Peter has previously been told to pray to God for help against the sorcerer, and this is apparently the sense which is to be supplied. But it is mentioned nineteen lines (and several events) earlier in the text, so direct linguistic retrieval seems unlikely to be in question. The implication is that the pragmatic principles which supply the meaning required in (13.b) may also cope with (13.a), which need not involve a linguistically supplied ellipsis.

(13) a. Clypa, ne ablin ðu, ac ahefe up þine stefne swa beme
'Cry-out, do not cease [lit.: not cease thou] but raise up your voice like (a) trumpet'
Sermon for the Third Sunday in Lent (*Angelsächsische Homilien und Heiligenleben*, ed. B. Assman, Bibliothek der angelsächsischen Prosa 3, Kassel 1889; repr. Darmstadt 1964, 138–143) 9.
b. Þa cwæþ he to Petre, 'To hwan ablinnest þu, Petrus?'
'Then said he to Peter, "Why ceasest thou, Peter?"' (Morris's translation)
BlHom 189.2

Or take the case of *lætan*. BT (*lætan*) says 'The ellipsis of a verb in the infinitive, the meaning of which may be inferred from the context, not unfrequently takes place after *lætan*.' But in at least the great majority of relevant citations the required sense is one of (abstract) position, motion or possession, and there is an object or predicate: these seem to be better interpreted straightforwardly in terms of the semantics of the combination of *lætan* with its complements rather than as elliptical uses (see the parallel suggestion made above for specific instances of verbs of group A).

Moreover, granted that there are some expressions without relevant absolute uses, this need only mean that the situation was akin to that in Present-day English. Today some expressions which are not auxiliaries may have the sense of a VP complement supplied from the linguistic context, though it cannot be retrieved from nonlinguistic context, for example *able* as in *I will come if I am able*, or *want* in *You may go if you want.* (For other instances see Jespersen 1909–49: V, §20.5 on the 'latent infinitive', Quirk *et al.* 1985: §12.65.) The properties of a word class are not typically absolute: what characterizes the class is a constellation of properties rather than any single one. Thus postverbal ellipsis is distinctive today for two reasons: first, because its regularity with auxiliaries contrasts with its much less general availability elsewhere; secondly because of its correlation with other properties. For Old English, then, the question is not whether these ellipses are totally absent elsewhere, but whether their distribution is potentially characteristic of groups A and B in correlation with other properties.

On an alternative view, the elliptical constructions exemplified above are interrelated, and their occurrence is a grammatical property of specific lexemes: a potential auxiliary group, including *don*. This is equally an interim view, but several considerations hold in its favour.

(i) It fits closely the data for the combination of postverbal ellipsis and pseudogapping in so far as it is reported in the major relevant sources for Old English. Antipova surveys a substantial range of texts (434 printed pages) and concludes that 'The composition of the group of substitute-verbs in OE does not differ much from that in Modern English' (1963: 136). Brown (1970) is explicit about the restriction of such constructions in *Cura Pastoralis*. And there is nothing to contradict this in the sections on ellipsis in Mitchell (1985), Visser (1963–73) and Wülfing (1894–1901).[16] Here the apparently restricted distribution of pseudogapping is particularly important.

(ii) The generalization of pseudogapping with postverbal ellipsis is supported by the overlap between the range of verbs with which pseudogapping is reported and those found with apparent postverbal ellipsis. It is suggestive for this generalization that *don* apparently occurs with both these constructions, since it does not appear without ellipsis as the periphrastic in Old English or all Middle English.

(iii) It is the introducing verb which should be characterized as permitting these 'elliptical' constructions (or 'pro-verbal' constructions: see the comment of my note 1). In the first place, this must hold for *don*. And it is difficult to resist generalizing the property to the verbs of A and even *beon/wesan*. Secondly, if postverbal ellipsis and pseudogapping are restricted as suggested, it is difficult to see how this could be appropriately stated otherwise. Note that the context of ellipsis cannot be given in semantic terms, since the range of senses involved in the examples cited above shows no sign of restriction (for example to prototypically 'modal' senses in the verbs of A). Nor can pseudogapping be stated as a purely semantic property, since both the semantic and rectional characteristics of the elliptical verb are involved. And any unrestricted syntactic statement will overgeneralize.[17] It is clear then that what is involved is well interpreted as a grammatical property of a lexeme.

(iv) The existence of a parallel situation in Present-day English, where there are two parallel interrelated constructions involving ellipsis which are licensed by (and therefore a property of) the introducing verb, shows that linguistic theory must permit this particular constellation of properties. Other things being equal, this account of Old English is therefore a linguistically natural one.

(v) The restrictive and empirical nature of the hypothesis is in its favour. It gives us a narrow characterization, and it makes clear predictions. In particular, pseudogapping should not be distributed independently of postverbal ellipsis, and if it is characteristic of an auxiliary group it should not be a normal construction with other verbs.

Thus the second hypothesis considered is preferable. It gives a much sharper characterization of the data, and it is linguistically 'natural'. The argument for it is oblique, but that is an unavoidable consequence of the fact that for Old English we have only partially recorded and partially investigated data. Strictly, then, what we can say at the moment (from the major sources surveyed) is that the following view is plausible: that some Old English verbs (a potential auxiliary group) shared the formal property of occurring in one or both of the two related elliptical constructions discussed in this section, and that in this they were distinct from other verbs. This generalizes across the two constructions, thus effectively generalizing the data (which is summarized in Table 5.1 at the end of the chapter). But this abstraction seems reasonable given the extent to which the occurrence of one (especially pseudogapping) predicts that of the other. To this we may add that the same situation apparently continues in Middle English.

So the occurrence of a distinctive formal property of our potential auxiliary group has been reasonably established as a plausible hypothesis (not, to be sure, as a fact) about the grammar of early English, and in what follows its essential correctness will be assumed. Now we must see whether it correlates with another formal property.

5.2 Transparency to impersonal constructions

5.2.1 Occurrence with impersonals

In Old and Middle English there occur impersonal constructions which have oblique arguments, but which lack a nominative subject. The verb if finite is third person singular.

(14) a. and hi wæron ða nacode, and him ðæs sceamode.
'and they were then naked, and they were ashamed of that [lit.: them (dat.) of-that (gen.) shamed].'
ÆCHom i.18.11

b. gif us ne lyst ðæra ærrena yfela ðe we ær worhton
'if we do not desire [lit.: us (acc./dat.) not pleases (3 sg.)] the former evils [gen.] we did [lit.: that we previously did]' (Sweet's translation)
CP 445.29

c. Me reweth soore of hende Nicholas.
'I am very sorry for courteous Nicholas [lit.: me (obl.) rues sorely of ...].'
*c*1390 Chaucer, *Canterbury Tales* I.3462

d. eet this when þe hungreþ
'eat this when you are hungry [lit.: you (obl. sg.) hungers]'
*c*1400 (?*a*1387) William Langland, *The Vision of William Concerning Piers the Plowman,* Text C (ed. W. W. Skeat, EETS 54) 16.252

A striking characteristic of some of Mitchell's '"modal" auxiliaries' and BE together with a very few other verbs at these periods is that they occur within such constructions, so that they too lack a nominative subject when their dependent nonfinite is impersonal. Thus the impersonal retains its constructional characteristics despite occurring in apparent subordination to another verb, and this other verb is in some sense independent of or transparent to the construction with which it cooccurs.

(15) a. þonne mæg heora wiðerwinnan sceamian, þonne hi hi geseoð mid sigores wuldre to heofonum astigan.
'then may (sg.) their enemies (acc. pl.) shame, when they see them [lit.: them see] rise up to heaven with the glory of victory [lit.: with victory's glory to heavens rise].'
Wulfstan: Sammlung der ihm zugeschriebenen Homilien (ed. A. Napier, Berlin, 1883; repr. Dublin and Zurich, Wiedmann and Max Niehans, 1967) 199.12

b. hine sceal on domes dæg gesceamian beforan gode
'he [lit.: him (acc.)] shall at Doomsday be-ashamed before God'
Wulfstan: Sammlung der ihm zugeschriebenen Homilien (ed. A. Napier, Berlin, 1883; repr. Dublin and Zurich, Wiedmann and Max Niehans, 1967) 238.12

c. Forþon ne þearf þæs nanne man tweogean, þæt seo forlætene cyrice ne hycgge ymb þa þe on hire neawiste lifgeaþ
'Because no man need have any doubt of this [lit.: because not need of-it no man (acc.) doubt], that the forsaken church (will) not take-care for those that live in her neighbourhood [lit.: in her neighbourhood live]' (Morris's translation)
BlHom 41.36

d. þonne ic wat þætte wile weoruldmen tweogan
'[if you now, Lord, are not willing to govern fate] then I know that human beings will doubt [lit.: will (3 sg.) human-beings (acc. pl.) doubt]'
The Meters of Boethius (ASPR V, 153–203) 4.51

e. Him may fulofte mysbefalle.
'He [obl.] may very often come to harm.'
(*a*1393) Gower, *Confessio Amantis* (ed. G. C. Macaulay, EETS ES 81, 82) 1.459

f. Ne schal me neuer schomye. louerd for þeo.
[Peter speaks] 'I shall never be ashamed [lit.: not shall me never shame], Lord, because-of you.'
*a*1300 *Passion of Our Lord* (ed. R. Morris, EETS 49: 37ff.) 138

g. He semed like an aungell. The more that a man beheld hym the bettre hym schuld like hym.
'He seemed like an angel. The more a man gazed-on him, the more he (obl.) should be-pleased-with him.'
*c*1450 *King Ponthus and the Fair Sidone* (ed. F. J. Mather Jr., *PMLA* 12, 1897: 1–150) 12.9

h. þink wheþer þee wolde schame as moche ... as þee wold and þou were mad stonde nakid bifore þe kyng & alle þe rewme.
'Think whether you (obl.) would be-ashamed as much … as you would if you were made to stand naked before the king and all the kingdom.'
*a*1425 (?*a*1400) *A Tretyse … þat Men Clepen Beniamyn* (*Deonise Hid Diuinite*, ed. P. Hodgson, EETS 231: 12–46) 37.9

Here we need to ask, first whether this is a formal property, secondly whether it is distinctive of a potential auxiliary group. Both the logic of the argument and the dictates of suspense require me to begin with the second question. In attempting to answer it I draw on a corpus of instances collected from entries for the major impersonal verbs in BT(S) and *MED*; from Breivik (1983), Elmer (1981), Mitchell (1985), van der Gaaf (1904), Visser (1963–73); and from a search through the Old English microfiche concordance (Venezky and Healey 1980) under the infinitives of the major impersonal verbs (sometimes also their participles), and through concordances to Chaucer, Gower and Malory. This gives me a collection of nearly fifty Old English examples of 'central' impersonal constructions (as in (15)) in the infinitive, and of nearly forty for Middle English (where, however, there are many more of the potentially relevant less central instances discussed immediately). I have not, however, generally attempted to collect such phrasal impersonals as *me is wel*, etc., since the labour did not seem worth the small additional data they were likely to yield. Denison (1990b) has also investigated this transparency for Old English: he gives a detailed and independent survey of the Old English data with plentiful exemplification.[18]

5.2.2 The range of verbs transparent to impersonal constructions

Not all instances of a potential 'auxiliary' plus 'impersonal' verb give equally convincing evidence of the type of transparency which is in question here. Examples like (15.a–c) above, where the only arguments are clearly oblique, are centrally relevant. But when one of the arguments is a following clause or infinitive, or is a noun phrase whose case is not distinctively oblique, the distinction between personal and impersonal rection may be neutralized. In such instances, the 'impersonal' verb has a potential overt subject, though the parallels available for a particular verb may lead us to prefer an 'impersonal' interpretation of the construction (as, for example, they do for OE *tweogan, tweonian* 'doubt' in (15.d).[19] The direct relevance of constructions with expletive *(h)it* is also doubtful (as is that of constructions with expletive *there*, which has arguably developed by Middle English, perhaps even from Old English; Breivik 1983). These give less satisfactory evidence for a syntactic property granted the possibility of a semantic account. We might also wonder whether at earlier periods these words should be analysed as referential pronouns of very broad sense (see Bolinger's suggestions for Present-day English 1973, 1977b, c), as is perhaps implied by the occurrence of lexical subjects with 'weather' verbs, for days dawn, snow snows, and hail, milk and a variety of liquids may rain in earlier English. I shall indeed argue below that impersonal constructions with an intervening verb are to be identified with 'raising' constructions in Old and Middle English; expletive 'impersonals' with an intervening verb will also be analysed this way, whether or not the dependency between the expletive pronoun and its verb is a syntactic or a semantic one. So such examples are relevant to my argument, and may for different reasons be thought relevant by other analysts. But since there is room for disagreement, I have concentrated here in the first instance on clear cases of the 'central impersonal' constructions of (15), and my statements will be based on examples of this type unless otherwise indicated. But reference will sometimes be made to 'less central' instances.

Verbs found in the type of (15) are:

A. The following members of Mitchell's '"modal" auxiliaries' and later counterparts:

OE *mæg*, (*mot*), *sceal*, *þearf*, *wile*;
ME *may*, (*mot*), (*mun*), ((*ouen*)), *shal*, ((*þarf*)), *wil*.

In my Old English data *mæg* and *sceal* are well attested, followed by *þearf* (see (15)). There are a couple of instances with *wile*, see (15.d), none with *mot*.[20] But both of these verbs also occur in less central types of example, as here.

(16) a. Me mæig . . . gif hit mot gewiderian, mederan settan
'One can . . . if it may be-fair-weather, plant madder'
LawGer 12

b. oðþæt hit wolde dagian
'until it was-about to-dawn'
ÆLS i.21.123

In my data for Middle English *may*, *shal* and *wil* are also well attested, but *mot* and *mun* only appear in less central instances. I have not found examples with CAN, DARE (in the sense 'dare'), or UTON in either Old or Middle English. But this is unsurprising. These three verbs presumably select their subjects,[21] so they cannot be transparent to the semantics of the construction that they enter. Moreover, the infinitive following UTON 'let's' regularly represents an action as under the control of its subject (as is at least predominantly true also of CAN and DARE), but this would not square with the type of semantics generally assumed for impersonal constructions (e.g. McCawley 1976, and see Fischer and van der Leek 1987). I have also not found examples with OE *agan*. There are potential examples with ME *ouen* and *þarf* (and with *dar* 'be necessary'). But there is the difficulty of interpretation that these verbs may themselves be 'impersonal' in Middle English, so that in examples like the following it is not possible to tell whether the impersonal construction belongs to the finite verb, to the infinitive, or to both (a problem which would also affect potential examples with 'impersonal' *mot*).

(17) a. þanne ne þarf us noðer gramien. ne shamien.
'then we will not need [lit.: not need us] either to-be-grieved or to-be-ashamed.'
*a*1225 (*a*1200) *The Trinity College Homilies* (*Old English Homilies*, ed. R. Morris, EETS 53) 69.21

b. he ... that dooth thyng for which hym oghte repente.
'he ... who does something for which he (obl.) ought to repent.'
(*c*1390) Chaucer, *Canterbury Tales* X.88

B. In Old English and early Middle English verbs which lack a direct (accusative) NP object but which have a nonpredicative NP or PP complement form an impersonal passive with BE or with *weorðan*. This construction parallels the one discussed above in that it is the participle which dictates the absence of a nominative subject and the case or preposition associated with the construction's NP arguments. BE or *weorðan* are transparent to these syntactic interrelationships. Two examples are given in (18) below (for others, see V§§1933, 1959; M§§849ff.). In Old English *beon/wesan* and *weorðan* also occur with the second participle of impersonal verbs; these are at least open to interpretation as perfects as in (19), (see Denison 1990a; M§734).

(18) a. forlæt þine anwylnysse. þæt ðinum life beo geborgen.
'Forsake thy self-will, that thy life (dat.) may-be saved.' (Skeat's translation)
ÆLS i.8.114

b. Swa wyrð eac gestiered ðæm gitsere ðæs reaflaces
'So also the avaricious man can be cured of extortion [lit.: so becomes also restrained (to) the miser (of) the plundering]' (Sweet's translation)
CP 341.11

(19) a. he ... ongan ... þus cweðan: 'wel is þe gelumpen, þu earma'
'he began to speak as-follows: "It has turned out well for you [lit.: well is you (dat.) happened], you miserable (being)"'
GDPref 3(c) 4.185.7

b. ac me todæg swa wundorlice is gelumpen
'but to-day it has befallen me so wonderfully' [lit.: me (dat.) today so wonderfully is befallen] (Skeat's translation)
ÆLS i.23.742

C. Examples with OE *onginnan* are plentiful, and Denison (1990b: 148) reports an instance with *aginnan*. In Middle English besides instances with *ginnen* I have noted a few with perfect *hauen* (alongside others which are less central to the class of impersonal constructions).[22] The relatively late appearance here of HAVE is not unexpected given that we would expect the perfects of impersonals to be formed initially with BE (as exemplified above) since they are distinct from the transitive prototype of the HAVE-perfect from which it traditionally spreads (see M§§724–33). There is also a possible Middle English example with *biginnen* followed by a *to*-infinitive.[23]

(20) a. Þa ongan hine eft langian on his cyþþe
'Then he later began to long [lit.: began him (acc.) later to-long] for his native-land'
BlHom 113.14

b. Hwæt, þe ongan lystan ure, nales us þin
'Indeed, you (acc./dat.) began to-desire us (gen.), not we (acc./dat.) you (gen.)'
Bo 7.19.13

c. He ... gan to sike
Wiþ Kyng Richard gan hym euyl lyke
'He ... began to sigh, he began to be very displeased with King Richard'
*a*1450–1509 Der mittelenglische Versroman über Richard Löwenherz (ed. K. Brunner, *Wiener Beiträge zur englischen Philologie* 42, 1913) 4800

(21) a. Him hadde be beter, he hadde hem slein!
'(It) would-have been better for him (if) he had killed them!'
*c*1330 (?*c*1300) *Sir Beues of Hamtoun* (ed. E. Kölbing, EETS ES 46, 48) 1204

b. Nyf oure lorde hade ben her lodeȝmon, hem had lumpen harde.
'If Our Lord had not been their pilot, it would have gone hard with them [lit.: to-them would-have happened hard (adv.)].'
*a*1400 (?*c*1380) *Cleanness* (ed. J. J. Anderson, Manchester University Press, 1977) 424

c. For alle myȝtest þow haue made . none mener þan other,
And yliche witty & wyse . if þe wel hadde lyked.
'For you might have made everyone, no-one poorer than another, and equally intelligent and wise, if (it) had pleased you well.'
*c*1400 (*c*1378) William Langland, *The Vision of William Concerning Piers the Plowman,* Text B (ed. W. W. Skeat, EETS 38) 14.167

(22) Þo bigan ham alle to agrise
'[When the Saracens saw that Otuel had killed Karnifees] then they all began to be terrified' [*ham* = 'them']
*c*1330 *Otuel* (The English Charlemagne Romances VI, ed. S. J. Herrtage, EETS ES 39, 65–116) 1604

The final example above implies that *begin to* at least sometimes showed this transparency; here it is used, as *ginnen* often is, to put the infinitive in rhyme and probably with weakened inceptive meaning (see *MED biginnen* v. 6, but Brinton 1988: 159). There are also early English examples of *onginnan, biginnen* and other aspectuals in construction with 'weather' *it,* which may show a similar transparency.

(23) a. Hit begann þa on æfnunge egeslice freosan
'It began then in (the) evening to freeze very hard [lit.: terribly to-freeze]'
ÆLS i.11.153

b. Ne blann itt nohht to reȝȝnenn
'It did not cease raining' [*blann* pa.t. 'cease']
?*c*1200 *The Ormulum* (ed. R. Holt, Oxford, 1878) 14565 (*OED*)

c. þe first day of his cristnynge hit bygan to reigne
'on the first day of his baptising [them] it began to rain'
(*a*1387) Trevisa, *Polychronicon Ranulphi Higden* (ed. C. Babington and J. R. Lumby, Rolls Series 41) 6.139

5.2.3 Characterizing the 'verb with impersonal' construction

5.2.3.1 Now that the range of verbs found in the 'transparent' position within impersonal constructions has been established, I will turn to the question of characterizing the construction, and for convenience I will call the verbs which 'intervene' 'I-verbs'. How then does this construction differ from that of other catenatives with a subordinate infinitive?[24] There are two clear differences from subject 'Equi' constructions in which the matrix verb and the subordinate infinitive both independently select the subject. First, there is no direct relationship of semantic selection between an I-verb and an NP to which oblique case has been assigned. In GB terms, the I-verb does not assign a theta role to such NPs. Thus the I-verb seems to show a semantic as well as a syntactic transparency to the construction. This also holds when I-verbs have a nominative subject, for they show evidence of semantic transparency in their occurrence with passives (see Chapter 7 below) and in the wide range of subjects they permit. Secondly, a distributional difference which follows from this is that distinctively Equi verbs do not intervene in impersonal constructions.

But semantic transparency is a property found with present-day 'raising' verbs like *seem*, as with auxiliaries.[25] Is the grammar of verbs which enter the 'verb with impersonal' construction distinct from the grammar of those which enter 'raising' constructions in Old and Middle English? Both distributional and theoretical considerations are relevant here, and I shall argue that neither gives good grounds for a distinction. At the moment, then, I have no reason to reject the view that the 'verb with impersonal' construction is simply what results when a 'raising' verb is married with an impersonal.

5.2.3.2 The distributional question is whether the set of verbs which 'intervene' in 'verb with impersonal' and 'raising' constructions are the same or different. If the 'verb with impersonal' construction is essentially just impersonal + 'raising' the two sets of verbs should be the same. But if there is a further constructional difference, we might expect the sets of verbs not to be identical. For Old English, however, there is a problem in the low incidence of 'raising' constructions outside the verbs listed above. One clear potential group is that of aspectuals, and we might wonder whether *onginnan*, *aginnan* are alone in appearing in impersonal constructions with the infinitive. But the apparent lack of examples needs to be interpreted in the light of two facts. One is the generally low incidence of such catenatives, apart from *onginnan*, which is clear from Venezky and Healey (1980), or from Callaway (1913). Thus Callaway's survey of Old English infinitives lists over a thousand examples with *onginnan* and *aginnan*, but gives only some 85 for *beginnan*, 40 for *(ge)wunian*, and fewer than 50 altogether with all the other infinitive-taking 'aspectualizers' Brinton lists for Old English (Brinton 1988: Ch. 3, Callaway 1913: 67–8, Appendix A.II). The other is the fact that some of these verbs are derived historically from senses in which they presumably selected their subjects. One may question to what extent individual verbs (such as *fon* and its compounds, or *gewunian*) had completed the transition to transparent 'aspectualizer' (or 'raising' verb) (I do not share Brinton's general confidence of this (1988: Ch. 3)). Perhaps then, the apparent absence of the 'verb with impersonal' construction with other aspectuals is simply an accident of the record, due to low frequency.[26]

In the case of other verbs, an inspection of Callaway (1913) shows a handful of undoubted examples of 'raising' catenative constructions like (24) with infinitives (including 'second passives') in glosses and close translation (esp. *Bede* and Wærferð's *Gregory*) (see particularly, but not only, 1913: 59–60, 72, 82). But there seem to be few serious possibilities elsewhere.[27] The apparent absence of the 'verb with impersonal' construction with these verbs, then, is even less remarkable. So it does not seem to be possible for Old English to discriminate on distributional grounds between a more general group of 'raising' verbs and a group of verbs which occur in the 'verb with impersonal' construction.

(24) hwilc cræft þe geþuht betwux þas furþra wesan?
Que ars tibi uidetur inter istas prior esse?
'Which (nom.) occupation to-you seems [lit.: second ptc.; supply "is"] among these to be superior [lit.: superior to-be]?'
ÆColl 211 [another example: 217]

5.2.3.3 The Middle English evidence is difficult to interpret. Among aspectuals *ginnen* shows clear evidence of transparency to impersonals, and there is a little with *biginnen* (see (22) above).[28] This might seem to point to the lack of a distinction between 'verb with impersonal' constructions and 'raising' constructions, were it not that *ginnen* may lack aspectual semantics (*MED ginnen* v. 3b; see the discussion of Brinton 1988: 152ff.), and *biginnen* apparently shows weakened semantics in (22) (and in the other examples referred to). This might distinguish them from aspectuals, and imply transfer into an 'auxiliary' group. I do not know any reports of other aspectuals in central 'verb with impersonal' constructions in late Middle English, but this is in any case the period when distinctively impersonal constructions were on the decline (van der Gaaf 1904). Other 'raising' constructions become more general only during this period of decline (see Warner 1982). Again, I have no relevant examples with such expressions as *semen* 'seem', *happenen* 'happen', *be lik* 'be likely', or *be said.* Moreover, *semen*, perhaps the commonest relevant verb, is itself found 'impersonal' (in constructions such as *him seemes werye* 'he seems weary', *him semed to be a kynges ayre* 'he seemed to be a kings heir') so that potential evidence would be neutralized. If distinctively transparent examples are absent, it would certainly be consistent with the possibility that only a restricted 'auxiliary group' occurred with impersonals. But there is a suggestive parallel in Icelandic. Here epistemic modals (including *kunna* 'may', *ætla* 'will'), aspectual verbs (including the perfect *hafa* 'have' and verbs for 'begin', 'stop') and *virðast* 'seem' may all occur in 'verb with impersonal' constructions, besides showing other evidence of transparency (Thráinsson 1979: §6.3; 1986: esp. 239, 248–58). Thráinsson analyses them all as one broad class, though he discriminates subclasses. To Thráinsson its members are 'AUX-like' in taking a VP complement and not assigning a theta role to their subject (1986: 258), though he refers to other work which analyses the class as 'raising'. So in a related language there is a similar (indeed wider) class of verbs in which the absence of theta-role assignment to a subject corresponds to occurrence in a 'verb with impersonal' construction, without that class's being distinct from (or within) a class of 'raising' verbs.

Without further data and arguments for Middle English (perhaps like those Thráinsson attempts to develop for Icelandic) the agnostic conclusion must be that there is (as yet) no good reason to suppose a distinction between 'verb with impersonal' constructions and 'raising' constructions in Old or in Middle English.

5.2.3.4 More purely theoretical considerations may also be relevant. In HPSG Pollard and Sag take the oblique case of the Icelandic 'verb with impersonal' constructions to be an automatic consequence of their analysis as 'raising' constructions (1987: 21). In their account 'raising' verbs have two distinctive characteristics: (i) they assign no semantic role to their subject; (ii) they require the unification of the syntactic and semantic properties of the two categories required as subject by matrix and subordinate verb. In the revised feature system of Chapter 3 the entry for *may* would include:

(25) may [SUBJ <NP1>, SUBCAT <V[+BSE, SUBJ <NP1>]>]

where the two 'NP1' values are unified (or shared). Then if we add to the grammar a default which assigns nominative case to subjects of finites unless another case is assigned lexically, we deal with oblique subjects in impersonals, and we predict the inheritance of oblique case by unification in 'raising' constructions, as exemplified for the combination *mæg hingrian* below, which is required to combine with an NP marked for accusative case.[29]

(26) a. hingrian V[+BSE, SUBJ <NP[ACC]>]
b. mæg [SUBJ <NP1>, SUBCAT <V[+BSE, SUBJ <NP1>]>]
c. mæg hingrian [SUBJ <NP[ACC]>, SUBCAT < >]

In this framework there is a straightforward identification of the constructions. Here then is some further support for the view that the 'verb with impersonal' construction is simply what results when a 'raising' verb is married with an impersonal.[30]

5.2.3.5 In conclusion, we lack both distributional and theoretical reasons for distinguishing the 'verb with impersonal' construction from a 'raising' construction. This means that the most straightforward account (on the basis of the limited investigation made here) will be to treat the 'verb with impersonal' construction as parallel to 'raising'. In HPSG this is partly a formal matter since syntactic as well as semantic properties are specified as undergoing unification. But this might be seen as motivated by, or a restatement of, the verb's lack of a semantic relationship with an NP argument. The formal property is interinvolved with the semantic property, and this weakens its value to any argument for a subcategory. Thus it seems likely that constructions of the type of (15) show at best a formal peculiarity which is semantically underpinned, rather than a more independent formal property.

5.3 Significance

Let us now return to the first two of my initial questions about the possibility of a grouping of 'auxiliary' verbs:

(i) Do these words have formal properties which distinguish them from other verbs?

(ii) If so, do such formal properties typically cooccur with each other, or with other properties which are uncommon in the general class of verbs, so that there is a measure of predictability between properties which might characterize a distinct group?

These questions depend on the view that word classes are defined by the correlation (or mutual predictability) of properties which stand in opposition to similar correlations for other classes, and that formal properties are of especial importance in such correlations. Thus the fact that a verb may 'intervene' in an impersonal construction is by itself a poor argument for its auxiliaryhood: it may simply identify a 'raising' verb (see Anderson 1991a). We need a set of interrelated properties, some of which are formal. Only two properties have so far been discussed, but we can already make preliminary points about the possibility of a relevant correlation.

(a) One of the properties investigated here is clearly formal, the other seems to be partly or more weakly so.[31] They are open to treatment as syntactic idiosyncrasies which are lexically specified. 'Ellipsis'-group verbs might be treated as proforms or as subcategorized for an elliptical construction; I-verbs will be lexically specified as 'raising' verbs. Here the property of permitting ellipsis is especially interesting since it does not seem to correlate directly with any semantic or other property. The property of occurring with impersonals, however, is less impressive as a formal criterion for classification since it seems likely to be the reflex of a semantic property.

(b) Despite the fact that these two properties are apparently independent of one another, there is a considerable overlap in membership of 'ellipsis'-group verbs and I-verbs, see Table 5.1.

Table 5.1 *Some properties of verbs in Old and Middle English*

Occurrence of verbs	In postverbal ellipsis	In pseudogapping	'Intervening' in impersonal constructions
CAN	(OE)(ME)		*
DARE	OE, ME	?ME	*
MAY	(OE)(ME)	OE, ?ME	OE, ME
MOT	OE, ME	ME	(OE)(ME)
ME *mun* (not in OE)	ME		(ME)
OWE	ME	?ME	ME!
SHALL	OE, ME	OE, ME	OE, ME
ÞARF	(OE), ME		OE, ME!
uton (not late ME)		(?)OE	*
WILL	(OE)(ME)	OE, ME	OE, ME
BE	OE, ME	?OE, ?ME	OE, eME
weorðan (not late ME)			OE, eME
on-/aginnan, ME *ginnen*	**		OE, ME
ME *biginnen*	**		?ME
perfect HAVE	ME	ME	ME
pro-verbal DO	OE, ME	?OE, ME	?*
ME semen, leornian 'learn', wenan 'expect', etc.			* (mainly)

OE, ME = attested in the construction at the period in question.
(OE) (ME) = instances which might be intransitive in the case of potential ellipsis, or less central instances in the case of impersonals.
ME! neutralized with use as impersonal verb in ME.
* subject-selecting verb.
** neutralized with use as intransitive verb.

Given the inevitable patchiness of the data, the extent to which these properties cooccur in the individual items is remarkable. The generalization of postverbal ellipsis and pseudogapping is justified not only by their close constructional similarity, but by this distributional parallel. The fact that CAN, OE *dearr*, *mot*, ME *mun*, and ÞARF have not been noted with pseudogapping may reasonably be interpreted as a consequence of their relatively lower frequency with the infinitive alongside the relative infrequency of the construction. I am also not aware of examples of I-group verbs with periphrastic DO in late Middle English, which may be a consequence of the decline of impersonal constructions and the fact that periphrastic DO is initially uncommon with stative verbs (Denison 1985). But *onginnan*, etc. and *weorðan* are striking as members of one class not yet reported for the other: note that Antipova (1963) and Brown (1970) do not report them with ellipsis.

The view of word classes, and subordinate word classes, developed in this book is one which is tolerant of a degree of mismatch between the occurrence of properties, but which predicts a core of 'prototypical' membership within a class. Here we have two unrelated properties (one formal, one with an important formal aspect) which have an impressive degree of overlapping membership. Moreover, these properties pick out a clear 'prototypical' membership: in OE *mæg*, *sceal*, *wile* and BE, and probably *mot* and *þearf*, verbs which must (hardly coincidentally) be central to anyone's list of potential auxiliaries for early English. Notice too that the mutual predictability of these properties seems to hold for the Middle English incomer perfect *hauen*, and that it seems to improve over time with the loss of *weorþan* in early Middle English and the typical restriction of *ginnen* to verse in Middle English (Brinton 1988: 120ff. and references).

The preliminary conclusion must be that there was already in Old English a striking correlation of properties. In the next chapter I will show that this picture of correlation can be considerably extended.

6 *Identifying an 'auxiliary group' before Modern English: further properties of 'modals'*

In the last chapter we saw that there was a rather striking correlation between apparently arbitrary properties of 'pre-auxiliaries' in Old English. In this chapter I want to pursue the same questions of (i) distinctive properties and (ii) their mutual predictiveness, widening the scope of discussion to include some properties which are not clearly formal, but postponing more straightforwardly semantic topics until the next chapter. The topics considered are these.

(1) a. Subcategorization for the plain infinitive, not for the *to*-infinitive.
b. Preterite-present morphology.
c. Restriction of some verbs to finite forms.
d. Use of past-tense forms without past time reference, outside a motivating context.
e. The availability of negative forms in *n*- in Old and some Middle English.
f. Absence of examples in which the verb is the antecedent to pro-verbal *do*.

Lightfoot (1979, and see 1991: 142ff.) discussed (a), (b) and (d) as factors preconditioning the development of the class of modals. I hope to show that the first in particular is a substantially more impressive distinctive attribute than he thought, and that more follows from their cooccurrence than in his account. But the last will be rejected as a useful criterion. The conclusion will be that there is a correlation of properties which would be mysterious and unexpected if we focussed simply on the sixteenth century as the point of recategorization.

In the next chapter I will argue that the verbs which these properties identify form a 'modal group' within an 'auxiliary group'. But here I shall simply call them 'group A verbs' as in the last chapter. For Old English this is Mitchell's '"modal" auxiliaries' without *agan*, but with *uton*. For Middle English the list differs marginally by the addition of *mun* (a preterite-present verb borrowed from Old Norse (*OED Mun*, *v.*, *MED monen* v. (2) and see *OED Maun*, *v.*[1])), and (sometimes) of *ouen*, but where precision is important I have referred specifically to these two verbs.

6.1 Subcategorization for the plain infinitive

Old English had both a 'plain' infinitive (in *-an*, as in *singan* 'sing', *lufian* 'love') and a *to*-infinitive (as in *to singenne, to singanne, to singan*). Here *to* was in origin a preposition of direction taking a dative, though *-enne* and *-anne* were no longer synchronic datives but part of the morphology of the verb even in Old English (see Warner 1983: 200f.). The combination must originally have expressed direction, purpose, etc. (*OED To, prep.* B), but in Old English it also occurs in variation with the plain infinitive in many of that infinitive's functions, and its history is one of steady encroachment on the plain infinitive. At some point *to* is interpreted as an infinitive marker. In his detailed study of infinitives in Old and Middle English, Bock (1931) concluded that this was not fully shown until the thirteenth century. The most clear-cut evidence is the occurrence of both the *to*-infinitive and the plain infinitive as subjects in the clause-initial position typical of nominal subjects, (see Bock 1931: 180–1 for thirteenth-century examples).[1] But the infrequency of the plain infinitive in this position in Old English, alongside the *to*-infinitive's increasingly general distribution and its occasional reinforcement by prepositional *for* towards the end of Old English makes one suspect that *to* had indeed already become a mere grammatical marker at the latest by late Old English.

Both the plain infinitive and the *to*-infinitive are found as complements to verbs in Old English, the plain infinitive being much more widely distributed than today. I will argue that verbs of group A already shared a distinctive property in the regularity with which they occurred with the plain infinitive, in contrast to the variation found with most other verbs, especially with other verbs having the same type of constructional semantics. If this is correct, then Lightfoot's apparent suggestion that a property distinctive of a class here appeared 'by the sixteenth century, if not earlier' (1979: 109) can be very substantially antedated, at least to late Old English. This view depends partly on my interpretation of the relevant opposition as one between plain infinitives and infinitives variably marked with *to*. Lightfoot (and others) seem in contrast to oppose the plain and the *to*-infinitive more directly. But this does not take sufficient account of the degree of variation in verbal complements, especially in late Old English. In the second place it depends on a re-examination of the Old English data, to which I now turn.

Callaway (1913) investigated and tabulated all infinitives in Old English. I shall rely here on his counts, which he regarded as 'approximate', since minor corrections will hardly affect the general picture. Callaway's data for the active infinitive as active object (this does not include 'group A' verbs which he classified as auxiliaries taking a predicative infinitive) show apparent selection: some verbs occur with only a plain infinitive, some with only a *to*-infinitive, others with both (Callaway 1913: Ch. 2, and App. A.II). The *to*-infinitive is well established here. It is true that the plain infinitive is considerably more frequent, but this is because it is selected by a handful of very common verbs. There are, however, more verbs with infinitive complements which are recorded with only *to*-infinitives (and not with plain infinitives) than *vice versa*, and outside the five commonest verbs the distribution is more evenly balanced, with the *to*-infinitive in fact being slightly more frequent.[2]

Now, if we leave aside verbs which Callaway records with an infinitive complement on two occasions or once only as giving too little evidence to establish a selectional preference then it is clear that a majority of verbs shows variation in choice of complement. Callaway classifies verbs under six headings in his Chapter 2. With one of these, 'verbs of sense perception', he records an infinitive complement as invariably plain, as it is also with the frequent *hatan* 'order', *lætan* 'permit'. Other verbs of 'commanding' or of 'causing and permitting' with one exception show variation rather than a *to*-infinitive.[3] Under Callaway's remaining three headings, 'verbs of mental perception', 'verbs of beginning, delaying and ceasing' and 'verbs of inclination and of will', we find both verbs whose infinitive complements are given as recorded with the *to*-infinitive only, and verbs which show variation. *Habban* 'have', which stands outside Callaway's classification, is also only recorded with the *to*-infinitive. With only two verbs is there any sign of a restriction to a plain infinitive in the complement, though the preference for the plain infinitive complement shown by *onginnan* (and *aginnan*) is notable.[4] The plain infinitive is, however, solidly regular with *cann, dearr, mæg, mot, sceal, þearf, uton* and *wile*. These never appear in Old English with a *to*-infinitive complement. *Agan*, however, is distinct in requiring the *to*-infinitive.[5]

The figures just discussed are crude in that they make no allowance for differences of register, dialect or period. But they seem to show clearly enough that avoidance of *to* in an infinitive complement was a remarkably restricted property in Old English, certainly by late Old English as the incidence of *to* increased. Occurrence with the plain infinitive only is found with verbs of 'sense perception', with *hatan* and *lætan*, and with verbs of group A.[6] Elsewhere variation or the *to*-infinitive is the norm. Only a couple of verbs show a possible restriction to the plain infinitive, and this is doubtful because of the small number of instances. Thus the restriction might stand by itself as a property isolating a rather small number of verbs, among which 'group A' verbs figure prominently.

But this pattern of distribution is interestingly related to the semantics of these constructions. Divide 'verb with infinitive' constructions into two types: those where the understood subject of the infinitive is that of the verb subcategorized for it ('subject equi' or 'subject raising' verbs like present-day *try* or *seem*), and those where that is not the case. The Old English verbs of sense perception (*seon* 'see', *hieran* 'hear' and derivatives), *hatan* and *lætan* clearly belong to the second type.[7] Verbs of group A clearly belong to the first. Callaway does not distinguish verbs with 'shared subject' semantics, and the data considered under his second set of three headings in Chapter 2 ('verbs of mental perception', etc.) include other types. But 'shared subject' relationships predominate, and each of the verbs in the subset of data discussed above (those occurring three or more times) which shows variation in infinitive marking is exemplified with the inflected infinitive in the 'shared subject' relationship. Thus among verbs whose subject supplies the subject of an infinitive complement, a restriction to the plain infinitive is regular virtually only with 'group A' verbs by late Old English. Moreover this restriction even extends to the less frequent members of the group, *dearr* and *þearf*. Thus we have a rather striking regularity. As I have interpreted it, this looks like an essentially formal criterion for 'group A' verbs.

In Middle English the *to*-infinitive (including the *for to*-infinitive) continued to displace the plain infinitive. But verbs of group A retained the distinctive property of taking a plain infinitive and not a *to*-infinitive. This remark deserves some immediate qualification. In the first place, it does not always hold of nonfinites; after nonfinite MAY at least *to*-infinitives also occur (see Chapter 8 for an interpretation of this).[8] Secondly, *to*-infinitives occasionally occur where a complement infinitive is separated from its governing verb. A majority of cases involves coordination, where a subsequent infinitive may have *to*, especially if it does not follow its conjunction directly. A minority of cases shows some noncoordinate material intervening between governing verb and infinitive. There are also cases where a fronted infinitive is marked by *to*. This all seems to be part of a general Middle English tendency to stronger infinitive marking (or perhaps to a tolerance of less constrained infinitive marking) in complement infinitives separated from their governing verb.[9] Thirdly, in the fifteenth century *will* is found in contact with a *to*-infinitive that it governs (V§1730).[10] But here we must reckon with the mutual influence of 'group A' *will* ~ *would* (*OED Will*, *v.*[1]) and the regular *will* ~ *willed* (*OED Will*, *v.*[2] from OE *willian*). As *OED* notes, these two verbs can be difficult to keep apart, and there are apparent syntactic blends (see *OED Will*, *v.*[1] 48, *Nill*, *v.* 1c, V§1730). *OED Wilne*, *v.* (OE *wilnian*) may also have been involved, with loss of *n* after *l* when *n* was word final (see Jordan 1974: §173). The survival of the *to*-infinitive here (especially in contact with finite *will* ~ *would*) into early Modern English points to the importance of interaction.

With these qualifications, the group of verbs in Middle English which takes a complement infinitive with 'shared subject' semantics and which is regular with the plain infinitive consists of the descendants of the eight 'group A' verbs listed above for Old English together with *mun*, and (later) periphrastic DO.[11] With other verbs which have 'subject equi' or 'subject raising' semantics, however, variation or (increasingly) the *to*-infinitive is the norm.[12] Thus only a minority of verbs of this type occurs with the plain infinitive in Chaucer, and though there are some (e.g. *kepen* 'care to', *ouen* 'ought', *wenen* 'think, intend') with which a considerable proportion of infinitive complements are plain, any verb occurring in more than a couple of instances is also found with the *to*-infinitive (Kenyon 1909: Ch. 10).[13]

Interestingly even uses of *ginnen* which have been classified as 'auxiliary' on semantic grounds seem to lack a restriction to the plain infinitive. The complement of aspectual *ginnen* varies (see *MED ginnen* v. 3a and examples cited in Brinton 1988). *MED* isolates meaningless 'auxiliary' uses. But even here there is variation between the *to*-infinitive and the plain infinitive (*MED ginnen* v. 3b).[14] Middle English *ginnen* may well show a preference for the plain infinitive, especially in weakened senses. But it occurs not infrequently with the *to*-infinitive, and it has yet to be demonstrated that any particular subset of its uses is restricted to the plain infinitive.

Outside the group of 'subject equi' or 'subject raising' verbs, verbs of sense perception are virtually regular with the plain infinitive, and a considerable proportion of occurrences of complement infinitives with particular verbs of ordering, permitting or causing is plain, for example, in Chaucer *bidden* 'order', *don* 'cause', *leten* 'permit', *maken* 'cause' (Kenyon 1909: Ch. 11, and elsewhere).

So the Middle English situation (as reported in the works referred to above) seems to parallel that for Old English. Only a small number of verbs regularly take a plain infinitive and not a *to*-infinitive complement. Verbs of group A are prominent among them. If we partition verbs according to the semantics of subject retrieval for the infinitive, the isolation of this group is again striking. Moreover the opposition between verbal complements restricted to the plain infinitive and those not so restricted itself became sharper in Middle English, as the *to*-infinitive increasingly became the norm in verbal complements (see Bock 1931: 216, 219, 248).

Table 6.1 *Preterite-present and other verbal conjugations. Late West Saxon preterite-present morphology compared with that of the regular weak present, and the regular strong preterite*

	Present of regular weak verb *hīeran* w.v. 1 'hear'	Present of preterite-present *sceal* 'shall'	*witan* 'know'	Preterite of regular strong verb *rīdan* s.v. 1 'ride'
Indicative				
Singular 1	hīere	sceal	wāt	rād
2	hīerst	scealt	wāst	ride
3	hīerð	sceal	wāt	rād
Plural	hīerað	sculon	witon	ridon
Subjunctive				
Singular	hīere	scyle, scule	wite	ride
Plural	hīeren	scylen, sculen	witen	riden

6.2 Preterite-present morphology

6.2.1 Morphological characteristics of preterite-present verbs

In Old English there are (if we include derivatives under the simple form) a dozen verbs which show preterite-present morphology. They include virtually all of our 'group A' verbs. Their present tense is derived from a type of Indo-European perfect formation (see also Latin *coepi* 'I begin', Greek *oida* 'I know'), and its conjugation is very like that of the regular strong preterite. The nature of the morphological contrasts can best be seen by comparing paradigms, as in Table 6.1.[15] The past finite forms of these verbs belong to a small and highly irregular group of weak preterites in the way they form their preterite stem, but they take the regular endings of the weak class.

6.2.2 Membership of the group of preterite-present verbs

The verbs which belonged to this group (or were associated with it) as a matter of synchronic grammar in Old English are listed in Table 6.2. Most of them are straightforward, but three deserve some comment. The invariable *uton, wuton* 'let's' is of debated origin. It seems clearly to be a form of *witan* 'go', but the nature of its original morphology is not settled. *OED Ute, v.* takes it to be an original subjunctive; see Seebold (1966) for some references and discus-

Table 6.2 *Preterite-present verbs in Old English and fourteenth century Middle English*

Old English	Middle English (Chaucer)	*OED*	
3 sg. pres., pret.	3 sg. pres.		
cann, cūþe	can	can (con)	
dearr, dorste	dar	dare	
mæg, meahte	may	may	
mōt, mōste 'may, must'	moot	mote, must	
–	(mun, munde) 'shall, must'	mun (see maun)	
sceal, sceolde	shal	shall	
þearf, þorfte 'need'	thar	thar(f)	dialectal after 1500
uton 'let's'	(ute)	ute	last *c*1275
āh, āhte 'have'	owe	owe, ought	also weak from late OE
ann, ūþe 'grant, give, permit'	(an)	unne	last *c*1320
dēag, dohte 'be strong avail'	(dow)	dow	dialectal after 1500, some weak forms earlier
geman, gemunde 'remember'	–	i-mune	weak in Anglian OE, last in eME
be-/ge-neah, -nohte 'need/be enough'	–		last in OE
wāt, wiste 'know'	woot	wit (and list of forms there referenced)	archaic or dialectal after sixteenth century, some weak forms earlier
eart, earon, sindon 'art, are, are' (only present forms cited)	art, arn	be	
(wile, wolde)	wil(e), wol(e)	will (nill)	

The forms are essentially illustrative. Old English forms are West Saxon. Middle English forms are Chaucerian, except where the verb is missing in Chaucer.

sion. In Old English it is clearly a verb (M§§916f.), and as a matter of synchronic grammar a preterite-present, and (surprisingly) an indicative. Note that its stem vowel is that of a majority of plural preterite-presents (*durron*, *sculon*, etc.) and that its termination is regularly the indicative *-on* (*-an*, *-un*), not the subjunctive *-en*.[16] The status of *-on* is borne out by a survey of Venezky and Healey (1980) since it is clear that *uten, ute* 'let's' are uncommon beside *uton*, etc. and are predominantly late (see also BT *witon*, *OED Ute*, *v.* and Callaway 1913: 96 n. 3 'occasionally *uten*' and n. 4). Moreover (and more impressively), the presence of a back vowel in the termination is vouched for by the normal form in (*w*)*u*-, whose development from *wi*- shows combinative back umlaut, a late prehistoric change dependent on a following back vowel, indeed virtually dependent on *u*, since the change is extremely limited before *a* (Campbell 1959a: §§218, 219). Thus historical phonology points to earlier *-*un*, and supports the synchronic classification of *uton* both as a preterite-present and as an indicative.[17]

Wile 'will, wish' largely has the morphology of a regular weak verb. But it has a 'contact preterite' as is typical of preterite-presents, and it has a distinctively preterite-present form in the second person of the present indicative, *þu wilt* 'thou wilt', which 'follows the pattern of the modal auxiliaries' (Prokosch 1939: §75d). It also has a uniquely anomalous form in the third person singular, *he wile*, which descends from an Indo-European optative. It looks like a synchronic preterite-present, however, if it is interpreted as an endingless form in which *-e* is part of the stem (as I think is plausible).[18] Besides these we may note that some of the forms of 'be' are also preterite-presents. *Earon* (pl.) 'are' and Anglian *earþ* 'art' probably derive from perfect formations, while *eart* 'art' additionally shows accommodation to the form of other preterite-presents (Prokosch 1939: 221–2, Onions 1966). *Sindon* (pl.) 'are', beside *sind*, shows an analogical secondary plural. Since (*e*)*aron* is largely Anglian (especially Northumbrian), while *sindon* is general across dialects (Forsström 1948: 218–19) this development may show a general analogy with preterite-presents as much as one with *earon*.

6.2.3 Word-class implications

From a word-class point of view, two points are especially worth noting. First, the special morphological characteristics of this group are of great antiquity, both as regards their 'preterite-present' formation (Prokosch 1939: §65), and the regularly associated 'contact' preterite (Prokosch 1927). Moreover, the group as such must itself be of considerable antiquity since a group with essentially the same properties and with substantially overlapping membership is found in all the Germanic languages. It is also clear that it has been a focus for developments; for example, particular verbs were attracted into it in Germanic times (see Prokosch 1939: §65 for *cann*, *OED* for *may*).

A second point worth noting about this group is that it is semantically restricted, being particularly rich in 'stative' verbs, appropriately enough given its origin in a perfect whose 'psychological emphasis lay on the state attained' (Prokosch 1939: 188). A notable subgroup within it is 'the chief Old English verbs meaning "to know" ... *witan* and *cunnan*' (Ono 1975: 33), to which we may perhaps add *gemunan* 'remember, bear in mind, consider' with *munan* and its other derivatives. *Uton* is not stative, but the 'modal' senses of other group A verbs are, as generally are their other senses, and the other verbs are also largely (though not entirely) stative. This morphological group thus has some semantic coherency even in Old English. And, interestingly, this identity is distinct from that of the transitive, dynamic prototype of the general class of verbs.

These points imply that there was already some real link between preterite-present morphology and nonprototypical verbal semantics in Old English. So the verbs of group A already 'belonged' here as part of a broader set of statives (or of nonprototypical verbs). A second implication is that this situation has its roots in Germanic, and that the association of preterite-present morphology with potentially grammaticalized 'auxiliary' items may antedate recorded Old English. This, at least, seems to follow from the development of *uton* (perhaps also, though less clearly, that of *wilt*, *sindon* and *eart*). In the case of *uton* a prehistoric **-un* does not seem to be the straightforward phonological descendant of any plausible (nonindicative) antecedent. Thus whatever its original analysis the form seems likely to have been accommodated to preterite-present morphology. This implies the importance of nonprototypicality as a verb, or association with the preterite-presents along some other dimension than stativity, since 'lets' is clearly dynamic, and it is presumably the moodlike semantics of *uton* which is most relevant.

6.2.4 Lexical losses and gains

During Middle English the morphology of these verbs remained distinctive, though their resemblance to strong preterites declined. In membership the group underwent both losses and gains. Some of these helped to focus preterite-present morphology more clearly on the verbs of group A; others did not. To this latter category belongs the loss of *ute* 'let's' which is last recorded in the thirteenth century (*c*1275, *OED Ute, v.*) and the fact that *þarf* 'need' becomes more typical of northern dialects in late Middle English and does not survive into Standard English, perhaps because of its attested confusion with DARE (see *OED Tharf, v.*; *MED durren* v. 2). A relatively neutral development is found with OE *agan* 'have'. This is distinct from the verbs of group A both in taking *to* with a following infinitive (regularly in Old English, commonly in Middle English) and in occurring relatively frequently with an NP object. It develops regular weak forms of the present in later Old English and both types of form are in use in Middle English.

There are other developments, however, which tend to focus preterite-present morphology on group A. *Wil* continues its process of accommodation (witness the identification of first and third person indicative singular, and the development of plural *willen* in some southern dialects which have regular *-eþ* plural: McIntosh, Samuels and Benskin 1986: vol. II, 120ff.), and two further preterite-presents appear in Middle English, both taking the plain infinitive and having 'modal' (or 'auxiliary') senses. One is northern and midland *mun* 'shall, must' (from Old Norse *munu*, itself preterite-present; *OED Mun, v.*). The other is the infrequent *can*, 'a modal verb stressing the fact of an act or event', which *MED* calls 'a peculiar variant of *gan*, p[ast] of *ginnen*' ('begin', etc.), *MED can* v.; see also *OED Maun, v.*[1] for a further preterite-present in Scottish English. Preterite-presents which ordinarily have other subcategorizations than the plain infinitive, and (presumably) nonmodal semantics, tend to be lost or to become weak; see Table 6.2. These changes improve the mutual predictiveness of preterite-present morphology on the one hand, 'shared subject' semantics and subcategorization for the plain infinitive on the other. And this improvement continues in the fifteenth century with the tendency of *can* to develop weak forms in nonmodal senses and constructions, and the decline of *witen* 'know'. These later developments will be discussed in Chapter 9. For the moment we may conclude that the mutual predictiveness of preterite-present morphology with 'shared subject' semantics and subcategorization for the plain infinitive improves steadily from Old English onwards. But it also seems likely that there was a weaker 'mutual predictiveness' already in Old English, and even before.

6.3 Restriction to finite forms

A striking feature of some 'group A' verbs in both Old and Middle English is the apparent absence of some nonfinite categories; the data for Old English and Middle English is summarized in Table 6.3. This absence is striking and

Table 6.3 *Recorded nonfinites of the major preterite-present verbs and* will

	Old English			Late Middle English (1300–1500)		
OE form	Inf.	Pres. ptc.	Past ptc.	Inf.	Pres. ptc.	Past ptc.
cann	+	–	+	+	+	+
dearr	–	–	–	+	–	15C
mæg	+	+	–	+	+	+
mōt	–	–	–	–	–	–
mun				+	–	–
sceal	–	–	–	–	–	–
þearf	?+	(adj.)	–	–	–	–
āh	+	+ (in compounds)	(adj.)	+	+	+
wile (uton)	+	+	–	+	+	+
dēag	+	+	–	+	+	+
geman	+	+	+			
ge-/be-neah	–	–	–			
an	+	+	+	+	–	+
wāt	+	+	+	+	+	+

Sources: *OED*, *MED*, BT(S), Visser, Long (1944), Rettger (1934), the major published grammars of Old English and Middle English, accounts of individual texts and the major detailed histories of the language. These sources are not always in agreement, and the more authoritative and standard works have been followed in cases of disagreement where no specific citations are given.

looks like a formal distinction from the wider class of verbs in these periods. On the other hand, as can be seen from the table, a rather fuller morphology for several of these verbs is recorded by late Middle English, and this apparent development (which was discussed in Chapter 4) argues that verbs of group A none the less remained within the more general class of verbs.

Recent major standard works do not give nonfinites of DARE and MOT for Old English, or of MOT and MUST in Middle English: see in particular Campbell (1959a), Brunner (1965) and the explicit statement of *MED moten* v. (2) that the infinitive and participles are lacking in Middle English. SHALL too seems to have lacked nonfinite forms early. It is clear from *OED* that its editors did not know any nonfinites after Old English and were doubtful about the occurrence of an infinitive even there: it is not given by Campbell (1959a) and is rejected by Onions (1966) and Mitchell (1985). There is one potential example in a gloss. But glossators often did not reproduce the categories of their original, so the evidence of a gloss without further support is dubious.[19] Nonfinites are not recorded in *MED*. Although there is a heading *shulen*, no nonfinites are cited and Professor Lewis, the editor-in-chief, kindly informs me that none have been found.[20] From *OED* and other sources it also seems likely that nonfinites of ÞARF are absent in Middle English, though major recent sources are apparently agreed that Old English had an infinitive and present participle (see especially Campbell 1959a: §767, Brunner 1965, Mitchell 1985.).

How seriously should we take these apparent gaps? Are they merely due to the accident of record, or to incomplete research? Frequency is one issue here, and it is worth pointing out that SHALL (though not DARE and ÞARF) is very common in both Old English and Middle English. It is not the vanishingly infrequent form of some modern American dialects. In Old English *sceal* is among the first hundred most frequent word-group lemmata in Madden and Magoun's (1964) grouped frequency word list of Anglo-Saxon Poetry (as is *mot*; see Venezkey and Healey 1980). In Chaucer's corpus *shal*'s frequency is second only to that of *may* among members of the modal group; in Shakespeare's, it is second only to that of *will* (my estimates, based on Tatlock and Kennedy 1927, Spevack 1968–80). So the absence of nonfinites is not simply due here to infrequent attestation.[21] In the case of Old English *mot* we have some interesting more direct evidence about the status of an infinitive from Ælfric's Latin Grammar. In the course of his discussion of impersonal verbs which take the dative we find the following for *licere*:

(2) *licet mihi bibere* mot ic drincan, *mihi licuit* ic moste, *tibi licet, nobis licet, si nobis liceret* gyf we moston; INFINITIVVM *licere* beon alyfed
ÆGram 207.1

Ælfric follows his normal procedure, citing representative elements of the Latin paradigm and giving some Old English glosses. In each case he glosses a Latin finite with a finite form of *mot*. But when he reaches the infinitive *licere*, instead of the infinite **motan*, which one might have expected, he uses instead the passive of *alyfan* 'permit'.[22] The clear implication is that he preferred to avoid **motan*, and this is consonant with its absence being a real fact about the language. I do not know of similar evidence for SHALL. But the notion of obligation is not of itself simply a finite one, nor is that of futurity. One might, for example, have expected the translators who devised the special *to + -ing* form to render the Latin future participle in the Wyclifite Bible and elsewhere (*transiturus erat = he was to passinge*) to have made use of a participle of SHALL had one been available to them. Nonfinites of the corresponding verbs are, moreover, found in both Old Norse and Old High German for SHALL, and in Old High German for MOT. So it seems that we should take these gaps seriously and regard at least MOT and SHALL as probably grammatically restricted to finite occurrence in Old and Middle English.

The maintenance of these gaps is puzzling. Could it simply follow from the nature of preterite-present morphology? If these verbs were for a period real preterite-presents, that is, if their present stem was morphologically [+PAST] but semantically nonpast, then perhaps they simply lacked the present plural stem from which Old English infinitives and present participles are formed. But it seems unlikely that the preterite-present status that this line of explanation requires can have survived for long enough. Even in Old English the second person indicative singular of preterite-presents has an ablaut grade distinct from that of strong preterites, and it sometimes ends in *-st* by analogy with other presents (*þu ahst, canst, dearst*). The inflectional ending of the plural becomes identical with that of the general present in midland dialects of Middle English, while it is sometimes replaced by the more general present ending *-eþ* in more southerly dialects as we saw in the last chapter. So, though the general defectiveness of the group may have helped to maintain the absence of nonfinites of MOT and SHALL, it hardly looks as if an account of this should be fundamentally morphological.[23]

There are however two suggestive facts about the status of finites. The first is that in Middle English nonfinites do not seem to be restricted to the plain infinitive, but sometimes occur with the *to*-infinitive (as noted above). So it is finites that are isolated by this criterion. Secondly there is apparently a generalization about the absence of nonfinites in Middle English in the period after the loss of *ute*, if we accept that nonfinites of *þarf* were missing.[24] It does not seem to have to do with the absence of 'full verb' constructions, since *shal* retains these (in the sense 'owe' and as an intransitive: *MED shulen*, v. (1) 1, 2). But the three verbs mainly involved at this period, *mot/most, shal, þarf*, share the semantics of obligation and necessity. I suggest that for Middle English the following statement may hold:

(3) Preterite-present verbs subcategorized for the plain infinitive which denote necessity, obligation and related notions of futurity are finite only.

This clearly holds for *mot* and *shal*. It is consistent with *OED*'s evidence for *þarf*. It is also consistent with a little further evidence. *MED* is silent on the question of nonfinites of *mun*, but the only nonfinite citation is in the sense 'be able', so here too the generalization may hold good (*MED monen* v. (2) 2). Infinitives and past participles of *dar* are found but none of the instances given by *MED* belongs to sense 2 'to be under necessity or obligation', nor do any of the instances in *MED*'s files.[25] *Ouen* clearly has nonfinites. But it is often found with the *to*-infinitive and weak verb morphology. So it is not straightforwardly restricted by the generalization.[26]

For Middle English, then, the position of finites looks potentially systematic. It should not be treated as an accidental collection of facts. So in the restriction to finiteness we apparently have a further formal property distinguishing (some of) group A. In Chapter 8 a particular interpretation will be put forward which attributes to such finites the property of opacity of mood which it was suggested in Chapter 3 was characteristic of present-day modals. If this interpretation is appropriate then the restriction to finiteness indeed reflects a formal property which exempts the item from automatic nonfinite categories. Nonfinites can be stated, and there is no general exemption from verbal morphosyntax as today, but finites and nonfinites need not share properties in the same manner as they do for other verbs; hence nonfinites may be subcategorized for variation in infinitive marking. Moreover as a lexical restriction the restriction to finiteness is subject to a lexical regularity, in its correlation with necessity. So I conclude that on general grounds the finiteness restriction looks a potential formal property characteristic of group A verbs, and that if the interpretation suggested in Chapter 8 is appropriate, then it is indeed such a formal property.

6.4 The developing independence of preterite forms

In today's English the overt past-tense forms *could, might, should, would* have only a limited availability for straightforward, 'non-modal' reference to the past. This is found in reported speech, but only restrictedly otherwise (see §1.2(k)). Indeed, the forms have substantial independence of the corresponding 'presents' and look much like separate lexemes. In Old English however the corresponding group of forms were preterites, with appropriate uses, though there are some signs of developing independence. Since there was already a substantial amount of ambiguity in weak preterite forms between indicative and subjunctive (even perhaps a general ambiguity between these categories in late West Saxon; see M§22), the preterite *sceolde* could be interpreted as an indicative 'had to' or as a subjunctive without specific time reference in a range of remote or tentative applications, for example in conditionals.

Lightfoot (1979: 103–5) discussed the developing independence of preterite forms, focussing on the fact that the relationship between present and preterite forms became increasingly opaque semantically. Hence, he reasoned, the items involved were becoming less like full verbs. The development can most clearly be seen in earlier English in cases where the preterite form has present time reference in a context where there seems to be no warrant for the interpretation appropriate to a preterite subjunctive, and indeed the reinterpretation of tentative or hypothetical preterite subjunctives which were motivated by pragmatic considerations is apparently a major strand in this development: see *OED Must, v.*[1] II 'The use as a present arose from the practice of employing the past subj. as a moderate, cautious, or polite substitute for the present indicative'; *OED Shall,* The past tense *should* with modal function, 18 'In statements of duty ... (originally, as applicable to hypothetical conditions not regarded as real).' But the development of other types of 'periphrastic subjunctive' is also relevant here, and the whole series of changes is interinvolved with the functional and formal decline of the inflectional subjunctive.

The first appearance of such opaque uses is very difficult to date, because of the infrequency of contexts in which one can be confident that the force of a preterite subjunctive is truly inappropriate. But, despite such difficulties for individual examples, it seems clear from *OED*, *MED* and Visser (1963–73: III, part 1) that the general development is well under way in Middle English in the case of *might, must, ought* and *should*; *would* seems to be exemplified by late Middle English at the latest; and Visser has a handful of potential Middle English instances with *could* and *durst.*[27] In the case of *should,* moreover, it seems clear that the development begins in Old English (for some discussion see Standop 1957: 98ff., Goossens 1987, tempered by Anderson 1991a). We find instances of *sceolde* apparently imposing a present obligation, as in (4). There is also a further separate possibility in that evidential or reportative *sceolde* (exemplified in Chapter 7) is not well paralleled by uses of *sceal*, and may be isolated.[28]

(4) a. æfter godes gesetnysse ealle cristene men sceoldon beon swa geþwære. swilce hit an man wære
'according-to God's decree all Christian men should be so united as if it were one man [lit.: one man were]'
ÆCHom i.272.23. (Example given in Goossens 1987; his translation)

b. Apostrophus ... tacnað þæt sum uocalis byð forlæten, þe on þam worde beon sceolde
'The apostrophe ... denotes that some vowel is omitted, which ought to be in the word [lit.: in the word be should]'
Byrhtferth's Manual (ed. S.J. Crawford, EETS 177) 184.15

The development of this independence is a long-term matter, not yet perhaps fully completed. One major milestone is the loss of straightforward reference to the past for particular senses. The relevant losses mainly belong to the Modern English period after 1500. For example, *should* 'did have to, was obliged to' is attested into the sixteenth century, 'was to, was about to' into at least the seventeenth (V§1527; *OED Shall*, 13 and V§§1528–9; but rejecting Visser's latest examples), while *might* of past permission, 'was allowed to', survived a good deal later (V§1662). It seems clear that a broadly similar series of developments affects verbs of group A individually, with *should* in the vanguard and *could* trailing behind, over a period of a thousand years or so, though development may have been most rapid during the Middle and early Modern periods.

The growing opacity of the semantic relationship between the present and the preterite was an irregularity from the point of view of relationships between verb forms. By the time that this irregularity had become a characteristic of several 'group A' verbs it must not only be seen as tending to distinguish these from other verbs, but also as tending to focus the group which shared this common property. This, then, is a further distinctive criterion, at least for Middle English. But it is also a development which is very suggestive for an eventual account of 'group A' verbs since it seems likely that what happened here was essentially that *should* (etc.) had ceased, at least sometimes, to be semantically compositional with a meaning derived as '*shall* + past + subjunctive' (or '+ indicative') and become an entity in its own right, with a partly independent semantics. This makes coherent sense in terms of the account of today's auxiliaries given in the first part of this book, and also ties in coherently with the restriction of some verbs to finite forms noted above. Thus I suggest that overall developments here were in fact rather wider than Lightfoot suspected, also involving opacity of the semantics of mood (a topic referred to in the preceding section, and taken up in Chapter 8).

6.5 Negative forms, and occurrence with *do*

Two further possible criteria which apply to potential auxiliaries, not just to group A verbs, are worth brief discussion.

6.5.1 Negative forms

Historically the negative particle *ne* cliticized onto 'certain common words' (*OED Ne, adv.*) which had an initial vowel, or with loss of initial [w] or [h].

These included forms of OE *witan* (*ic nat, nyste*, etc.), *willan* (*ic nylle, nolde*, etc.), *agan* (*ic nah, nahte*, etc.), BE (*ic nam, næs, we næron*, etc.), and *habban* (*ic næbbe, næfde*, etc.) (see Campbell 1959a: §§265, 354, 469). Similar forms are found in some Middle English dialects, where there is also a more general cliticization of *ne* before verbs with an initial (often unstressed) vowel (*MED ne* adv. 4, and see Levin 1958, McIntosh, Samuels and Benskin 1986 for information on dialect distribution). At both periods other words are also involved: OE *nan* 'none', *næfre* 'never', *nænig* 'not any', etc. The loss of initial [w] shows that synchronically for some items this involves the specification of a negative form, rather than a cliticization, as does its relevance to word formation in *nytenness* 'ignorance' with the backformation *nyten*. The verbs involved are either preterite-present or members of a potential auxiliary group, though not all preterite-presents that might be thought syntactically and phonologically possible occur, for *unnan* 'grant' lacks such forms. So too does *weorðan* 'become', although it occurs in impersonal constructions. Thus it does not seem that there is a unitary generalization here. But among verbs the property of possessing negative forms overlaps substantially with a potential auxiliary group, and may have helped contribute to its definition.

6.5.2 Occurrence with DO

Examples of pro-verbal DO with a 'modal' or with perfect HAVE as antecedent do not seem to have been reported for Old or Middle English (I am not convinced by the example in V§187). There are examples with antecedent BE, but these are uncommon, and even slightly dubious (V§§187, 188). Perhaps this parallels the modern situation, where such examples sometimes occur in text, though ungrammatical in Standard English. For an example with antecedent possessive HAVE in Middle English see V§1476. If pro-verbal DO avoided (or virtually avoided) members of the 'auxiliary group' as antecedent in Old and Middle English, this might look like a further formal criterion for such a group. But it is in fact open to a largely pragmatic account, since the verbs involved were themselves available in elliptical constructions. Thus the occurrence of DO would have stood in opposition to a repetition of the 'auxiliary' verb. Since these verbs are common in ellipsis in early English, we may be confident that this opposition was a real one. So if DO was available with such an antecedent, the choice of DO might have led to a preference for some other antecedent: an infinitive or participle associated with the 'auxiliary', or (particularly in the case of BE + PRED) some other verb in context. This may clearly be the pragmatic basis for the origin of the grammatical distinction.

Unfortunately its plausibility (together with some uncertainties about the data) makes it difficult to say when the distinction became grammatical, and this subverts a possible line of argument for the formal distinctness of an auxiliary group in early English (despite Plank 1984: 319, Kroch 1989b: 218).

It is not clear that the apparent absence of periphrastic DO with BE and HAVE in Middle English is significant. Before 1475 this DO is uncommon (Ellegård 1953), and it tends to prefer to occur with verbs of activity, achievement or accomplishment (Denison 1985a). These factors may be thought to provide a sufficient account, though periphrastic DO may have shown such a grammatical restriction early, perhaps adopting it from pro-verbal DO.[29]

6.6 Conclusion

It is clear that in addition to the properties discussed in the preceding chapter there are several further properties of verbs which show a high degree of mutual predictiveness and which are characteristic of the subset of 'group A' verbs. They imply both distinctness from the general class of verbs and potential identification as a subgroup. To the properties (a)–(b) we may therefore add (c)–(g).

(5)
a. Occurrence before contexts of ellipsis.
a′. Occurrence in pseudogapping contexts.
b. Transparency to impersonal constructions.
c. Subcategorization for the plain infinitive, not for the *to*-infinitive.
d. Preterite-present morphology.
e. Restriction of some verbs to finite forms.
f. Use of past-tense forms without past time reference, outside a motivating context.
g. The availability of negative forms in *n*- in Old and some Middle English.

The high degree of mutual predictiveness of these properties, which is set out in Table 6.4 for (a)–(f), is very striking, particularly for (a/a′), (c) and (d). Note too that the properties of Table 6.4 are drawn from several domains (or subdomains) of linguistic analysis; that some of them are formal, or partly so, that is, they encode abstract grammatical properties; and that from a synchronic perspective their constellation is apparently arbitrary. These facts imply that their correlation is highly significant for the establishment of word-class (or subclass) status.

It is 'group A' verbs which are identified by (c)–(f), not BE, HAVE, or other verbs which allow ellipsis or are transparent to impersonals. But some properties are shared: BE has some forms with preterite-present morphology (c), or

Table 6.4 *Properties of verbs in Old and Middle English*

Occurrence of verbs	In ellipsis	'Intervening' in impersonal constructions	Synchronic pret.-pres.	Complement inf. only plain	Fin. only	Opaque pret.
CAN	(OE)(ME)		+	+		?ME
DARE	OE, ME		+	+		?ME
MAY	OE, (ME)	OE, ME	+	+		ME
MOT	OE, ME	(OE)(ME)	+	+	OE, ME	ME
ME *mun* (not in OE)	ME	(ME)	+	+		
OWE	ME	ME!	+/–	–		ME
SHALL	OE, ME	OE, ME	+	+	OE, ME	OE, ME
ÞARF	(OE), ME	OE, ME!	+	+		
uton (not late ME)	(?)OE		+	+	OE, eME	
WILL	OE, ME	OE, ME	(OE), ME	(+)		ME
BE	OE, ME	OE, eME	partly	–		
weorðan (not lME)		OE, eME	–			
on-/aginnan, ME *ginnen*	*	OE, ME	–	–		
ME *biginnen*	*	?ME	–	–		
perfect HAVE	ME	ME	–			
pro-verbal DO	OE, ME		–			
periphrastic DO			–	?+		
other verbs	?–	?	+/– F	+/– N		

F = few and declining.
N = limited and poorly supported with 'shared subject'.
OE, ME = property attested at the period in question.
(OE) (ME) = instances which might be intransitive in the case of potential ellipsis, less central or clear instances in the case of impersonals, preterite-present morphology.
ME! neutralized with use as impersonal verb in ME.
* neutralized with use as intransitive verb.

with initial negative *n-* (g); periphrastic DO probably takes only the plain infinitive; and several verbs have additional subcategorizations (and senses) which seem to align them with the more general class of verbs. So if this is a significant grouping it is one focussed on (some of) the verbs of group A, but it is not clear where we could put a boundary without an *ad hoc* treatment of criteria. The grouping does indeed seem to be fuzzy. But the notion of a grouping here is impressively well defended for core instances.

In order to interpret the significance of this I return to the discussion of Chapter 4. There I noted that in more general work on categorization (e.g. by Rosch and her associates on cognitive categorization) in which classes are defined in terms of clusters of associated properties which oppose one another, classes do not have clear-cut boundaries, and are not homogeneous in the sense that members all share the same set of properties. Moreover, at subordinate levels of classification (and I shall argue later that it is indeed such a level which is involved here) classes are relatively less clearly defined. They also have fewer distinctive properties, and share more properties with the subclasses they oppose, just as verbs of group A share word-order properties, agreement and some subcategorizations with other verbs. The fuzzy grouping just described looks very much like what one would expect of a subordinate level of classification on Rosch's account. The intersection of a series of sets (defined in the first instance most plausibly by the properties (a)–(d) and (f) above, perhaps also by opacity of tense and mood in the finite) defines the core of a subclass whose boundaries and precise membership are poorly defined because that is the nature of subclasses, but in which some of the verbs of group A are presumably prototypical. So despite the fact that each of the criteria above defines a different group of verbs (or uses of verbs), it seems clear that there is a clustering even in Old English which would be a candidate for a weakly defined subordinate-level category. Moreover, some of the criteria involve formal properties, and there is a correlation between criteria from different linguistic levels. Both of these points are particularly characteristic of word classes. There is one further general point which argues for the reality of the grouping discussed here: it is a grouping which becomes less fuzzy as Middle English progresses. There are changes (like the loss of *uton* or development of *shulleþ*) which do not reduce the fuzziness of definition of this group. But the general trend is particularly for preterite-present morphology and subcategorization for the plain infinitive to become better criteria for 'group A' verbs, and for the group as a whole to become better defined.

It is clear, then, in answer to the first two questions put in Chapter 4, that there is a range of properties from different linguistic levels which have a high level of mutual predictiveness, and which are focussed on the verbs of group A. The range of apparently unconnected properties, including formal ones, speaks for the linguistic reality of this grouping, at some level even in Old English. Moreover there is some evidence for a degree of group identity even before this. But to follow the logic of the line of argument laid out in Chapter 4, I need now to turn to the question of the notional characteristics of this group to see whether its identity as a group is linguistically plausible and whether it can be cross-linguistically identified. I take the question to be centred in that of the semantics of its prototypical members. Accordingly the next chapter is devoted to discussing the historical semantics of 'group A' verbs.

7 *The developing modal semantics of early English 'modals'*

7.1 Introduction

Formal criteria are primary to the establishment of word classes, but such classes typically have a notional core. Moreover, the diachronic relationship between formal and semantic characteristics needs investigation, particularly in the light of Brinton's recent claim that in a closely related area semantic change precedes syntactic change and that it is abrupt (1988: 161f.). So in this chapter I turn to two topics central to the history of modals: the development of recognizably 'modal' uses within a small group of verbs, the ancestors of today's group of modals, and the growing semantic coherency and isolation of that group.

The existence and status of distinctively modal uses in Old English especially needs clarification. BT gives headings which correspond to some of the distinctive areas of present-day modality in Old English, but on the whole cites less than fully convincing examples in support (see Goossens 1982 for discussion: I am rather more sceptical than he is about some of these instances). The most important semantic account for Old English is Standop (1957). He identifies the central members of the group as *modalen Hilfsverben*, and isolates the parameters which structure their semantic space. But he is concerned to classify the majority of uses within a historically oriented framework of sense development. Thus the synchronic significance of potentially modal uses is never focussed on as a distinct topic. On the other hand, Traugott's (1972) discussion of the sense changes undergone by these verbs from Old English is focussed on the development of grammaticalized realizations of performatives. More recently there has been some discussion of the status particularly of epistemic modality and the lack of subject selection in Old English (Goossens 1987, Kytö 1987, Traugott 1989, Denison 1990b), and of the development of epistemic modality (Traugott 1989). Here I want to discuss the potentially modal semantics of these verbs in Old English and later periods as a more general topic, focussing on the two most distinctive parameters suggested in Chapter 1 for the semantics of modality in Present-day English.

The chapter will begin by recapping these parameters (see §1.4 for a brief outline of the semantics of the area). Then earlier English will be examined for uses which show signs of these, and related, properties. Here, of course, I depend substantially on previous writers. But considerable use has also been made of the Toronto concordance of Old English (Venezky and Healey 1980). There are, however, limitations on what is attempted here. A fully adequate assessment would require a detailed survey (as begun in Kytö 1987). The citation of particular uses carries its own dangers of misinterpretation and lack of balance. The reader must remember in particular that 'modal' uses need not reflect a predominantly 'modal' semantics in earlier English, although the written record is probably poorer in such distinctive uses than the spoken language. A more rounded (but still incomplete) view will also be possible with the completion of the Toronto dictionary of Old English. I am not, then, presenting a complete account, but am attempting to review what is established, and to make some further headway in this important area.

7.1.1 Parameters of modality in the present-day modals

In Chapter 1 epistemic, dynamic and deontic modality were distinguished. Epistemic modality involves the status of the truth of a proposition. 'Root' modality is subdivided into the deontic modality of permission and obligation, and the dynamic modality which involves possibility and necessity within a circumstantial frame of reference. In this chapter some discussion of futurity and hypothetical uses will also be necessary, but these topics will be dealt with as they arise.

The most important general semantic characteristics identified in Chapter 1 as identifying prototypical modals are the following.

(i) The fact that modals typically qualify the event or proposition as a whole, and do not generally select their subjects.

(ii) Subjectivity: a striking characteristic of modals which distinguishes them sharply from (indicative) verbs as a group is their typical use in utterances which give expression to a speaker's judgements and will.

(iii) A further possible candidate is the interlinked system of semantic notions central to modals: necessity, probability, possibility; obligation and permission; futurity, volition and intention.

The dimension of subjectivity is important for epistemic and deontic modality. It is dynamic uses that may be 'subject oriented' (to use Palmer's term, 1979, 1988) in that they involve their subject's ability, willingness, etc., and contract a selectional relationship with their subject. These uses are those most like nonauxiliary verbs. Indeed they are not categorized as modal by all linguists. Most centrally modal are the subjective epistemic and subjective deontic areas which lack subject-selecting instances.

7.2 Verbs of group A and typically modal meanings in Old English

The coherency of verbs of group A has been discussed in the course of the last three chapters *à propos* of their formal properties. This chapter will be focussed on potentially 'modal' uses of verbs in this group when in construction with the infinitive. But remember that such uses for the most part occur alongside uses with clearly 'nonmodal' semantics, as well as in 'nonmodal' constructions (see §4.3). Two further points about the broader group of preterite-present verbs are worth making. The first is that they have a semantic coherency, being predominantly (though not entirely) stative. The second is that there is an important subgroup of verbs of knowing, in *witan* 'know' and *cann* (note also *gemunan* 'remember') where *witan* is the general Old English equivalent for PE *know*. Thus the semantics of the preterite-present group is by no means solely focussed on an area related to present-day modality (see esp. Tellier 1962). Finally, dynamic and deontic necessity and a future of appointment or arrangement can also be expressed by BE with a *to*-infinitive from Old English, and HAVE later developed a construction with the infinitive in which it denoted dynamic and deontic necessity. But I will not be discussing these constructions in this chapter.

7.2.1 Problems of evidence

An important further caveat concerns the difficulties of making the relevant assessments for a dead language. Here I shall principally be discussing evidence for uses of verbs as sentence modifiers which do not select their surface subject and as subjectives (both deontic and epistemic), since these are the major semantic properties which distinguish modals from verbs in today's English. We can feel most confident when we have evidence both from distribution and from translation. An argument for the absence of subject selection is supported not just by translation but also by distributional evidence, since these verbs may occur with impersonal constructions. But where translation, that is, our own interpretations of contextualized written utterances, is the sole basis of our evidence it is harder to be confident, because of the presence of contextual effects and the potential interplay of semantic and pragmatic factors. It may be impossible to make a sensible assessment as to whether we have an instance of a particular category or whether contextual effects lead to a result which looks to us indistinguishable from an instance of that particular category. This may affect assessments of type of modality and of subjectivity. Thus today it is often polite to issue directives indirectly, or to understate opinions, and the virtual irretrievability of such factors may lead us to misinterpret the Old English data. Consider, for example, Standop's discussion of the refrain in *Deor* (Standop 1957: 22):

(1) Þæs ofereode, þisses swa mæg!
'That passed away, so may this!' (*ofereode* impersonal with genitive *þæs, þisses*)
Deor (ASPR III, 178–9) 7, etc.

He notes the possibility of taking *mæg* as an epistemic, and considers the suggestion that it is an understatement for 'will'. But this surely raises the possibility of a basically dynamic semantics, since to say that it is possible for an event to occur may in context make the point that it will occur. Thus this particular example is not necessarily good evidence for an epistemic sense for *mæg*. Moreover there is a good deal of indeterminacy of meaning in today's English (Coates 1983). This is a worse problem for earlier English, where apparently plausible examples can often be referred to other senses of the words in question. Epistemic modality involves the further difficulty that the major classes of instances are future or future related in sense in Old English, and there is disagreement over the epistemic status of such cases in Present-day English. I have tried to be sensitive to alternative possibilities of interpretation within the linguistic context, but there is bound to be a measure of disagreement between individuals, and my citations should be interpreted as 'likely, rather than certain, examples', to borrow Traugott's cautious phrasing (1972: 68). Finally, in making an assessment, it is worth bearing in mind that today formal and written language contains a much lower proportion of epistemic instances than does informal conversation (Coates 1983: 247 and *passim*). The same must be true for subjective deontics for most classes of writing. Standop gives some evidence which implies that his *modalen Hilfsverben* were considerably more frequent in spoken than in written Old English (1957: 170), and it would be reasonable to suppose that subjective modality was commoner in spoken Old and Middle English than in our written record.

7.2.2 Necessity and obligation

In this field the relevant verbs in Old English are *sceal* (later SHALL), *þarf* and *mot* (later MUST). *Sceal* initially meant 'owe', a sense which appears until late

Middle English. From it had developed senses of obligation or constraint of various kinds, both dynamic and deontic. *Þarf* is glossed 'need to' in BT. It is centrally dynamic, but also expresses deontic modality. *Mot* most often expresses permission and possibility, but it is also used for dynamic and deontic necessity. This only becomes common in late Old English; indeed it has been claimed that this sense only develops round about the year one thousand (Solo 1977). But it develops rapidly, and is the predominant sense by the mid thirteenth century (Ono 1958: 67, Tellier 1962). The change may have taken place because *mot* had a historically basic sense 'to be allotted' which tolerated both developments (Standop 1957), or because of a sense change originating in negative (and other) contexts where the distinction was neutralized ('not possible' = 'necessary not', see *OED Mote*, *v.*[1]). Many instances in Old English texts occur in such neutralized contexts and this implies that the distinction drawn here between major sense branches may be an artificial one.

7.2.2.1 Lack of subject selection

Sceal, *þarf* and perhaps *mot* resemble modern modals in that each may appear in sentences where there is no selection of its subject. Evidence for this is necessarily indirect, but it seems to be the most reasonable interpretation of occurrence in impersonals, like those of Chapter 5; see Denison (1990b) for some discussion. This is supported by the occurrence of passives like those below, in which it seems unlikely that the subject is selected (though in some passives it may be). If the notion of 'being allotted, meted out' is still associated with *mot* as Standop (1957) suggests, there may be selection of the subject in (4), though the fact that *mot* is elsewhere attested with an impersonal implies that it may be a sentence modifier. It is worth noting that the existence of examples like (2.c) (and (4.a)) suggests that *sceal* (and *mot*) could be sentence modifiers in Old English even when deontic, like their present-day counterparts, despite the obvious temptation to take a subject noun phrase as itself an argument of the verb.

(2) *Sceal* with impersonals and passives

a. Hwy ne sceolde me swa þyncan?
'Why should it not seem so to me [lit.: not should to-me so seem]?'
Bo 38.119.9

b. Se mægðhad sceal beon mid ðæs modes godnysse Criste sylfum geoffrod
'(The) virginity ought to-be offered to Christ himself with holiness of spirit [lit.: with the mind's goodness (to) Christ himself offered]'
ÆAdmon 1 7.21

c. getacnod wæs, hwær gesette beon sceoldon þa lichaman haligra fæmnena.

'(it) was shown where the bodies of holy virgins should be buried [lit.: where buried be should, etc.].'
Bede 18.16

(3) *Þarf* with impersonals and passives

a. Ne þearf þe þæs eaforan sceomigan
'You will not need to be ashamed of this son [lit.: not need to-you (of) the son to-be-ashamed]'
Genesis (ASPR I, 1–87) 2329

b. ac witodlice þæt gesegen beon mæg, ne þearf þæt beon gelyfed
'but indeed what can be seen [lit.: seen be can], does not need [lit.: not needs that] to-be believed'
GD 269.15

(4) *Mot* with passives (no impersonals have been noted with this sense)

a. manna gehwylc, ... mot he beon ærost ðinga gemynegad & gewisod þæt he cunne hu he of hæþendome mæge to cristendome ... cuman.
'each man [lit.: of-men each] ... must (he) be above all things [lit.: first of-things] warned and instructed so-that he should-know how he may come from heathendom to christendom [lit.: from heathendom may to christendom come].'
WHom 8c.8.

b. swa þa lærendum þam preostum se papa geþafode, þæt Equitius moste [*vr* sceolde] beon gelæded to Romebyrig
... ut ad Romanam urbem deduci debuisset
'so then to those priestly advisors [lit.: (to) advising those priests] the pope granted that Equitius should (??might) be brought to Rome'
GD 35.19

7.2.2.2 Subjectivity

The possibility of subjective deontics or epistemic modalities is harder to discuss. There do, however, seem to be examples which show the imposition of the speaker's will. Examples are clearest with *sceal*: see *OED Shall*, 5.a. 'In the second person, equivalent to an imperative'; *OED* 6 'expressing the speaker's determination to bring about ... some action, event or state'; Standop's dubbing *ðu scealt* ('thou shalt') a usage similar to the imperative (1957: 94); and BT *sculan* II.(4); (but *OED* 5.a notes 'Chiefly in Biblical language... rendering the jussive future of ... the Vulgate', and this distribution is perhaps consistent with a lower degree of speaker involvement). Mitchell (§918) notes that *þearf* too may 'serve to express commands or wishes', but examples seem less direct. He does not note instances with *mot*, and Visser (§1693) indirectly suggests that they are missing for Old English.

(5) Subjective deontic *sceal*

a. Hælend him þa ondswarede & cwæþ, 'Þu scealt fylgean me, & lætan þa deadan bergean heora deade.'
(How the Lord spake to Peter when he asked that he might go and bury his father.) 'The Saviour answered him [lit.: Saviour him then answered] and said, "Thou shalt follow me, and let the dead bury their dead." ' = Vulgate imperative in Matt 8.22. (Morris's translation).
BlHom 23.14

b. Wend þe from wynne! Þu scealt wæpnedmen
wesan on gewealde
(God's words to Eve at the expulsion from Paradise.) 'Turn (yourself) from joy! You shall be under man's control [lit.: to-man be in control]'
Genesis (ASPR I, 1–87) 919

Clear cases of epistemic modality which parallel today's sentence modifiers in evaluating past- or present-tense propositions do not seem to appear until Middle English. But *mot* and *sceal* both occur in examples which are open to interpretation in terms of the less clearly epistemic area of inevitable or expected futurity. In the examples of (6) it might be argued that *mot* simply shows a contextually dependent use of the sense 'be allotted'. But if subject selection may fail with *mot*, an interpretation as sentence modifier becomes available, and this is epistemic here. Thus in the first example, 'it is necessarily the case that we will die' is appropriate rather than, 'it will be necessary for us to die'. This cannot be a certain interpretation. But it is reasonable, and it is easy to believe that these instances contain a subjective element.

(6) Future epistemic *mot*

a. Ealle we moton sweltan.
Omnes moriemur.
'We will all necessarily die [lit.: all we must die].'
(The Egyptians force the Jews to leave Egypt, saying: if you Jews do not leave Egypt, we Egyptians will all necessarily die; but see comment on (6.b).)
The Old English Version of the Heptateuch (ed. S. J. Crawford, EETS 160) Exodus 12.33

b Dryhten hæl us we moton forweorðan.
Domine, salva nos, perimus.
(The disciples wake Christ during the storm, saying) 'Lord, save us: we must perish', or possibly 'we might perish', following Solo 1977: 228–9, but again corresponding to modern epistemic modality.)
The West-Saxon Gospels (ed. M. Grünberg, Amsterdam, Scheltema and Holkema, 1967) Matthew 8.25

In the case of *sceal,* BT and BTS give a sense 'must, shall' 'because a conclusion is inevitable' without, however, citing any fully convincing examples.[1] The two best candidates I have come across are given below. The first is from

OED (*Shall*, 3) the other from a scanning of the Ælfredian Boethius in the microfiche concordance. Each of these occurs in a context of logical argument, and would be well rendered by a modern epistemic. In the first, (7.a), the conclusion is supported by logical inference. In (7.b) it is a truth which has been previously established and the context is one of rational discourse, not teaching by authority. It is however notable that the Old English Boethius does not use *sceal* as an epistemic with the abstract proposition under consideration (as *must* is used in *unity and goodness must be one thing*) although Chaucer used MOT in just this sense in his translation of Boethius. Granted this, it seems safest to suggest that these examples (and similar instances elsewhere) are of rather indeterminate status between epistemic and dynamic, perhaps best interpreted as related to the inevitable future, which will be discussed below.

(7) Future epistemic *sceal*

a. gif þu þonne gelefst þæt hit swa sie on Gode, þonne scealt þu nede gelefan þæt sum anwald sie mara þonne his
'if you then believe that God is such [lit.: that it thus is (subjunctive) in God], then must you necessarily believe that some power is greater than his'
Bo 34.84.24

b. Đa cwæð he: þu scealt þeah gelyfan ðæt sio annes & sio godnes an þing sie. Đa cwæð ic: Ne mæg ic þæs oðsacan.
'Then said he: "You must however believe that (the) unity and (the) goodness is [= *sie*, subjunctive] one thing." Then said I: "I cannot deny [*oðsacan*] that."'
Bo 34.90.20

7.2.3 Possibility and permission

In this field the relevant verbs in Old English are *mot* (later MUST) and *mæg* (later MAY). *Mot* 'be allowed, may' (BT *motan* I) 'expressing permission or possibility that comes from permission' (BTS) is centrally deontic. But there are many examples which seem to combine a notion of objective possibility with the sense that it is allotted by fate or deity. This is often difficult to distinguish from the fully neutral dynamic possibility into which it shades, though Standop concluded that the distinction was indeed systematically present and that *mot* was never a simple equivalent to *mæg* (1957: esp. 72–3). *Mæg* with the historically primary sense 'be strong or able, have power' is often subject-oriented, and Traugott (1972: 72) notes that 'be able' is its most important sense in Old English. But like modern *can* it is also available as a neutral dynamic of objective possibility (*OED May*, *v.*[1] 3, BT *magan* III) and as a deontic (*OED* 4, BT IV).

7.2.3.1 Lack of subject selection

The occurrence of impersonals and passives with *mæg* and *mot* leads to the reasonable interpretation that they did not always select their subjects, and that they may be sentence modifiers even when deontic.

(8) *Mæg* with impersonals and passives

a. Mæg þæs þonne ofþyncan ðeodne Heaðobeardna
'That may then [lit.: may of-that then] displease (the) prince (dat.) (of the) Heathobards'
Beowulf (ASPR IV, 3–98) 2032

b. be þam mæg þæt apostolice word cweden beon
de quibus apostolicum illum licet proferre sermonem
'concerning whom may the apostolic word be repeated [lit.: said be]'
Bede 472.10

(9) *Mot* with impersonals and passives

a. Me mæig ... gif hit mot gewiderian, mederan settan, linsed sawan.
'One can ... if it may be-fair-weather, plant madder, sow linseed.'
LawGer 12

b. þa ongunnon þa broðor þæs mynstres ... geornlice biddan, þætte mid him þa halgan reliquias ... gehealdne beon moston.
'then proceeded the brethren (of) the monastery ... earnestly to-beg that with them the holy relics ... might be preserved [lit.: preserved be might].'
Bede 182.31

7.2.3.2 Subjectivity

Both *mot* and *mæg* occur in instances which show evidence of subjective deontic modality in that an interlocutor is the authority granting permission. *Mot* is also common after verbs of granting whose subject is the source of permission (see M§1995, Tellier 1962: 86) and it occurs after verbs of asking whose indirect object is the source of authority (see Standop's examples in 1957: 84–6). In discussing MAY Traugott (1972: 118) notes that 'the full performative use of *may*, as in *You may go* "I permit you to go", did not gain wide currency until the sixteenth century'. But there are some apparent examples in Middle English (as we shall see below), and Venezky and Healey (1980) yielded several Old English cases where permission is apparently conferred or withheld, and which look like early instances of this category. Note the occurrence of imperatives in context in (10) and (11.a).

(10) Subjective deontic *mot*[2]

a. God ... him to cwæð, 'Ealra þæra þinga þe on neorxnawange syndon þu most brucan ... buton anum treowe ... ne hrepa þu þæs treowes wæstm
'God ... (brought Adam into Paradise and) ... said unto him [lit.: him to said], '(Of) all the things which are in Paradise [lit.: in Paradise are] thou

mayest eat, ... save one tree ... touch thou not the fruit of this tree [lit.: not touch (imperative) thou that tree's fruit]' (Thorpe's translation)
ÆCHom i.12.34
Cf. Ex omni ligno paradisi comede, de ligno autem scientiae boni et mali ne comedas, ... Genesis 2.16–17.

b. Ða clipode se Wisdom & cwæþ: Mot ic nu cunnian hwon þinre fæstrædnesse, ...? Ða andwyrde þæt Mod & cwæð: Cunna swa þu wille.
'Then spoke Wisdom [lit.: the Wisdom] and said, "May I now enquire somewhat (into) your fixedness-of-mind, ...?" Then answered the Mind and said, "Enquire as you wish." '
Bo 5.12.12

c. Ða cwæð placidas, Drihten leof mot ic þis cyðan minum wife, and minum cildum, þæt hi gelyfan on þe? Þa cwæð drihten to him, far nu, and sege hiom þæt hi fulwiht onfon
'Then said Placidas, "Dear Lord [lit.: lord dear] may I make this known (to) my wife and (to) my children, that they may believe on Thee?" Then said the-Lord to him: "Go now and bid them receive baptism [lit.: that they baptism should-receive]' (Skeat's translation)
ÆLS ii.30.70

(11) Subjective deontic *mæg* [3]

a. Ah ic þe hate þurh þa hehstan miht
þæt ðu hellwarum hyht ne abeode,
ah þu him secgan miht sorga mæste,
þæt ðu gemettes meotod alwihta
(God speaks to Satan, banishing him to hell. Imperatives precede and follow this passage.)
'But I order you through the highest power that you do not announce hope to the inhabitants of hell [lit.: to-inhabitants-of-hell hope not announce], but you may tell them the greatest of sorrows [lit.: to-them say may of-sorrows greatest], that you met (the) Lord of-creation'
Christ and Satan (ASPR I, 135ff.) 693

b. Cwædon him to: Gif þu ne wilt us geðafian in swa æðelicum þinge, þe we biddað, ne meaht þu in usse mægðe ne ussum gemanan wunian. & dreofon hine onweg, & heton þæt he ... gewite.
.. aiebant: 'Si non uis adsentire nobis in tam facili causa, quam petimus, non poteris iam in nostra prouincia demorari'. Et expulerunt eum, ac de suo regno cum suis abire iusserunt.
'(The kings of the East Saxons) said to him: "If you will not consent to-us in so easy (a) matter, as we request, you may not remain in our province or our society [*wunian* = remain]", and (they) drove him away, and ordered that he ... should-depart.'
Bede 112.22

Denison (1990b: 153) gives some possible examples of epistemic uses of possibility–permission *mot* in Old English; the best is (9.a) above. *OED* does not give epistemic senses for MAY until Middle English, and although BTS provides the category 'expressing the admissibility or certainty of a supposition' (BTS *magan* IIIi(2)) none of the instances cited is clearly epistemic. Standop (1957: 22f.) pointed out the difficulty of discriminating epistemic instances from uses of the present tense to refer to the future, but had no doubt that there was at least one straightforward epistemic in Old English, the first cited below, and he also cites transitional instances (p. 21). Goossens (1982: 78) refers to the use of *eaþe mæg* to render Latin *forte, forsitan* in glosses and suggests that elements of epistemic meaning are involved in some other instances cited elsewhere in BT. Since *eaþe* 'easily, possibly, perhaps' is found with *mæg* in subject-oriented as well as in neutral dynamic senses *eaþe* cannot be the sole carrier of epistemic meaning here, and I suggest that the examples (taken from *eaþe* in the Toronto microfiche) given below in addition to Standop's support the position that *mæg* could be used in epistemic contexts, even if this did not form an important part of its meaning and was partly restricted to contexts which neutralized the epistemic–dynamic distinction.[4] I have not cited the commoner but less satisfactory generalizing and future referring examples, but *mæg* is also compatible with such neutralized contexts.

(12) Epistemic *mæg*

a. and hi ða ealle sæton, swa swa mihte beon fif þusend wera
(Part of the narrative of the feeding of the 5,000 with loaves and fishes)
'And they then all sat, so that (there) might-have been five thousand (of) men'
ÆCHom i.182.16
Cf. John 6.10: numero quasi quinque millia

b. Swa hit eaþe beon mæg þæt se halga heahengel of heofenum cumen wære, & wære gemyndig manna tyddernesse, þæt he hine geeaðmedde þæt he hie mid his sylfes handum gesette & geworhte
'So it easily may be that the holy archangel came from heaven [lit.: from heavens come was (subjunctive)], and was mindful (of) men's infirmity, so-that he deigned [lit.: himself humbled] that he established and made it [= the cave which forms St Michael's church] with his own hands [lit.: he it with his own hands established and built]'
BlHom 197.10.

c. Eaðe mæg gewurðan þæt þu wite þæt ic nat, ðu þe þar andweard wære.
Potest enim fieri ut quod ego minus novi, tu intelligas qui praesens affuisti.
(The king gives Apollonius a letter to read in the hope that he will be able to explain what it means, and says:) '(It) easily may be that you know what I do-not-know, you who were present there [lit.: there present were].'
The Old English 'Apollonius of Tyre' (ed. P. Goolden, Oxford University Press, 1958) 21.10

7.2.4 Reference to the future

The simple present (better, 'nonpast') tense is the normal verb form found with future reference in Old English. But both *wile* (later WILL) and *sceal* (later SHALL) also occur in contexts of future reference. Futurity is difficult to isolate from volition and obligation, and there has been disagreement as to when (or indeed whether) these two words became markers of the future, discussion not aided, as Visser (§1483, n. 1) remarks, by the lack of clear or defined notions in this area. *OED*'s assessment is that already in Old English WILL 'was not unfrequently used as a future auxiliary, sometimes retaining no trace of its original sense' but that SHALL retained some tinge of obligation or necessity until Middle English, although it was plainly used for a prophetic future or future of appointment (*OED Shall*, 8). But *OED*'s examples for WILL are not beyond doubt; contrast Storms' statement that he has not found 'unquestionable instances of the pure future tense use of *will*' until after 1300 (1961: 304–5) with Visser's claim that there is 'incontestable proof' for such a usage in Old English (V§1581, and see Wekker 1976: 24ff. for further references). Standop (1957) and Mitchell (1985) are both cautious. Standop interprets both *sceal* and *wile* as available for marking future time reference, but only secondarily and contextually. Mitchell (1985 §1023) suggests 'that **sculan* and *willan* at times come pretty close to expressing futurity with no undertone of compulsion or volition'.

The central senses basic to *wile* are 'to will, intend, wish, be willing' (cp. BT *willan*), and they may occur with an infinitive, as here, as well as with noun phrases and *þæt*-clauses as illustrated in §4.3.

(13) Hwilcne hafoc wilt þu habban, þone maran hwæþer þe þæne læssan?
'Which hawk do you want to have, the larger or the smaller?'
ÆColl 134

An extension of such senses to a characteristic predisposition or property of the subject (which may be inanimate or even abstract) also appears, as in (14); see *OED Will*, *v.*[1] 8 'habitually does; sometimes connoting "may be expected to"'.[5]

(14) elpendes hyd wile drincan wætan, gelice an [MS &] spynge deð
'elephant's hide will absorb liquid, like a sponge does'
Or 230.26

But *wile* also seems to occur in sentences which involve a 'simple' or 'pure' future, and in sentences of future prediction where there is no question of the subject's volition or internal properties being relevant. The best evidence for this (as with other verbs in the group) is occurrence in impersonals (like (15.a,

b) below) and passives (c) and (h), but *wile* also appears with nonvolitional subject and stative verb as in (d) and (e). See Denison (1990b: 151–2), who cites further impersonal examples to illustrate the futurity of *wile*.

(15) Future *wile*

a. ic wat, þæt hine wile tweogan, hwæðer heo him soð secge.
'I know, that he [lit.: him (accusative)] will doubt, whether she tells him the truth [lit.: she him truth tell (subjunctive)].'
Wulfstan: Sammlung der ihm zugeschriebenen Homilien (ed. A. Napier, Berlin, 1883; repr. Dublin and Zurich, Wiedmann and Max Niehans, 1967) 3.7

b. Sumum menn wile þincan syllic þis to gehyrenne, forþan þe ylpas ne comon næfre on engla lande.
'(To) some man (it) will seem wonderful to hear this [about the martial use of elephants] because elephants (have) never come within England.' (Here the position of *þis* makes it an unlikely subject.)
ÆLS ii.25.564

c. Gif me seo godcunde geofu in ðære stowe forgifen beon wile, þæt ic lifgan mote be minum hondgewinne, ic ðær lustlice wunige.
'If the divine grace that I may live by the labour of my hands will be vouchsafed to me in that place, I will live there cheerfully [lit.: If to-me the divine grace in that place vouchsafed be will, that I live may by my hand-work, I there cheerfully will-live].'
Bede 366.5

d. Ic wat soþlice hwæt þeos axung bion wile. ymbe þas halgan rode þe ure yldran þone nazareniscan hælend on ahengon.
'I know indeed what this question will be: [it will be] about this holy cross that our ancestors hung the Nazarene saviour on [lit.: the Nazarene saviour on hung].'
Legends of the Holy Rood (ed. R. Morris, EETS 46) 9.5

e. Gif we deoplicor ymbe þis sprecað, þonne wene we þæt hit wile ðincan ðam ungelæredum to manigfeald.
'If we speak more deeply about this [lit.: more-deeply about this speak], then we think that it will seem too complex to the unlearned [lit.: (to) the unlearned too complex].'
ÆCHom ii.582.25.

f. Wucan & monðas sind mannum cuðe æfter heora andgite, & ðeah ðe we hi æfter boclicum andgite awriton, hit wile ðincan ungelæredum mannum to deoplic & ungewunelic; ...
(After naming and glossing the seven hours of the night.) 'Weeks and months are clear to men [lit.: to-men clear] from their (native) understanding, and even if we (do) describe them according to scholarly understanding [lit.: we them after scholarly understanding describe (= present subjunctive)], it will seem to unlearned men too profound and unwonted.'
ÆTemp 3.26

g. Se untruma eac wacode oðþæt hit wolde dagian.

'The sick-man also stayed-awake until it was-about to-dawn.'
ÆLS i.21.123

h. Gif ge nu gesawan hwelce mus þæt wære hlaford ofer oðre mys, & sette him domas, ... hu wunderlic wolde eow ðæt þincan. ... & mid hwelce hleahtre ge woldon bion astered.
'If you now saw some mouse that was lord over other mice, and set them judgements ... how wonderful would that seem to you [lit.: to-you that seem]; ... and with what laughter you would be moved!'
Bo 16.35.32

Here (c) is apparently a simple future, dependent on reference to the speaker's 'now', (g) is the past tense of the simple future. The example in (e) however is contingent on the condition expressed and belongs to *OED Will*, *v.*[1] 15 an 'auxiliary of future expressing a contingent event', which *OED* refers to Old English. This corresponds to Coates' (1983) epistemic category of 'prediction' for today's English; (a) and (b) may also belong here, as probably does (d), though this may be neutralized between 'prediction' and the simple future. Standop (1957: 139) deals with the instances of *OED* 15 as an extension of examples like (14) which express an attitude or characteristic property of their subject. But although the implied subject selection could hold for (e), it cannot for the impersonal (a) (see Warner 1990: 543 for the impersonal status of this example). This surely shows us that a predictive sense has indeed developed by Wulfstan's period, and this therefore seems to be the most reasonable way of construing such instances in Ælfric. 'Predictability' of a present or past event is, however, only dubiously found. Visser (§1587) cites a supposed Old English instance, but it is not easy to be sure of its interpretation. *OED Will*, *v.*[1] 15d only cites instances from the fifteenth century.

The preterite *wolde* of (15.h) occurs in an unreal condition corresponding to a present-tense real condition like that of (e); its conditionality may depend on the fact that it is the preterite and presumably subjunctive, though the form is not distinctive of mood. But this may have been reanalysed as a property of *wolde* as an item; *OED* 42, from which this example was taken, refers to *would* as a marker of conditionality, and this is Palmer's treatment of the corresponding modern type (1979: 138f.) which Coates classifies as an epistemic hypothetical (1983: 213ff.). But either way, WILL is epistemic. It is worth noting that *wolde* might as easily be the preterite of 'predictability' as of 'prediction' WILL to the modern reader. (See V§1610, M§3611 for further relevant Old English examples.)

Thus it seems clear that already in Old English *wile* could be used in sentences where it functioned as a sentence modifier, imposing no selection restrictions on its subject, and that it could have a very general sense: involving simple futurity, epistemic prediction and (in the preterite) epistemic hypotheticality (or the conditional).

Sceal with the infinitive need not select its subject, and evidence for the development of a future sense is less easy to interpret than with *wile*. But Old English uses *sceal* for a future of arrangement (*OED Shall*, 4 'Indicating what is appointed or settled to take place') and for an inevitable future (*OED* 8a 'announcing a future event as fated or divinely decreed'). Instances without subject selection may be found for both of these categories. A gloss including the words 'inevitably' or 'certainly' often seems appropriate, but whether such futurity is essentially epistemic or not is unclear.

(16) *Sceal* as inevitable future

a. him sceal sceamian ætforan gode ælmihtigum ... æt ðam micclan dome
'he [lit.: him (dative)] shall be-ashamed before God Almighty ... at the great judgement'
ÆLS i.12.169

b. we sceolon, wylle we nelle we, arisan on ende þyssere worulde mid flæsce ond mid bane
'we shall, whether we will or not [lit.: will we, not-will we], arise at (the) end (of) this world with flesh and with bone' (Thorpe's translation)
ÆCHom i.35.532.7

(17) *Sceal* as future of appointment
Eala þu eadige Maria, ... Adames gylt þurh þe sceal beon geþingod
'Oh thou blessed Mary' (... God hath appointed thee as a surety here in this world, and) 'Adam's guilt through thee is-to be interceded-for'
BlHom 9.6

There are, however, also examples which present the necessary consequences of preceding acts or states of affairs. These are presumably to be related to the inevitable future (though *OED* does not give such a subcategory of the future until early Middle English, see *Shall*, 8g) and seem potentially epistemic. They resemble, and may be associated with, the potentially future epistemic examples of (7) above.

(18) *Sceal*: possible 'future epistemics'

a. Niede sceal bion gebrocen ðæt mod ðara hieremonna, gif se lareow & se hierde agiemleasað ðæt he hiera utan ne helpe
'Necessarily shall be broken the spirit (of) the subjects, if the teacher and the shepherd neglects helping them in external things [lit.: that he of-them outwardly not help]'
CP 137.13

b. Swa swa seo beo sceal losian þonne heo hwæt irringa stingð, swa sceal ælc sawl forweorðan æfter þam unrihthæmede, buton se mon hweorfe to gode.

'As the bee shall perish when she stings anything angrily [lit.: anything angrily stings], so shall every soul perish after (the) unlawful-lust, unless the man turn to good.' (Fox's translation)
Bo 31.71.6

7.2.5 *Other categories*

Four other uses of these verbs are important to us here. The first is the occurrence of *sceolde* (the preterite of *sceal*) in indirect speech, whether or not in a subordinate clause, to show that the writer is not committed to the truth of the report (cf. German *sollen*; see *OED Shall*, 15; BT *sculan* II.(13); Standop 1957: 101f., M§§2037–8. The last two discuss the possible status of *sceal* here). This clearly encapsulates the writer's attitude to the proposition and is subjective epistemic, though it does not belong to the traditional area of modality (but see Palmer 1986: 51ff., 66ff.).

(19) a. & to þam Pentecosten wæs gesewen innan Barruc scire æt anan tune blod weallan of eorþan. swa swa mænige sædan þe hit geseon sceoldan.
'And at that Pentecost blood was seen to well from the earth at a village in Berkshire [lit.: was seen within Berkshire at a village blood to-well from earth], as many said who supposedly saw it [lit. who it see should].'
ChronE 235.15 (1100.6)

b. Þa sceolde þæs Iobes fæder bion eac god; þæs nama wæs Saturnus
'Then this Job's father was also alleged to be a god [lit.: should (of) that Job father be also (a) god]; his name was Saturn'
Bo 38.115.27

The second is the use of *mot* in clauses expressing a wish. This is common in Middle English (see *MED moten* v. (2) 9–12). The use is firmly assigned to late Old English by Standop (1957: 78f.), but perhaps Visser is right to show more caution, since there are few instances and at least some might be interpreted as volitional subjunctives of a full sense of *mot* (V§1692; see also Ono 1958: 73f., Behre 1934: 30f., 36). This use expresses the involvement of the speaker and is clearly subjective.

The third is *uton, wuton* 'let's'. This may occur with a subject *we* though it is more commonly absent. This restriction on the subject may imply selection and that *uton* is not a sentence modifier. It is however strongly subjective, encapsulating the writer's or speaker's attitude. Note that in view of the regularity of the primarily indicative termination *-on*, this aspect of *uton*'s meaning cannot be ascribed to its mood.

Fourthly, and finally, what of the use of these verbs as subjunctive equivalents? A much repeated view is that expressed by Mustanoja (1960: 453) 'the subjunctive mood begins to be indicated periphrastically by means of modal auxiliaries'. The equivalence implied here is, however, misleading. Rather, some of the particular functions discharged by the inflectional subjunctive begin to be discharged by modal verbs, without any simple replacement or equivalence. This complex series of developments is generally later than Old English, but we may point to two particular categories: (i) the possibility, discussed briefly above, that *wolde* functions as a conditional or hypothetical and (ii) the use of *mæg* as a subjunctive (and future) auxiliary in Northumbrian, and perhaps in particular constructions in other dialects.[6]

7.2.6 Conclusion

To what extent, then, did these verbs show uses in Old English which tended to separate them from prototypical verbs and to unite them as a distinct group? It is clear from the preceding discussion that these verbs in construction with the infinitive already showed distinctive properties which relate them to the modern modals. I will first summarize these properties, and then go on to suggest how we may assess their significance.

(i) With the apparent exception of *uton*, the Old English verbs discussed here may be 'sentence modifiers' in that there are instances with no relationship of selection between the verb and its subject, or its infinitive complement, both with epistemic and (apparently) with deontic modality. (For a discussion of this with root modality in general, see Denison 1990b.) The evidence for this is weakest for *mot*, where there is room for doubt, but its occurrence with impersonals ((9.a) above, Denison 1990b: 147) implies that it too may be a 'sentence modifier'. In Present-day English this property is found with such verbs as *seem*, *happen* and *begin*. But this is in general a Middle English development (though OE *onginnan* 'begin' clearly shows it; see the discussion of §5.2.3). Impersonals such as *sceamian* 'be ashamed' etc. are not relevant here, since although they lack subjects, they apparently select their arguments. Thus verbs of group A were rather sharply distinguished from prototypical verbs by this property. Its importance is interestingly shown by the occurrence of an instance where it is extended to DARE already in Old English, as in modern examples noted in §1.4.1 (Callaway 1913: 83, Denison 1990b: 160).

(20) be þam ne dorste us nan wen beon geðuht, þæt ...
de quibus nil coelestis gloriae praesumi posse videbatur
'concerning whom no expectation dared seem to us, that ... [lit.: not dared to-us no expectation be seemed, that ...]' (See M§1049–51 on *beon geþuht* 'to seem'. I have taken *nan wen* as subject, but this is not beyond doubt.)
GD 232.7

(ii) The sentence modifiers involved are broadly similar to those involved today: necessity and possibility, obligation and permission, futurity, prediction, hypotheticality, and report, to name the major ones discussed above. These are distant from the verbal prototype of event or action.

(iii) Subjective modalities occur, and subjectivity is not a property associated with prototypical verbs. Most striking is the *uton* of first-person imperatives. *Sceal* (of obligation) and *mot* (of permission), perhaps also *mæg* (of permission), give apparently clear evidence of subjective deontic modality, supported by the *mot* of wishes. The development of strong subjective epistemic modality is later, in line with Traugott's predictions that epistemic modalities develop after dynamic (deontic) modalities and that weak subjectivity precedes strong subjectivity (1989). But epistemic modality which is at least weakly subjective is apparently shown by prediction *wile*, by *sceolde* of report, less clearly by future-based senses of *mæg*, *mot*, perhaps *sceal* and hypothetical *wolde*. Present or past referring epistemics seem possible with *mæg*. Thus deontic *uton*, *mot* and perhaps *sceal* show strong subjectivity, and epistemics already show some weak subjectivity. Moreover, most clearly with deontics but also with some epistemics, there are examples where subjectivity is apparently independent (or relatively independent) of verbal context, and this is consistent with the interpretation of subjectivity as a lexical property of individual items (whether pragmatic or semantic).[7] The question of the extent to which subjectivity is a lexical property of modals is in general a difficult one (see the discussions of §§2.4, 7.2.1), and the argument for today's English was based on indirect evidence. But Old English *uton* is clearly subjective as an item, and this suggests that subjectivity may in fact be a lexical property of some of these words, most clearly the deontics, in Old English.

Finally, how can we assess the importance of the properties listed above? This difficult question will perhaps not permit a generally agreed answer. But there are some relevant considerations. Firstly, the verbs discussed here occur relatively commonly with the infinitive in Old English (though much less so than today), and for each of the verbs considered here the construction is considerably more frequent than its 'full verb' constructions (as is not the case for CAN; Kytö 1987: 210–11). Secondly, the evidence of impersonals (and passives) strongly implies that these verbs could be 'sentence modifiers'. But since traditional interpretations have tended to classify examples according to basic senses which tend to be subject-selecting, admitting that selection may fail widens the possibility for (and plausibility of) epistemic interpretations in particular, whose presence has perhaps been understressed in the past. Finally we must recognize that both subjective deontic and subjective epistemic modality, as well as the use of *wile* for futurity, will have been considerably more frequent in speech than in the surviving written record where examples especially of epistemic modality are uncommon (though Kytö 1987 found as much as 4 per cent epistemic *mæg* in Old English prose). Given these considerations, I suggest that these properties discussed above were indeed significant enough within Old English to form part of the characterization of a grouping of 'modals' (whose reality is supported by other evidence) although the semantic field is less focussed than today, and the correlation with morphological properties is weaker. Thus these properties not only tend to distinguish these verbs from other verbs; they also tend to unify them as a subordinate grouping.[8] The nature of this grouping will be discussed in the next chapter, but enough has already been said to justify the use of the pretheoretical term 'modal' for the relevant senses of these verbs in Old English, and I will henceforth refer to a 'modal group' of verbs in Old and Middle English.

7.3 The modal group and typically modal meanings in Middle English

The later semantic development of the modal group shows two features of particular interest to us. Firstly there is the further development of (or further evidence for) the expression of epistemic and subjective deontic modality, and of futurity and hypotheticalness. Secondly the group becomes more coherent semantically as semantic changes and lexical losses increase the correlation between modal uses and preterite-present morphology. Here I will briefly (and rather selectively) indicate the most important Middle English developments without attempting a complete picture, and without recapitulating elements which continue with little change from Old English.

7.3.1 Necessity and obligation

Here *mot* gives evidence of a fuller range of senses, both epistemic and subjective deontic. By the fourteenth century epistemic uses are well attested: there are a good many in Chaucer's translation of Boethius (mainly in collocation with *nedes* or a similar adverbial). The earliest examples I know are cited in *MED moten* v. (2) 4, but the first ((21.a) below) strikes me as less clearly epistemic in context than *MED* takes it to be. Deontic senses of necessity *mot* become more frequent in early Middle English, and examples which seem possibly subjective appear.

In the course of late Middle English *mot* is replaced by *must*, and *mot* hardly survives into the sixteenth century except in dialect or as a literary archaism (*OED Mote*, *v.*[1]). *Must* owes its origin to the remote or subjunctive preterite (OE *moste*) (*OED* and Ono 1958: 76ff.) and second person singular present indicative (OE *most*) of MOT, and is evidenced in a similar range of senses of necessity and obligation. There is also some evidence that *should* is found as an epistemic of necessity at the end of this period (V§1530). *Mun* and *ouen* both occur as deontics, and *mun* is found as a future epistemic. But I have not noted clearly subjective instances with *ouen*.

(21) Epistemic *mot*

a. He moste kunne muchel of art
Þat þu woldest ȝeue þer of part.
'He would-have-to know much (of) art, that you would yield part of this [lit.: there of part].'
c1300 (c1250) *Floriz and Blauncheflur* (ed. J. R. Lumby, rev. G. H. McKnight, EETS 14) Cambridge MS, 521

b. for as god passiþ men, so goddis lawe mut passe in autorite mannus lawe, ... goddis word mut euere be trewe ȝif it be wel vndirstondun
'for as God surpasses men, so God's law must surpass man's law in authority. ... God's word must always be true if it is understood properly'
*a*1500 (?c1378) *De Officio Pastorali* (*The English Works of Wyclif Hitherto Unprinted*, ed. F. D. Matthew, EETS 74: 405–457) 438.4

c. yif preisynge make gentilesse, thanne mote they nedes ben gentil that been preysed.
'If praising creates nobility, then they who are praised must necessarily be noble.'
?*a*1425 (*c*1380) Chaucer, *Boece* III, Prosa 6.41

(22) Subjective deontic *mot*

a. Þa spæc Merlin; ...
ȝe mote neh gon; & neodliche heom fon on ...
and cumeð mid strengðe; ȝif ȝe hine maȝen sturien.
'Then spoke Merlin: "... You must go near, and forcibly take hold of [= *fon*] them ... and return [imperative] with strength, if you can move it."'
*a*1225 (?*a*1200) Laȝamon, *Brut* (ed. G. L. Brook and R. F. Leslie, EETS 250, 277) Caligula MS, 8681

b. Ac ðanne hit is þin wille ðat ic ðe loc ofrin mote
'But if it is Thy will that I must offer Thee (a) sacrifice [= *loc*]' Holthausen's translation
(*c*1200) *Vices and Virtues* (ed. F. Holthausen, EETS 89) 85.5

c. Whane þescheker is forþ ibroȝt
Biþute panes ne plei þu noȝt.
Þu most [*vr.* shalt] habbe redi mitte
Twenti Marc ine þi slitte.
'When the gaming board is brought out, don't play without money. You must have ready at hand twenty marks in your sleeve.'
(part of a passage of instruction to an individual for a particular plot)
*c*1300 (*c*1250) *Floriz and Blauncheflur* (ed. J. R. Lumby, rev. G. H. McKnight, EETS 14) Cambridge MS, 347

7.3.2 Possibility and permission

Here MOT had been of major importance in Old English, and senses of permission and possibility continue (now including clear dynamic possibility), though less frequently, and in more restricted, especially subordinate, environments (see Ono 1958, Tellier 1962). As it becomes a modal of necessity and obligation, much of its range is taken over by MAY, which becomes less subject-oriented than in Old English (Tellier 1962: 150) and gives better evidence both of general deontic uses and of subjective uses. Middle English has clear subjective deontic instances, including some from the beginning of the period in the *Ancrene Wisse* (see Tellier 1962: 147) on the reasonable assumption that the author sometimes wrote as if he was himself the source of authority for the anchoresses' rule, as his common use of imperatives implies. Clearer instances of epistemic MAY are also found in Middle English.[9] Reference to a future possibility is found from early Middle English, as is the preterite *mihte* with a cotemporal possibility.

(23) Subjective deontic *may*

a. to ower wummen ȝe mahen þah seggen wið lut word hwet se ȝe wulleð. ȝef eani god mon is of feorren icumen; hercnið his speche & ondswerieð wið lut word to his easkunges.
(on keeping silence:) 'to your women you may however speak with short speech whatever you wish. If any good man comes from a distance [lit.: is from far come], hearken-to (imperative) his speech and answer (imperative) his questions briefly [lit.: answer with short speech to his questions]'.
*c*1230 (?*a*1200) *Ancrene Wisse* (ed. J. R. R. Tolkien, EETS 249) 38 f.17b.8

b. Þou mait saien al þine wille,
And I shal herknen and sitten stille
'You may say everything you wish [lit.: all your will], and I shall listen and sit still'
?*a*1300 *Dame Siriȝ* (*Middle English Humorous Tales in Verse*, ed. G.H. McKnight, Boston, Heath, 1913) 49

c. Ye mowe, for me, right as yow liketh do
'As far as I am concerned, you may do just as it pleases you'
(*c*1395) Chaucer, *Canterbury Tales* IV.1554

(24) Epistemic *may*

a. sæidon, þes þe heom þuhte, þet þær mihte wel ben abuton twenti oðer þritti hornblaweres.
'(they) said, as (it) seemed to-them, that there might well be about twenty or thirty hornblowers.'
*a*1131 *The Peterborough Chronicle* (ed. C. Clark, 2nd edn. Oxford, Clarendon Press, 1970) 1127.70

b. Þu þohhtesst tatt itt mihhte wel
Till mikell frame turrnenn,
3iff Ennglissh follk, forr lufe off Crist,
Itt wollde ʒerne lernenn
'You thought that it would probably be beneficial, if English people were willing to learn it eagerly for the love of Christ' (see *MED mouen* v. (3) 12(f); *frame* = 'profit, benefit')
?*c*1200 *The Ormulum* (ed. R. Holt 1878) Dedication 17

c. It may wel be he looked on hir face
In swich a wise as man that asketh grace
'It may well be that he gazed on her face in just the manner of one who begs favour'
(*c*1395) Chaucer, *Canterbury Tales* V.957

d. And seide, 'Ther is manye of yow
Faitours, and so may be that thow
Art riht such on
'And said, 'There are many of you imposters, and so it may be that you are just such a one'
(*a*1393) Gower, *Confessio Amantis* (ed. G. C. Macaulay, EETS ES 81, 82) I.174

The primary sense of Old English *cann* with the infinitive was 'know how, be able' of intellectual (perhaps learned) ability, in contrast with the more general or physical capacity of Old English *mæg*. But, presumably in response to MAY's shift in sense, CAN also develops a sense of more general ability. This is difficult to date since the original sense 'passes imperceptibly into the current sense' (*OED Can, v.*[1] 3–4). *OED* finds it before 1300, Tellier (1962) assigns it to the period between the early thirteenth century and the late fourteenth century. But the very beginnings of this development were perhaps already apparent in Old English.[10] Subsequently there develop senses which are not subject-oriented. Neutral dynamic possibility seems to be established by the fifteenth century at the latest when passive examples are first noted (see (25)), though there are earlier instances like (25.c) which show much reduced subject agentivity and which are probably well taken as neutral dynamic.[11] Epistemic possibility is problematic. *OED* (*Can, v.*[1] 5) and Visser (§1628) assign it to early Middle English, but their evidence seems open to dynamic interpretation. If it is possible before Modern English it is apparently very infrequent. Deontic modality is also later, and clear subjective instances are not found until the nineteenth century (V§1630, discounting unsatisfactory earlier citations).

(25) Neutral dynamic *can*

a. bi men and in men can not ne may not eny parfiter service be doon to þee, god
'by men and among men neither can nor may any more perfect service be done to thee, God'
(*c*1443) R. Pecock, *The Reule of Crysten Religioun* (ed. W. C. Greet, EETS 171) 227–228

b. neuere man ȝitt wroote enye notable book whiche couþe so suerli sett his wordis þat noon inpugnacioun couþe be made þere aȝens
'never has a man yet written any notable book who could so surely place his words that no attack could be made against it/them.'
*c*1475 (*c*1445) R. Pecock, *The Donet* (ed. E. V. Hitchcock, EETS 156) 6.20

c. We olde men, I drede, so fare we:
Til we be roten, kan we nat be rype
'we old men, I am afraid, we are like that: until we are rotten we cannot be ripe'
(*c*1390) Chaucer, *Canterbury Tales* I.3875

7.3.3 Futurity

From early Middle English the use of the simple nonpast to refer to the future becomes very much less frequent, except in particular contexts such as temporal clauses where it may survive today. *Shal* and *wil* become the normal means of indicating futurity, and *shal* predominates, especially in earlier texts, though a higher proportion of *wil* seems to have been typical of less formal usage which was less influenced by Latin (Mustanoja 1960: 489ff., Tellier 1962: 133ff., and see Jespersen 1909–49: IV, 275–6).

For the *Ancren Riwle* of *c*1225 Tellier (1962: 135) concluded that both verbs had futurity as a basic part of their meaning. From this period the statistics of occurrence of these verbs with different grammatical persons in different types of clause show clearly the impact of *wil*'s subject-oriented volition and *shal*'s external (or perhaps subjective) obligation which was to result in their interchange within the future paradigms established for Standard English some centuries later (see Tellier 1962; for Old English, Standop 1957).

7.3.4 'Subjunctive equivalents' and hypothetical uses

Should retains the modality of qualified report found in Old English into the Modern English period (*OED Shall*, 15, V§1549). More generally, modal group verbs, especially *may* and the preterites *might*, *would* and *should*, have tended to develop senses which appear where earlier English would have used a subjunctive form of the nonmodal verb. For this reason they are sometimes referred to as 'periphrastic subjunctives', though this implies too strong an equivalence. The expressions could indeed be equivalent in particular contexts, and the modals are sentential modifiers, as is the subjunctive. But the systems they belong to are distinct. However, the decline of the inflected subjunctive is interinvolved with the development and establishment of some uses of modals (see Mustanoja 1960: 453, 457 for a brief statement with some examples). Here we must distinguish as far as we can uses in which the apparent equivalence depends on the fact that the modal is itself in the 'remote' preterite (or even the preterite subjunctive), or is preterite in indirect speech: for example, uses of Old English *sceolde* after preterite verbs of ordering may simply represent a preterite of SHALL, not a more independent status of *sceolde*. Then the most important categories here in Middle English for the development of senses which do not simply fall under the general headings given above are the following.[12]

(i) *Clause complements of verbs of willing, commanding, wishing, etc.* Here *should* is common by late Middle English. *May* also appears where wishes, permissions, etc. are involved.

(ii) *Clauses subordinate to various expressions of attitude: surprise, sorrow, wonder, fear, etc.* Here again *should* is found in late Middle English (Behre's 1955 'Meditative–Polemic' *should*).

(iii) *Hypothetical clauses of unreal and rejected condition.* Here *would* may appear in Old English (see above), and *would, should* and *might* occur by late Middle English.

(iv) *Purpose clauses,* in which *may* and *should* in particular gain over the inflected subjunctive by late Middle English.

(v) *Main clauses expressing a wish (etc.),* in which *mot* is common beside the inflected subjunctive from early Middle English (or late Old English). These express the involvement of the speaker and are clearly subjective.

(26) a. 'Amen,' þat es 'sua most [*vr* mot] it be'
'Amen, that is: so may it be'
*a*1400(*a*1325) *Cursor Mundi* (ed. R. Morris, EETS 57, 59, 62, 66, 68, 99, 101) 25387

b. Wele mot William cheue & alle þat lufes pes!
'May William and all who love peace prosper!'
?*a*1400 (*a*1338) R. Mannyng, *Peter Langtoft's Chronicle* (ed. T Hearne, Oxford, 1725) 146

7.3.5 Conclusion

The changes in sense discussed above, particularly those involving *can*, much improve the semantic coherency of the modal group during Middle English, as do some of the losses noted in Chapter 6. By Chaucer's period, the late fourteenth century, the semantics of the modal group has become more evidently 'modal' (or 'nonverbal') than it was in Old English. In particular there are more clearly developed epistemic senses in *mot* (*must*) and *may*, better established modifiers of futurity and (increasingly) of the hypothetical, and a clearly established subjective use in the *mot* of wishes. Subjective deontic modality is also maintained; *shal* continues to express obligation, and *may* takes over permission senses from *mot*. Moreover *can*'s development of non-subject-oriented senses increases the coherency of the group, as do various lexical losses and other changes. *Wite* 'know' is by the fifteenth century isolated as the only surviving nonmodal preterite-present in the developing standard language. The modal group continues to have other 'nonmodal' functions, and the modal senses differ from today's in frequency of use, in the way they interact with tense, and in respect of many particular details. But, granted this, it is very clear that by the late fourteenth century the semantics of *may*, *mot/must*, *shal* and *wil* is largely concerned with modality, in sharp distinction to the semantics of other verbs.

7.4 Modern English developments

As we have seen, by Chaucer's time the modal group shows a range of uses which are substantially like those of the modern modals, alongside their other uses. The sharpness with which this group is distinguished increases in early Modern English with the loss of *wite* 'know' and the better integration of *can* as a modal (and its split from *con* 'study'). *May* also loses intransitive senses ('have power') by the late fifteenth century (*OED May*, *v.*[1] 1). *Must*, replacing *mot*, shows epistemic uses probably from the late fifteenth century (see examples under *MED moten* v. (2) 6a (c), (d)) but certainly both epistemic and subjective deontic in the sixteenth (Kakietek 1972: 63, 66); and *should* develops further epistemic uses from the fifteenth century, including its modern one, losing its earlier sense that the speaker is uncommitted to the truth of a report later in Modern English (V§§1530, 1550; *OED Shall*, 18, 15). Thus Ehrman, who was concerned to characterize the semantic system of the modals instead of focussing as I have done on specific properties, concluded that 'it looks as if the PDE [Present-day English] modal semantic system was established by

Shakespeare's time' (1966: 97), except that subject-oriented volitional *will* deserved a full place in the system, partly on the grounds of its frequency, whereas she analysed such uses today as an 'overtone' of the basic nonvolitional sense. Otherwise, she suggested, differences mainly involve the frequency of occurrence of different semantic categories. This statement masks some interesting differences however. Thus Shakespeare's use of *shall* for an uncoloured future, though commonest in the first person, is found in all three persons, whereas later Standard English restricted this use to the first person (Taglicht 1970), and today it is absent in some dialects, and generally formal in those where it survives (Palmer 1979: 112, Wekker 1976: 47).

There are also some more systematic differences between early Modern English and Present-day English, which reflect a continued semantic focussing of modality. Firstly, modals continue to lose past-referring uses of their preterite forms, so that the tense-relationship becomes more opaque. Secondly, there is a continued reduction in the relevance of subject-oriented uses. *Will* loses the sense 'desire' (which *OED* characterizes as '*Obs.*, or *arch.*, or merged in other senses'; *Will*, *v.*[1] 5) and volitional instances decline in frequency. *May* finally loses the potentially subject-oriented sense 'be able' to *can* in the course of Modern English (*OED May*, *v.*[1] 2). *Can* itself loses the sense 'know' and the object construction, but also senses with the infinitive in which 'know how' is prominent and the subject is selected (*OED Can*, *v.*[1] 3; V§1622); note that Ehrman (1966: 82) assigned the sense 'know how to' to nearly a quarter of the instances of *can* in her Shakespeare corpus.

Finally, there are some further developments in *can* and *may*. *May* retreats from the more verblike dynamic senses into the more distinctively modal epistemic and deontic areas. Figures cited by Kytö (1991: 91ff., 153) show an incidence of under 5 per cent for epistemic *mæg* in Old and Middle English corpora, some 18 per cent for epistemic *may* in an American corpus of 1620–1720, but from 65 per cent to 79 per cent for modern corpora. This is consistent with a major development of the epistemic function of *may* during the Modern English period. Similar figures for an increase in epistemic *may* from the fifteenth to the nineteenth century are given by Simon-Vandenbergen (1983), who also charts a decline of dynamic senses from the fifteenth century, when nearly half the instances of *may* in his sample are dynamic, to the nineteenth century, where only 5.5 per cent are. Today dynamic *may* is effectively absent except in formal registers (Coates 1983: 131f., 142; Palmer 1979: 157f.). *Can*, on the other hand, develops nondynamic modal senses. Instances from Shakespeare which may well contain an element of objective deontic modality are cited by Visser (§1630) and by Kakietek (1972: 58), but it is only from the nineteenth century that Visser gives really convincing instances, or cites subjective deontic examples. Epistemic modality is also clear for the nineteenth century, but earlier examples given in Visser and *OED* seem less convincing (V§1628, *OED Can, v.*[1] 5).

Thus although the semantic system of Shakespeare's modals is essentially the modern one, the semantic focussing of the modal group does not cease with the sixteenth century, but continues throughout Modern English.

7.5 Conclusion

In this chapter I have argued that there was already a 'modal group' in Old English which was distinctive in that it had uses interpretable in terms of parameters essentially similar to those which hold for the present-day modals. The clearest evidence is for occurrences which lack a relationship of selection with their grammatical subject, and are apparently sentence modifiers. This is supported by their occurrence in impersonal and passive constructions. There also seems to be quite a range of uses with a subjective component, especially deontic but also epistemic (though *uton* which is strongly subjective apparently selects its subject). I do not want to overinterpret the kind of data that I have produced for this period, or neglect the gap between my individual citations and the systematic analysis that might be undertaken on a more complete data collection. But the frequency of the occurrence of the modal group with impersonals, and the range over which subjective or partly subjective uses apparently occur makes it seem possible that there is already a 'modal' component associated with these words in Old English. There is increasing evidence for these parameters in Middle English, so that the semantics of the modal group in Chaucer seems to be quite substantially similar to the modern system, although it is less isolated. Further developments mean that the present-day 'modal semantic system was established by Shakespeare's time' in all major respects (Ehrman 1966: 97). But the focussing of the semantics of modals continues throughout the modern period, so that modals have continued to become both a more semantically coherent group and one that was more distinct from nonauxiliary verbs.

This outline of the development of the modal semantics of modals leads me to make two immediate points. The first concerns the major semantic changes involved, which include the loss of subject-oriented senses, the development of deontic and epistemic senses, and the strengthening of subjectivity, as is partly in line with the accounts of Traugott (1982, 1989). These changes (and the lexical losses) which focussed the semantics of the modal group took place gradually though at varying rates over the whole period from Old English until the present day (and may still be continuing). Secondly, it seems possible that from Old English (and even perhaps before) the semantic coherency of the modal group and its correlation with other properties was itself a factor which led speakers and learners to prefer developments of this group to other forms of expression. Thus at any moment there would have been a 'trading relationship' between the availability of some member of the modal group and the inflectional subjunctive, or an adverbial of futurity, or some other expression, in which the modal group tended, over a long period of time, to have an advantage. This is a point to which I will return in the next chapter. But it is already clear that it is too simple to attribute the rise of modals to the decline of the inflectional subjunctive (with Steele *et al.* 1981: 278ff.). There is a major interrelationship, but it is hardly a simple causal one, and other semantic areas are also involved.

8 *The status of modals and auxiliaries before Modern English*

8.1 The full range of properties

To the largely formal properties discussed in Chapters 5 and 6 we can now add semantic (or semantic–pragmatic) properties of the modal group. One, their occurrence as sentential modifiers, is a property already identified in the narrower context of impersonal constructions. But since 'subject-raising' constructions with other verbs become more prominent in late Middle English, this is a less distinctive property at this period. More significant is occurrence as subjectives, both deontic and epistemic; this parameter is incorporated into Table 8.1 (p. 186) along with others already established. Here 'prediction' uses are included as subjective epistemics. Among other verbs, subjective deontic and epistemic uses in early English are associated with verbal mood rather than with individual lexemes, though 'hortative' *let* may be a partial exception to this statement (*MED leten* v. 10a) and particular context-bound instances (e.g. of *seme*) may be subjective; there are also (as today) adjectives (e.g. *lik* 'likely') and adverbs (e.g. *certain, douteles*) which may presumably be subjective epistemic. This additional criterion, along with the further evidence that these words are sentential modifiers, reinforces the picture of the mutual predictiveness of properties, and of the prototypical status of the verbs of group A: this seems very clear for late Middle English, less so for Old English. Indeed, for late Middle English there is virtually a further criterion. As 'nonmodal' senses and subcategorizations are lost, members increasingly occur only with the plain infinitive or with a directional complement, and this restriction begins to correlate well with the other properties of Table 8.1.

The mutually predictive properties listed in Table 8.1 are generally rather salient. They belong to a range of linguistic levels, and are not *a priori* interconnected with each other (though I effectively gave an account of some possible interconnections in Chapter 2). Their mutual predictiveness (and its historical tendency to become more focussed) requires some account. Thus these words clearly share some type of category status even from Old English.

As we saw in Chapter 4, we can distinguish different levels of category structure, which crucially have different properties. At the central, basic level categories (interpreted in terms of clusters of mutually predictive distinguishing properties) are best defined. At the subordinate level below this, categories are less distinct. They typically share more properties with each other, and are distinguished by fewer properties. I suggest that the status of the auxiliary group (and the modal group within it) was that of a subordinate-level category in Old and Middle English. This is consistent with the fact that the clustering shares with the main class of verbs the various properties discussed in Chapter 4: oppositions of person and number (to some extent tense and mood; see below), the possibility of subject selection and typically verbal complementation, and parallels in word order. One would also expect that subordinate-level categories will tolerate a lower mutual predictiveness between their properties, as a corollary of the fact that it is at the cognitively fundamental 'basic' level that the distinctiveness of categories is sharpest. In this way too they will tend to be less well defined. Hence the rather ragged or fuzzy nature of the grouping is also merely what we should expect of a subordinate-level category.

8.2 Notional correspondences: identifying the group

Now for the third of the questions of my §4.4. It can be rephrased here: 'Is there a notional correspondance between this candidate category and the cross-linguistic "auxiliary"?' In Chapter 1 it was suggested that the notional characteristics of the semantic prototype of today's auxiliaries would be candidate members of a universal set identifying such a category cross-linguistically. The two major characteristics pointed to were occurrence as sentence modifiers, and subjectivity. A third involved the semantic area of necessity and possibility and its generalizations. Being a sentence modifier is clearly a central property of 'auxiliaries' both in present-day English and generally; and the general importance of subjectivity to modality is also clear (see Lyons 1977: Ch. 17, Palmer 1986: 16f. and *passim*, and the recent discussion of 'aspectualizers' in Brinton 1988). If this is good sense, then group A verbs can be identified as an auxiliary and modal group by the fourteenth century at the very latest. Earlier, it is possible to doubt how central to the category these characteristics were, though their early common occurrence with impersonals, the argument of Chapter 7, and the morphosyntactic opacity of some group A verbs (especially *uton*) which will be discussed below imply that there was a modal (hence auxiliary) group as early as Old English.

Table 8.1 *Further properties of verbs in Old and Middle English*

Occurrence of verbs	In ellipsis	'Intervening' in impersonal constructions	Synchronic pret.-pres.	Complement infinitive only plain	Fin. only	Opaque pret.	Potential subjective modality
CAN	(OE)(ME)		+	+		?ME	
DARE	OE, ME		+	+		?ME	
MAY	OE, (ME)	OE, ME	+	+		ME	(OE) ME
MOT	OE, ME	(OE)(ME)	+	+	OE, ME	ME	OE, ME
ME *mun* (not in OE)	ME	(ME)	+	+			(ME)
OWE	ME	ME!	+/–	–		ME	
SHALL	OE, ME	OE, ME	+	+	OE, ME	OE, ME	OE, ME
ÞARF	(OE), ME	OE, ME!	+	+			
uton (not late ME)	(?)OE		+	+	OE, eME		OE, eME
WILL	OE, ME	OE, ME	(OE), ME	(+)		ME	OE, ME
BE	OE, ME	OE, eME	partly	–			
weorðan (not lME)		OE, eME	–				
on-/aginnan, ME *ginnen*	*	OE, ME	–	–			
ME *beginnen*	*	?ME	–	–			
perfect HAVE	ME	ME	–				
pro-verbal DO	OE, ME		–				
periphrastic DO			–	?+			
other verbs	?–	?	+/– F	+/– N			

Table 8.1 (*cont.*)

F = few and declining.
N = limited and poorly supported with 'shared subject'.
OE, ME = properties attested at the period in question.
(OE) (ME) = attested by instances which might be intransitive in the case of potential ellipsis, less central or clear instances in the case of impersonals, preterite-present morphology, less clear or more marginal in the case of subjective modality.
ME! neutralized with use as impersonal verb in ME.
* neutralized with use as intransitive verb.

This table is based on incomplete information particularly for subjective modality in *mun*, OWE and ÞARF (*MED* is not yet available for the last). There are possible instances for the latter two, but particularly in the case of OWE they seem better interpreted with reference to an external framework of established moral requirements.

Another approach to this question of identification is to list the properties of 'auxiliaries' across languages to see how early English corresponds. We might take the characteristics claimed for the syntactic node AUX by Steele *et al.* (1981; and see Steele's 1978), and interpret at least some of them as potential class properties of 'auxiliary'. Tense and modality are central; aspect is listed among the 'limited and specifiable set of notional categories which may be marked there [sc. in AUX]' (1981: 146).

Modality is involved in 'modal group' verbs from Old English, as discussed in the last chapter. Deontic modality is found, and there is some development of the subjective deontic (and even the subjective epistemic) uses which I take to be most characteristic of modality. *Uton* is also clearly a subjective deontic. If mood and modality are closely connected, it is worth noting the evidence that particular uses of some words show a developing equivalence to the subjunctive even in Old English. *Sceolde* may be evidential, thus manifesting another of Steele's 'limited set of notional categories'. In Middle English the range of subjective deontic and subjective epistemic uses increases, as does that of apparent subjunctive equivalents. Tense in Steele's terms is shown in the form of the verb. But *wile* may arguably already convey a 'pure' future sense in Old English and this is true for both SHALL and WILL in Middle English. It is clear that 'modal group' verbs can be justifiably given that title, and that they would be the semantic prototype of an auxiliary group.

Outside the modal group, aspect is shown in perfect HAVE, and in the partial accommodation of *weorðan* and *ginnen* to the group (I do not interpret BE as aspectual at any stage of English); tense is perhaps shown in periphrastic DO. Nonpast forms of Old and early Middle English *beon/wesan* show a contrast (*is* : *bið,* etc.) which is both temporal and aspectual. I suspect, however, that from a notional point of view the placing of BE in the same group as 'modals' reflects the fact that it is (in effect) a sentence modifier which is typically stative and of very general meaning. These properties may point to a better fit with the modal than with the full verb prototype. Thus from a notional point of view BE may be a secondary member of this group, and the same might also hold of the later developing HAVE and DO.

This alternative approach also points to the notional identification of the group as 'auxiliary' in its semantics. But on either approach there is an important caveat. Such semantics is less central to the group than it becomes later in several ways. For one thing, it is for most items found alongside other usages to a greater extent. For another, the semantics of deontic and epistemic modality is less developed. Thus, though the group is identifiably 'auxiliary' it would be misleading to pigeonhole it under the notional label if this implied a simple equivalence to the present-day category. It differs by being a relatively less well defined, less distinct category (a 'subordinate-level category'), and (perhaps as part and parcel of this) in corresponding less fully to the notional category. The reasonable conclusion is that Old and Middle English did indeed have 'auxiliary verbs', but in the following sense: 'a linguistically significant "subordinate-level category" of verbs with some of the identifying characteristics of the notional "auxiliary" '.

This conclusion raises the question of interconnections between the properties of the members of the group, and I shall develop a partial account of this in discussing the grammaticalization of these words.

8.3 The special position of finiteness

In both Old and Middle English some members of the modal group are found only in finite forms. It was argued in Chapter 6 that this was probably a real restriction in grammar. The fact that this property is itself lexically restricted can readily be accounted for along lines suggested for Present-day English in Chapter 2: the items involved are interpreted as having subjective uses in which the contribution of indicative mood is opaque. This differs from the modern situation in that there is no systematic failure of verbal morphosyntax: instead the items show a lexically based exceptionality. They can be analysed as unitary lexical formations in which the Old English finites [+FIN, +INDIC] may be assigned an interpretation which is not a function of the normal contribution of [+FIN, +INDIC].[1] Like other 'frozen' word formation these forms may have both 'transparent' and 'opaque' interpretations. But the fact that *mot* and *sceal* [+FIN, +INDIC] did not manifest productive rules of composition inhibited the production of nonfinite categories. These categories would not have been impossible, but they would have required a separate statement, something akin to a nonce backformation albeit one supported by the status of these words as verbs. This analysis implies that the subjunctive of these items should also be analysed as noncompositional in the same way. I do not know of evidence in favour of this for Old English, but there is some for Middle English where *MED shulen* v. (1) notes specifically that historically subjunctive forms can no longer be distinguished in meaning from indicatives. Note that *uton* becomes a coherent member of the group under this interpretation. It is morphologically indicative, but a unitary form with a subjective semantics which would otherwise have required the subjunctive. Note too that the development of the opaque preterite shows essentially the same process in operation; indeed it may follow partly as a consequence of the initial listing if this involved tensed combinations from the beginning. Finally, the apparent Middle English correlation of this restriction with the semantics of necessity is readily stated as a lexical redundancy rule.

This account depends essentially on the existence of subjective deontic modality in Old English, argued for in the last chapter. There we saw that it was in deontic modality that subjectivity was strongest and best evidenced; subjective epistemic modality was less clear. And strikingly it is the three verbs which best showed subjective deontic modality that are clearly restricted to finites in Old English: *mot*, *sceal* and *uton*.[2] On my account this is no accident. Subjective deontic modality emerges and is clearly marked before subjective epistemic modality; this can be partly interpreted in terms of the type of general historical semantic processes discussed by Traugott (1989). It is therefore subjective deontics that are first reanalysed as having opacity of finiteness, and it is these verbs that will be likely first to show the finiteness restriction. The *sceolde* of report is also interesting as a subjective epistemic which may well show a restriction to the preterite (see §6.4); this would imply an early potential opacity of tense, and it is notable that it is precisely with SHALL that opacity of tense is marked earliest in other constructions (e.g. in deontic uses of *sceolde*). The irregularity of the inherited morphology of these verbs (perhaps indeed some semantic opacity since *-on* selects preterite stems outside preterite-present verbs) was presumably also a factor motivating this reanalysis.

There are two possibilities for group A verbs which lack the finiteness restriction. One is that they lack grammaticalized subjective uses, and simply show the normal range and interpretation of verbal categories. This was presumably the case for OE *cann* (and *dearr* but see note 2). The other is that their finites are analysed noncompositionally in respect of mood (and tense), and are open to subjective (alongside nonsubjective) interpretation, but that they have an additional nonfinite stem stated in their (nonredundant) lexical entries. This may be implied for MAY in late Middle English by the fact that finites occur strictly with the plain infinitive, nonfinites are occasionally also found in contact with a *to*-infinitive.[3] This minor difference of subcategorization of forms which are not connected by inflectional rule is not a problem, but a natural consequence of the independent statement required.

If this approach is appropriate, we have a further reason for identifying a class of modals or auxiliaries in Old English, since at least a subset of group A verbs shows a special property which distinguishes them from other members of the general class of verbs, and which is characteristic of modals and auxiliaries today.

What are the implications of the special status of finites for accounts in which the restriction to finite forms is a property of occurrence in a particular syntactic position, AUX, or INFL (or I), or its successor categories T, Agr (see Lightfoot 1979, 1991, Steele *et al.* 1981, Roberts 1985, and others)? What of the possibility that those words restricted to finite forms could be generated directly in INFL from Old English? Two kinds of point arise here. First, this would reduce the importance of the changes to modals in early Modern English, which will not be as dramatic as Lightfoot (1979) or Roberts (1985) imply, and it highlights the contribution of an essentially lexical treatment (see van Kemenade 1989, Lightfoot 1991: 152). Secondly there are questions about the characterization of functional categories in an account in which some items are (or may be) generated in INFL. We might consider van Kemenade's (1989) suggestion that epistemic modals were already generated in INFL in Old English, but that the bigger group of deontic (and dynamic) modals were full verbs; or we might consider whether MOT, SHALL and *uton* (at any rate) should always be generated in INFL. The properties of an item in the INFL position are normally taken to include a lack of the ability to assign theta roles (Roberts 1985, Pollock 1989, but cf. Chomsky 1986: 20, 69ff.). In early English MOT and SHALL are restricted to finite forms equally in epistemic and deontic uses, and *uton* is only deontic. If we take this restriction seriously, then van Kemenade's epistemic/deontic split seems unattractive, since it should predict nonfinites of deontic uses.[4] But generating MOT and SHALL, etc. in INFL would be plausible given the position of my Chapters 1 and 7 in which deontic modality does not necessarily assign theta roles. This hardly seems appropriate, however, for *uton*, which occurs both with and without *we* (which it presumably selects) throughout its history. There is a further problem in the fact that SHALL 'owe', 'be pertinent to' with ditransitive or transitive complementation is also not recorded as having nonfinite categories. This restriction looks much more like a property of the lexeme than of a syntactic position.[5] A further point is that the properties of the developing group are not solely those of finites. Occurrence with ellipsis is found with nonfinite as well as with finite verbs of the modal group, and this looks like a property which holds straightforwardly across the various uses of a lexeme. So it seems clear, firstly, that developments are consistent with a word-class model, and there is no need to appeal to a designated syntactic position to support the restriction to finiteness; and secondly, that if INFL is to be appealed to as a basis for this restriction then (adjunct) theta-role assignment in this position must have been more systematically available in early English than today, and it would be good to have some principled account of this difference.[6]

8.4 A speculative historical sketch to the fifteenth century

8.4.1 Old and Middle English show an apparently coherent long-term development of an auxiliary group. Accounting for such linguistic 'drifts' is notoriously difficult, and the causation of any historical process is bound to be complex. But two particular factors are of long-term importance:

(i) the decline of the effectiveness of oppositions of mood, especially indicative vs. subjunctive;

(ii) the internal dynamics of the developing auxiliary (especially modal) group.

Here (i) is partly a drag-chain effect which results from independent phonological and morphological changes. Already by Old English the indicative–subjunctive opposition lacked much of its earlier distinctness (see M§§21, 22, 601, 601a), and some of its functions are taken over by modal group verbs. But (as discussed in the last chapter) there is no simple equivalence between these forms of expression. Moreover the range of alternatives available among modal group verbs must have meant that preciser or more emphatic alternatives to a subjunctive expression were available even when mood was robust. Thus push-chain mechanisms may also have been involved from an early date. Later, of course, the growing frequency, coherency and grammaticalization of these verbs must of itself have been a factor in the decline of the subjunctive. A particular view of long-term historical changes of this type in the general case is developed at length in Samuels (1972; see esp. pp. 80–4 for a summary, and cf. Plank 1984: 359f., but note that I am departing from Samuels' general position in suggesting the early importance of push-chain mechanisms in this case). The situation in Old English is sufficiently independent of detailed interaction with the subjunctive for Standop's view to seem appropriate: 'It becomes quite evident in studying the OE auxiliary verbs that the loss of grammatical forms cannot under any circumstances be held responsible for the introduction of the auxiliary verbs' (1957: 45, translated in M§1014). In the historical period, certainly, push-chain mechanisms must have had considerable importance, and Steele *et al.*'s view that morphological decline causes the rise of modals in the mediaeval period is too simple (1981: 278ff.).

The possibility of (ii), some 'internal dynamic' for the development of the auxiliary group (which has in part just been discussed), may be interpreted in two ways. Both depend on aspects of Rosch's principle of 'cognitive economy', which asserts that 'the task of category systems is to provide maximum information with the least cognitive effort' (1978: 28). She interprets category structure as organized so as to maximize both the mutual predictiveness of attributes within categories and the sharpness of distinctions between categories. Given this, it seems plausible that once some level of mutual predictiveness of attributes has been achieved, this coherency will itself tend to promote a better differentiated categorization, as complying better with the demands of cognitive economy (though it is an open question when a stage of 'sufficient' coherency is reached). This suggestion corresponds to one of the specific hypotheses developed by Rosch according to which correlated attributes are more important for the formation of prototypes than uncorrelated attributes are (1975: 194). Since 'prototype formation can be understood as part of the general processes through which categories themselves may be formed' (Rosch and Mervis 1975: 599) and 'a reasonable hypothesis is that prototypes develop through the same principles ... as ... categories themselves' (Rosch 1978: 36–7), this essentially holds of category formation. The implication is that an increasing correlation may itself tend to promote further coherency. The second possibility follows from Rosch's suggestion that frequency and salience are related to prototype formation: 'the frequency of items and the salience of particular attributes or particular members of the categories ... undoubtedly contribute to prototype formation' (Rosch and Mervis 1975: 599, and hypotheses (3)–(5) of Rosch 1975: 194). This need not always be the case: frequency did not correlate directly with prototypicality for the artificial categories investigated by Rosch, Simpson and Miller (1976). But there is a potential relationship. Rosch provides no general application of her ideas to change (though she suggests that if a category system 'becomes markedly out of phase with real-world constraints it will probably tend to evolve to be more in line with those constraints' (1978: 42)), but it seems straightforward. As modal group verbs became more frequent and salient, because of the decline of the subjunctive or their expressive utility in other respects, this will have promoted the formation of a prototype based on their 'family resemblance'. The demands of cognitive economy will presumably have reacted to these changes in category structure by tending to develop a better differentiated categorization for modal (and auxiliary) group verbs, so that this factor will have counted in favour of the succession of minor changes which promoted this end. If we can accept the relevant underlying principles we have a rather simple and general account which says that an increase in the frequency and salience of some potential association of properties may lead to its becoming clearer and sharper, hence accounting for one general aspect of linguistic drift. Modal group verbs did indeed become considerably more frequent in the course of mediaeval English, and their characteristics became accordingly better defined.

The ideas here are traditional in that considerations of function and frequency have often been referred to in linguistic change. Thus Roberts (1985) refers to the ability of modals 'to functionally substitute for the subjunctive' as it declines in frequency. On Roberts' view, though, this precedes the grammatically interesting part of the change. What is new in my account is some level of warrant or more general grounding for specific instances of such ideas, which have a theoretical basis in Rosch's cognitive categories, and therefore become more justifiable as part of a serious account (though I do not pretend that there is not a long way to go). The account is a limited one, dealing with one aspect of categorization. But it will surely form one component of a modular account, and its construction is defensible as a necessary step towards the better understanding of the area. It is subject to the caveat 'other things being equal', without an ability to specify the 'other things'. It is necessarily only weakly predictive (strictly, nonpredictive), and some might argue that this makes it empty (Lass 1980). I prefer to see it as an interpretive rationalization which has some weak (*post hoc*) explanatory value, and would argue that the historian is necessarily involved in the construction of such accounts. I am also here taking for granted the linguistic appropriacy of the potential association and subsequent developments, for example, that it is in line with a universal specification of 'auxiliary', or with a coherent set of discourse functions, and that it would constitute some *prima facie* evidence for such specifications.

8.4.2 Using these ideas, we are now in a position to outline a speculative history of the auxiliary group.

(a) In Germanic and Primitive Old English preterite-present verbs largely have stative semantics. Thus within the category of verbs two nonprototypical characteristics, one formal and one semantic, are associated with each other.

(b) Some preterite-present verbs developed uses expressing modality. This may have been partly in response to the loss of the optative in Germanic, and to a presumed weakening of the distinctiveness of the subjunctive mainly at later periods. The loss of the inflected first-person imperative may have motivated the development of *uton*. The grouping became more focussed and developed further properties under two pressures:

(i) the decline of the effectiveness of oppositions of mood, especially indicative vs. subjunctive;

(ii) the independent focussing of the developing group.

(c) Contemporaneously another kind of development took place. Some preterite-present verbs typically occurred in utterances expressing a subjective deontic (and epistemic) modality, so that they were fully compatible with such subjectivity (though they may indeed have tended initially to occur with it because they offered an indirect or potentially objective form of expression). Then this is reinterpreted as a lexically encoded property in at least *mot* and *sceal*, so that their finite forms become opaque to mood.[7] The fact that their morphology was nonprototypical for verbs must also have encouraged (or been a precondition for) reanalysis. A lexical encoding must also have occurred in the case of *uton*, at the latest when analysis as an imperative became impossible as *-aþ* became the imperative plural form for preterite-presents (a development which is early and general in Old English (Campbell 1959a: §767)); see §6.2 for phonological evidence that *uton* had the same termination as a preterite-present plural indicative well before recorded Old English.[8] Indeed its reinterpretation as a preterite-present indicative may have been a crucial event for the lexicalization of subjectivity in this formal category.

This is the stage reached by recorded Old English.

(d) In Old and Middle English (i) and (ii) continue as long-term pressures which motivate the increasing focus of the class. There is a gradual development in which further properties characteristic of the class emerge and the individual properties become clearer in themselves and better as mutual predictors.

8.5 Comments on grammaticalization

Grammaticalization has commonly been taken to be a process whereby an autonomous word becomes a grammatical element; where a word ends up as a bound morpheme this typically means that it is reduced in form, restricted in distribution and generalized (perhaps 'bleached') in semantics in the process. In the case of auxiliaries we have a related shift from (more) lexical to (more) grammatical. This can be seen under two headings: one, the specific reanalysis of finites discussed above; the other, more general (or long drawn out) processes of focussing of the class. These seem to involve the following.

(i) At a semantic–pragmatic level, the lexical encoding discussed above is a conventionalizing of previously contextual elements of meaning. This reanalysis arguably shows the 'strengthening of informativeness' typical of the metonymic changes discussed by Traugott (1989), Traugott and König (1991), rather than a loss of the force associated with the indicative, since the indicative is the unmarked term in the system of mood. At a grammatical and lexical level there is a specific development of opacity in a morphosyntactic combination, so that a small number of items become exceptions to normal rules for the semantics (or pragmatics) of combination. This was presumably both formally and semantically motivated. The development of lexical exceptionality is important here, though it may be that the development is already supported as a group phenomenon (see (b.ii) above)

(ii) The general semantic developments of epistemic modality and of increased subjectivity show the tendencies of semantic–pragmatic change discussed in Traugott (1989), towards meanings based in the speaker's subjective belief state/attitude towards the proposition. Traugott's 'Tendency II', towards 'meanings based in the textual and metalinguistic situation' (1989: 35), is presumably also shown by the fact that these words have developed general elliptical or pro-verbal uses. The grammaticalization of auxiliaries as a class involves general principles of class formation (internal coherence and external opposition) which would presumably also apply to 'nongrammatical' classes. Rosch's general principle of cognitive economy gives us a way of understanding some of this process of diachronic focussing.

Finally, grammaticalization is not here led by semantics as suggested for aspectualizers in Brinton (1988), whether we focus on the development of morphosyntactic opacity, or on the more general and later developments. Brinton claims 'grammaticalization is initiated by a semantic shift … the syntactic actualization or realization of this semantic change proceeds gradually, and the syntactic changes are a consequence, not a cause, of the earlier semantic reanalysis' (1988: 237). In the case of modals, however, it seems that from Germanic there is an association of formal and semantic–pragmatic properties. Even a contextual association with subjective modality may have included reference to preterite-present morphology. Then the initial development of lexicalized subjectivity in some items must be related to their nonprototypical morphology, which is surely relevant at the point of reanalysis of finites: the opacity is a morphological as well as a semantic fact. And the syntactic property of ellipsis is present from the earliest time for which we can expect evidence. So, while semantic developments are clearly crucial, they do not have the clear-cut independence and priority apparently envisaged by Brinton.

In the more general and later developments, it is clear that the semantics of individual items (as of the group) continues to develop, as discussed in the last chapter. Moreover, both formal and semantic criteria are clearly important and mutually predictive in varying degrees, and the semantic criteria do not seem to have a special or predominant importance. It is the formal properties which seem more impressively cohesive in the Old English modal group. OE *cann* 'know how to' conspicuously lacks the semantics of epistemic or deontic modality, has a substantial proportion of uses in 'full verb' constructions, and is apparently related in the first instance to *witan* 'know' despite its increasing occurrence with the infinitive (see Ono 1975, Kytö 1987). But it is solid with the plain infinitive (§6.1) and occurs in potential ellipsis. A similar situation is found with OE and ME DARE, which is also solid with the plain infinitive and found in ellipsis (though this might be interpreted as having modal semantics along lines suggested by Perkins 1983 or Joos 1964). In each case one is bound to suspect that the cohesion of formal properties (ellipsis ~ plain infinitive complement ~ preterite-present) takes precedence over the semantics, and indeed bears some responsibility for CAN's development of modal semantics. The fact that OWE partly accommodates to 'modal group' properties in Middle English is presumably attributable to its morphology as well as to its semantics. This is in line with the traditionally structuralist account of Chapter 4 in which formal criteria are prior in establishing the membership of language-particular classes. It is however in apparent contradiction of the view developed by Brinton (1988) in which the development of an appropriate semantics for aspectualizers preceded the development of syntactic properties. In the present case it seems that formal properties, and the establishment of a poorly focussed subgroup based on them, have been important not only during Old and Middle English but from the earliest point at which we can make a definite statement. Grammaticalization, then, is not here a semantically led development in the particular sense that Brinton proposed for aspectualizers.

9 *Auxiliaries in early Modern English and the rise of* do

This chapter will focus on the period of particularly rapid change in early Modern English in which the status of modals and auxiliaries was substantially clarified. Lightfoot (1979) interpreted this as showing the development of a class 'modal'. My views differ from his in many respects. But we agree that the beginning of early Modern English saw a particularly significant set of changes, as (with less enthusiasm) does Plank (1984, see 348). In discussing this, I will need to recap some work familiar particularly from these authors, but my interpretation will differ and I will cover a wider range of data than Lightfoot.

We can conceptualize early Modern English changes affecting auxiliary group verbs under three headings. First comes a series of changes to earlier properties which further differentiate the modal group from full verbs: these are (A)–(D) of §9.1 below. Second is a striking further series of changes which look like new developments. These tend to make the auxiliary group more coherent and distinct. I will argue that both these sets of changes are illuminatingly interpreted as the development of a 'basic-level' category within Rosch's approach to categorization. Finally there is the general adoption of periphrastic DO. This must surely be interinvolved with these other changes if only because of the striking coincidence of date, but the nature of the connection is less clear. I will consider what other factors might be involved, and will sketch a speculative account relating changes in the status of finiteness to changes in word order, the obligatoriness of subjects, and the rise of periphrastic DO.

9.1 Apparent generalizations of earlier properties

A major group of changes apparently focussed on the second half of the fifteenth century and the first half of the sixteenth substantially sharpens the distinction between modal group verbs and full verbs:

(A) Loss of nonfinites of CAN, MAY, WILL and perhaps DO.

(B) Loss of nonmodal senses and constructions in CAN, MAY and WILL, and the development of lexemic splits in CAN, DARE and NEED.
(C) Further restriction in distribution of the plain infinitive.
(D) Full correspondence of preterite-present morphology with the modal group when WITE 'know' is lost.

Dow, *mun* and *tharf* will not be discussed in what follows because they do not enter Standard English but (with rare exceptions) are dialectal after 1500.

(A) Loss of nonfinites of CAN, MAY, WILL *and perhaps* DO

As we saw in Chapter 6, MOT/MUST and SHALL have always lacked nonfinites in recorded English. But nonfinites of CAN, MAY and WILL are found until early Modern English.

MED has plentiful nonfinite forms for CAN and MAY in the fourteenth and fifteenth century (*connen* v., *mouen* v. (3) 10, 11), and they continue to appear in the late-fifteenth-century works of Caxton who was born *c*1422, and died in 1491 (Kellner 1890: §19, Wienke 1930: 102ff.). But it seems clear from Visser that in the works of More (1478–1535) nonfinites of CAN followed by an infinitive are no longer found, while nonfinites of MAY are 'obsolescent' and very infrequent (1946–56: §§492, 512–17, 659; V§1649ff.). Later in the century none is remarked in Shakespeare by Franz (1939) or Schmidt (1962). The most relevant categories here are clearly nonfinites followed by an infinitive or which occur in clear cases of ellipsis. The latest straightforward examples given in *OED* or Visser (1963–73) for Standard English are cited below (for CAN see V§1649ff.; for MAY see V§1684–7; for both see V§§2042, 2134). The participle *cunning* is not cited here: a verbal use does not seem to survive Middle English (see *OED Cunning, a.*; *MED connyng* ppl.; V§1651).

(1)
a. To conne deye is to haue in all tymes his herte redy.
1490 Caxton, *The Arte and Crafte to Knowe Well to Dye* 2 (*OED Can, v.*[1] B.3) Inf.
b. And sure maye you be that if he had coulde, he wold not haue fayled to haue done the tone.
1533 More, *Works* (London, 1557) 975 C 10; *The Complete Works of St. Thomas More*, Vol. 10 (ed. John Guy, R. Keen, C. H. Miller and R. McGugan, New Haven, Yale University Press, 1987) 104.7 Past ptc.
c. that appered at the fyrst to mow stande the realme in great stede
1533 More, *Works* (London, 1557) 885 C I; *The Complete Works of St. Thomas More*, Vol. 9 (ed. J. B. Trapp, New Haven, Yale University Press, 1979) 84.5 Inf.

d. yf we had mought conuenyently come togyther
1528 More, *Works* (London, 1557) 107 H 6; *The Complete Works of St. Thomas More*, Vol. 6 (ed. Thomas M. C. Lawler, G. Marc'hadour and R. C. Marius, New Haven, Yale University Press, 1981) 26.20 Past ptc.

e. Maeyinge suffer no more the loue & deathe of Aurelio.
1556 *The Historie of Aurelio and Isabell* (1608) M ix (*OED May, v.* A.5.) Pres. ptc.

In giving late examples of a construction in this way there is the problem of isolating an appropriate range of 'standard' usage. Nonfinite CAN survives to this day in dialect, and *OED* gives nineteenth-century uses indicating that they are 'Scotch' or 'dialectal' (*Can, v.*[1] A.5.; and see modern examples below). There are also uses postdating the examples above whose significance is less clear: senses referable to CON, instances in glossaries, instances in later editions of texts, or the several infinitives of CAN in absolute (or in some cases perhaps elliptical) uses cited by *OED* after 1550 as 'used for the nonce' (which presumably implies at least their infrequency, see B.4.b.). But it seems clear that a real change is evidenced soon after the turn of the century.[1] The latest of this final group is (c) below.

(2)
a. *Possum* ... To may, or can
1565 T. Cooper, *Thesaurus* (*OED May, v.*[1] A 1) Inf.

b. dyscrecion to canne kepe peace. on all partyes.
The Myroure of our Ladye (ed. J. H. Blunt 1873, EETS ES 19) 148. The work was composed *c*1450, printed in 1530.

c. If from this love thy will thou canst unbind,
To will is here to can.
1633 P. Fletcher, *The Purple Island, or the Isle of Man; together with Piscatorie Eclogs* ... VI.xxvi (*OED Can, v.*[1] B.4) Inf.

Nonfinite forms of WILL also occur in Old and Middle English. Here the existence of a regular verb (past *willed*) alongside the modal creates problems of distinction and mutual influence. The last nonfinite of the latter cited by *OED* (and V§2042) and attested by its morphology is given below. (The last instance of a nonadjectival participle *willing* is hardly to be discriminated.) Nonfinites are, however, certainly very unusual in the sixteenth century (Weida 1975 gives (3.b); see Visser 1946–56: §659 on the infinitive).[2]

(3)
a. If hee had would, hee might easily ... occupied the Monarchy.
1633 J. Done, *Aristeas' Auncient Historie of the Septuagint* 216 (*OED Will, v.*[1] B.49)

b. I might haue been Fellow if I had would
1596 T. Nashe (Weida 1975: 36)

Nonfinites of periphrastic DO are found in the fifteenth century, but they do not seem to occur in Standard southern English certainly after the mid sixteenth century, probably after the turn of the fifteenth.[3] On the face of it this shows a loss of nonfinites roughly contemporary with that affecting CAN and MAY, and it looks as if it should be assigned to the same cluster of changes. The question of how these changes are interconnected will be discussed below.

Within the kind of analysis developed for Present-day English in Chapter 2 the loss of nonfinites implies the generalization of the opaque status of finite forms, and their systematic independence of this aspect of verbal morphosyntax. This lexical account does not (of course) entirely rule out the possibility of nonfinites for early Modern English or for modern dialects; but such forms require an additional (marked) statement which is no longer supported by the morphosyntactic properties of the (sub)class of modals or the class of verbs. Hence the survival of nonfinites of WILL, and occasional forms of CAN is consistent with a more systematic distinction from the first half of the sixteenth century.

(B) Loss of nonmodal senses and constructions in MAY, WILL and CAN, and the development of lexemic splits in CAN, DARE and NEED

MAY, WILL and CAN lose their nonmodal senses and constructions in the late fifteenth or the sixteenth century, although SHALL as a transitive and impersonal MOT/MUST are last recorded in the fifteenth century.[4]

MAY occurs in early English as an intransitive in the sense 'be strong, prevail', and it is also found in this sense with a 'cognate' object or (more rarely) as a full transitive. The first two are recorded throughout the fifteenth century (see *MED mouen* v. (3) 1, 6). The latest clearly relevant instances cited in *OED*, *MED* and V§§177, 557 are these.

(4) a. enuy where it may ouer, doth al the hurt it can.
c1531 More, *Works* (London, 1557) 85 B 1 (V§177. Possibly directional, but cooccurrence with *over* is normal, see V and *MED*.)

b. 3e xall not choppe my jewellys, and I may.
'You shall not chop my jewels [sc. testicles] if I can help it.'
c1475 *Mankind* (*The Macro Plays*, ed. M. Eccles, EETS 262: 153–84) 441 (*MED mouen* v. (3) 6(i))

c. If it had beene the pleasure of him who may all things
1597 T. Morley, *A Plaine and Easie Introduction to Practicall Musicke* 2 (*OED May, v.*[1] 9.c.)

WILL is again problematic because of the two verbs involved. *OED* gives the preterite-present *Will, v.*[1] with a nominal object in senses 'desire', 'wish for' into the eighteenth century. The latest clear instances with distinctive 'modal' morphology or clitic forms cited in *OED* or Visser belong to the seventeenth century: such uses are exemplified below as (a)–(c).[5] The use with a clausal object, as in (d), survives longer, and remnants of it are found today.

(5) a. When we would no Pardon they laboured to punish us.
1643 J. Angier, *Lancashire's Valley of Achor* ... 18 (*OED Will, v.*[1] 22)
b. and in that I'll no gainsaying.
1616 Shakespeare, *The Winter's Tale* 1.2.19
c. I'll none of that
1678 J. Dryden, *All for Love* 5.1 (V§559)
d. He would that Captain Credence should join himself with them.
1682 J. Bunyan, *The Holy War Made by Shaddai upon Diabolus* 263 (*OED Will, v.*[1] 23)

CAN is found throughout Middle English as a transitive with the senses 'know', 'learn', and this is lost in early Modern English. Examples for 'know' are cited by *OED* (*Can, v.*[1]) and V§551ff. (discounting dialect and probable literary archaisms) until the mid seventeenth century for prose, though these are post-dated by verse.[6]

(6) a. Can you no succours, sir?
1616 B. Jonson, *The Divell is an Asse* 3.1 (V§551)
b. No Skill of Musick can I, simple Swain.
1710 A. Philips, *Pastorals* iv.23 (*OED Can, v.*[1] 1.b)

Alongside these losses CAN, DARE and NEED each show a split development which suggests a sharpened distinction between modal and nonmodal categories. In CAN, the sense 'learn' becomes established in the spelling *con* as a distinct verb taking regular inflections. In Middle English both <a> and <o>/<u> (representing [u]) occurred in the present paradigm. Forms with <a> gradually spread, though the sense 'learn' and certain phrases, such as *con thank* 'thank' tend to resist this process and to develop regular forms in Middle English.[7] The differentiation of forms and senses, however, belongs mainly to the sixteenth century (*OED Can, v.*[1]; *Con, v.*).

Before the sixteenth century DARE is a preterite-present verb taking as its complement a plain infinitive or directional phrase (very rarely, a finite clause), and it develops nonfinite forms in the course of Middle English. In early Modern English the forms and constructions typical of a modal group verb continue. But DARE developed a complex category membership at this period. It appears also with new regular tensed forms *dareth* (later *dares*) and *dared*, and as a transitive ('to venture upon', etc.), though this does not have the distinctively preterite-present *he dare* or *durst*. It may also have a *to*-infinitive, which in Shakespeare at least is virtually restricted to *dares* or to nonfinites, and in the seventeenth century *dare* + *to*-infinitive starts to occur with periphrastic *do*.[8] Since transitive constructions are not found with distinctively preterite-present forms, transitive DARE has the characteristics of a 'full', nonauxiliary verb. Occurrences with the *to*-infinitive are also largely distinct from the finite modal. There is some blurring of a modal/verb category distinction especially in the occurrence of a plain infinitive after nonmodal forms. But in general these developments are strikingly consistent with a sharpening of the distinctness of modals.

NEED does the reverse of this. In Old and Middle English it is a regular verb. In Middle English it occurs in a range of personal and impersonal constructions, including ones with a dependent infinitive. But in the sixteenth century it starts to show modal characteristics, perhaps partly in response to the loss of THARF 'need' in southern English. (See *OED Need, v.*[2], *MED neden* v. (2), V§1345ff.). As an intransitive in construction with the infinitive it develops preterite-present *need* alongside *needs*, and instead of disappearing, the plain infinitive continues and even strengthens its position: it seems to be the less favoured infinitive in late Middle English (to judge from *MED* and other sources) but it is the commoner in Shakespeare, except that infinitive form *need* itself strongly prefers *to* (Warner 1987). There is otherwise no sharp distinction between modal and nonmodal NEED. But the correlation of modal properties shown in this development is again consistent with the development of an enhanced opposition between modal and nonauxiliary verbs at this period.

(C) Further restriction in distribution of the plain infinitive

Variation between the *to*-infinitive and the plain infinitive in complements of verbs had declined to virtually the modern situation in the sixteenth century, and occurrence with the plain infinitive became effectively distinctive of the modal group. Because of the gradual nature of this change it is difficult to establish when a sufficiently 'modern' situation is reached. Bock thought that the present-day situation was practically reached by the late fourteenth century (1931: 216, 219, 248). There is, however, quite a degree of continuing variation in Chaucer (Kenyon 1909) and in Pecock in the mid fifteenth century (Schmidt 1900: 97ff.).[9] By the sixteenth century, however, the situation looks like today's, except that there are more verbs which occasionally appear with the plain infinitive. This is shown for the century as a whole by the data of Visser's survey, where the plain infinitive is very little cited (V§897ff., 1177–342), and it holds for Shakespeare (Franz 1939: §650). For the first half of the century, Visser reported that 'by More's time *to* + infinitive had succeeded in crowding out the simple or bare stem to almost the same degree as in Pres. D. standard English' (1946–56: §244), and in his survey of More's usage in V + VP he only notes instances with *hear (say), let (flee), like, list, lust, gan, hap, come, go* and the phrase *have lever.* This is very different from Chaucer's usage. It is not sensible to cut the continuum of development up in any sharp way. But it is clear that by the beginning of the sixteenth century at the latest the opposition 'modal + plain infinitive vs. nonmodal + *to*-infinitive' was established for 'shared subject' verbs.

To this statement there is, as today, the puzzling exception of OUGHT. Moreover, OUGHT went on to generalize the *to*-infinitive. In Middle English it is found with both the plain and the *to*-infinitive, and there was considerable variation between different texts (see Sanders 1915: 52 for some figures). The plain infinitive is 'by no means rare' in More, but it 'becomes outmoded about the end of the sixteenth century' (Visser 1946–56: §537, V§1718). How can we make sense of this remarkable development? I suggest that OUGHT did not belong to the core group of modals in the sixteenth century because it retained the possibility of past time reference and its preterite was interpreted as formed according to the full verb schema of *bought, brought, fought, rought (<reck), sought, thought, wrought,* and (after identity of ME ou and au) *caught, fraught, taught* (Brunner 1963: §13 note 11, Dobson 1968: ii §240). This is a 'production-oriented schema' for the preterite (in the sense of Bybee and Slobin 1982, Bybee and Moder 1983), that is a formation target which is not related to a present-tense base form.[10] This relationship was supported by the fact that *ought* remained the past of OWE until the second half of the seventeenth century.[11]

(D) Full correspondence of preterite-present morphology with the modal group when WITE *'know' is lost.*

In the fifteenth and sixteenth centuries the preterite-present WITE 'know' both developed regular forms and declined sharply in frequency.[12] In Chaucer's works and in the Wyclifite Sermons of *c*1390 it is the commonest verb of knowing, occurring several times as frequently as KNOW (though it has a more restricted distribution). In Shakespeare, however, WITE is very uncommon. Chaucer used it over 800 times, while in Shakespeare's much larger corpus it occurs only forty times, mainly in verse (my estimates from Tatlock and Kennedy 1927, Spevack 1968–80). And in Shakespeare its use is very restricted. The preterite-present third person singular occurs only four times, in the parenthetical *God wot.* A picture of extreme infrequency and restriction also emerges from concordances to Lyly, Spenser, Sidney and Jonson. A similarly limited use was earlier described for the fifteenth-century *Paston Letters* by Tellier (1962: 215), who remarks that the verb is virtually restricted to recurrent collocations characteristic of letter writing and to the phrase *God wot*, though the verb is frequent in Malory's *Morte D'Arthur* (*c*1470) and in Caxton's revision (see Kato 1974, Sandved 1968).[13]

WITE was the last preterite-present verb which lacked modal constructions and semantics, if we except BE and admit the oddity of OUGHT. OWE 'own, owe, ought' had already generally adopted a regular present formation from the fourteenth century in the south (Brunner 1963: §72), and the last instance of *he owe* outside the north given in *OED* is from Caxton. Thus the loss of preterite-present WITE meant a substantial improvement in the coherency and distinctness of the modal group.

As a result of the changes of (A)–(D) the modal group became considerably more coherent within itself and distinct from nonauxiliary verbs. If we return to Table 8.1, by the middle of the sixteenth century, perhaps even by 1525, there was, in the developing standard, a one-to-one relationship between preterite-present morphology and membership of the modal group (excepting some forms of BE) and only WILL retains (uncommon) nonfinite forms. There is also a striking correlation between membership of the modal group and subcategorization for only the plain infinitive or a directional complement: witness the generally slightly later developments with CAN, DARE and NEED, which show this. By the end of the century only WILL of the central group retains other subcategorizations, and its position here (as with the retention of nonfinites) may be a result of contact with *will – willed.* The less central DARE and NEED admittedly show some fuzziness of boundary, and OUGHT differs. But this also holds today.

If we take seriously the evidence of More's infrequent use of nonfinite CAN and MAY in contrast to Caxton's, and admit that exceptional forms may survive as special items without being well integrated into the grammar, then it seems plain that this striking coherency and isolation became sharply clearer for the incipient standard in the period 1475–1525, and we might look to conditions in the late fifteenth century, when the writers of 1525 were children, for the immediate causes of these developments. The most striking single fifteenth-century development is the decline of WITE, partly because other Germanic languages retain the cognate verb of knowing and do not develop an auxiliary category comparable to that in English. The speed of its loss may point to motivation from the growing coherence of the modal group. Or it might be seen as a response to the changing semantics of CAN (itself perhaps a response to changes in MAY and MOT), which led to the isolation of WITE as a preterite-present verb of knowing. Perhaps both factors were relevant. Given the dating of its loss it must seem very possible that it precipitates or is the first significant change among the cluster of changes *c*1500.

9.2 New developments

The changes outlined above sharpened the opposition between modals and full verbs because properties that were formerly shared became restricted to one class. This is the culmination of Old and Middle English developments, and it results in modals with very much their modern properties (though they retain agreement). How should this be interpreted? An answer must take account of the striking series of further changes which affect auxiliaries (and modals). These differ in that they involve the development of new properties as much as the restriction of old ones. Moreover these changes do not cluster in a way which permits the idealized extraction of a period of fifty years as particularly crucial or central, as I have suggested for the four discussed above. The changes affect both the internal coherency of auxiliaries and their distinctness from verbs. Let me begin by discussing the four most striking developments which imply greater external distinctiveness.

(E) Movement of lightly stressed adverbs before the verb.
(F) Appearance of 'tag questions'.
(G) Appearance of a series of clitic forms.
(H) Appearance of contracted negatives in *-n't*.

(E) Movement of lightly stressed adverbs before the verb

Ellegård (1953: 183ff.) discusses the placement of lightly stressed adverbs, such as *never, always, seldom,* etc. He notes that in the Middle English of Chaucer and Rolle adverbs may appear before or after the finite verb, commonly following the verb in main clauses, varying in position in subordinate clauses. But in the case of *never,* which he investigated in detail, the possibility of postposition after a nonauxiliary is lost by the end of the sixteenth century, and 'It appears that the rate of change was fastest in the late 15th and early 16th centuries' (1953: 183). There is some evidence that 'other adverbs of indefinite time' were 'not far behind' (1953: 184). Such adverbs continued to occur after modals, BE, HAVE (and DO) (Jacobson 1981), and this suggests that the grammar differentiated between auxiliary and nonauxiliary contexts from the sixteenth century.[14]

(F) Appearance of 'tag questions'

In the mid sixteenth century appear what look like the first instances of today's tag-question construction. Visser gives examples with *do* and also cites seventeenth-century examples with BE (V§§202f., 310ff.). A search in Spevack's concordance to Shakespeare (1968–80) shows that by the turn of the sixteenth century the construction is established with DO, BE, perfect and possessive HAVE, and a range of modal group verbs, as exemplified below.

(7) I sent him a full answere by you, dyd I not?
*a*1553 N. Udall, *Ralph Roister Doister* 3.4.19 (V§202)

(8) a. You heard what this knave told me, did you not?
1598 Shakespeare, *The Merry Wives of Windsor* 2.1.151

b. She comes of errands, does she?
1598 Shakespeare, *The Merry Wives of Windsor* 4.2.153

c. You are grand-jurors, are ye?
1596 Shakespeare, *The First Part of King Henry IV* 2.2.87

d. You have not heard of the proclamation, have you?
1603 Shakespeare, *Measure for Measure* 1.2.89

e. I think I have done myself wrong, have I not?
1603 Shakespeare, *Measure for Measure* 1.2.40

f. You have me, have you not? – My lord, I have.
1602 Shakespeare, *Hamlet, Prince of Denmark* 2.1.68

g. How now, Simple! Where have you been? I must wait on myself, must I? You have not the Book of Riddles about you, have you?
1598 Shakespeare, *The Merry Wives of Windsor* 1.1.181

h. Come, come; thou'lt do my message, wilt thou not?
1588 Shakespeare, *Titus Andronicus* 4.1.118

i. Why, and I trust I may go too, may I not?
1598 Shakespeare, *The Taming of the Shrew* 1.1.102

The construction here is apparently the one described for today's English in Quirk et. al. (1985: §§11.8–9). In it the question tag follows without a conjunction (*or*, *and*, etc.) or complement (*so*, *that*, etc.) and without a change of speaker, and it may show retained or altered polarity. The early Modern examples just given seem natural instances. As far as I know, this construction has not been reported for Middle English.[15] Greater confidence requires more work. But on the face of it this looks like the development of a distinct construction restricted to auxiliaries.

(G) Appearance of a series of clitic forms

Evidence for a system of clitic forms for the auxiliary group verbs BE, HAVE, WILL (and SHALL) is also first found in the sixteenth century, when forms like the following appear:

(9) a. I'm, thou'rt, he's (= he has), we'll, thou'lt, she'ld; weis (= we shall), yoush (= you shall). (All given as sixteenth century in *OED*, see relevant verbs.)
b. He's (= he is), you're, thou't (= wilt), he'd (= would), thou'dst, thou'ldst, I've. These can be added for Shakespeare from Spevack's concordance (1968–80).

Others follow in the succeeding period. The reductions of *will* and *would* in particular suggest that what was involved here went beyond the low stress reduction rules of the language and required the listing of distinct allomorphs.[16] There is apparent evidence for the cliticization of pronouns and auxiliary group verbs in Middle English (e.g. *ichulle = ich wulle, woltou = wolt thou*) as with other verbs (e.g. *icherde = ich herde, ichot = ich wot*), but the conspectus of forms provided by *MED* and McIntosh, Samuels and Benskin (1986) gives no indication of Middle English reductions with apparent desyllabification like those above.[17]

(H) Appearance of contracted negatives in -n't

The contracted negative *-n't* is first evidenced in writing in the second half of the seventeenth century with modals, BE and HAVE. Note that phonologically irregular forms are already attested here so that an inflection rather than a clitic is in question (see Zwicky and Pullum 1983), and auxiliaries might be interpreted as verbs which potentially had a negative form, as traditionally.

(10) mayn't 1652, shan't 1664, won't 1666, don't 1672, can't 1674, ar'n't, a'n't (= are not, am not), e'n't, ain't (= is not) 'since 17th. c.' (*OED*, but illustrations are later. Information from *OED*; see individual verbs and *not*, and Jespersen 1909–49: V, §23.)

The dating of the characteristics of (F), (G) and (H) raises the question of the gap between their becoming established, presumably as part of the more colloquial language, and our first awareness of them in the record. There certainly seem to be representations of reasonably colloquial speech in earlier literature, though much of the writing of the late fifteenth and early sixteenth century is relatively formal. There are also representations of cliticized or reduced forms in Middle English spelling (though they are more typical early than late). An antedating of half a century or so, as Jespersen suggested for *-n't* (1909–49: V, §23.1_5ff.), seems not implausible. But it is difficult to make a case for any very substantial antedating.[18]

The four developments of (E)–(H) comprise a syntactic differentiation, a distinctive construction, a series of clitic allomorphs, and a morphology for negative forms. All are special to auxiliaries. The first three seem likely to develop in the period after the sharpening of status represented by (A), (C) and (D). The fourth follows perhaps *c*1600 or soon after. Here we have a fresh set of formal properties which characterize auxiliaries and set them apart from verbs. They are moreover appropriate from a general linguistic point of view. Cliticization is typically a property of closed-class items and it is often associated with auxiliaries (Kaisse 1985: 101ff.). It is striking that such a development should follow so rapidly on the firming up of the status of modals. Moreover there is a notional appropriacy for the other developments, since Steele *et al.* note that negation may be marked within AUX (1981: 146), and the tag-question construction has subjective semantics. With these developments the status of BE, HAVE and DO within the broader class of auxiliaries becomes very clear.

There is also some evidence for the external distinctiveness of auxiliaries in the fact that periphrastic (nonimperative) DO is never found in construction with *be* or *have* in the developing standard in early Modern English or in the Middle English dialects which most directly underlie Standard English.[19] This implies that DO is subcategorized for V[–AUX] at some point. It is difficult to pin this down because there are other restrictions which may have the same effect, semantic in the fourteenth century (Goossens 1984, Denison 1985a), and collocational in the sixteenth (Ellegård 1953: esp. 166–7, 201, 206). I am inclined to say 'late sixteenth century at the latest', though if the origin of this subcategorization is a generalization of the parallel restriction on pro-verbal DO (see Chapter 6) it may be much older.

To conclude the discussion of (A)–(H). The 'modal group' becomes sharply more coherent and distinct during a period centred on the end of the fifteenth century. Probably in the course of the sixteenth century the auxiliary group developed significant formal peculiarities (involving adverb position, the tag-question construction and clitic forms), and at the turn of the century (or in the first part of the next) auxiliaries develop the further peculiarity of a series of negative forms. There is clearly a rather rapid series of changes in which the classification of modals and auxiliaries is sharpened (and whose importance is underlined by the coincidence with developments in periphrastic DO as we will see below). If there is a difference of some kind in the classification of these words between early English and today's English (as I am disposed to believe) then this must be the period in which that change is centred.

9.3 A category-based account of early Modern English

9.3.1 The development of a 'basic-level' category

We have to deal with a focussing of the modal group followed by the development of significant formal attributes by the auxiliary group. New properties appear, and it seems clear that there is a succession of changes spread over a period of time. I suggest that this all makes excellent sense if we interpret the changes as the development of 'basic-level' category status in Rosch's sense for the modal and auxiliary group.

Let me begin by recapping two of the ideas about categories presented at the end of Chapter 4.

(i) The establishment of a category depends both on the extent of resemblances (for some set of attributes) between members of the category, and the extent of differences between members of the category and the members of other categories.

(ii) Categories are not all at the same level as one another, and categories of different levels may differ in the sharpness with which they are bounded.

Rosch (and other taxonomists) claim that there are different levels of categorization, and, crucially, that they have different properties. There is a central level which Rosch calls 'basic'. At this level categories are at once most internally coherent within themselves and most sharply distinguished from one another. I cite one of Rosch's examples in (11). Here the subordinate-level terms *kitchen chair* and *living-room chair* share many attributes in common, and are distinguished from one another by fewer attributes than the category *chair* is from other basic-level categories such as *table*. The superordinate-level term *furniture* on the other hand is less internally coherent. Rosch and Mervis (1975) noted that few attributes were common to all members of the superordinate categories they investigated, and that they tended not to be distinctive of the category.

(11) Example of taxonomy used in basic object research, Rosch (1978: 32)

Superordinate	*Basic Level*	*Subordinate*
	Chair	Kitchen chair Living-room chair
Furniture	Table	Kitchen table Dining-room table
	Lamp	Floor lamp Desk lamp

Rosch (and her co-workers) have shown that the basic level of cognitive categorization of objects is central to a range of different aspects of human behaviour, having priority in perceptual and processing tasks, as well as developmentally. This is the level at which we best identify categories in terms of perceptual and functional gestalts, and it is the level of our most complete categorization of the world. Thus it is psychologically a central level. It is also the most informative level in the sense that it is here that the internal coherence of classes and their differentiation from each other are at a joint maximum. As Rosch *et al.* put it:

> categories within taxonomies of concrete objects are structured such that there is generally one level of abstraction at which the most basic category cuts can be made. In general, the basic level of abstraction in a taxonomy is the level at which categories carry the most information, possess the highest cue validity, and are, thus, the most differentiated from one another.
> (Rosch, Mervis, *et al.* 1976: 383)

The cue validity of an attribute for a class is (roughly) a measure of the probability that possession of the attribute goes along with membership of the class. This principle is essentially one of cognitive economy: basic-level categories represent the best use of both similarity and difference. At a superordinate level, similarities between members of classes are outweighed by differences, so that the coherency of the classes is lower. At a subordinate level, the number of properties shared between classes is higher, so that the classes are less well distinguished. The basic level represents the most efficient utilization of these contrasting class properties.

In Chapter 4 I discussed why Rosch's theories are relevant to linguistic categorization, and noted the possibility of marrying her ideas with those of other theorists who posit a selection of innate properties, or who seek to derive properties from discourse. Here let me just point out that the ideas that we crucially need to borrow from Rosch are very general ones. They are not tied in any way to the specific areas she investigated, but seem like plausible general principles of considerable abstractness. We do not need the notion of a strict taxonomy in the sense that simple class inclusion holds between levels, or even a basic level which itself lacks layering.[20] Crucially we need the two ideas which began this section, and immediately, the notion that categories may differ in degree of internal coherency and external distinctness according to the position within a general framework of categories assigned to them by principles of cognitive economy.

Given this, it is clear that the cluster of changes discussed here which affects the auxiliary group in the period whose centre is 1500 is to be interpreted as showing the development of a basic-level category status by this group. Basic-level categories are distinguished by more attributes, and the attributes themselves are more distinctive. The culmination of mediaeval developments discussed in §9.1 had just this effect. What had previously been a 'subordinate-level' category, relatively fuzzy in definition with attributes and membership overlapping with nonauxiliary verbs, rather rapidly became a strikingly coherent and well-defined basic-level category. Properties were still shared with nonauxiliary verbs, but the more general category which subsumed both auxiliaries and nonauxiliary verbs itself became a less coherent 'superordinate-level' category at the latest by the seventeenth century. The core of the auxiliary category was the modal group of preterite-presents. But BE, HAVE and periphrastic DO continue to belong to it for the reasons noted in Chapters 1 (esp. §1.4) and 8, that they are distant from the verb prototype, and like central uses of modals they do not select their subjects. DO is subcategorized for the plain infinitive; BE retains some preterite-present morphology; and the subcategorization of perfect HAVE for the active second participle is not paralleled among verbs, but is found after modal group verbs and BE in early Modern English, as in earlier English (V§1895). Thus both formally and notionally they have more in common with the modal than with the nonauxiliary prototype. Hence they are 'secondary' auxiliaries.

These proposals have some interesting further consequences for historical change, some of which were discussed briefly at the end of the last chapter. It seems reasonable to suppose that the demands of cognitive economy which play a part in structuring the classification of words are relevant to linguistic change. Perhaps these demands contribute directly to the learning of language by children (with the effect of a kind of evaluation metric); perhaps they also correlate with the relative accessibilities which impact on use in adults. Whatever the mechanisms involved, I suppose that language will tend (other things being equal) to change so that its word-class structure accords better with the demands of cognitive economy.

Now, as noted in Chapter 8, 'the task of category systems is to provide maximum information with the least cognitive effort' (Rosch 1978: 28), and 'cognitive economy dictates that categories tend to be viewed as being as separate from each other and as clear-cut as possible' (1978: 35). Thus there is a tendency for basic-level categories to be formed with reference to their attributes in such a way as to maximize both the distinction between categories and the internal resemblance of their members. Given that this holds for linguistic categories, we should expect potential diachronic consequences. The first of these is clear, the second more speculative.

(i) As a category distinction becomes basic it may tend to be reinforced in two ways. Its internal coherency may tend to increase. And externally its distinctness from other basic categories may tend to rise: that is, shared properties may become restricted, and fresh differentiations may arise. Thus we should expect a succession of changes, rather than the set of ideally instantaneous changes which corresponds to Lightfoot's 'cataclysmic' reanalysis.

Now it is clear why there is a succession of changes which further characterize auxiliaries in the sixteenth century and later. The prediction is that as (and after) a category becomes 'basic' there may be a succession of changes, potentially of quite varied types, tending to promote the internal coherency and external distinctiveness of the auxiliary category. This is just what we found in §9.2 above, in the case of tag questions, clitic formation, etc. Here too probably belong the lexemic split of CAN/CON and the more gradual attrition of WILL's nonauxiliary properties noted in §9.1. There are also other relevant changes, which will be discussed below. It is worth noting that the dynamic aspect of cognitive economy makes a contribution here to our understanding of a linguistic 'drift'.

(ii) A possible further consequence follows from reflection on the properties of the basic level of categorization as presented in Rosch and other taxonomists. It is the level of maximum structuring of attributes and greatest distinctness of categories. Rosch also hypothesises that 'correlated attributes' have a 'special salience' in prototype formation (hence category formation). 'Our hypothesis is that conjoint frequency (correlated attributes) will influence the prototype more' (1975: 194). These properties may imply that as a subordinate-level category approaches the basic level and the correlation of attributes increases, the demands of cognitive economy do not rise monotonically, and that we might expect the final stages of such a development to be rather sudden.

This second prediction is also borne out. It accords with the fact that the developing basic category involves a relatively rapid cluster of changes. Putting the two predictions together we get what looks like the standard S-curve of change, with the rapid clarification of basic status in the middle of the curve, followed by a continuing tendency to further differentiation.

So we have a rather complete interpretation of an aspect of the history of English auxiliaries in terms of a simple and general theory of categories. It is 'rationalized history' rather than 'explanation', but it is illuminating. It makes clear the nature of events in early Modern English, and shows how they are consistent with the appearance of categorial distinctions at earlier stages of the language. And since the theory interprets categories in terms of their attributes it is flexible enough to deal with a succession of changes, lasting well beyond the sixteenth century.

9.3.2 Some further consequential changes

Finally, I will review some of the further changes which can arguably be interpreted as results of a tendency to improve the differentiation of basic level categories. These I have divided into two groups, though the subdivisions are necessarily somewhat artificial. Secondly I will briefly discuss the relationship between verb, auxiliary and modal in early Modern English.

Changes mainly promoting internal coherency

(I) The reinforcement of preterite-present BE. In Chapter 6 it was pointed out that some forms of BE in Old English were essentially preterite-present in formation. In Middle English this verb shows much dialectal variation, but typically in the south and the central midlands the second person present indicative singular (*thou art*) is formally unrelated to the plural (*we been, beeþ, be*) (see McIntosh, Samuels and Benskin 1986: I, 334ff., II, 81ff., etc., and Forsström 1948 for a detailed survey of forms). Such is also the general usage of Caxton in the late fifteenth century. But a century later Shakespeare has *thou art – we are*, and *thou wert* (*wast*) – *we were* has replaced *thou were – we were*. Thus BE shows the formal interrelationship (*art – are*) of SHALL and WILL (2nd sg. -liquid+t ## ~ pl. -liquid##). (Remember that postvocalic [r] is not lost in British English until the eighteenth century, Jespersen 1909–49: I, Ch. 13). The *are* type was common in Lincolnshire and parts of the north in Middle English. By the fifteenth century it can be found in Norfolk, and it also occurs infrequently in London. Why did it become general in London in the sixteenth century? At this date a refreshed contrast between indicative and subjunctive seems an unlikely motivation. Other northern forms enter Standard English, so perhaps sociolinguistic factors were involved. But why did they give just this result? I suggest that the rapidity of the adoption of *are* is due to its structural relationship to *art* (reflected in the creation of *wert* beside *were* at the same period), and that this reflects the enhanced evaluation of preterite-present morphology as a badge of auxiliaryhood which follows from its basic category status.

(J) The development of *could* with [-ld] by analogy with *should, would* (alongside earlier *coud*, and replacing earlier *couth*). *OED* first gives written forms with <l> for the sixteenth century (noting that '*l* began to be inserted about 1525', A.2); earlier examples are rare.[21] In the sixteenth century orthoepists show [l] and the form is supported by rhymes (Dobson 1968: II, §4, Wyld 1923: 130). *Could, should, would* form a set characterized by their similarity, not by their synchronic relation to the corresponding 'present'. They presumably constitute a minor 'production-oriented schema' in the sense of Bybee and Slobin (1982), which is restricted to the modal group.

Two minor developments which improve the coherency of the group are the following.

(K) The semantic developments discussed in §7.4, especially the increasingly deontic and epistemic semantics of CAN and MAY.

(L) The occasional appearance of auxiliary 'preterite-present' *he do* (*come*) from the mid sixteenth century, and perhaps the partial acceptance of periphrastic *he don't* from the late seventeenth century (*OED Do, v.*).[22] One must suspect that such forms would have made more headway had English not been standardized. Note that a similar contrast develops in some dialect (see §2.2.3).

Changes mainly promoting external distinctiveness

Here belong the developments of §9.2 above (E)–(H). We may more tentatively add the following.

(M) The final development of the modern situation in which BE and HAVE (and therefore auxiliaries in general) lack verbal morphosyntax involves the cluster of changes discussed in §2.5. Although this is partly dependent on developments in DO and the loss of *thou*, this is none the less a striking addition to the external distinctiveness of the class.

(N) The fact that the adoption of periphrastic DO 'went to completion', so that an auxiliary became obligatory in particular contexts. In §9.5 below I suggest a particular motivation for the adoption and generalization of periphrastic DO in interrogatives. But its generalization with *not* makes sense if interpreted as a consequence of a continued structural pressure for a sharpening of the 'basic' distinction. The steady direction of this development, the fact that it goes to completion, and the fact that this takes an extended period of time (even until the ninteenth century for negatives, see Rydén 1979: 31, but cf. Tieken 1987) all make sense from this perspective.

(O) The nineteenth-century tendency to differentiate auxiliary *thou dost, he doth*, nonauxiliary *thou doest, he doeth* (*OED Do, v.* A.2.b.; Jespersen 1909–49: VI, §§3.7, 2.3_3). There are also differentiations between the paradigms of auxiliary and nonauxiliary DO and HAVE in some dialects, as noted in (L) (see §2.2.3 for references).

(P) The loss of directional complements after modals. It looks as if this construction type, which was common in Shakespeare and More, contracted and was generally lost in Standard English in the seventeenth and eighteenth centuries. See especially *OED*, V§128, Söderlind (1951–8), also Plank (1984: 325). There is a more general loss of directional phrases after nonauxiliary verbs, but they also survive, for example after verbs also taking an object (*order, ask*, etc.) and are characteristic verbal adjuncts which presumably have some function as verbal identifiers. Arguably the loss of this construction improves the 'cue validity' of the distinction between modals and nonauxiliary verbs.

(Q) The losses of forms of HAVE (perhaps BE) discussed below.

9.3.3 The relationship between verb, modal and auxiliary in early Modern English

Modals are clearly the prototype of the category auxiliary, and they have the opacity of mood (and tense) found in today's modals, in that they are not 'composed' by the regularities of verbal morphosyntax. Moreover they no longer show the oppositions of finiteness found in full verbs. This represents a generalization from what in Middle English had been a lexical property of particular finites to a formal property of a class. Grammaticalization here is the reanalysis of this lexical opacity as a formal restriction on the systematic availability of verbal categories (in the context of a general sharpening of the opposition between modals and verbs). Thus there is now no general expectation that modals will partake in the morphosyntactic categories of verbs (except possibly for agreement as discussed below). This differs from Middle English, when there was such an expectation but it was frustrated by the opacity of some finite forms, for example in the case of SHALL. Hence the obsolescence of nonfinites in Modern English.

Modals did, however, retain overt agreement forms for some time, and if the analysis of *is* given in §§2.3–4 is correct the morphosyntactic opacity typical of modals did not hold for the nonprototypical auxiliaries BE and HAVE until the eighteenth century (see §2.5). Thus instead of moving directly to the modern position, the availability of verbal morphosyntax became partly restricted when the class became more distinct from that of verbs, in such a way that nonfinite verbal categories ceased to be available for prototypical auxiliaries and DO, that is, those subcategorized for a plain infinitive. The status of agreement is less clear. Such forms as *should(e)st* look overtly transparent, and if the broad coincidence of date between the loss of second-person inflections and the opacity of *is* is significant, then it is possible that agreement in modals remained an inflectional and verbal property until this point, as suggested in §2.5.

It also seems likely that possessive HAVE at least lacked the verbal property of automatic progressive and passive participles, and BE may have done so. Indeed, there is a rather remarkable development, for the progressive and passive participles of possessive HAVE occur in Middle English, but are absent (or virtually so) in early Modern English. Visser (§1841) gives no examples of the progressive of possessive HAVE for early Modern English, though he cites Middle English instances, and Söderlind (1951–8: I, 81) notes the absence of the form in Dryden.[23] Visser accounts for this absence by claiming that only later did HAVE develop the senses 'enjoy', 'endure', 'experience', etc. But this explanation will not do. HAVE is found in both Middle and early Modern English in nonstative senses.[24] We need a nonsemantic account for this absence of progressive *having* in early Modern English. Turning to the passive participle, *had*, this was very common in Old and Middle English. It becomes much less common in Modern English, and is today restricted to a narrow range of actional senses. Visser (§1928) remarks these differences and gives a large number of early examples. In More, for example, 'There is a conspicuously great number of passive constructions of the verb *to have*' (Visser 1946–56: §570). But it is very uncommon in Shakespeare and seventeenth- and eighteenth-century writers for whom the form is concordanced.[25]

There is a straightforward account of this given that the greater distinctiveness of auxiliaries involves the rejection of some verbal properties in early Modern English. Since **he is being* is also unavailable in early Modern English (though not perhaps in late Middle English; V§1834) I suggest that progressive and passive participles of auxiliaries became unavailable (or marked) at this period.[26] The restriction can be simply stated as a default to [–PRD] (as today). This predicts that a past participle of perfect HAVE should occur at this period, and this surprising prediction is apparently borne out: see *OED* 26. The default, however, bars a progressive.[27]

So we have evidence here for a particular kind of relationship between auxiliaries and verbs, one which is less distinct than today's, particularly in the case of nonprototypical auxiliaries BE and HAVE. If we assume a modern feature system, it can be briefly stated in terms of two default conditions. The first says that the morphosyntax of nonfinite categories does not hold for auxiliaries subcategorized for a plain infinitive; hence modals and DO are finite only. The second says that participles of auxiliaries may not be predicative, that is, progressive or passive.

(12) a. [+AUX, SUBCAT <[–TO, +BSE]>] ⊃ [+FIN, –BSE]
(or: [+BSE] ∨ [+ING] ∨ [+EN] ⊃ ¬([+AUX, SUBCAT <[–TO, +BSE]>])
b. [+AUX] ⊃ [–PRD]

9.4 Lightfoot revisited

Clearly, I owe a great deal to Lightfoot's original insightful proposal that the class of English modals emerged in the sixteenth century. But there are major differences of interpretation which it may be helpful to review. Lightfoot claimed that the development of a class 'modal' in the sixteenth century (interpreted in 1991 as their recategorization as instances of INFL) was preceded by independent changes which 'had the effect of isolating the premodals' as 'an emerging class' (1991: 148, and see 1979: 109). The three precursor changes were among those discussed in my Chapter 6: (a) inflectional distinctness after the loss of other preterite-presents; (b) increasing opacity of the present-preterite relationship in pre-modals; (c) increasing isolation of the plain infinitive as a complement.[28] Then the reanalysis of premodals 'was manifested by the loss of their nonfinite forms ... and their direct objects' (1991: 142; see my §9.1 (A) and (B)).[29] In 1979 Lightfoot took this change to be motivated by a 'Transparency Principle' forbidding more than a certain level of exceptionality, and to be a cataclysmic development. In 1991 he saw the development as motivated by preceding morphological changes, and as being not necessarily as cataclysmic as he earlier suggested. Subsequently English develops its modern restriction on the distribution of periphrastic *do*, and in 1991 (pp. 152f.) Lightfoot suggested that this reflected the loss of general V-to-INFL, and that it was somehow a consequence of the lexicalization of modals.

With the suggestion that developments in *do* and modals should be seen as interconnected I fully agree, and this is discussed in the next two sections. But from the present perspective Lightfoot's account of Old and Middle English needs some revision. First he sees the developments as a chance piling up of irregularities. Second, the early date of the restriction to finiteness of SHALL and MOT is unexpected. But these fall into place given the extra evidence (particularly occurrence in ellipsis and impersonals, and the interpretation of the distribution of the plain infinitive) that I have been able to adduce for an earlier categoriality of auxiliaries. Their properties in Old and Middle English are interrelated, then, because they belong to a developing classification with a notionally appropriate core, and throughout they constitute a subordinate regularity. So there is no intolerable level of exceptionality, or support for a 'Transparency Principle'. The group tends towards a steadily more coherent and distinct status for the functional and word-class reasons discussed in the last chapter. Thus what is mysterious and unprincipled in Lightfoot's account becomes rational and orderly. There is no 'cataclysmic' change or radical restructuring in the sixteenth century but a culmination of earlier developments, which come to a head.[30] Then there is a change in category status (rather than in simple category identity) with an expected rather sudden 'tidying up' of properties in a cluster of changes. But it is the word class 'auxiliary' that is affected, not just a class 'modal'. And the changes are not ideally simultaneous, as in Lightfoot's 1979 account, but form a smallish cluster occurring in the space of only a few generations. Moreover, unlike Lightfoot we have grounds for predicting a succession of further changes, though not the individual identity of the changes, except that they will tend to be appropriate to a universal category auxiliary. (More may of course follow given a more structured universal theory.) Lightfoot focussed on the loss of properties shared between 'pre-modal' and verb, such as the pre-modals' loss of non-finite categories, and on direct consequences (particularly for *do*). But within this framework we should expect not only such losses and direct consequences, but also changes which widen the gap between auxiliary and 'full' verb by adding distinguishing properties to one category but not the other, such as the development of negative or clitic forms for auxiliaries only. Finally, these points of interpretation not only seem entirely appropriate, at each stage of this history they give a closer modelling of events than Lightfoot's account, and a fuller interpretation. Both in theoretical interpretation and coverage of the data, then, this present account is superior.

9.5 Periphrastic *do*

I want finally to discuss the place of periphrastic *do* among the changes reviewed in this chapter. I will first say why I believe that *do* must indeed be integrated into the account (as is accepted e.g. by Roberts 1985, Lightfoot 1988, 1991). Then in an unashamedly speculative section I will try to show

how the development of full-scale lexical/morphosyntactic opacity in the modals led naturally to the adoption of periphrastic *do*.

9.5.1 The adoption of periphrastic do *and the changing status of modals*

I will not discuss the complex problem of the origin of this construction (for which see in particular Ellegård 1953, Denison 1985a). It first becomes available during Middle English. But its general adoption in the south-east seems to be closely associated with the developments in auxiliaries discussed here.

According to Ellegård's (1953) detailed survey, periphrastic *do* spreads from thirteenth-century south-western verse into east midland verse in the fourteenth century, into western prose in the late fourteenth century, and into eastern prose in the fifteenth. As it advances clearly causative instances of *do* decline. In the sixteenth century it is normal in London English and the developing Standard, and it becomes very common. But it is rare or absent in northern dialects until considerably later. We need to distinguish the use of *do* in simple, unemphatic, affirmative declaratives from its use in negatives and interrogatives. The first seems to be a marker of high style, at least when it is frequent. In colloquial speech as reported in Shakespeare's plays it is 'very rare', whereas *do* is a common enough option here in negative sentences and a predominant one in inverted interrogatives, so that by this time it is clearly a vernacular element (Salmon 1965: 277ff., Rankova 1964: 571). In the fifteenth century *do*'s status is less clear. Ellegård suggests, however, that its frequent use had a literary stylistic value ('a mark of the highflown style, or of the pedantic one' (1953: 165)) but that interrogatives (which had a higher proportion of *do* than other clause types from the beginning of the fifteenth century) may already have reflected colloquial usage.

Ellegård's figures for *do* show a remarkable surge in its incidence in the late fifteenth and early sixteenth century, which is most marked in interrogatives. This is partly masked in the much-reproduced graph of the spread of *do* (1953: 162), because before 1500 Ellegård gave figures only for texts which had instances of periphrastic *do*. A page count of the data reported in his appendix shows that he used only 40 per cent of his data for the period 1425–75, and only 75 per cent for 1475–1500. The texts of the other 60 (or 25) per cent showed no instances of periphrastic *do* and were omitted. As Ellegård notes: 'It is obvious that the 15th century frequencies would become even smaller than they are if all the texts read had been allowed to contribute' (1953: 159). In the sixteenth century, however, *do* is found in all his texts. Thus there is both a general acceptance of periphrastic *do* and a substantial proportionate increase in usage in inverted interrogative sentences with the opening of the sixteenth century. This increase can be seen from the figures in Table 9.1 cited (or worked out) from Ellegård (1953: 159ff.).[31]

Table 9.1 *Overall incidence of periphrastic* do *as a percentage of simple finite V plus* do ... *V*

	In all sentences	Positive and negative inverted interrogatives	Positive inverted interrogatives	Negative declaratives
1425–75	0.3 (0.1)	4.8 (1.9)	4.2 (1.7)	1.2 (0.5)
1475–1500	1.8 (1.3)	7.7 (5.8)	7.0 (5.3)	4.8 (3.6)
1500–25	1.8	33.6	22.7	7.8
1525–35	3.3	42.4	32.4	13.7
1535–50	9.5	53.6	44.9	27.9
1550–75	10.8	64.2	56.3	38.0
1575–1600	8.5	61.5	60.3	23.8

In this table the figures in parentheses are my estimates of likely proportions including Ellegård's omitted data. Figures for interrogatives are for *yes/no* questions and for those opening with a *wh*-adverb; object-initial interrogatives (for which figures are lower) are treated separately by Ellegård.

Since it is interrogatives which seem most likely to represent colloquial usage at this period, it is tempting to suppose that the remarkable surge in their incidence in particular classes of question 1500–25 coincides with or follows shortly after the general adoption of *do* as a vernacular element in the east midland and London dialects. Since both this development and a more general increase seem to begin in the last quarter of the fifteenth century, and the surge in interrogatives might be referred to learning done by children in that period, perhaps we should generalize this shift to the period 1475–1525. This is the period identified as central to the cluster of changes sharpening the coherency and isolation of modal group verbs (especially (A) and (D)), which suggests some interconnection with this series of events. Ellegård interestingly characterizes Caxton (who had lived abroad for much of his adult life) as an adult who was adopting *do* in the 1480s (1953: 165), but *do* is well established in More's works of *c*1530. Recall that earlier these two men provided convenient points of reference for the retention and (virtual) loss of nonfinites of CAN and MAY. The coincidence of date here strongly suggests that developments in modals and in *do* are interconnected. Any linguistic history must give some account of this interconnection if it is to be convincing. The relationship can of course be looked at in reverse: then we have some further evidence to add to that surveyed earlier in the chapter that a change of some importance affects auxiliaries in the late fifteenth and early sixteenth century.

There is a further, less convincing reason for suggesting that the rise of periphrastic *do* is connected with these other developments: the dialects of the north and Scotland to which periphrastic *do* last penetrated, and in which it only later became obligatory in interrogatives and negatives (in the last century or even early in this) are the dialects in which nonfinite modals have been best preserved, as in the modern Newcastle examples below.[32] This is not the same connection as that of early Modern English, but it also points to the interrelatedness of these developments.

(13) a. He'll can get a try on Tuesday.
b. What's it been like? – Terrible, I haven't could sleep.
c. A good machine clipper would could do it in half a day.
(McDonald 1981: 187–9)

9.5.2 Other factors

Not only is there a potentially close relationship between the modals' acquisition of basic-level word-class status and the rise of *do*, the loss of verb-second order in English may also be involved. This is suggested by the fact that verb-second order declines rapidly in early Modern English, while *do* is initially proportionately commonest in inverted questions as noted above (Ellegård 1953: 160ff.; see Table 9.1 above). Here I would like to take for granted the plausibility of an interconnection between these three areas of change, and try to provide an abstract (and speculative) interpretation of their interaction. I do not want to deny the relevance of other considerations and approaches. Indeed, it would clearly be possible to integrate *do* into the word-class account developed earlier in this chapter. But this can be done in various ways, so that it is insufficient for the more precise questions which arise, and I take the view that an interpretation at the level of abstract grammar will itself be part of any general account of these changes. But a range of other factors may be involved. Thus in inversion *do* is most frequent with transitive verbs and when the subject is a full noun phrase rather than a pronoun (Ellegård 1953: 189ff., Kroch, Myhill and Pintzuk 1982, Kroch 1989a). Kroch and Ellegård take this to show the relevance of word order; in Kroch's (1989a) interpretation it involves pressures for clear surface identification of the object as the NP directly following V (and see Kroch, Myhill and Pintzuk 1982, Salmon 1965). Thus with transitives, inverted *do*SVO (in which the object is clearly identified) has an particular advantage over VSO (in which it is not). Aside from this functional (or psycholinguistic) factor, others include the complex of social, stylistic and semantic considerations investigated by Stein as well as the phonotactically motivated distribution he discusses (1986, 1990). Furthermore, a source for *do* relevant to its diffusion may be shown by the fact that similar lexical tense forms occur in nonstandard dialects of Dutch and German, particularly when associated with child language, and in creoles and contact situations (Poussa 1990, Tieken 1988, and references there). The adoption and diffusion of *do* may then have involved a whole range of factors. Major headings are:

(i) some kind of 'analogy with the modal auxiliaries' (references in Ellegård 1953: 124);
(ii) pressures for surface SV(O) word order;
(iii) preference for combinations with *do* as a way of avoiding complex consonant clusters as the syllabic independence of verbal affixes declines;
(iv) social and stylistic motivation, and semantic changes;
(v) contact-based or learner-based development of lexical expression of tense.

But here I will focus on an abstract grammatical characterization. First, I will give an account of the extension of *do*, then turn to an account of the interrelatedness between the loss of verb-second order, the consolidation of modals and the development of periphrastic *do*.

9.5.3 Two stages of change

It looks at first sight as if the connection between the category change of modals and the rise of *do* might be that it involved a reanalysis of *do* as a unitary item expressing tense/mood in the late fifteenth century, when this characteristic in modals became central to a basic-level word class; or if this had already happened, some favouring of *do* because of the word class's new status. But it must be more complex than this because there is a striking apparent dislocation in the steady development of *do* which occurs in the second half of the sixteenth century when the incidence of affirmative *do* begins to decline. Kroch (1989b) has recently argued convincingly that there was a shift in underlying grammar at this point. Traditionally there is a period of 'extension' of *do* followed by a period of 'regulation'. From the beginning of the sixteenth century, the incidence of *do* increases in all contexts. Moreover, in the various negative and inverted interrogative contexts isolated by Ellegård, Kroch demonstrates that it shows the same rate of increase until the period 1550–75. In affirmative contexts it also increases during this period, but at a slightly lower rate. Kroch interprets this as consistent with his 'constant rate hypothesis', that linguistic change proceeds at the same rate in different contexts. The following period, 1575–1600, shows a shift, and thereafter the development of inverted, negated and affirmative contexts is no longer parallel. In positive inverted questions the incidence of *do* continues to increase; in negative contexts (whether inverted or not) it declines sharply, but then recovers and continues to increase at a lower rate than in positive inverted questions; finally, in affirmative contexts the incidence of *do* begins a steady decline. Kroch (1989a, 1989b) convincingly interprets this as a turning point in the development of *do,* and as evidence for some kind of grammatical reanalysis at this period. For Stein (1990) too there is a turning point at the end of the sixteenth century, which he interprets in terms of partial grammaticalization and a shift in the semantics of *do*.

There are then two points of change to characterize, and it looks as if either might be the stage at which *do* was reanalysed as a unitary item expressing tense/mood. I suggest, however, that a better answer might somehow distinguish a late-fifteenth-century 'unitary' *do* from the late-sixteenth-century identification of *do* and tense/mood. This might follow if we accept the view maintained by Traugott (1972, 1982) that periphrastic *do* initially had a range of pragmatic functions, including 'affirmation of speaker truthfulness' (1982: 257). Stein (1990) argues for a distinct but related position, and surveys a range of data which might support such an interpretation of early Modern English. Such interpretations are broadly consistent too with Denison's (1985a) persuasive suggestion that periphrastic *do* arose as a semantic weakening of *do* 'achieve'; we simply need to flesh out the stages of this weakening. What these approaches share is a stage at which auxiliary *do* is not simply a grammaticalized equivalent of tense and mood. If such a view is reasonable we may interpret developments as follows.

Stage I. From the late fifteenth century *do* expresses tense and mood within a unitary lexical item, like the modals of the newly delineated class. It has some advantage in inverted structures (a topic which will be taken up below) and its use in such contexts increases as the occurrence of tense/mood in inverted structures with full verbs declines. It is in inverted structures that it occurs most strongly.[33] But *do* has a range of pragmatic/discourse functions and is not yet merely the expression of tense and mood. It has a lexical identity, and it is also available in other contexts, both negative and affirmative. The first choice facing the language user who wants to realize tense is '*do* or full verb'. Consequently the development of *do* proceeds at a 'constant rate' across different contexts. The exception is that affirmative contexts develop *do* more slowly. This may be attributed to some (relatively stable) interfering factor, possibly the well-attested social and stylistic evaluation of this category (see Ellegård 1953: 169, Stein 1990 esp. Ch. 6).[34] This account predicts that non-finites of periphrastic *do* should decline as this analysis is adopted generally in recorded texts, that is, from the turn of the fifteenth century, and this is correct (see §9.1).

Stage II. In interrogative inversions the pragmatic/discourse functions of *do* are restricted to focus on the truth value/polarity of the proposition. As such structures become more common, *do* is reanalysed as having simply (or centrally) the semantics appropriate to tense and mood. This is essentially a variant (or reinterpretation) of the semantic account given by Stein (1990). Now *do* and affix are both realizations of tense/mood, as in today's English, and this choice is context-dependent (in this way *do* and affix are like allomorphs of a single category). The choice facing the language user who wants to realize tense/mood is '*do* or affix in the context of this V and construction'. Consequently the development of *do* fragments, and proceeds at different rates in different contexts. The phenomenon of 'blocking' begins to affect affirmative *do*, which declines, though it takes over a century before this preference against synonymy results in the absence of unemphatic *do*. This must be referred to the eighteenth century, and where *do* – adverb – verb is concerned, even to the ninteenth century (Sweet 1891–8: §2180, Tieken 1987: 118ff.). Thus the function of 'affirmation of speaker truthfulness' declines except in so far as it is conveyed contextually by specific combinations, or by emphasis. Note that Stein interprets the modern contrast of polarity found in 'emphatic *do*' as first attested at the close of the sixteenth century (1990: 273), and he sees this as consistent with his proposed semantic reanalysis of *do* at that period.

The change to stage II is relatively abrupt, and it may well be due to child learning: the language experience of learners may well have contained a higher proportion of interrogative *do*, and a smaller proportion of affirmative *do* than is shown by Ellegård's figures, given the evidence that the first is particularly frequent in colloquial registers, the second in certain literary styles (Ellegård 1953: 166ff.).[35]

9.5.4 The decline of verb-second order

This account of the two stages of the development of *do* does not yet interconnect its rise with the decline of verb-second order and the changing status of modals. Discussion of this requires an account of the major principles of word order in earlier English, and this will be couched within HPSG in terms of the way subjects are realized.

The typology of subcategorization for subject

Chapter 3 gave an account of English clause structure in terms of two lexical features, SUBJ and SUBCAT, and two corresponding universal Immediate Dominance rules, which are repeated in an abbreviated form below.

(14) a. *Rule 1*
[SUBJ < >] → H[–LEX, SUBJ <C>], C

b. *Rule 2*
[SUBCAT < >] → H[+LEX, SUBCAT <C*>], C*
In these rules H stands for 'head', C for 'complement (or subject)', and C* for any number of complements (including none). The attribute LEX distinguishes lexical items [+LEX] from phrasal categories [–LEX].

c. *'Subcategorization Principle'*
'A category that is on the SUBCAT list of a head and not on the SUBCAT list of its mother or on the SUBJ list of a head and not on the SUBJ list of its mother must be matched by a sister of the head' (Borsley 1987: 6).

The features SUBJ and SUBCAT define an item's subject and complements, and the 'subcategorization principle' of (14.c) requires a head category to occur with appropriate sisters. The relevant Immediate Dominance rule establishes mother–daughter relations of constituent structure, and left–right order is the province of separate rules of linear precedence. Thus the *puts* of *He puts any windfalls in the bank* will be entered in the lexicon as V[SUBJ <NP[nom., 3sg.]>, SUBCAT <NP, PP>]. When *puts* occurs with the appropriate sisters: NP (*any windfalls*), PP (*in the bank*), the value of its SUBCAT feature is satisfied, and its mother carries the 'saturated' feature SUBCAT < >. This is in accordance with rule 2. Similarly when *puts any windfalls in the bank* occurs with the appropriate sister NP[nom., 3sg.] (*he*) the value of its SUBJ feature is satisfied and its mother carries the 'saturated' feature SUBJ < >. This is in accordance with rule 1. Thus as applied to English clauses rule 1 corresponds to the traditional S → NP VP (modulo order), rule 2 to VP → V (+ complements).

Rule 2 also defines 'flat' inverted structures for auxiliaries, corresponding to S → V[+AUX] NP XP, from their derived lexical entry [+AUX, SUBJ < >, SUBCAT <XP, NP>], where the fact that the subject is sister to the auxiliary and its complement is encoded by entering it in the SUBCAT list alongside a saturated SUBJ list. In what follows I will for convenience refer to these two types of clause structure as 'VP structure' and 'flat structure' respectively.

Let us suppose that the notion 'subject' (or 'least oblique complement') is parameterized in the following way: that it may be entered as a value of either SUBJ or SUBCAT (see Borsley 1992 for some evidence for this general position). This is already the implication of the analysis of the contrast between the treatment of uninverted and 'flat' inverted structures for auxiliaries. Then in Old English both flat and VP structures occur. Verb-initial sentences and inverted verb-second sentences will be analysed as having the subject sister to the head V. VP structures will result in SVO ordering (with V initial in its constituent), and will also occur in subjectless nonfinite clauses. SOV order may show either a flat or VP structure; in either case the V is final (or late) in its constituent. Now given the reasonable assumption that subcategorization is essentially a relationship between a head and the categories on its SUBCAT list, we can give an account of a series of differences between Old English and late Middle English as follows. In Old English the flat clause structure is basic, V subcategorizes for its subject, and VP structure is secondary and derived by lexical redundancy rule. In late Middle English the VP structure is basic, V does not subcategorize for its subject, and the flat structure is secondary and derived by lexical redundancy rule.[36] Here I illustrate the analysis from ditransitives, using S (= subject), O (= object), IO (= indirect object) informally to indicate relationships on the 'obliqueness hierarchy'.

(15) Old English
a. Basic lexical entry:
V[SUBJ < >, SUBCAT <IO, O, S>].
b. Derived lexical entry:
V[SUBJ <S>, SUBCAT <IO, O>].

Late Middle English
c. Basic lexical entry:
V[SUBJ <S>, SUBCAT <IO, O>].
d. Derived lexical entry:
V[SUBJ < >, SUBCAT <IO, O, S>].

In both languages V may be initial in its constituent; in Old English it may also be final. Thus given the two universal Immediate Dominance rules of (14), both languages allow clauses with VP-structure and flat structure. Hence in topicalized sentences where some element appears before a clausal structure, that clausal structure may be flat or VP in type. When it is flat with V initial in its constituent we have the inverted verb-second structures typical of these periods.[37]

But in Old English the subject is within SUBCAT in basic lexical entries: hence it is 'strictly subcategorized' by the verb. This means that the verb may not merely select its semantics, but may impose formal or syntactic conditions on it. In particular it may be optional, as in the case of 'weather' verbs such as 'rain'; it may be marked with an oblique case as with central impersonals (both illustrated in Chapter 5). By the fifteenth century, however, subjects are obligatory, and they may no longer be marked with an oblique case by their lexical verb. This is captured if in Old English the default value for SUBJ is < >, but in the fifteenth century it is <S>. This is the 'subject' parameter.

There is a further consequence if we suppose (with Borsley 1987) that unbounded dependencies may only be terminated when they represent values of SUBCAT, not SUBJ. This essentially requires a trace to be sister to a lexical head, thus capturing within HPSG an insight which overlaps with the GB principle that an empty category must be properly governed. The subject of a *that*-clause is a not sister to a lexical head within the VP-structure of Present-day English, hence the **that*-t effect. But in Old English the subject of a *þæt*-clause may indeed be the sister to a lexical head within a flat structure. So in Old English we find instances of '*þæt*-t' like (16) below (Allen 1977: 81ff., 122), though *þæt* and trace need not be contiguous. Note that examples like *the fellow I thought was foolish* are generated with a bare VP complement to the verb in Present-day English (Pollard 1985, following Gazdar *et al.* 1985), so that this type is not a violation of the principle above.

(16) Ac hwæt sægst ðu ðonne ðæt sie forcuðre ðonne sio ungesceadwisnes?
'But what say you then that is wickeder than the foolishness?' = 'But what do you say (that) is wickeder than foolishness?'
Bo 36.109.1

Thus a range of differences between Old English and late Middle English are accounted for by a single parameter. For languages with similar differences between sets of properties see Insular and Mainland Scandinavian (Icelandic, Faroese versus Danish, Norwegian, Swedish); Platzack (1987) gives a summary of major distinctions.

Decline of V2 and the development of 'opaque' modals

So English changes from one 'subject' parameter type to another probably by the second half of the fifteenth century when nominative subjects are effectively obligatory in indicative clauses; subjectless constructions survive this century in only a small number of items and in restricted use (Fries 1940, Elmer 1981, V§3ff.). But the verb-second situation is not stable. Rather, verb-second constructions themselves decline. This seems to be a long-term process, lasting well into the early Modern period. Both Jacobsson (1951) and Ellegård (1953: 188) found that inversion of the simple verb after a fronted element survived comfortably into early Modern English. It is difficult to discern significant turning points, particularly as many types of inversion survive today (Green 1980, 1985). But Jacobsson's (1951) survey of the data pointed to a markedly steep decline at the end of the sixteenth century; in Ellegård's summary: 'For some of the commoner adverbs the proportion of inverted instances was 44% in the 15th, 34% in the 16th, and 7% in the 17th century' (1953: 188). So although there is much uninvestigated complexity here (and note in particular the relevance of the shift away from orally based types of writing; see Stein 1990: 279), it seems safe to suggest that the decline of 'verb-second' structures in affirmative clauses had begun in the fifteenth century, but that such structures certainly survived beyond the end of the sixteenth.[38] Why should English have been different here from other Germanic languages with verb-second constructions? I suggest that we may find an answer in the different realization of mood in these languages. English is distinct in two ways. It has very few morphological distinctions of mood: the imperative, the 'base' form of the indicative, and the subjunctive had become formally identical by the early sixteenth century, and they were not distinct from the infinitive. Past-tense forms were then also largely identical to the second participle. And English had a distinct subclass which realized mood lexically. In contrast the modern Scandinavian languages have formal mood distinctions: imperative, indicative and infinitive must be distinguished, as generally must the subjunctive (though its range of use is very narrow) despite some formal coincidences (Haugen 1976). And their modals are much more like full verbs in construction and morphology. Perhaps then the answer lies here. As morphological contrasts of mood decline in English, it is increasingly realized lexically as modals replace the subjunctive. Tense is presumably also to be included here since it is incorporated into the modals, and on verbs it is morphologically realized along with the indicative (or subjunctive) mood. This may have promoted the lexical realization of other finite moods (indicative and imperative) by periphrastic *do*. But crucially for my argument I suggest it meant that the assignment of agreement, tense, mood and nominative case within flat structures with full verbs became marked (as I will explain directly), hence that such structures tended to decline, though particularly with some individual items they can survive quite late.[39]

In HPSG's lexical approach, finite verbs enter the syntax fully specified for tense, mood and for the case and agreement features of their subjects. These last are assigned via the SUBJ or SUBCAT feature of verbs. In a verb which will enter a VP structure the case and agreement information must be carried on the value of SUBJ, and the less specified (17.a) will be related to the more fully specified (17.b). But in a verb which will enter a flat structure it is carried on the value of SUBCAT, and the less specified (17.c) is related to (17.d). (Here I continue to use S, O, IO informally as above.)

(17) a. V[SUBJ <S>, SUBCAT <IO, O>].
b. V[SUBJ <S[nom., 3sg.]>, SUBCAT <IO, O>].
c. V[SUBJ < >, SUBCAT <IO, O, S>].
d. V[SUBJ < >, SUBCAT <IO, O, S[nom., 3sg.]>].

Now let us suppose that the marking of a verb for tense/mood etc. applies simultaneously with lexical redundancy rules which give 'derived' values of SUBJ and SUBCAT, and that it is combined in a monotonic fashion, so that the combination remains essentially transparent. Since mood/tense is so heavily interinvolved with syntax and since its presence does not block retrieval of the verb without mood and tense in ellipsis this seems to be the appropriate assumption.[40] Then the features required to cope with the 'subcategorization' of tense/mood/agreement (which may be interpreted as a possibly null verbal 'affix') for its verb will be as follows.

(18) a. In combination with a verb that will enter a VP structure (see (17.a)):
SUBCAT <V[SUBJ <S>, +LEX]>.
b. In combination with a verb that will enter a flat structure (see (17.c)):
SUBCAT <V[SUBCAT < … , S>, +LEX]>.

Compare with these the comparable feature specifications for modals and *do* where tense/mood etc. is lexically encoded. Here for both VP and 'flat' structures the modal's subcategorization includes a VP, *viz.* V[SUBJ <S>].

(19) a. For a modal that will enter a VP structure:
SUBJ <S[nom.]>, SUBCAT <V[SUBJ <S>]>.
b. For a modal that will enter a flat structure:
SUBCAT <V[SUBJ <S>], S[nom.]>.

Here note first the degree of overlap between the information which characterizes the 'affix' and modals when a VP structure is involved, in contrast with the considerable differences in the case of flat structures. It is clear that there is a potential generalization between modals and 'affixes' in VP, not clear that there is such a generalization in flat structures. Secondly, a more speculative idea. Note that modals, like other raising predicates, make reference to the value of the SUBJ feature of the VP they combine with (since it is identical in relevant respects to their subject). This holds for both types of structure. The verbal affix also has access to this feature in (18.a), necessarily since it will attach nominative case to it and must agree with it. But the type of reference found in (18.b) into the subcategorization (SUBCAT) feature of a subcategorizand is not paralleled within the syntax of Modern English in a restrictive lexicalist model of grammar. In this type of framework it is isolated as a distinctively morphological property, being typically associated with word formation. If inflection differs from derivational morphology and syntax in its properties (as often suggested; see e.g. Anderson 1982) then we might speculate that there is a difference here between the distinctively morphological (18.b) and the more neutral (18.a) and (19). There may also have been a more strictly syntactic factor in the type of agreement involved. The 'subject' in SUBCAT is classified as a syntactic complement. Thus agreement here holds between a verb and a syntactic complement. It seems possible that this may have been syntactically marked in comparison with subject–verb agreement with a subject in SUBJ. Clearly neither this factor, nor the preceding factors, can stand alone; in particular agreement in inverted structures is perfectly stable in other languages. But cumulatively they may have been decisive for acquisition, particularly if we suppose that periphrastic *do* was particularly common in the colloquial language addressed to children.

One historical possibility then is as follows. Suppose that mood, modality and tense belong together as (part of) a coherent subjective verb-related category which will be subject to the Roschian principle that it is more highly valued as its membership has more unitary properties. Then as modals become more frequent, the importance of their properties to this category must increase. Hence their increasing lexical opacity means that the occurrence of full verbs in flat structures will tend to become increasingly marked in respect of combination with mood/tense. Moreover the independent evidence which would support a distinctively morphological subcategorization for the affix has declined: the overt morphology is weak, and flat structures no longer have a basic status attested by the occurrence of empty or case-marked subjects. A further factor may have been that evidence for the marked type of agreement involved in flat structures declines as the frequency of *do* increases. Here, then, we have a basis for a 'parameterization' of types of inflectional category, those which have the more typically morphological characteristic of reference to the subcategorizational properties of their stem as in (18.b), and those which lack such reference and in that are parallel to syntactic combination. Present-day English has the second, but Old and Middle English had both the second and the first. To put it crudely then, among the factors promoting the loss of V2 structures in English are the opacity of mood and tense in the modals, which represents a lexicalization of these categories, and the weakening of overt distinctions of verbal inflection, perhaps coupled with the comparative markedness of agreement in flat structures.

There is, moreover, a clear implication for the rise of *do*. It offers a lexicalization of mood and tense which avoids the markedness problems of full verbs in inverted structures. Hence the fact that periphrastic *do* is first adopted in, and first goes to completion in, inverted structures. Adoption presumably may begin to occur at any point after verb-second order starts to become marked, and *do* becomes morphosyntactically opaque. This opacity must be motivated by identification with that property in modals, which occurred to some extent in earlier English, but is most obviously to be aligned with the systematizing of the property as auxiliaries become a basic class. Hence the coincidence in date between the rapid adoption of *do* in inversion and the development of basic class status of auxiliaries. This does not, however, account for the distinction between structures in which inversion is retained (contexts of interrogation and negation) and other contexts in which it is lost, and this is an important fact which ought to be integrated in a serious account. This line of explanation may also seem to cause problems for the transparency of *is* in early Modern English, as attested by ellipsis facts (§2.5): should it not too develop an opaque analysis in the sixteenth century? But inversion (and hence the availability of a marked combination with tense) continues with nonauxiliaries for a considerable period, and the factorization of BE is supported by the existence of its nonfinite categories. So the retention of transparent *is* seems justifiable (though its incidence may indeed have been declining in early Modern English). More striking is the point that if the interpretation offered here is correct, the final loss of inversion in nonauxiliaries would motivate the development of opacity in *is*, as was suggested in §2.5.

Summary

Let me summarize the suggestions I have sketched above.

In the course of late Middle English lexical items develop a basic subcategorization which distinguishes subjects from complements, a derived subcategorization which identifies both as values of SUBCAT.

In the fifteenth century verb-second order begins to decline. It has become marked with full verbs because it requires a distinctively morphological combination of tense/mood with the verb, which is at odds with the increasing loss of mood morphology, and with the lexicalized status of tense and mood in the modals. It may also have involved a comparatively marked type of agreement.

Do is reinterpreted as a 'unitary' combination with tense and mood as part of the changes whereby modals acquire 'basic' word-class status. Inversion therefore favours the lexicalized tense and mood of *do* over the morphological tense and mood of full verbs. Hence the striking coincidence of these developments. But *do* remains an independent lexeme, and its occurrence therefore increases across a range of contexts, until *c*1575.

Then, *c*1575, *do* is reanalysed as a unitary 'opaque' combination representing only tense/mood. Its occurrence in distinct subcategorizational contexts is differentiated and the different contexts show separate lines of development. The phenomenon of 'blocking' begins with the decline of affirmative *do*.

This account is necessarily a speculative sketch dependent on a series of assumptions, and the reader may reject some of what I suggest without rejecting all. In particular, my account of the markedness of V2 structures with full verbs is largely independent of the account of the extension of *do*, which can stand by itself.

Alternative accounts

Lightfoot (1991: 153) noted as a problem requiring solution 'Somehow Universal Grammar must enforce a connection between the new lexicalness of INFL and the loss of V-to-INFL in order to explain the obsolescence of *Came John to London?* and the like.' Here, within a different framework, I have tried to show how some of the relevant events might have been interconnected. I have also tried to integrate this with the decline of V2 order, taking the markedness of flat structures to be basic to the change. This more complex characterization is a strength: more data is covered, and the peculiarity of English among Germanic standard languages is more plausibly accounted for in terms of a complex of properties. Moreover, the prediction that inverted structures spearhead the introduction of *do* is consistent with its rapid development in inversion at just the appropriate time, so the account has the apparent advantage of fitting the progression of the historical data closely. Thus we have a coherent alternative to accounts which interpret these changes in terms of growing restrictions on V-to-I movement dependent on the changing status of an agreement parameter, or in terms of the status of *not* (Roberts 1985, Pollock 1989, Weerman 1989).[41] Changes in morphological agreement may indeed be important, though note that any parameterization which focusses on this must involve its abstract properties, since English retains a distinction between the three persons of the singular well beyond 1500 (especially in language addressed to children where *thou* will have been much more common than in the written record).[42] It must also allow for the fact that the mainland

Scandinavian standard languages lack number agreement but retain verb-second constructions, hence V-to-I (Platzack 1987). If the development of *not* as a 'blockade' to the transfer of finiteness features from V to S is crucial (Weerman 1989), it seems curious that the period of the most rapid adoption of the occurrence of *do* with *not* (the centre of the s-curve of change) is as late as the last quarter of the seventeenth century on Ellegård's account and that it does not become categorical until the nineteenth (Rydén 1979: 31). From a historical perspective this looks much more like a secondary development. (See van Kemenade 1989 for a series of problems for Weerman's account.) Kroch (1989b), however, has recently mounted a sophisticated defence of the view that the parameters of diffusion of a change do not 'reflect the forces pushing the change forward' but rather 'the functional effects, discourse and processing, on the choices speakers make among the alternatives available to them in the language as they know it; and the strength of these effects remains constant as the change proceeds' (1989b: 238). I cannot deny the potential of Kroch's argument, especially for cases where parameters are only convincingly attested for part of a change (as with Stein's phonotactic parameters). But he has really only argued for the view that the distribution of parameters is not necessarily relevant; the possibility that they none the less are must remain open. And at least in the present case, the question arises of just why it is that the alternatives available in the language show the pattern of distribution that they do. The answer to this may indeed well be that at least the prominence of inversion reflects the forces pushing the change forward. (This can surely be consistent with the 'constant rate hypothesis', and need not imply 'successive actuation' in any meaningful or detectable sense.) So despite Kroch I am disposed to believe that the fact that periphrastic *do* is initially prominent and first goes to completion in interrogative inversion is no accident, and I suggest that the degree of 'fit' between my account and the historical data is a substantial argument in its favour.

9.6 Conclusions

In this chapter I have presented a detailed account of early Modern English developments in auxiliaries including the general adoption of periphrastic *do*. I have shown how changes in modals and auxiliaries are well interpreted within the framework of a Roschian theory of classes as the development of a basic-level category. This deals with a wider range of data than Lightfoot (1979), and in a more structured way than Plank (1984). It also differs from Lightfoot's (1979) account in that the development is not (ideally) 'cataclysmic'; instead we can account for a series of subsequent developments which further the distinctiveness of the class (and in earlier chapters we accounted for the coherency of antecedent developments). It has been shown how the generalization of the restriction of modals to finite can be interpreted as the reanalysis of a lexically based property, so that modals and *do* systematically lack the nonfinite morphosyntactic categories of verbs. This is consistent with developments in BE and HAVE which lack predicative categories, though they are not as close to the modal prototype in their general properties as they later become, and the whole account is consistent with the grammar of present-day auxiliaries argued for in Chapters 2 and 3. It therefore underpins the 'lexical' account of the first half of the book by showing that it can deal with history.

I have also provided a speculative but coherent account of the development of *do*, making essentially three claims. First, the decline of verb-second order in English was promoted by the lexicalization of mood and tense in the modals and the decline of inflectional morphology. Second, the rise of *do* followed from the markedness of full verbs in verb-second order and the fact that when *do* was reinterpreted as 'opaque' to mood/tense as a consequence of the reanalysis of modals, this meant that inverted structures with *do* avoided the markedness of inverted structures with full verbs. Hence the rise of periphrastic *do* is closely associated with the development of basic status for auxiliaries. Thirdly, its predominance in interrogative inversion meant that *do* was reinterpreted *c*1575 as simply equivalent to tense/mood, and it thereafter developed the complementary distribution with the affix characteristic of today.

10 *Conclusions*

In this book I have tried to offer a relatively nonabstract account of major aspects of the grammar and history of English auxiliaries, not simply relying on reinterpretations of established data, but undertaking some further investigations as appropriate. I do not (of course) pretend to have provided a complete account, but have focused on specific topics which I am confident will need to be integrated within a more complete statement. My conclusions can be best presented under four headings.

Synchrony. I have argued for a new analysis of English auxiliaries, claiming that a series of their properties has a natural interpretation if they are analysed as a word class which is distinct from verbs particularly in that they are not subject to the regularities of verbal morphosyntax. What look like inflected forms are not, but (with the partial exception of *being* and *having*) are holistic or unitary items incorporating tense, mood or nonfinite categories lexically. This gives a rational account of the ordering of auxiliaries, of the absence of particular categories, of some curious facts about ellipsis, and of a range of other particular properties. It also accounts for the learnability of such properties. A formal analysis within the account of the lexicon given in HPSG was outlined, and a small set of lexical redundancy rules was shown to give a rather complete account of auxiliary constructions. It was more speculatively suggested that the distinct categoriality of auxiliaries in the case of modals (whose properties are central to the class) partly but crucially involves the interaction of subjectivity with their formal distinctness from verbs.

Diachrony. Arguments have been mounted against the view that 'pre-auxiliaries' were ordinary members of the class of verbs in Old and Middle English, showing that (at the present stage of research) it is reasonable to suppose that they manifested a substantial correlation of distinctive formal properties at these periods and that the grouping is identifiable as 'auxiliary' on the basis of its prototypical semantics. A version of a traditionally structuralist account of word classes in which classes may be cross-linguistically identified on notional grounds was spelled out, and arguments based solely on semantics or on hypothetical universals were carefully avoided. Thus there is a responsible distributional basis for the position that Old and Middle English had 'auxiliary verbs', but that they formed a subordinate, relatively less well defined class. An extended series of early Modern English changes was interpreted as the development of 'basic-level' category status for this class and the consequences of that development. This included the systematic generalization of what had been a lexically based finiteness restriction in modals, a property which it was suggested was relevant to the loss of verb-second order and to the rise of periphrastic *do*. The full rejection of verbal morphosyntax for *be* and *have* followed later in the eighteenth century, and the historical account is fully compatible with the grammar presented for Present-day English.

Lexical syntax. I hope to have shown the plausibility of a rather lexical, nonabstract approach to the syntax of this area both in synchrony and diachrony. If my arguments hold, the importance of such types of account for some areas of grammar is enhanced. Three particular points are worth remarking. (i) The finiteness restriction on modals has been dealt with lexically in a motivated way, not simply as an accidental exceptionality, without positing a special syntactic position or restriction. (ii) Relevant generalizations can be stated without overpredicting. This ability to state partial generalizations illustrates a strength of unification formalism. (iii) The speculative interconnection between the morphosyntactic opacity of the modals, the loss of V2 order, and the rise of periphrastic *do* involves the parametricization of the interaction of inflection with the subcategorization properties of lexical items, but does not require an operation of V-to-I Movement. Moreover, the learnability of the obsolescence of nonfinite *may*, of *Came John?*, of *being acting a part*, of *I wish our opinions were the same but in time they will* have all been accounted for. This lexicalist treatment is not open to the type of objection raised by Lightfoot (1991: Ch. 6) against limited lexicalist accounts which deal with exceptionality by means of the accumulation of exception features on lexemes. Indeed, if it is viable, it implies that there is a substantial place for the 'lexical' treatment of properties even of a highly grammaticized area, which may indeed prove to be integrable as a modular component within a more abstract account but which carries an implicit challenge to more abstract accounts of this area of syntax.

Grammaticalization. A central process here is the development (later, the generalization) of the semantic (or semantic–pragmatic) opacity of inflectional categories in particular lexical items. The formal process started apparently when a small group of items (perhaps only *mot, sceal, uton*) which had been associated with subjectivity (perhaps as a conventional implicature) were reinterpreted as holistic items having opaque morphosyntax. This encoding of exceptionality within the lexical item was supported by formal regularities before recorded Old English (as the history of *uton* makes plain), and I would speculate that there was previously an association or correlation between subjectivity and the preterite-present morphology of these items. There is no evidence that semantic developments preceded associated syntactic and morphological changes as was suggested by Brinton (1988) in the development of aspectuals. But correspondence with cross-linguistic, notional universals is perhaps important. The major candidate property here is subjectivity. Another is being a 'sentential modifier' (lacking selection of subject and complement, or failure to assign 'theta roles'). Both of these properties are very fully developed by the time that the category is focussed as a basic-level category *c*1500. But in Old English being a 'sentential modifier' may have been secondary: its status depends on the analysis assigned to deontics, and *uton* in particular does not look like a sentential modifier.[1] Occurrence before ellipsis (or as a proform), however, is well developed in Old English, and this may be a candidate for a more general formal property.

The later history was interpreted as involving principles derived from a synchronic account of category formation. To the traditionally structuralist account of word classes was added the distinction drawn by Rosch between different levels of categorization and their properties for general cognitive categories; these are presumably also relevant to open classes, not just to auxiliaries. They give us some partial theoretical basis for implicitly functionalist accounts.

(i) A central 'basic' level of categorization tends to maximize coherency and distinctness.
As auxiliaries become basic-level categories they develop a sharply higher level of coherency and distinctness from nonauxiliary verbs, and over the following centuries there is a continuing tendency to favour further such developments.

(ii) More speculatively, in some circumstances an increase in frequency and salience of items or attributes may make a category more coherent and distinct. In mediaeval English a subordinate-level category became steadily better defined as its members and attributes (and their association) became more frequent and salient. This happened partly because of the decline of the morphology of verbal mood, partly because of the internal dynamic of the group's own development.

This account of categorization proved insightful in interpreting the history of auxiliaries, and it seems reasonable to suggest that this reflects an aspect of the behaviour of linguistic categories which may be referred to general cognitive properties. It is not reflected in the formalism of feature systems, but linguists none the less need to take account of it.

Notes

1 Basic properties of English auxiliaries

1 The major criteria here are often referred to as NICE properties after Huddleston (1976b: 333), where NICE is an acronym for 'Negation, Inversion, Code, Emphasis'. As will be clear from what follows, I prefer not to regard the characteristic emphatic uses of auxiliaries as a distinctive constructional or other 'property' (as Huddleston and Palmer apparently do), though it leads to a workable criterion. The convenient acronym NICE can alternatively be interpreted as 'Negation, Inversion, Contracted/Clitic, Ellipsis', where 'contracted' includes *-n't*. The 'floating' of the quantifiers *all* and *both* from subject to postverbal position has not been included as a test for auxiliaryhood, although it is given by Pullum and Wilson (1977) and Quirk *et al.* (1985: §3.28), and it is treated as an auxiliary phenomenon by Pollock (1989). But it seems equally to be found with other catenatives, especially raising verbs, and is not apparently restricted to auxiliaries. See in particular the discussion of Huddleston (1980: 74). There is a perhaps related but much less clear difficulty over the criterion involving adverb position, see Chapter 2 note 10.

2 The term 'verbal group' will be used for any sequence of auxiliaries which is not itself dependent on an auxiliary, together with any following dependent nonauxiliary verb (see Huddleston 1976a: 57ff.).

3 There are also parallel constructions with pro-verbal *do* at least in British English. This may 'stand for' an entire preceding verb phrase, in parallel to post-auxiliary ellipsis, or it may take (in whole or in part) the construction of another verb which is its antecedent, in parallel to pseudogapping (see (i) – (iii) below). It seems to be the nonauxiliary verb which has these otherwise auxiliary properties. The fact that the properties go together implies that there is a generalization across these constructions.

(i) I rely on friends, just as you have always done.
(ii) I rely on my friends, as you can surely do on yours.
(iii) Probably drives him crazy to have her call him up all the time. It would do me.

4 Including asyndetic coordinations, as in (10.a) without *and*. But gapping may also make some restricted contribution to ellipsis in comparatives. Levin (1978) identified post-auxiliary ellipsis and pseudogapping, but in 1980 she distinguished them. Her reasons, however, all involve particular restrictions on pseudogapping which are absent on post-auxiliary ellipsis. This type of argument merely shows that

pseudogapping is a subcase of post-auxiliary ellipsis with a more limited distribution. And many of the restrictions she cites are readily understandable as limitations on a more marked construction containing a contrastive element; see her perceptually based account of the 'like-subject condition' on pseudogapping, or the claimed absence of pseudogapping after *to* (but see §1.3.2), which may merely show a lexically based restriction on this item.

5 See Palmer (1979: 6, 29f.), and discussions of individual verbs; Quirk *et al.* (1985: §§4.50, 4.59ff.); Coates (1983: discussions of individual verbs).

6 For example by Jespersen (1909-49: IV, esp. §9.5), Joos (1964), Huddleston (1971), Perkins (1983: 107f.).

7 The first problem remains if *would* (etc.) are analysed as having the same form in both present and preterite. This is unusual in verbs, but found, as in *shed, outbid.*

8 But see Palmer's suggestion that basic discourse functions which do not modify propositional content are characteristic of the NICE properties (Palmer 1983: 207, 1986: 91).

9 Imperative *do/don't* is rather idiosyncratic but seems to belong better here than under (iii). *Don't* fulfils more tests: it has inversion with the subject, which *do* lacks. *Do* is also not clearly one item in that *do not* seems not to involve the 'emphatic imperative' *do* which has a special semantics. But both pass the tests for ellipsis, and for adverb position: *Don't ever touch me*; *Please do sometimes touch me.*

10 This is essentially why I avoid the terminology of Palmer, who calls modals 'secondary auxiliaries', *be*, *do* and *have* 'primary auxiliaries'. As auxiliaries it is modals that are primary, *be*, *do* and *have* that are secondary. Palmer's use of the terminology seems to depend on a distinction between 'paradigms': 'primary' *takes, is taking* etc., 'secondary' *must take*, *must be taking*, etc. (Palmer 1988: 26ff. and *passim*). Quirk at al. (1985), on the other hand, refer to *be*, *do* and *have* as 'primary verbs', see their §2.29 for a rationale.

11 Schachter's nonfinites in tag questions as in *John shouldn't have been smoking, should he have?* (1983: 150) are presumably not a separate test from ellipsis.

12 Examples (18)–(21.a) and (22) (and their glosses) are from Coates (1983), (21.b, c) from Palmer (1979).

13 The exception is *have* + past participle, a unique subcategorization in Standard English. I assume that *help* is subcategorized for the plain infinitive among other possibilities.

14 Zagona (1988) analyses perfective *have* and 'progressive' *be* as head of their phrase, but the arguments she deploys depend on specific assumptions in X-bar theory and do not carry over to my framework.

15 See especially Sag (1977), Neijt (1980) and Sag *et al.* (1985: 156ff.) for examples and discussion of gapping. Van Oirsouw (1987) surveys the literature.

16 Akmajian, Steele and Wasow (1979: 18, n. 17) claimed that Pullum and Wilson's argument failed because nouns and adjectives also underwent gapping, so that there was no simple generalization across auxiliaries and full verbs. See Schachter (1983: 195f.), Warner (1989b) for rebuttals of their argument.

17 I use the descriptively convenient term 'small clause', but do not intend to imply that such sequences should necessarily be analysed as constituents.

18 Perfect *have* and 'progressive' *be* were analysed as (underlying) heads with a VP complement (ASW assigned the complements distinct bar levels, as in (45)). Others assigned less structuring here, or took them as specifiers within VP. Copula *be*, and possessive *have* were taken to be (underlying) heads within VP.

19 As well as '*Have/be* shift', which ensures that finites of *be* and auxiliary *have* are operators and that these words do not follow periphrastic *do*, a rule of '*Do* deletion' is required to prevent the occurrence of unstressed periphrastic *do* + full verb.

20 But Roberts (forthcoming) and others place AgrP above TP (an order which would reflect the morphological structuring of Romance languages).

2 The morphosyntactic independence of auxiliaries

1 Moreover, it depends on the *ad hoc* adoption of particular restrictions and features; see Warner (1985: 17) for some comments. An account along similar general lines was offered in Warner (1985). But this also did not offer the more general justification required for plausibility.

2 But Schachter (1983: 157ff.) would in fact permit all the 'impossible' combinations of aspectual *be* and *have* given an appropriate context (though he stars **John has had eaten* on the ground 'that there is unlikely to arise any situation to which such niceties [i.e. the relative past of a relative past] are suited' (1983: 165)). Thus he suggests that in a particular context 'it might be possible for me to say … *?Whenever I see you, you're always just having returned from a vacation*' (1983: 161). But such examples are surely straightforwardly ungrammatical, not 'marginally tolerable' as Schachter would have it.

3 I shall suppose that progressive and nonprogressive *ing*-forms are to be distinguished either syntactically (as in my Chapter 3) or semantically (but this is less plausible; see my comments above) so that there is indeed a category 'progressive participle'. The pragmatic treatment of the difference offered by Stump (1985) seems unconvincing. In either case, *having* simply lacks the relevant property (which the learner has no basis for acquiring).

4 Here and below I shall suppose that the coordinations of (35) in Chapter 1 are zeugmatic. But this may not be the best decision.

5 Together of course with whatever principle ensures that the head of the complement carries the category of its mother. Note that I have for simplicity omitted auxiliary *to* and imperatives, as well as nonprogressive *ing*-forms, from the following discussion.

6 There are three sets of facts here:

(a) the requirement of each individual item that it should be followed by a specific morphosyntactic category;
(b) the availability of morphosyntactic categories of individual items;
(c) the ordering of morphosyntactic categories.

It is clear that either the second or the last of these is redundant, that is that

(a) & (c) ⊃ (b);
(a) & (b) ⊃ (c).

In Warner (1985) I took (a) and (c) to be basic and predicted (b). But I now believe that it is better to take (a) and (b) to be basic and predict (c).

7 Those familiar with the analyses of ASW and Lapointe will be interested briefly to note that they both generate structures for the 'verbal group' which come very close to encapsulating the morphosyntactic ordering of (8), though their structures are imposed by very different principles (including the use of a series of bar-levels in VP) and show configurational differences. Lapointe (1980a) generates auxiliaries in stacked verb phrases which reflect my ordering except in one minor respect which he does not defend. ASW generate initial structures which look very different, but they argue for restructuring rules which have the effect of moving BE and HAVE to positions which correspond to morphosyntactic categories, and their transformation of *Do* Replacement ensures that finite BE and HAVE occur in the same position as other finites (modals and *do*). For details of the correspondence in both cases see Warner (1985: 68-70).

8 The rare attestations of a progressive *ing*-form after a gerund *being* in British and Australian English noted by Halliday (1980), are taken here to be strictly ungrammatical. Their infrequent occurrence shows the pressure of semantics on grammar; see Halliday's discussion of their expressive function.

9 *Neededn't* and *daredn't* might of course have become *needn't* and *daren't* by an essentially phonological reduction (see Jespersen 1909-49: I, §7.72; IV, §§1.7(4), 1.8(1)). But examples of preterite *need* and *dare* are not restricted to instances with a following *not*. See Visser, for *dare*; also Quirk and Duckworth (1961).

10 There is also the evidence of adverb positioning to consider. Since adverbs such as (i) *often, always, never, scarcely, seldom, virtually,* etc.; (ii) *probably, certainly, evidently, clearly,* etc. may occur after *being* and *having* this may seem to show that they are [+AUX] (see §1.2(f)). But I am sceptical that reference to [+AUX] is required to state the positioning of adverbs. Note that many adverbs of the classes above may occur after a raising verb before VP without a separate intonation contour.

(i) a. George often/always/never/scarcely seems to enjoy himself on holiday.
b. George seems often/always/never/scarcely to enjoy himself on holiday.

(ii) a. George certainly/evidently/clearly seems to be the best candidate.
b. George seems certainly/evidently/clearly to be the best candidate.

In the case of (i) there are differences of scope, but these do not need syntactic statement via [+AUX]. Instances like (ii) seem impeccable to me (and other speakers of British English I have consulted) though they are limited. There are restrictions on such adverb placement which I suggest depend on the fact that many sentence adverbs not only require to be in a syntactic position where they can be interpreted as having a clause within their scope, they also require to be closely associated with the deictic and mood properties of some (perhaps reported) speech act or 'tensed' proposition (which may have nonfinite syntax), perhaps because they have a subjective element (sometimes a strong one, as with *probably* or *frankly*). They therefore resist embedded position within the clause. In some dialects when medial in *John would have been singing* they are restricted to occurrence before or after *would*. Other dialects add the position after *have*. The position after *been* is always difficult. So reference to [+AUX] does not seem helpful. (Note incidentally the impossibility of **John has probably the money* in British English which also implies that reference to [+AUX] is also not sufficient). Although I have no account of the restrictions on their placement I suggest that the syntactic element in it is simply 'before VP or predicate phrase', and that no reference should be made to [+AUX]. The occurrence of *having evidently enjoyed himself on holiday* is then evidence not that *having* is [+AUX] but that the proposition has sufficiently independent status to permit subjective modification.

11 Does this make the lack of a progressive interpretation for *having* a puzzle? No, because I'm not claiming there is a productive relationship with the other forms of the verb (which are anyway [+AUX]), just a transparent analysis for the *ing*-form.

12 ASW claim straightforwardly that the only form of BE which may be fronted is *being* (see their (77), p. 28), though there is no explicit discussion of the crucial instances of (k) and (l), which their analysis predicts to be ungrammatical, either here or in Akmajian and Wasow (1975). GPS's analysis makes the reverse prediction for (k) and (l). The examples of (l) seem clearly ungrammatical. Those of (k) also seem generally unacceptable, though the judgement is not so clear. It seems best to accept the judgements implied by ASW.

13 It may also provide a basis for an account of the claimed failure of stranded *being* after a fronted complement (ASW: 28 and Iwakura 1977, 1983) as in *They all said that John was being obnoxious before I arrived, and obnoxious he was being!* Note that Huddleston's (1980) reported judgements of the fronting of predicative and VP complements generally allow '[+AUX] – gap', disallow '[–AUX] – gap'. GPS, however, claim that (with appropriate stress patterns) such instances are grammatical (GPS: 630-1).

14 There is a recent account of fronting in Zagona (1988), but she does not discuss the status of *being* in such examples.

15 But nonfinites may be possible for some. Seppänen (1979: 17-18) claims that infinitives and nonprogressive *ing*-forms may be acceptable in particular instances (though her examples sound questionable or unacceptable to me). Coates found only finites in her collection of examples (which included the Lancaster corpus) (1983: 52).

16 In some American English 'nonaspectual' auxiliary *have* is apparently restricted to the present tense (Akmajian and Wasow 1977; and see LeSourd 1976 for *have got*). This also fits well with my lexical account.

17 The examples of (20) are all, of course, acceptable with a final *to*, but then we have no reason to interpret *have* as the auxiliary.

18 My suggested analysis must raise the question: how far does this phenomenon go? Clearly, present and preterite may have distinct properties in the case of modals (see also GPS: 611, n. 17 for the semantics of modals in inversion, and note the absence of *would*, but not other preterite modals, in conditional inversions: *if she would admit ... /*would she admit ...*). Note the idiosyncrasies of HAVE just discussed in (vii) and note 16, and the possibility that the present (or finite) of perfect HAVE has a distinct semantics (see Salkie 1989 for references. and discussion). The paradigm of BE also shows added distinctions: *if I were* and (for some) *if he be*, and the inverted *aren't I* beside **I aren't*. The dialect reported by Myhill (1988) appar-

ently shows inflected forms of auxiliary BE in inversion and with *not*, but invariable finite *be* in straightforward affirmative sentences, reflecting the distinct subcategorizational properties of these paradigms. Thus it is arguable that the possibility of idiosyncratic properties can hold within the finite paradigm and even for individual forms. And perhaps we should add clitics: compare *There's a man been attacked* but **There is/has a man been attacked* (Kaisse 1985: 43). One possible analysis here is that *there* may provide the limited context in which *'s* neutralizes *is/has*.

19 Coordination differences argue for a categorial distinction between *my* and *John's*, but this may be determiner versus NP rather than a difference of case category; compare **John's and my book*; *those books of John's and mine*; **John's and mine book*.

20 Elsewhere, note that *wh*-words can also be interpreted as showing individual properties, for example *whose* may be inanimate when relative, not when interrogative, *how* is not available in relatives with an antecedent.

21 But some retrieval from derivatives is relatively acceptable: this point will be taken up below.

22 Different principles may actually be involved in cases of coreference and of identity of sense. Inflected forms may refer, whereas the parts of derived stems do not have independent reference (despite Postal's discussion of *orphan* cited above); the failure of coreference into anaphoric islands may depend on this. If so, then in cases of sense retrieval some different principle will be involved.

23 Schachter (1978) has argued that this retrieval may be based in the nonverbal situation, but instances of apparent retrieval without a verbal context are very restricted, and it seems more satisfactory to interpret them as a distinct phenomenon.

24 Some parallels to Postal's examples are neutralized with pseudogapping.

25 More precisely, it is the phrase headed by the verb which is transparent rather than just the verb. But word and 'phrase headed by word' seem equally to result in anaphoric islands and to be similarly tolerant of violations: compare *?*Tobacco-smokers really shouldn't, ?*Smokers of tobacco really shouldn't* [sc. *smoke tobacco*]. Thus the simpler formulation is sufficient for the contrast between verbs and auxiliaries which will be discussed below.

26 Akmajian and Wasow (1975) suggested a separate process of auxiliary ellipsis for reasons which do not survive the criticisms of Iwakura (1977), Sag (1977) and Huddleston (1978). Nor is there a separate process of auxiliary ellipsis in comparatives, see Napoli (1983) (and Kuno 1981).

27 Some examples of these types (33.b) and (34.b) were included in the questionnaire reported immediately below. Virtually all respondents found them highly unacceptable, (*) with a few (?*); none found them acceptable.

28 I am grateful to the students taking English language degree papers in 1985 who provided the data. Similar results were found for an earlier questionnaire with five respondents reported in Warner (1985: 60 and n. 29).

29 Only a minority of judgements (4 per cent) favoured an ellipsis with V over one with BE, and they were found equally in all three groups.

30 In my 1985 questionnaire seven individuals showed a marked dislike of ellipsis of perfect HAVE with a nonidentical antecedent, and preferred examples with identical

antecedent. But among other individuals there were a few scattered instances where this judgement was reversed (with a narrow difference of acceptability), and there was a proportion of cases where retrieval was rejected whatever the antecedent. Thus the picture was less sharp than with BE. In the case of possessive HAVE thirteen of the respondents rejected (as *, ?*, or ??) its ellipsis when it followed a nonidentical HAVE which showed auxiliary behaviour (as in (45.a)), though most of these found acceptable instances with a potentially nonauxiliary antecedent of identical morphosyntactic category (as in (45.b)). I have not discussed ellipsis after *having* because this is so generally unacceptable (Huddleston 1980: 70).

31 I suggested above that for some speakers nonfinites of possessive HAVE may be nonauxiliary. If this is so, then difficulties of retrieval from an auxiliary antecedent might be attributable to the difference between nonauxiliary and auxiliary, rather than to differences of morphosyntactic category.

32 If the ellipsis of BE-phrases and HAVE-phrases was only permitted when the immediate context was given information, their morphological identity would follow. But this is not so: consider *John should be there by now, and I expect Paul will too*, and other examples cited above.

33 Antecedent imperative *be*, which I have not discussed here, straightforwardly permits retrieval of infinitive *be*, but not of *been*, *being*. Thus if imperatives are finite as I argue in the next chapter, the relevant notion of 'morphosyntactic category' must permit the neutralization of finiteness between imperatives and infinitives: that is, it must essentially involve the 'base form' whether finite or nonfinite. But this hardly seems implausible given their invariable identity of form, and perhaps of semantics; see Huntley (1984).

34 In Welsh English *will* appears in such examples as: *Is he ready? No, but he will in a minute* (see Trudgill and Hannah 1982: 29). This, however, may be a calque on Welsh *bydd* 'will be', which is used to form a future tense of other verbs, and which may occur before parallel ellipses.

35 Thus the retrieval of 'can/be able to swim 10 metres at age eight' may be impossible in (i) either because nonfinites of *can* do not exist, or because they cannot be retrieved from the finite.

(i) If John could swim 10 metres at age eight, then surely Paul will.

But the fact that I find the retrieval of **stridden* as in (ii) grammatical although the form does not exist in my idiolect may imply that there is indeed an argument here for the morphosyntactic opacity of finite modals.

(ii) I asked if he ever strode across the room, and he replied that he frequently had [sc. stridden across the room].

In dialects with modal nonfinites it may be possible to test this opacity, but the variability found in Standard English, and the possibility of retrieval where there is some degree of morphological transparency may mean that results are not simple to interpret.

36 The weakness of the opposition of tense (in the time-reference sense) is also argued by the fact that where there is no secondary modal the present-tense form is

available with past sense in a past context (with *must, need, dare*). Note here the recent extension of uses of *may* into contexts where *might* was previously normal.

37 There may seem to be a possible difficulty here and with the parallel suggestion made below for mood, that it will get scope relations wrong. But recent work by Enç (see esp. 1986) has called into question the notion that tense is a scope-assigning operator.

38 I am not convinced that English has a real subjunctive (except perhaps for BE), but would treat examples like *demand that he not go* as nonfinite *that*-clauses. Modals only occur in such clauses in so far as indicatives also may, and it seems clear that in the most straightforward account they are simply indicatives.

39 For example, it may be possible to devise one in which deontic modals are indicative, the specification of deontic source is left open (as e.g. in Perkins' 1983 treatment of modals), and there is an account based on conversational implicature to the directive illocutionary force of subjective deontics.

40 Palmer posits a distinct modality component where 'a single simple judgement is made' so that 'we should expect the modals not to cooccur' (1983: 209). But he gives no reason for supposing that the modality component should be so simple: illocutionary forces may after all be rather complex.

41 Some writers admittedly seem to avoid the construction, perhaps because of its 'jingle'. But note that Dryden, who is such a writer, none the less has at least one instance (Söderlind 1951-8).

42 There is not enough data to comment sensibly on ellipsis of BE with nonfinite antecedent (see incidental examples in V§§1756, 1759, 1763), or HAVE with finite antecedent. That there may be a similar situation in this last case is implied by the following example. But I do not have the relevant more general data.

> Have you never been there? No, you never can. (1814 Jane Austen, *Mansfield Park*, ed. J. Lucas, Oxford University Press, 1970: 50)

Since eModE preterite modal + infinitive can correspond to PE modal + *have* + infinitive some apparent examples are not necessarily relevant, for example, those cited for the eighteenth century in V§1758 (and for 1742 in §1756).

43 It may have been lost earlier in particular registers, since it is restricted to her letters and to reported speech in the novels.

44 See Warner (1986) for two further possibilities here: that *am*-forms lose inflectional morphology with the loss of *art, wert, wast*; and that this loss leads to the hypercharacterization of the indicative paradigm of BE.

3 A formal interlude: the grammar of English auxiliaries

1 Borsley treats 'SUBJ as a feature that takes as its value a single member list' (1987: 6). We need to distinguish the values of SUBJ (and SUBCAT) when they are 'saturated', that is after combination with the complements they specify, from instances of simple underspecification. This is one way of doing it for SUBJ, which I adopt without enthusiasm as a minor 'matter of execution'.

2 See Kornai and Pullum (1990) for arguments that the essential content of X-bar theory can be reformulated by reference to headedness, without the concept of bar-level.

3 See Borsley (1987: 6, 1989: 335) for similar formulations of these rules; see also Pollard and Sag (1987: 150ff.).

4 The disjunction here is resolved in terms of a common property in Borsley (1993) where SUBCAT and SUBJ are identified as 'valency features' along with the attribute SPEC which is proposed for NPs. The 'Subcategorization Principle' is then restated as applying to 'valency features'.

5 Here as below I present category information informally suppressing the detailed structuring of the theory. In general I broadly follow Pollard and Sag (1987) (Pollard and Sag (forthcoming) only became available to me in prepublication form at a late stage of revision) except for the adoption of SUBJ, and my substitution of Boolean valued attributes for major category distinctions and for morphosyntactic categories of the verb. Phrasal categories are themselves attribute-value matrices containing an attribute DAUGHTERS, though structures are normally presented as trees for the reader's convenience.

6 Radford (1988: 330) calls such sentences 'semi-echoic' and this might seem to open the possibility of retrieval of the semantics of (progressive) *be* from a preceding verbal context. But (8.a) is a perfect initial utterance in a context where Major is on the television. Thus such sentences are not restricted to 'echoic' contexts.

7 But note that a syntactic distinction is not essential for the analysis of my Chapter 2 to hold. This requires only that there be some distinction between progressive and nonprogressive *ing*-forms which requires to be stated; it may as well be semantic as syntactic (provided an account of the strict, and therefore apparently grammaticalized, prohibition against perfect **is having* can be given).

8 See the analyses of gerunds in Schachter (1976), Pullum (1991). Do we, however, need to characterize a class of 'predicative adjuncts' which includes perfect *having*? I suggest that what is striking about adjuncts is the freedom with which different phrasal categories may occur, and do not see that there is any need to isolate a 'predicative' subset except perhaps with [+N] categories.

9 Here I assume a couple of transparent features: DIR encodes the directionality of the complement of *been* and GOT is justified in Warner (1985: 45 and n. 23). Imperative *do* and *don't* (for which see below) are not included, nor is identificational *be*.

10 Pollard and Sag (1987: 193ff., 207) imply a substantial reduction in redundancy; Flickinger (1987: 7) adopts the stronger position that 'each new piece of information, each distinct property exhibited by one or more elements of the lexicon, is introduced exactly once in the lexicon'. In general Flickinger's view strikes me as unrealistically strong.

11 I will use Flickinger's more informal terms 'class' and 'subclass'. Flickinger states that the labels assigned to classes 'can be thought of simply as a convenient name for some collection of properties that define the named class' (1987: 20).

12 Flickinger's account differs in a good many details from that given in Pollard and Sag (1987). But I follow Flickinger here without discussion because Pollard and Sag only refer briefly to defaults, and because for my purposes the differences between the two accounts are unimportant.

13 But in Warner (1992b) this class is split into two. This is required to integrate equative *be* in the most coherent way.

14 I shall assume not that VP is inherited from some superordinate class in the COMPLEMENTATION hierarchy with Flickinger (1987: 26), but that a more general account is required in which the values of SUBCAT are by default phrasal, and [+BSE, –FIN, –TO, –PRD] can only be V. This implies that the values of SUBCAT themselves enter the word-class hierarchy under VERB FORM. Pollard and Sag (1987: 204) assign SUBCAT values without generalization, at the level of individual lexemes.

15 This 'merging' is no longer straightforward unification, and neither Flickinger (1987) nor Pollard and Sag (1987) provide a formal statement; see Kaplan's comments on what he calls 'Priority Union' (1987: 180f.).

16 The statement of (14.c) permits *to* to be [+PRD]. That this is appropriate is argued by fact that *seem* occurs with [+PRD] (but not with [–PRD]) complements, and that a *to*-infinitive may be conjoined to the adjectival complement of *seem*.

(i) They seem alike/alive/asleep/ready/*former/*mere.
(ii) They seemed vibrantly alive and to want to enjoy life to the full.
(iii) He seemed quite ready and to have everything he needed.

17 Here I am supposing an account of 'priority unification' (to adapt Kaplan's term) which applies recursively within category-valued categories, in an extension of the account of unification in Gazdar *et al.* (1986). Thus the 'priority unification' of SUBCAT <[+PRD, –BSE]> with SUBCAT <[+BSE, –FIN, –TO, –PRD]>, where SUBCAT <[+PRD, –BSE]> has priority, retains feature values which are consistent with [+PRD, –BSE]. The result is SUBCAT <[–BSE, –FIN, –TO, +PRD]>.

18 *Not* may occur 'within' ellipsis after a nonfinite when it represents one of the remnants of pseudogapping. But the construction requires stressed contrastive *not* and will tend to be limited in acceptability, since it combines two marked constructions (pseudogapping and constituent negation) which exhibit a range of little-understood constraints on acceptability. This seems to be correct. Compare the difference between such pairs as (i)/(ii) and (iii)/(iv).

(i) *Mary may be not eating and Paul may be not too.
(ii) ?*Mary* may be *eating* but *Paul* may be *not*.
(iii) Mary may not be eating and Paul may not either.
(iv) Mary may be eating but Paul may not.

So, in so far as examples like (20.b) above are occasionally acceptable, this is why.

19 This structure creates problems for the derivation of *Have you the money?* which is normal in some British English. But this generally recessive construction might perhaps be treated as an unpredicted peculiarity, in effect a historical relic, without straining credulity.

20 The possibility that SLASH categories would be predicted to percolate into the 'subject' without also percolating into the complement under the SUBCAT analysis, as in (i) beside (ii), is also raised by Pollard and Sag (forthcoming: §9.6).

(i) *Which rebel leader did rivals of e assassinate the British Consul?
(ii) Which rebel leader did rivals of e assassinate e?

But this should be ruled out by their 'Subject Condition'. Since in subject-raising structures information about the subject is shared by the valency statements for the lower and higher predicates, the lower verb (here *assassinate*) will have a value for SUBJ which contains SLASH. But the Subject Condition (which prevents subjects from having nonparasitic gaps) will hold for it. Hence *assassinate* must also have a SLASH within its SUBCAT (see Pollard and Sag forthcoming: §4.5, §9.2).

21 Pollard and Sag do not say what formal condition must be met for a lexical redundancy rule to obtain. I shall assume that lexical redundancy rules apply to (fully) specified lexical entries with which their 'source' (the left-hand side) has a unification. Then since the unification of list valued features requires lists of identical length (Pollard and Sag 1987: 45f.), SUBCAT<XP> will identify only items with a single item on their SUBCAT list. So Negation may not reapply to its output. Inversion may not either. As stated Ellipsis may, but with vacuous effect. This could be avoided by adding [–ELLIPSIS] to the statement of the rule's input.

22 The obliqueness hierarchy is extended by Pollard and Sag (1987: Ch. 7) to include adjuncts and even perhaps phrasal heads, so the inclusion of *not* seems unremarkable.

23 Quirk *et al.* (1985: §11.7) observe that 'some speakers accept' the 'rather formal' construction of *Is not history a social science?* and that this order is especially likely in formal contexts where the subject is lengthy. If some principle of weight ordering is also involved this may account for the exceptional status of tags: *aren't they?*, *are they not?*, **are not they?*

24 Periphrastic *do* does not include imperative *do* for which see the next section.

25 So of course is pro-verbal *do*; see Pollock's identification of this with periphrastic *do*.

26 Fabb (1988) suggests that there are instances of affixes attaching to affixes. But if he is right, this is a highly marked situation, and alternative accounts of his data might be envisaged.

27 The occasional occurrence of unemphatic affirmative *do* (in the spoken English of the London–Lund corpus and the Lancaster–Oslo/Bergen corpus) has been investigated by Nevalainen and Rissanen (1986), who show that its uses seem to involve some kind of textual prominence.

28 A simple formulation within a lexical inheritance hierarchy is to put in DO FORM (where the paradigm of *do* is stated) the condition:
'SUBCAT <[–ELLIPSIS, –AUX]> & *do* ⊃ semantic prominence'.
I assume that 'prominence' is a very general semantic property assigned high in the hierarchy. This can be read as 'if the word properties of elliptical context, subcategorization for more than one category, and morphology are lacking then the word property of prominence must be present'.

29 This may also be supported by evidence that historically it declined faster in writing than speech (Rissanen 1985, Tieken 1987: 115f.), which implies the relevance of the tendency to reduce functionless variation found in the process of standardization (Milroy and Milroy 1985).

30 This clearly requires something further to restrict the distribution of imperative clauses to root sentences. A simple possibility is that they are [+INV] (where complements default [–INV]).

4 Distinguishing auxiliaries and verbs in early English

1 The history of English is conventionally divided into three periods: Old English (OE, with substantial records from the ninth to eleventh century), Middle English (ME, twelfth to fifteenth century) and Modern English (Mod E, sixteenth century to the present), also sometimes called New English (NE). Present-day English is abbreviated PE.

2 Perhaps other verbs such as *hætan*, *lætan*. But I shall only refer to these in passing.

3 This is least clear in the case of invariable *uton* 'let's'. But this is discussed below in Chapter 6.

4 Thus AB language (early thirteenth century) still has a formal indicative: subjunctive distinction in the 'modal' group (d'Ardenne 1961: 249). But *MED* comments under *shulen* that even in early ME there is no apparent semantic distinction between historical indicatives and subjunctives. See M§22 for neutralization of the indicative: subjunctive contrast where this depended on *-on* : *-en*.

5 For *mot* see M§1001. There are, however, possible instances of 'nonmodal' constructions in Middle English (see *MED moten* v. (2) 5b), and BT cites *uton þæs* 'let us that' (Bo 33.75.17), where *þæs* is presumably the genitive object of a verb of desiring (M§1082) but is anaphoric in context (another: W. Endter (ed.) *König Alfreds des Grossen Bearbeitung der Soliloquien des Augustinus* (Bibliothek der angelsächsischen Prosa 11). Hamburg 1922: 2.55.15), compare PE 'you may that', etc. *Dearr* is restricted in Alfredian OE (Wülfing 1894-1901: §391), but permits other constructions in Middle English, possibly already in late Old English (*MED*).

6 For a brief statement on (a) and (b) see Traugott (1972: 106-8). For more detail on all three orders see Bacquet (1962: esp. Chs. 2, 8 and 9 (passives)), and Mitchell (1985: Ch. 9 and references). Note that these three orders are those which Mitchell describes as 'common' for modal passives (in §758; v = 'modal', V = 'be', C = second participle) except that Mitchell's comments are not restricted to subject-initial sentences. Note also that in Bacquet's Chapter 9 he argues that (c) rather than (a) is the 'ordre de base' in main clauses for *beon* and *habban* with the second participle (despite the admitted frequency of (a)).

7 These need not order the head peripherally in its phrase, but may be responsive to the weight of complements and adjuncts (see Uszkoreit 1986a). Thus medial verb positions can potentially be coped with.

8 For forms in general see relevant entries in *OED*, *MED* (note that *MED*'s initial conspectus of forms for *connen* is very incomplete). For forms and distribution of *shal/shulleþ* see McIntosh, Samuels and Benskin (1986). *Witeth* is typically fifteenth century, so probably too late to be relevant here. In the midlands the contrast in the present indicative plural between preterite-present verbs and other verbs is lost when *-e(n)* becomes the general termination for this category.

9 This can be seen by comparing dot maps 153 and 166 in McIntosh, Samuels and Benskin (1986, vol. I). At least ten of the dialect survey's 'linguistic profiles' of individual texts show *shulleþ* (etc.) beside *wole, wollen* (etc.). The county and profile reference number under which these linguistic profiles are listed in vol. III are: Devon 5040, 9330; Hampshire 5511; Monmouth 7250, 7271; Oxfordshire 6890;

Somerset 5200, 5280; Wiltshire 5331, 5362/3. *Willeþ* is not of course the only point of contact; *oueþ* may also have been relevant. But it is much less common, and tends to leave the preterite-present paradigm, so my point remains plausible. Data of the type given above is not available for *oueþ*.

10 CAN also develops a present participle in Middle English but it has marked adjectival characteristics and it is not cited with the plain infinitive in *MED connen* v., *conning* ppl. So it may not be relevant here.

11 See *MED ouen* v. 3, 4d, 4e; *moten* v. (2) 8; and *OED Must, v.*[1] 10; *Tharf, thar, v.* But note that BTS *beþurfan* III gives an impersonal example. *Ouen* tends to lose its preterite-present status from late Old English.

12 MAY is not found as an impersonal verb in Middle English, despite *MED mouen* v. (3) 9; cf. M§734 on possible impersonal *mæg* in Old English. Note also that DOW occurs as an impersonal (see *OED Dow, v.*; *MED douen* n. (1) [*sic*, for v. (1)]), and the striking reinterpretation of *bus* (< *bihoves*) as an endingless singular without nonfinites, with new preterite *bust* (*MED bihoven* v., *OED Bus, v.*).

13 Van Kemenade (1989) suggests that the root/epistemic distinction is reflected in the possibility or impossibility of verb raising in Old English. But I am sceptical that there is (at least as yet) sufficient evidence involving epistemics for confidence in this possibility.

14 There are further types of category structuring for which this characterization does not hold; see, for example, the discussion of Lakoff (1987). But I shall suppose that, in the first instance at least, these are not relevant to my concerns here. Note that the question of semantic structuring is a further issue, and that it need not be of this type.

5 Identifying an 'auxiliary group' before Modern English: sentence-level syntax

1 The occurrence of *do* here raises the question whether these constructions with *do* and with auxiliaries are fundamentally elliptical or contain a verb proform (or 'substitute' verb), as suggested (for example) by Napoli (1985). The analysis of §3.4.1 partly neutralizes this question, but I will continue to use the convenient word *elliptical* not only for the constructions with auxiliaries but also with *do*.

2 To exemplify rejected types of example:

(i) þæt hie of his rice uuoldon
'that they were-willing (to go) out-of his kingdom'
ChronA 76.14 (878.20)

(ii) Hige sceal þe heardra
'Resolution must (be) the tougher'
The Battle of Maldon (ASPR VI, 7-16) 312
(See in particular BT(S), M§3863, and V§§234, 1895 for further examples of (ii).)

(iii) Eft ne mot nan mann ne ne sceal secgan
'Neither again may any man (say), nor ought he to say, ...' (Skeat's translation)
ÆLS i.1.177

(iv) þonne beo we urum Hælende fylgende, swa se blinda wæs
'then are we following our Saviour, as the blind man was'
BlHom 23.11

3 Further distinctions are of course required (see Quirk *et al.* 1985: §§12.31ff.). Following Hankamer and Sag (1976) we might interpret *try* as showing 'Null Complement Anaphora', *start* as an intransitive verb of rather open sense (1976: 412, n. 21).

4 In the types of (i) and (ii) in note 2 and in cases where the sense 'do' is supposedly to be supplied, the meaning of the infinitive which is supplied in translation corresponds to (and is predictable from) an aspect of the complementation of the verb. This is a distinct category from a more general intransitive or absolute use which would be appropriate to postverbal ellipsis contexts. Besides these types BT(S) *durran* and [*motan*] I(b) 'with ellipsis of infinitive' only have instances like (2) or (6) with retrieval from linguistic context. To judge from BT(S) the same might hold for *willan*, but there seem to be absolute examples elsewhere. As well as all of these types, [*sculan*] III 'without an infinite' has instances meaning 'be necessary', 'be appropriate', 'avail'. But these do not give suitable sense in postverbal ellipsis contexts.

5 The 'construction' might be accounted for in semantic terms, as requiring the sense of a verb and its complements to be retrieved from linguistic context. The point would however remain that a distinct statement must be made to characterize such uses. But a semantic account of pseudogapping will not be possible since the rectional characteristics of the retrieved verb are retained and 'Case/theta-role correlations in OE are not entirely systematic' (Anderson 1986: 173).

6 Although Antipova (1963: 131) takes this example to be elliptical (and see Fox's translation), it is conceivable that it is not, but shows *wesan* + dative 'to belong to, for a person to have something' (BT *wesan* I(8)(a)): 'but it belongs to all men'. The parallels given in BT, however, retain the full sense of their gloss, which is not really appropriate here: the crown is offered to all men, but is only achieved by the virtuous. On the whole a pseudogapping interpretation seems preferable, but a contextually weakened sense of *wesan* + dative cannot be ruled out with confidence. A possible instance within a comparative occurs at Or 120.9. The example given by V§1745 I take to be postverbal ellipsis in type, not pseudogapping.

7 It is possible that two more of their criteria also held: that the missing expression should be precisely recoverable, and that its insertion should result in a grammatical sentence with the same meaning as the elliptical sentence. These four criteria are those met by today's post-auxiliary ellipsis and pseudogapping to which the Old English constructions are on the face of it straightforwardly parallel.

8 Similar comments to those of note 4 above apply; see *MED moten* v. (2) 5b. for a range of examples in which the sense of an infinitive (mainly of motion including abstract motion) is apparently to be supplied in translation from the verb in construction with its complement. *MED* and *OED* give *ouen*, and *þarf* in absolute or intransitive senses, but not ones appropriate for postverbal ellipsis contexts. *Mot* and *shal* occur in senses 'be necessary, appropriate', etc. (see in particular *MED moten* v. (2) 5b. esp. (d), (e), and *shulen* v. (1) 2, 27; *OED Shall*, 25, 26) but again

not in senses appropriate for particular contexts of ellipsis. *MED durren* v. 1a.(b) has an intransitive example but it is from the Early Version of the Wyclifite Bible and is rejected in the Later Version, so it is not good evidence; see Warner (1982: Ch. 6) for some discussion of the relationship of these versions.

9 Wülfing (1894-1901: §§389-97), Antipova (1963). Besides these for Old English see especially BT(S), Brown (1970), and, for all periods, V§§309, 573, 1743ff. and *OED*. Wülfing (§388) cites an instance with *cann* (Bo 24.55.15), as does Antipova (p.127, ChronE 251.32 (1123.32)), but they seem less satisfactory than (2.e) as potential ellipses (though (2.e) is itself not certain). Visser is wrong to imply that pseudogapping occurs only from late Old English: Wülfing gives plentiful examples from early Old English.

10 There are also a couple of glosses where a Latin subjunctive has been rendered merely by *uton* as in this example (where there is no form of *caraxare* in the preceding context).

> caraxemus (glossed) utan
> 'let us write' 'let's'
> Aldhelm, De Laude Virginitatis (*Old English Glosses: a Collection*, ed. H. D. Meritt, MLA general series 16, New York, 1945: no. 2) 179.

11 For Middle English see especially Visser (as in note 9), *OED* and *MED* under relevant entries. For Middle English examples may be found especially under the following headings in *MED*:

> *connen* v. 1(b), 2(b);
> *durren* v. 1a(b);
> *moten* v. (2) 5a;
> *mouen* v. (3) 5a, 5b;
> *ouen* v. 4c, 4e, 5(f), 5(i).
> *shulen* v. *passim*

Wil and *þarf* have not been published in *MED* at the time of writing. For *wil* in ME see Visser as above, *OED Will, v.*[1] 17ff., 34. For postverbal ellipsis with *þarf*: Chaucer, *Troilus and Criseyde* ii.1661; *Cursor Mundi* 23443, *OED Tharf, v.* A 3aβ (possibly pseudogapping).

12 For BE see especially V§309 and *MED ben* v. 16. Chaucerian examples are cited incidentally in the sections on verbal ellipsis in Karpf (1930). V§1745 gives the example of pseudogapping from Middle English cited above as (9), and an OE instance which could well simply be postverbal ellipsis. V§1756 gives a supposed instance with OE *weorðan* from early Middle English, but it is inadequate.

13 For perfect HAVE see in particular *MED hauen* v. 13, and V§1753, which includes a late Middle English example with pseudogapping. Note that the putative Old English example of ellipsis after perfect *habban*, which Visser (§1753) takes from BT, is not a good one (see M§1004).

14 I have avoided comparative constructions in citing data so far because of the possibility that the relevant ellipsis is a property of the comparative construction; *swa* might also sometimes be taken as a verbal complement. But examples like those cited here show an ellipsis which is not required by the comparative construction,

and it would plausibly be identified with more general processes of postverbal ellipsis and pseudogapping. On *swa* as potential complement see Nummenmaa (1973: 18) who claims that it 'may obtain the character of a quasi-object' with *don* in Old English, and M§§2379-82, 3265f. for distributional arguments that it does not in fact achieve the status of object or pronoun at this period.

15 Instances of gapping seem to be more widely distributed across clause types in earlier English than today, which raises the possibility of a different interrelationship between elliptical constructions than holds today. See Warner (1992a) for some examples.

16 Or in Kohonen's remarks on ellipsis (1978: §5.6), or the other (brief) accounts of ellipsis involving verbs that I know in the monograph literature. The possibility of a parallel to pseudogapping with infinitive taking verbs more generally is not raised in Mitchell's survey of elliptical patterns (§§3858ff.) or sections on nonexpression of the infinitive (see index), or in Visser's discussions of gapping and pseudogapping (§§186, 586, 595; 573).

17 For example the statement 'any plain infinitive governed by a verb may undergo ellipsis' would predict a very wide distribution for these ellipses.

18 Denison also claims that this evidence points rather directly to auxiliary status for the verbs involved: but I believe the argument is necessarily a more indirect one.

19 BT(S) give *tweogan* with experiencer subject, or impersonal. With the impersonal an NP object of doubt is in the genitive. Here *þætte* is either the complementizer or (less plausibly) the relative pronoun ('I know what human beings will doubt'), cf. BT *þætte* conj. and *þætte* pron. Either way the construction is impersonal. The potential subjecthood of a following clause or infinitive in earlier English has been much debated; see M§1507 for a brief comment.

20 Possible: *Elene* (ASPR II, 66-102) 915, *The Judgement Day I* (ASPR III, 212-5) 80. Denison (1990b: 147) says there are two probable examples of his type (i) (which includes my 'central' impersonals, but allows nonargument *hit* subject), but only cites the ambiguous *HomS* 25 412 (which I prefer to take as his type (ii), with nominative subject) and, later, my (16.a).

21 But note the transparent 'passive' with *dearr* at GD 232.7 cited in §7.2.6 below.

22 On the face of it the examples given in (21) are simply impersonal. But they might perhaps be construed as having a sentential argument (empty or understood in the second two cases), so they are not as convincing as examples available for group A. The constructional parallels of *Herkne nou hwat me haueth met* 'Hear now what I have dreamed' *c*1300 *The Lay of Havelok the Dane* (ed. W. W. Skeat, 2nd edn. rev. K. Sisam, Oxford, Clarendon Press 1915) 1285 are not sufficient for us to claim that it is impersonal.

23 Other possible examples with *begin to*: *c*1300 *The Lay of Havelok the Dane* (ed. W. W. Skeat, 2nd edn. rev. K. Sisam, Oxford, Clarendon Press 1915) 497; *c*1300 *The Middle English Evangelie* (ed. G. H. Campbell, *PMLA* 30 (1915) 545-80) 348 (correcting *MED*'s 378); *c*1300 Mary Magdalene (*The Early South-English Legendary*, ed. C. Horstmann, EETS 87: 462-80) 201 (the last two given under *MED grisen* v. 1(c) impers). Regrettably, these could be interpreted as a reflexive whose subject is not expressed, so they are potential rather than certain examples. *MED* does not give *agrisen* v. as a reflexive (though *King Horn* 867, cited under 1(b), might be a possi-

ble example) and *Otuel* 1604 seems unlikely to be a subjectless reflexive.

24 Denison (1990b) did not find any relevant impersonal constructions for Old English with the first (or present) participle, nor have I noted any for Old English or Middle English, so the question here involves constructions with subordinate infinitives.

25 I will use 'raising' for the preciser 'subject-raising to subject'.

26 To give some idea of the significance of these numbers, here is a sum whose assumptions should not be taken too seriously. I have noted about a dozen impersonal infinitives with OE *onginnan, aginnan, ginnan*. This represents just over 1 per cent of Callaway's 1,000+ instances of this verb with the infinitive. If this proportion held for 175 examples with other verbs, we would expect one or two with an impersonal infinitive in my data. If we compensate for the higher incidence of subject selection which I believe holds for *beginnan, onfon*, etc. we might expect to find one impersonal instance, and should not be surprised to find none. Absence may well be accidental, not systematic.

27 Kageyama (1975), Traugott (1972: 102) remark this general absence. Note that the construction of *Hy ... wyrðe þinceað* 'They seem worthy ...' (*Beowulf* ASPR IV, 3-98: 368) is not under consideration here since it is not catenative.

28 For some analysts there will be further relevant evidence in the occurrence of aspectuals with 'weather' *it*, and this will imply the identity of 'verb with impersonal' constructions and 'raising' constructions.

29 In Chapter 9 below I shall analyse Old English subjects as corresponding in the lexicon to values of either SUBCAT or SUBJ, where SUBCAT is basic. Only one of these possibilities is illustrated here, and I have assumed for the sake of simplicity of illustration that an impersonal could have an oblique case NP as value of SUBJ.

30 In GB the situation is less clear, but see Lightfoot (1991: 145-6), Warner (1992a: 198-9) for suggestions that would essentially identify 'verb with impersonal' and 'raising' constructions in Old English.

31 Transparency in impersonal constructions is presumably 'weakly' formal in other theories too. So in GB, constructional properties of 'raising' predicates are associated with the lack of subject theta-role assignment.

6 Identifying an 'auxiliary group' before Modern English: further properties of modals

1 A single instance of a *to*-infinitive in such a position in Old English is cited by Callaway and Mitchell (beside a couple with the plain infinitive), though the position reflects and is perhaps influenced by the order of the Latin which is being rendered (Callaway 1913: 7, 10; M§1537; Bock 1931: 149ff., esp. 153).

2 Callaway (1913: Ch. 2) gives thirty-six verbs as occurring with the 'uninflected' infinitive only (our 'plain' infinitive), beside sixty with the 'inflected' infinitive only (except for very rare instances where the 'inflection' occurs without *to* this is our *to*-infinitive; Callaway 1913: 2) in the construction 'active infinitive as object of an active verb'. Thirty-six verbs occur with both types of infinitive. There are few passive infinitives, or passive matrix verbs. If we restrict discussion (as below)

to verbs which Callaway records with an infinitive complement on three or more occasions, seven verbs are given as found taking the 'uninflected' infinitive only, and sixteen with the 'inflected' infinitive only. Some thirty show variation. Callaway's overall figures for this active 'objective infinitive' are 2,709 'uninflected' : 529 'inflected'. But if we omit the five most frequent verbs (*hatan* 'order' 1124 : 0, *onginnan* 'begin' 977 : 37, *ðencan* 'think, intend' 92 : 34, *lætan* 'permit' 121 : 0, *wilnian* 'wish' 45 : 76) these figures reduce to 350 'uninflected' : 382 'inflected'. Callaway's 'objective infinitive' (Ch. 2) does not include the 'predicative infinitive with accusative subject' (Ch. 8), the few examples classified as 'predicative infinitive with dative subject' in Ch. 9, or the predicative infinitive after *beon/wesan* (Ch. 7).

3 In Callaway's data only *liefan* 'allow' is recorded with the *to-* but not the plain infinitive, but in only four examples. The position of verbs of 'sense perception', *hatan* and *lætan*, corresponds to that of their construction with a predicative infinitive with accusative subject in Callaway's Ch. 8, where they are also restricted to the plain infinitive in their complement (*hatan* and *lætan* with over 400 examples each).

4 The plain infinitive is better represented here in early texts, and in verse; see Bock (1931: 170ff.), Callaway (1913: 66ff.) for discussion of verbs of beginning and ceasing. The two verbs with the plain infinitive only are *blinnan* 'cease', with seven examples (all from the early Bede) and *hogian* 'intend', with six examples. (But *ablinnan* is found with the *to*-infinitive, and note that *blinnen* with infinitive, which is absent in late Old English, appears with *to* in early Middle English; *MED*, V§1292). Callaway's figures for *onginnan* are 977 'uninflected' : 37 'inflected', for *aginnan* 28 'uninflected' : 5 'inflected' but these five are late (1913: 68). *Myntan* 'intend' 17 : 1 is also late with *to*. Bock suggests that the *to*-infinitive was first found with senses of *ginnen* (and derivatives) which involve intention, referring to their use to render Latin *conari*. But it seems unlikely that instances of the two infinitives can be reliably discriminated here on semantic grounds (see Callaway 1913: 67).

5 M§996; for *uton* Callaway (1913: Ch. 6). Callaway argued that *cann* did occur with the *to*-infinitive, but his examples are surely to be rejected (Callaway 1913: 81-2, Bock 1931: 156-7). Mitchell lists these and other doubtful 'inflected' exceptions with references to discussions in his §996, and notes an example in coordination after *wile*, for which see below.

6 Here one might want to add the infinitive with verbs of motion and rest (as in *com fleogan* 'came flying') which is invariably plain (Callaway 1913: Ch. 5), although this is not a complement infinitive. See also M§§967, 1543.

7 Although *hatan* can mean 'promise', BT(S) does not give this sense in construction with an infinitive (but see BTS *gehatan* for this sense with an inflected infinitive). *Lætan/leten* with 'subject equi' senses ('cease, refrain' etc.) is a later development (see BT(S), *MED*, *OED*).

8 For examples see *MED mouen* v. (3) 10(c), 11; V§§1686, 1687, 1732; instances with separation are of course not necessarily relevant (as discussed immediately). With other verbs the evidence is less clear, but the situation may be similar. Nonfinites of WILL with *to* in contact are found, but should perhaps be assigned to

the regular weak verb. With CAN I only know examples with some separation (*to konnen parfiȝtly to axson*; *English Wyclifite Sermons*, vol. I, ed. A. Hudson, Oxford University Press, 1983, Sermon 51.8) or after the participle *cunnynge*, which is arguably distinct. The only Middle English nonfinite with *to*-infinitive I know for DARE involves separation (V§1366); I do not know an instance for MUN.

9 For this general topic, see Mustanoja (1960: 522), *OED To, prep.* B.19, Ohlander (1941), V§1728-34, Warner (1982: 127-33), M§996 for an Old English example. In later Middle English I have noted a few instances which, while not showing contact with a finite, come very close; see Quirk and Svartvik's reasonable practice of taking examples with 'short intervening elements such as *not, wel,* and *fully*, as well as subjects (in inversion)' as not showing 'separation' (1970: 403). Here are the two most striking instances noted from *MED*; for another from the Stonor letters see V§1733. The presence of *noght* in (i) is especially remarkable if this is the *not* of sentential negation.

(i) For al this world I myhte noght
To soffre an othre fully winne,
Ther as I am yit to beginne.
(*a*1393) Gower, *Confessio Amantis* (ed. G. C. Macaulay, EETS ES 81, 82) 2.510

Here *noght* is stressed, rhyming with *thoght*. Is *myhte* here intransitive with an infinitive of consequence, or is *noght* a 'cognate object' ('I would have no capacity at all [so as] to endure another's success')?

(ii) That as we refuse grete dignite and fame,
So he must nedely to refuse the same
(MS variants: *do*, omission; ?='too') ?*c*1500 (*c*1477) T. Norton, *Ordinal of Alchemy* (ed. J. Reidy, EETS 272) 222

10 Sanders gives several purported early Middle English examples of a 'group A' verb with a *to*-infinitive, of which three are in contact (1915: 47-51). But they are all to be rejected. In all but one the infinitive is adverbial, or *to* is a verbal prefix, a preposition or the numeral *two*. The other, which requires discussion, is:

þe alle weren eateliche to bihaldene and muchele strengre þen eani þurg to þolien
'which were all horrible to behold, and much harder than anyone dare endure' (Morris's translation)
*a*1225 *The Lambeth Homilies* (*Old English Homilies*, 1st. series, ed. R. Morris, EETS 29, 34) 41.28

But *þurg* is a curious graph for either the indicative or subjunctive of *þarf*, though straightforward for 'through'. A better translation is surely 'and much harder to suffer through ['endure'] than any'.

11 We might add *MED can* v., a 'peculiar variant of *gan*, p[ast] of *ginnen*' which *MED* cites with plain infinitive except where separation is involved.

12 For infinitive marking in Middle English in general see Bock (1931), Fischer

(1992), Mustanoja (1960) and their references; for early Middle English prose see now the authoritative statement of Jack (1991). For individual verbs see *MED*. Note that ME *gon* + infinitive 'proceed to, begin to' is not restricted to the plain infinitive (see *MED gon* v. 11a(a), but Mustanoja 1960: 535). Impersonal verbs should perhaps be included in this discussion since a following infinitive in construction with them might be interpreted as a complement rather than as a subject (see Fischer 1992). Some (e.g. *listen* 'please') clearly prefer a plain infinitive. But *to*-infinitives are also found with these verbs from Old English, where Callaway reports only one verb as occurring with a plain infinitive more than twice without also being found with a *to*-infinitive (*gelystan* 'please' three times; cf. *lystan* 61 plain, 4 inflected. Callaway 1913: Ch. 1 and App. A). For a similar picture in Middle English see especially Sanders (1915), Kenyon (1909).

13 For *kepen* in contact with a *to*-infinitive (not given for Chaucer by Kenyon), see Gower, *Confessio Amantis* (ed. G.C. Macaulay, EETS ES 81, 82) 5.5754 and other references in *MED kepen* v. 2.

14 But the criteria developed by Brinton (1988: 152ff.) for nonaspectual *ginnen* may lead to a sharper and different view. For aspectuals generally see Brinton Chapter 3 and the comment of her note 20 (on p. 270).

15 The similarities between preterite-presents and the strong preterite lie in the first and third person singular of the indicative without termination, the plural in *-on*, and the general existence of a vocalic alternation between these forms which for some preterite-presents is clearly referable to a particular class of strong verbs. The major differences lie in the possibility of *i*-mutation in the preterite-present subjunctive, and in the formation of the second person singular of the indicative. This does not show the same ablaut pattern as the strong preterite, and has either a form in *-t* which is peculiar to these verbs (*scealt, meaht*, etc.), or in *-st* which generally parallels the normal present-tense ending. Historically the form in *-t* is, like the rest of the paradigm, an Indo-European perfect in origin, whereas the regular strong preterite is syncretistic, taking its second person indicative singular from an original aorist.

16 The fact that *-en* tends to be replaced by *-on*, especially in late West Saxon (Campbell 1959a: §735) is not involved here.

17 *Uton*'s sense might seem to imply analysis as a morphological imperative (and historically an imperative or injunctive form may indeed have been involved, though it is not a straightforward phonological development of such an earlier form; alternatively, it might perhaps simply show the equivalence 'imperative plural = indicative plural' found in other verbs). But Campbell (1959a: §767) only gives preterite-present plural imperatives in *-aþ* (*munaþ, witaþ* and see *willaþ,*) or subjunctival imperatives. So this is not a plausible analysis synchronically.

18 The analyst of Old English verbal forms has a choice between allomorphy of stem and allomorphy of termination. I prefer the first, which gives identical endings for the present of all weak verbs, thus: *ic fremm-e, hier-e, lufi-e*; *he freme-þ, hier-þ, lufa-þ*; *we fremm-aþ, hier-aþ, lufi-aþ*; etc. The predicted stem form for the third person singular of the indicative of *willan* is *wile*. This lacks the weak-verb termination *-þ*, and is without termination, like a preterite-present.

19 & þæt getiwe under ealdre us scealan beon he fylige
et ut ostendat sub priore debere nos esse subsequitur dicens
'And that he-should-show under prior us shall be he follows (subj.)'
= 'And in order to show that we should be under a superior, he goes on to say ...'
The Rule of St Benet, Interlinear Version (ed. H. Logeman, EETS 90) 32.10

Another example from this text is referred to in a note by Goossens as a potential infinitive (1987: 142, n. 9). But in it *we sculan* glosses *debere*, and the form is finite.

20 I know of two references to nonfinites in the literature, which are inadequate. Long (1944: 297) cites a past participle *shulde* ((?*a*1439) Lydgate, *Fall of Princes*, ed. H. Bergen, EETS ES 121-3: vol. I, 12/432). But the reference is to a straightforward preterite. Visser (1946-56: 834) cites an infinitive of SHALL (*Le Morte d'Arthur*, ed. H. O. Sommer, London, Nutt 1889-91: 535.3). But the instance is clearly better taken as finite with omission of the subject 'I', as Sommer interpreted it (vol. II, 23), and note the presence of *I* before *shall* in the Winchester MS (*The Works of Sir Thomas Malory*, ed. E. Vinaver, Oxford, Clarendon Press 1967: 736.26). It is not repeated in Visser (1963-73).

21 The lemma for *dearr* in contrast is eight times less frequent than that for *mot*, over twenty times less frequent than that for *sceal*. So the absence of nonfinites here may indeed be accidental.

22 It seems as if Ælfric also avoids the infinitive *magan* though the form is found fifty years later, and this has been discussed above.

23 Since preterite-presents form a new weak preterite, forming the past participle should be morphologically straightforward. Its partial absence in Old English might be ascribed to the late spread of the *habban* perfect with the various classes of intransitive verb; note that in Old English the preterite of 'group A' verbs is found in conjunction with the adverb *furðum* to give the sense of the perfect (Campbell 1959b). But by Middle English at the latest we might surely expect to find instances.

24 Here I rely on *OED*, the most authoritative grammars (especially Brunner 1960, 1963) and other accounts which supply references. But more positive assurance on this point must await further volumes of *MED*.

25 I am grateful to Professor Lewis, editor-in-chief, for kindly supplying me with references from *MED*'s files.

26 Note also that according to *MED* the northern contraction of *bihoves* to *bus*, which is apparently interpreted as having preterite-present morphology since it leads to a new preterite *buste*, is only found in finite forms (*MED bihoven* v.).

27 *Would* is difficult. *OED Will, v.*[1] 42 and V§1610 give 'conditional' instances from Old English. But although this might represent a distinct 'conditional' use, it seems as satisfactory to interpret such examples as the preterite subjunctive of *wile*, as suggested in Chapter 7. Then more 'independent' examples seem to belong to late Middle English (though *MED* is not yet available at the time of writing). Similarly the Old English examples with *meahte* in V§1673, *wolde* in V§1604 seem to be possible preterite subjunctives of *mæg* and *wile*.

28 For discussion see in particular Standop (1957: 101-2), M§2038. The possibility of

this usage in the present apparently depends on two examples from *Leechdoms* cited in BT *sculan* II (13), and quoted in M§2038. But I do not see why these are apposite. *OED* places them under *Shall*, 9.c 'the idiomatic use of the future to denote what ordinarily or occasionally occurs under specified conditions' (see also *Shall*, 15) and this is surely appropriate. Mitchell quotes a further possible instance (ÆCHom ii.572.16), but it seems to me this might equally be *OED Shall*, 4 (of what is appointed to take place). So I am dubious about evidence for this category in the present. At the same time, one would expect it to be relatively infrequent, since contexts of report typically involve the preterite in recorded Old English.

29 Note that 'empty' GINNEN is found with complement BE; see *MED ginnen* v. and compare the analysis of Pollock (1989) in which periphrastic and pro-verbal DO are closely related.

7 The developing modal semantics of early English 'modals'

1 Goossens (1982: 79) accepts the words of God to Adam *ðu scealt deaþe sweltan* (*The Old English Version of the Heptateuch*, ed. S. J. Crawford, EETS 160: Genesis 2.17): '(If you eat of the tree) you shall suffer death'. But in context the Vulgate future *morieris* is possibly, even probably, deontic, so that this is not a convincing instance.

2 Another instance: Bede 266.21

3 Further possible instances: *West Saxon Gospels*, Luke 16.2 (cited in *OED May*, *v.*[1] 4, BTS *magan* IV) *Agyf þine scire, ne miht þu lencg tunscire bewitan*, = *iam non poteris vilicare*, 'Give-up your office, you may no longer control (the) stewardship' (but is the speaker the source of authority behind *miht*?); two other renderings of the same passage: *Homilies of Ælfric: a Supplementary Collection*, ed. J. C. Pope, EETS 259, 260: 16.9, 16.92; Bede 74.5; *Genesis* (ASPR I, 1-87) 543.

4 In the case of (12.c), although the editor characterizes the text as a 'faithful translation', he notes 'the independent character of the Old English style' in which 'Latin constructions are carefully avoided' (*The Old English 'Apollonius of Tyre'*, ed. P. Goolden, Oxford University Press, 1958: xxiii–xxv). Other instances: ÆLS ii.30.267; Bede 410.24; Bo 40.137.4; *Beowulf* 2032 (= (8.a) above), but see my comment on (1); Bede 96.22 (from Goossens 1982); Revival of Monasticism (*Leechdoms, Wortcunning and Starcraft of Early England*, ed. T. O. Cockayne, Rolls Series 35, vol III, 432-44) line 5 (from Denison 1990b: 153); *Christ and Satan* (ASPR I, 135ff.) 22. Kytö 1987 gives my (12.b, c) and cites other examples, the best of which is Or 18.30.

5 Traugott assigns (14) to her category 'prediction' which includes the future (1972: 69 and see 1989: 39). But for Old English it seems safer to regard it as an extension of the basic sense which refers to the internal properties of the subject (see Standop 1957: 138-9).

6 For MAY as a subjunctive (and future) auxiliary see BT *magan* V, M§1014, *OED May*, *v.*[1] 8, Krzyszpień (1980) (cp. M§2975a). For more details and for verbs of this group as subjunctive equivalents in Old English in general see Mitchell's (1985) general index under 'verbs, "modal" auxiliary, with infinitives as periphrases for simple subjunctive', and more especially his comments on noun

clauses in §§1995-9, 2036, final and consecutive clauses in §§2974-5a and conditional clauses in §3706.

7 But see Traugott for the claim that subjectivity in Old English epistemics derives 'largely from invited inference' (1990: 510f.). With reference to *eaþe mæg*, note that *eaþe* is normally found in collocation with *mæg* but is common with root (including subject-oriented) senses (see Venezky and Healey 1980), so that *eaþe* is not simply a carrier of epistemic modality.

8 There may be some further evidence for this in their interaction with negation. With Old English *sceal* and *mot* of obligation and necessity preverbal *ne* is interpreted not as sentential negation but as negating the subordinate proposition (for *mot*, see Tellier 1962: 114). Indeed the equivalence 'not possible' = 'necessary not' may underlie *mot*'s shift of sense. Moreover *þearf* + infinitive seems to occur most frequently in negative and virtually negative (or 'affective') contexts, as do modern *dare* and *need*. Thus *ne þearf* 'not necessary', hence 'possible not', might be seen as effectively suppletive to *ne sceal*, *ne mot* 'necessary not' and *ne mæg*, *ne mot* 'not possible', and the modals can be seen to be behaving as a coherent group in imposing this general distribution on *þearf*.

9 V§1663-4; *OED May*, *v.*[1] 5; *MED mouen* v. (3) 12(d)(f) and elsewhere, especially 3, 4 and perhaps 7.

10 See BTS, Standop (1957: 66, 168) and Wallum (1973); and see Ono (1975) for figures some of which are stronger in Standop's support than Standop's own figures. But I am less convinced by BTS's instances than Standop is.

11 See *MED connen* v. 2. I am unconvinced by earlier instances given in V§1629. For passives see especially V§1656; Traugott (1972: 171) cites another of 1445.

12 Major references for major uses in the five categories listed here (see also the general index to Mitchell 1985 for Old English).

(a) *OED Shall*, 22a, *May*, *v.*[1] 8a(c), V§§1546, 1620, 1678, Mustanoja (1960: 459), Warner (1982: 192ff.).
(b) *OED Shall*, 22c, e, V§1544 (cf. §§1540, 1541, 1543, 1545), Behre (1950, 1955).
(c) *OED Will*, *v.*[1] 42, 45, *Shall*, 19b, *May*, *v.*[1] 6, V§§1532, 1551, 1555, 1558, 1610, 1618, 1619, 1671-3.
(d) Mustanoja (1960: 466), *OED May*, *v.*[1] 8a, V§1676, Tellier (1962: 122, 147).
(e) *MED moten* v.(2) 9, 10, 11, 12, *OED Mote*, *v.*[1] 1.c., V§1692, Ono (1958: 73ff.).

8 The status of modals and auxiliaries before Modern English

1 The opacity of [+FIN, +INDIC] may be stated for stems which then undergo agreement marking (appropriately in the preterite where normal verbal agreement is shown) and even perhaps tense marking in early stages of the development; or for word forms such as *sculon*, *uton* which contain a minority agreement pattern; or (most plausibly) for a combination of the two.

2 *Dearr* also lacks nonfinites in recorded Old English, but this is plausibly attributable to its very much lower frequency (see §6.3).

3 See §6.1. Granted that separation may 'motivate' a *to*-infinitive and the presence

of the weak verb *will* – *willed*, the evidence for CAN, DARE and WILL is so far unclear. If CAN has noncompositional finites in Middle English this would be consistent with some level of subjectivity; see the attribution of epistemic semantics to CAN in Middle English by *OED* and Visser (but see my §7.3 above). It could however also imply that the lexicalization of mood has become a formal (unmotivated) property of group A verbs already in late Middle English.

4 Van Kemenade's claimed epistemic/deontic split would be supported if word order possibilities distinguished between epistemic and deontic 'modals' in Old English in a way that her account would predict, as she suggests is the case. But, as noted in Chapter 4, it is not clear that there is (yet) enough evidence for epistemics to have confidence in this possibility.

5 For Roberts (1985) there would also be the theoretical difficulty that finites show normal agreement (despite the fact that a minority conjugation is involved), and this would presumably imply government by an affix in INFL. But if elements generated in INFL lack theta roles this contradicts the proposition that 'V assigns theta-roles iff V is governed' on which his account crucially depends ((17), p. 29). See Denison (1990b: 159f.) for further discussion of Roberts (1985).

6 Note that epistemic modality in itself does not necessarily imply a restriction to finite, as noted in §2.4.

7 Here we move from contextual effects to a lexicalized grammatical statement. This may involve a move from (say) a conversational implicature ('the unspecified source of authority is the speaker') to a lexically based lack of the conventional implicature for indicative; or to a semantic opacity. Details of analysis here (and there are other possibilities) will depend in part on the treatment of the meaning of finiteness.

8 If the form *uton* is partly analogical, this lexical encoding may even have been associated with its adoption of preterite-present morphology.

9 Auxiliaries in early Modern English and the rise of *do*

1 Allan (1987) seems to me to overinterpret some of this evidence; for example, *They had cand their lesson* (1587) is hardly a late premodal nonfinite, but a weak transitive verb to be assigned to CON, see *OED Can*, *v.*[1] III 'Senses now written CON.'

2 *OED Nill*, *v.* gives nonfinites for 16, 17C (see *Will*, *v.*[1] A 1), but note the contemporary weak preterite.

3 See *OED Do*, *v.* 31; Visser (1946-56: 502-4; partly also in V§§1414a, 2022, 2133) has unconvincing sixteenth-century examples which leave the possibility open. I suspect that it was indeed absent from the early sixteenth century outside Scots (unless the limited legal causative use is to be identified with periphrastic *do* at this point).

4 The example of transitive *shal* in 1530 (*Court of Love* 131) is verbally identical to Chaucer, *Troilus and Criseyde* (iii.1649) and occurs in a poem written in deliberately archaic language which abounds in imitations of Lydgate and Chaucerian reminiscences (see Skeat 1897). It is not good evidence for sixteenth-century English (as Lightfoot noted; 1979: 101, n. 1) despite Allan's (1987) defence of its relevance.

5 V§558ff. and *OED* give later examples, but they can be analysed as elliptical or taken as archaisms, except for the the recurrent *what will/would you?* and *I'll none (of)* ..., as in (c) below, which may be idiomatic fixed phrases.

6 But note that the phrase *can skill* (as in V§554) may contain the verb *skill* (see *OED Skill, sb.*[1] 5, *v.*[1] 4).

7 Regular forms are of course more general in some southern dialects (see §4.3), and <a> also has a dialectal distribution (McIntosh, Samuels and Benskin 1986: I, 477f.).

8 For the general development: see *OED Dare, v.*[1]; *MED durren* v.; V§1355ff. For Shakespeare: Warner (1987). Periphrastic *do* + *dare* + plain infinitive seems to be nineteenth century (V§1360).

9 See also Kellner (1890: §26), Baldwin (1894: §237). Some of the difference is due to the fact that impersonals tended to occur more with the plain infinitive.

10 It is restricted to full verbs after the loss of *mought* 'might' in Standard English: this is uncommon in Caxton (Wienke 1930: 104), and occurs only once each in Shakespeare, in Marlow and in Sidney's verse (Franz 1939: §178, and see concordances), though it is occasionally found to the end of the seventeenth century as a literary device or a vulgarism (*OED*, Sweet 1891-8: §1481).

11 Stress may also be relevant. I note that in verse Shakespeare always uses OUGHT on a potential ictus, and that today OUGHT is typically stressed (Coates 1983: 75f.).

12 Regular third person singular forms are dated 'from the 14C' by *OED*; see also Long (1944: 298), Rettger (1934: 185).

13 This may reflect dialectal differences, but Tellier suggests that the use is a literary archaism, of a piece with other archaic usages (1962: 214-15). It is suggestive that the distinctive preterite-present third person singular is all but absent (Sandved 1968: 369, Kato 1974); for this more generally at this period see Price (1910: 29).

14 This might be stated as the development of a restriction on adverb placement in VP[–AUX], showing the availability of (perhaps the development of) the feature AUX for such a syntactic differentiation. But see Chapter 2 note 10 for some doubts about the relevance of auxiliaries to the parallel restriction on adverb placement in today's English.

15 I have looked through nominative pronouns in Kato's (1974) concordance to Malory without finding examples, and I have searched the standard works and monographs for Middle English which are available to me. But they give no hint of any earlier availability for this construction.

16 See Kaisse (1985: 39ff.); note that *would* had pronunciations both with and without [l].

17 Except for a very late reduction given in *MED*: *is* 'I shall'. But *MED* only cites one instance of this, in the first line of *Is tell yw* 'I shall tell you (my mind)', (*shulen* v. (1) 11(a); *Secular Lyrics of the XIVth and XVth Centuries*, ed. R. H. Robbins, 2nd edn., Oxford, Clarendon Press, 1955, no. 6). *MED* dates composition *c*1500. The manuscript is early sixteenth century, the language 'N. W. Midland' (McIntosh, Samuels and Benskin 1986). This may imply a late-fifteenth-century reduction in this combination in this area. Note that *MED willen* has not appeared at the time of writing.

18 There is what may be a special negative form of WILL in late Middle English: *wyn-*

not (pl.) (See *Will, v.*[1] A.6.b. *OED* dates this text *c*1420, *MED a*1475). But a work in the same manuscript and by the same hand as the text from which it is cited also has *shyn* 'shall' (pl.) (McIntosh, Samuels and Benskin 1986, Linguistic Profile 43), and elsewhere the fifteenth century occasionally has plural *wyn* (*OED Will, v.*[1] A.4). If this underlies *wynnot* it is not as a negative form that it is idiosyncratic. But *wynnot* in any case would represent a single lexical idiosyncrasy, not the systematic development of the seventeenth century.

19 This cautious wording allows for the instances of *do be* in *Zir Egir, Zir Gryme* cited in V§1451. The original of this is Scottish, and I suggest that we have here an overextension in the usage of an adult whose vernacular lacks periphrastic DO and who is adopting it as a feature of literary language (partly to put *be* in rhyme) without observing the southern restriction. V§1438 cites another example from early Modern English, but it is poor evidence since *be* is the second infinitive in a coordination which is itself separated from DO.

20 Rosch herself seems to suggest that there may be further structuring of some kind at this level (1977: 42ff., Rosch, Mervis, *et al.* 1976: 430ff.).

21 *MED* cites one incidentally (*c*1450 *The Gest Hystoriale of the Destruction of Troy*, ed. G. A. Panton and D. Donaldson, EETS 39, 56: 2529); for others see Sandved (1968: 206), Wienke (1930: 102).

22 Here it is necessary to distinguish dialectal *he do* which may be endingless for other reasons; see *OED*'s citation of Bale, who is from East Anglia and has endingless forms more generally (V§840). Note that Pepys normally has *he do*, but he does not restrict it to the auxiliary, Voglsam (1951: 126 and *passim*). *He don't* is probably developed independently (Jespersen 1909-49: V, §23.2); what is in question here is its partial acceptance.

23 Middle English instances are not numerous, but the progressive itself was much less common then. There is a relevant early Modern English instance in 1611 Bible, Authorized Version, Zechariah 9.9 *he is just and having salvation, lowly, and riding upon an ass, ... veniet tibi iustus et salvator; ipse pauper et ascendens super asinam, ...* But the evidential value of this is weakened by its occurrence in coordination, and by the possibility that a nonprogressive participle is used to render *salvator*.

24 See citations under *MED hauen* v. 7d, 8, 9; *OED Have, v.* 9b, 11, 11b, 14, 17; More's frequent use of such phrases as *have sport* (Visser 1946-56: §63, §103); the occurrence of imperative *have* in Shakespeare and Pope (see concordances).

25 V§1928 gives few seventeenth-century instances and none for the eighteenth century. There are about a dozen instances in Shakespeare, half a dozen or fewer in the verse of each of Jonson, Milton and Pope, and none in the works of Blake according to my examination of concordances. Some sense changes are no doubt involved in this shift (in particular the loss of *OED* 10 'to consider or regard as'), but they are not adequate to account for it.

26 V§1834 gives one early Modern English example: *is being* ('is in existence') for 1532, so the category may have been available in this absolute sense (or in the type of traditional religious context involved here).

27 From the late eighteenth century progressive *having* reappears; but both this and passive *had* are then better taken as [–AUX] in line with their actional semantics.

An alternative account of **is being* before 1800 would subcategorize BE for [–AUX], like DO. But this gives a less general account of the data for the period. Note that before the late eighteenth century *being* and *having* will not be [–AUX] as today if forms of BE, HAVE are morphosyntactically interrelated since they will share a common (abstract) stem which is [+AUX].

28 Lightfoot (1979) added two more: the loss of direct objects with pre-modals, and the special marking of epistemic pre-modals to avoid SVOM structures. The first is better taken as (mainly) a consequence of the reanalysis, as in 1991, the other was based on the (false) view that the epistemic–root distinction is syntactic (see Warner 1983: 196).

29 Lightfoot (1979: 112) added the development of quasi-modals: *be going to, have to, be able to*, and here he is followed by Roberts (1985). But see Warner (1983: 199, n. 9), and note the potential importance of semantic developments, that (for example) *be able* may acquire the sense 'have the ability to' in the mid fifteenth century because CAN is increasingly used for neutral (nonsubject-selecting) possibility.

30 The question of actual trigger for these developments is not resolved. If properties of agreement are involved (a claim put in some detail in Roberts, forthcoming), then it may be possible to claim (with Lightfoot) that the trigger was essentially morphological rather than a mix of formal and semantic changes. But the sharp morphological distinction which arose with the loss of *wite* 'know' may also have been a factor.

31 The contracting dialectal base of the sample underlying these figures is no doubt also a contributory factor.

32 See *EDD*, Murray (1873), Wright (1892), Wilson (1915: 125ff.), Grant and Dixon (1921), Ellegård (1953: 164, 200, n. 1, 207, n. 1).

33 Kroch (1989b) suggests that the early high incidence of interrogatives with *do* has nothing to do with functional motivation, but merely shows the pattern of diffusion of the change. I discuss this briefly below. For the moment note that the pattern of diffusion is at least consistent with the hypothesis that inverted structures are initially important for the adoption of *do*, and Kroch's intercept values for interrogatives are also consistent with their early prominence (1989b: Table 4).

34 Kroch (1989b: 231) interprets this as due to an interaction with Affix-hopping. But all the maths points to is the relevance of some further reasonably constant factor(s).

35 There may seem to be a possible problem for this account in that *is* is clearly transparent to tense/mood in 1750, on the evidence of retrieval in post-auxiliary ellipsis, and this might seem to imply a more general transparency for nonmodal auxiliaries, including *do*. But the status of *is* will have been supported by the existence of nonfinites of *be*, as well as by the retention of properties shared between auxiliaries and full verbs. So this need not imply a parallel analysis of *do* at the same period, whereas the loss (or lack) of nonfinites of DO implies its opacity. See the account at the end of §9.3.3.

36 Expletive *it* and *there* are characterized by means of a referential index in Pollard and Sag (forthcoming), so the fact that they are possible subjects reflects the limits of semantic selection rather than syntactic subcategorization.

37 General word-order distinctions between root and subordinate clauses might depend on a feature [+INV], where categories in SUBCAT default [–INV], and V[+INV] is initial, V[–INV] is typically late or final in Old English.

38 Here I will assume verb-second order declines independently of *do* in the first instance at least, since it seems clear that verb-second order begins to decline from the beginning of the fifteenth century, before *do* is heavily represented in our surviving texts as an alternative in inversion. But this may be inappropriate. Note that van Kemenade sees a turning point 'around 1400', for the beginning of the process of loss (1987: 228).

39 The further contraction of the range of inversion from word-order freedom to a construction restricted to interrogative, negative and a few other contexts is more puzzling. Stein (1990) may be right to see this as a consequence of the changed semantics of *do*, but it is arguably a process which had already started before *do* became an important factor.

40 For examples of retrieval from a preceding verb-second structure in Old English: see Or 260.5 cited in Wülfing (1894-1901: §391), Or 166.31 cited in Wülfing (1894-1901: §395).

41 There is also a rationale for the movement of lightly stressed adverbs before the verb associated with the rise of *do*, though it does not follow automatically from my account. See §9.2 (E) and note 14 above.

42 Pollock suggests two stages of loss (1989: 420), but the second (which goes with loss of overt second person singular agreement) is not obviously well timed to suit the decline of affirmative *do* from *c*1575, and the need to posit variation in the property of inherent barrierhood seems unappealing (despite Pollock's defence in his note 49). Roberts (forthcoming) suggests that the loss of an opposition of number in which both singular and plural are overt is a crucial parameter. This may be interpretable within my suggestion above, if it can be taken as crucial for the status of a distinctively morphological combination.

10 Conclusions

1 Note also the relatively poor evidence for lack of subject selection with *mot,* and see Standop's comment on the pervasiveness of the sense of 'being allotted' with this verb in Old English (1957: 169-70).

References

Abbott, Barbara. 1976. Right Node Raising as a Test for Constituenthood. *Linguistic Inquiry* 7.639–42.

Abney, S. 1987. The English Noun Phrase in its Sentential Aspect. MIT dissertation.

Akmajian, Adrian, Susan Steele and Thomas Wasow. 1979. The Category AUX in Universal Grammar. *Linguistic Inquiry* 10.1–64.

Akmajian, Adrian and Thomas Wasow. 1975. The Constituent Structure of VP and AUX and the Position of the Verb BE. *Linguistic Analysis* 1.205–45.

1977. More on *Have got*. *Linguistic Inquiry* 8.772–6.

Allan, W. Scott. 1987. Lightfoot noch einmal. *Diachronica* 4.123–57.

Allen, Cynthia. 1975. Old English Modals. In Jane B. Grimshaw (ed.) *Papers in the History and Structure of English* (Occasional Papers in Linguistics 1). 89–100. Amherst: University of Massachusetts.

1977. Topics in Diachronic English Syntax. Dissertation, University of Massachusetts. Amherst: Graduate Linguistic Student Association.

Allen, M. R. 1978. Morphological Investigations. Dissertation, University of Connecticut.

Anderson, John M. 1971. Some Proposals Concerning the Modal Verb in English. In A. J. Aitken, Angus McIntosh and Hermann Pálsson (eds.) *Edinburgh Studies in English and Scots*. 69–120. London: Longman.

1986. A Note on Old English Impersonals. *Journal of Linguistics* 22.167–77.

1991a. Should. In Dieter Kastovsky (ed.) *Historical English Syntax*. Berlin: Mouton de Gruyter.

1991b. Grammaticalisation and the English Modals. In Piotr Kakietek (ed.) *Problems in the Modality of Natural Language*. 9–27. Opole: Pedagogical University of Opole.

Anderson, S. R. 1982. Where's Morphology? *Linguistic Inquiry* 13.571–612.

Antipova, Ye Ya. 1963. Glagol'noe zamescenie v drevne angliiskom yazyke. *Vestnik Leningradskogo Gosudarstvennogo Universiteta. Series: Literature, History, Language*. 8, 2: 125–36.

Aronoff, Mark. 1976. *Word Formation in Generative Grammar*. Cambridge, Mass.: MIT Press.

Bach, Emmon W. 1979–80. In Defense of Passive. *Linguistics and Philosophy* 3.297–341.

Bacquet, P. 1962. *La Structure de la phrase verbale à l'époque alfrédienne*. Publications de la Faculté des Lettres de l'Université de Strasbourg, Fasc. 145.

Baker, C. L. 1981. Learnability and the English Auxiliary System. In C. L. Baker and John J. McCarthy (eds.) *The Logical Problem of Language Acquisition*. 296–323. Cambridge, Mass.: MIT Press.

Baldwin, C. 1894. *The Inflections and Syntax of the Morte D'Arthur of Sir Thomas Malory*. Boston: Ginn.

Behre, Frank. 1934. *The Subjunctive in Old English Poetry* (Göteborgs Högskolas Årsskrift 40). Göteborg: University of Gothenburg.

1950. The Origin and Early History of Meditative–Polemic *Should* in *That*-clauses. *Göteborgs Högskolas Årsskrift* 56.273–309.

1955. *Meditative-Polemic 'Should' in Modern English 'That'-Clauses* (Gothenburg Studies in English 4). Stockholm: Almqvist and Wiksell.

Bendix, E.H. 1966. Componential Analysis of General Vocabulary: the Semantic Structure of a Set of Verbs in English, Hindi, and Japanese (Indiana University Research Center in Anthropology, Folklore and Linguistics, 40). Bloomington: Indiana University. Also published as Part 2 of *IJAL* 32, no. 2.

Bock, H. 1931. Studien zum präpositionalen Infinitiv und Akkusativ mit dem *to*-Infinitiv. *Anglia* 55.114–249.

Bock, M. 1938. Der stilistische Gebrauch des englischen Personalpronomens der 2. Person im volkstümlichen Dialog der älteren englischen Komödie. Inaugural dissertation, Innsbruck.

Boertien, Harmon. 1979. Toward a Unified Semantics of Aspectual Verbs with *to* and *ing* Complements. In Paul R. Clyne, William F. Hanks and Carol L. Hofbauer (eds.) *Papers from the Fifteenth Regional Meeting Chicago Linguistic Society*. 42–52. Chicago: Chicago Linguistic Society.

Bolinger, Dwight. 1973. Ambient 'It' is Meaningful Too. *Journal of Linguistics* 9.261–70.

1977a. *Meaning and Form*. London and New York: Longman.

1977b. *There*. In Bolinger 1977a: 90–123.

1977c. *It*. In Bolinger 1977a: 66–89.

Borsley, Robert D. 1983. A Welsh Agreement Process and the Status of VP and S. In Gerald Gazdar, Ewan Klein and Geoffrey K. Pullum (eds.) *Order, Concord and Constituency*. 57–74. Dordrecht: Foris.

1986. A Note on HPSG. *Bangor Research Papers in Linguistics* 1.77–85.

1987. *Subjects and Complements in HPSG* (Report No. CSLI–87–107). Stanford: Center for the Study of Language and Information.

1989. An HPSG Approach to Welsh. *Journal of Linguistics* 25.333–354.

1992. NPs and Clauses in Welsh and Syrian Arabic. University College of North Wales, Bangor: unpublished paper.

1993. Heads in HPSG. In G. Corbett, N. Fraser and S. McGlashan (eds.) *Heads in Grammatical Theory*. Cambridge University Press.

Breivik, Leif Egil. 1983. *Existential 'There': a Synchronic and Diachronic Study* (Studia Anglistica Norvegica 2). Bergen: Department of English, University of Bergen.

Bresnan, J. 1982. The Passive in Lexical Theory. In J. Bresnan (ed.) *The Mental Representation of Grammatical Relations*. 3–86. Cambridge, Mass. and London: MIT Press.

Brinton, Laurel J. 1988. *The Development of English Aspectual Systems*. Cambridge University Press.

Brown, W. H., Jr. 1970. *A Syntax of King Ælfred's 'Pastoral Care'*. The Hague: Mouton.

Brunner, Karl. 1960. *Die englische Sprache*. 2nd edn. 2 vols. Tübingen: Niemeyer.

1963. *An Outline of Middle English Grammar*, translated by G. Johnston. Oxford: Blackwell.

1965. *Altenglische Grammatik nach der Angelsächsischen Grammatik von Eduard Sievers*. 3rd. edn. Tübingen: Niemeyer.

Bybee, Joan L. and Carol Moder. 1983. Morphological Classes as Natural Categories. *Language* 59.251–70.

Bybee, Joan L. and Dan I. Slobin. 1982. Rules and Schemas in the Development and Use of the English Past Tense. *Language* 58.265–89.

Callaway, Morgan, Jr. 1901. The Appositive Participle in Anglo-Saxon. *PMLA* 16.141–360.

1913. *The Infinitive in Anglo-Saxon.* Washington: Carnegie Institution of Washington.

Campbell, A. 1959a. *Old English Grammar*. Oxford: Clarendon Press.

1959b. Review of Standop 1957. *Review of English Studies* n. s. 10.186–7.

Charleston, Britta Marian. 1941. *Studies on the Syntax of the English Verb* (Swiss Studies in English 11). Bern: Francke.

Cheshire, J. 1982. *Variation in an English Dialect: a Sociolinguistic Study.* Cambridge University Press.

Chomsky, Noam. 1957. *Syntactic Structures*. The Hague: Mouton.

1980. *Rules and Representations*. Oxford: Blackwell.

1986. *Barriers*. Cambridge, Mass.: MIT Press.

Coates, Jennifer. 1983. *The Semantics of the Modal Auxiliaries*. London: Croom Helm.

Cremers, Crit. 1983. On Two Types of Infinitival Complementation. In Frank Heny and Barry Richards (eds.) *Linguistic Categories: Auxiliaries and Related Puzzles*, vol. I. 169–221. Dordrecht: Reidel.

d'Ardenne, S. T. R. O. 1961. *Þe Liflade ant te Passiun of Seinte Iuliene* (EETS OS 248). London: Oxford University Press.

Denison, David. 1985a. The Origins of Periphrastic *Do*: Ellegård and Visser Reconsidered. In Roger Eaton, Olga Fischer, Willem Koopman and Frederike van der Leek (eds.) *Papers from the 4th International Conference on English Historical Linguistics*. 45–60. Amsterdam: John Benjamins.

1985b. Some Observations on *Being Teaching*. *Studia Neophilologica* 57.157–9.

1990a. The Old English Impersonals Revived. In S. Adamson, V. Law, N. Vincent and S. Wright (eds.) *Papers from the 5th International Conference on English Historical Linguistics, Cambridge 6–9 April 1987.* 111–40. Amsterdam and Philadelphia: John Benjamins.

1990b. Auxiliary + Impersonal in Old English. *Folia Linguistica Historica* 9.139–66.

Dennis, Leah. 1940. The Progressive Tense: Frequency of its Use in English. *PMLA* 55.855–65.

Di Sciullo, Anna-Maria and Edwin Williams. 1987. *On the Definition of Word.* Cambridge, Mass.: MIT Press.

Dobson, E. J. 1968. *English Pronunciation 1500–1700.* 2nd edn. 2 vols. Oxford: Clarendon Press.

Downes, William. 1977. The imperative and pragmatics. *Journal of Linguistics* 13.77–97.

Dowty, David R. 1988. Type Raising, Functional Composition, and Non-Constituent Conjunction. In Richard Oehrle, Emmon Bach and Deirdre Wheeler (eds.) *Categorial Grammars and Natural Language Structures.* 153–97. Dordrecht: Reidel.

Ehrman, M. E. 1966. *The Meanings of the Modals in Present-day American English* (Janua Linguarum Series Practica 45). The Hague: Mouton.

Ellegård, A. 1953. *The Auxiliary 'Do': the Establishment and Regulation of its Use in English.* Stockholm: Almqvist and Wiksell.

Elmer, W. 1981. *Diachronic Grammar: the History of Old and Middle English Subjectless Constructions.* Tübingen: Niemeyer.

Emonds, Joseph E. 1972. A Reformulation of Certain Syntactic Transformations. In Stanley Peters (ed.) *Goals of Linguistic Theory.* 21–62. Englewood Cliffs, N.J.: Prentice-Hall.

1976. *A Transformational Approach to English Syntax: Root, Structure-preserving, and Local Transformations.* New York: Academic Press.

Enç, Mürvet. 1986. Towards a Referential Analysis of Temporal Expressions. *Linguistics and Philosophy* 9.405–26.

Evers, Arnold and Tineke Scholten. 1980. A Dutch Answer to the Luiseño Argument. *Utrecht Working Papers in Linguistics* 9.87–101.

Fabb, N. 1988. English Suffixation is Constrained only by Selectional Restrictions. *Natural Language and Linguistic Theory* 6.527–39.

Falk, Yehuda N. 1984. The English Auxiliary System: a Lexical-Functional Analysis. *Language* 60.483–509.

Fischer, Olga C. M. 1992. Syntax. In N. Blake (ed.) *The Cambridge History of the English Language,* vol II: *1066–1476.* 207–408. Cambridge University Press.

Fischer, Olga C. M. and Frederike C. van der Leek. 1987. A 'Case' for the Old English Impersonal. In Willem Koopman, Frederike van der Leek, Olga Fischer and Roger Eaton (eds.) *Explanation and Linguistic Change* (Current Issues in Linguistic Theory 45). 79–120. Amsterdam and Philadelphia: John Benjamins.

Flickinger, D. 1987. Lexical Rules in the Hierarchical Lexicon. Stanford Dissertation.

Flickinger, D., Carl Pollard and Thomas Wasow. 1985. Structure-Sharing in Lexical Representation. *Proceedings of the 23rd Annual Meeting of the Association for Computational Linguistics* 262–7.

Forsström, G. 1948. *The Verb 'to be' in Middle English: a Survey of the Forms* (Lund Studies in English 15). Lund: Gleerup.

Francis, W. Nelson. 1968. Modal *Daren't* and *Durstn't* in Dialectal English. *Leeds Studies in English* 2.145–63.

Franz, Wilhelm. 1939. *Die Sprache Shakespeares in Vers und Prosa* (Shakespeare-Grammatik, 4th edn.). Halle: Niemeyer.

Fridén, Georg. 1948. *Studies on the Tenses of the English Verb from Chaucer to Shakespeare, with Special Reference to the Late Sixteenth Century* (Uppsala Essays and Studies on English Language and Literature 2). Uppsala: Almqvist and Wiksell.

Fries, C. C. 1940. On the Development of the Structural Use of Word-order in Modern English. *Language* 16.199–208.

1952. *The Structure of English*. New York: Harcourt, Brace.

van der Gaaf, W. 1904. *The Transition from the Impersonal to the Personal Construction in Middle English* (Anglistische Forschungen 14). Heidelberg: Carl Winter.

Gazdar, Gerald, Ewan Klein, Geoffrey K. Pullum and Ivan A. Sag. 1985. *Generalized Phrase Structure Grammar*. Oxford: Blackwell and Cambridge, Mass.: Harvard University Press.

Gazdar, Gerald, Geoffrey K. Pullum and Ivan A. Sag. 1982. Auxiliaries and Related Phenomena in a Restrictive Theory of Grammar. *Language* 58.591–638.

Gazdar, Gerald, Geoffrey K. Pullum, Robert Carpenter, Ewan Klein, Thomas Hukari and R. D. Levine. 1986. *Category Structures* (Cognitive Science Research Paper CSRP 071). Brighton: University of Sussex.

Goossens, Louis. 1982. On the Development of the Modals and of the Epistemic Function in English. In A. Ahlqvist (ed.) *Proceedings of the 5th International Conference on Historical Linguistics*. 74–84. Amsterdam: Benjamins.

1984. The Interplay of Syntax and Semantics in the Development of the English Modals. In N.F. Blake and Charles Jones (eds.) *English Historical Linguistics: Studies in Development*. 149–159. Sheffield: Centre for English Cultural Tradition and Language, University of Sheffield.

1987. The Auxiliarization of the English Modals: a Functional Grammar View. In Martin Harris and Paolo Ramat (eds.) *Historical Development of Auxiliaries*. 111–43. Berlin: Mouton de Gruyter.

Grant, W. and J. M. Dixon. 1921. *Manual of Modern Scots*. Cambridge University Press.

Green, G. A. 1980. Some Wherefores of English Inversions. *Language* 56.582–601.

1985. The Description of Inversions in Generalized Phrase Structure Grammar. In M. Niepokuj, M VanClay, V. Nikiforidou, D. Feder, C. Brugman, M. Macaulay, N. Beery and M. Emanatian (eds.) *Proceedings of the Eleventh Annual Meeting of the Berkeley Linguistics Society*. 117–45. Berkeley: Berkeley Linguistics Society.

Griffiths, Patrick D. 1987. Constituent Structure in Text-copying. *York Papers in Linguistics* 12.75–116.

Halliday, Michael A. K. 1980. On Being Teaching. In Sidney Greenbaum, Geoffrey Leech and Jan Svartvik (eds.) *Studies in English Linguistics for Randolph Quirk*. 61–4. London: Longman.

Halliday, Michael A. K. and Ruqaiya Hasan. 1976. *Cohesion in English*. London: Longman.

Hankamer, Jorge and Ivan A. Sag. 1976. Deep and Surface Anaphora. *Linguistic Inquiry* 7.391–428.

Harris, Zellig S. 1951. *Structural Linguistics*. Chicago and London: University of Chicago Press.

Haugen, E. 1976. *The Scandinavian Languages*. London: Faber and Faber.

Healey, Antonette diPaolo and Richard L. Venezky. 1980. *A Microfiche Concordance to Old English: the List of Texts and Index of Editions* (= Parts I and II of Venezky and Healey 1980). Newark, Del. and Toronto: Pontifical Institute of Mediaeval Studies.

Hopper, P. J. and S. A. Thompson. 1984. The Discourse Basis for Lexical Categories in Universal Grammar. *Language* 60.703–52.

Huddleston, Rodney D. 1970. Two Approaches to the Analysis of Tags. *Journal of Linguistics*. 6.215–22.

1971. *The Sentence in Written English*. Cambridge University Press.

1974. Further remarks on the Analysis of Auxiliaries as Main Verbs. *Foundations of Language* 11.215–29.

1976a. *An Introduction to English Transformational Syntax*. London: Longman.

1976b. Some Theoretical Issues in the Description of the English Verb. *Lingua* 40.331–83.

1978. On the Constituent Structure of VP and Aux. *Linguistic Analysis* 4.31–59.

1980. Criteria for Auxiliaries and Modals. In Sidney Greenbaum, Geoffrey Leech and Jan Svartvik (eds.) *Studies in English Linguistics for Randolph Quirk*, 65–78. London: Longman.

1984. *Introduction to the Grammar of English*. Cambridge University Press.

Hudson, Richard A. 1984. *Word Grammar*. Oxford: Blackwell.

1987. Zwicky on Heads. *Journal of Linguistics* 23.109–32.

Hughes, Arthur and Peter Trudgill. 1987. *English Accents and Dialects*. 2nd edn. London: Arnold.

Huntley, Martin. 1984. The Semantics of English Imperatives. *Linguistics and Philosophy* 7.103–33.

Iatridou, Sabine. 1990. About Agr(P). *Linguistic Inquiry* 21.551–77.

Iwakura, Kunihiro. 1977. The Auxiliary System in English. *Linguistic Analysis* 3.101–36.

1983. A Filter on Auxiliary Verbs. *Linguistic Analysis* 11.285–94.

Jack, George. 1991. The Infinitive in Early Middle English Prose. *Neuphilologische Mitteilungen* 92.311–41.

Jackendoff, Ray. 1972. *Semantic Interpretation in Generative Grammar*. Cambridge, Mass.: MIT Press.

1975. Morphological and Semantic Regularities in the Lexicon. *Language* 51.639–71.

1977. *X-bar Syntax: a Study of Phrase Structure*. Cambridge, Mass.: MIT Press.

Jacobson, S. 1981. *Preverbal Adverbs and Auxiliaries: a Study of Word Order Change* (Stockholm Studies in English 55). Stockholm: Almqvist and Wiksell.

Jacobsson, B. 1951. *Inversion in English with Special Reference to the Early Modern English Period*. Uppsala: Almqvist and Wiksell.

Jespersen, Otto. 1909–49. *A Modern English Grammar on Historical Principles*. Published and reprinted, London: George Allen and Unwin.

Joos, M. 1964. *The English Verb: Form and Meanings*. Madison and Milwaukee: University of Wisconsin Press.

Jordan, R. 1974. *Handbook of Middle English Grammar: Phonology*. Revised by H. Matthes, translated and revised by E. J. Crook. The Hague: Mouton.

Kageyama, T. 1975. Relational Grammar and the History of Subject Raising. *Glossa* 9.165–81.

Kaisse, Ellen M. 1985. *Connected Speech: the Interaction of Syntax and Phonology*. Orlando: Academic Press.

Kakietek, Piotr. 1972. *Modal Verbs in Shakespeare's English* (Seria Filologia Angielska 3). Poznań: Adam Mickiewicz University.

Kaplan, R. M. 1987. Three Seductions of Computational Psycholinguistics. In Peter Whitelock, M. M. Wood, H. L. Somers, R. Johnson and P. Bennett (eds.) *Linguistic Theory and Computer Applications*. 149–88. New York and London: Academic Press.

Karpf, Fritz. 1930. *Studien zur Syntax in den Werken Geoffey Chaucers* (Wiener Beiträge zur englischen Philologie 55). Vienna: Bräumuller.

Karttunen, Lauri. 1984. Features and Values. *Coling 84: Proceedings of the Tenth International Conference on Computational Linguistics*. 28–33.

Kato, Tomomi. 1974. *A Concordance to the Works of Sir Thomas Malory*. Tokyo: University of Tokyo Press.

Keenan, Edward L. 1980. Passive is Phrasal (not Sentential or Lexical). In Teun Hoekstra, Harry van der Hulst and Michael Moortgat (eds.) *Lexical Grammar*. 181–213. Dordrecht: Foris.

Kellner, L. 1890. *Caxton's Blanchardine and Eglantine* (EETS ES 58). London: Oxford University Press.

Kemenade, Ans van. 1987. *Syntactic Case and Morphological Case in the History of English*. Utrecht dissertation. Dordrecht: ICG printing.

1989. *Syntactic Change and the History of English Modals* (Dutch Working Papers in English Language and Linguistics 16). Leiden: Rijksuniversiteit te Leiden.

Kenyon, J. S. 1909. *The Syntax of the Infinitive in Chaucer*. London: Chaucer Society.

Klima, Edward. 1964. Negation in English. In J. A. Fodor and J. J. Katz (eds.) *The Structure of Language*. 246–323. Englewood Cliffs, N.J.: Prentice-Hall.

Kohonen, Viljo. 1978. *On the Development of English Word Order in Religious Prose around 1000 and 1200 A.D.: a Quantitative Study of Word Order in Context*. Åbo: Research Institute of the Åbo Akademi Foundation.

Kornai, András and Geoffrey K. Pullum. 1990. The X-bar Theory of Phrase Structure. *Language* 66.24–50.

Kroch, A. 1989a. Function and Grammar in the History of English: Periphrastic *Do*. In R. W. Fasold and D. Schriffin (eds.) *Language Change and Variation*. 132–72. Amsterdam and Philadelphia: Benjamins.

1989b. Reflexes of Grammar in Patterns of Language Change. *Journal of Language Variation and Change* 1.199–244.

Kroch, A., J. Myhill and S. Pintzuk. 1982. Understanding *Do*. In Kevin Tuite, R. Schneider and R. Chametzsky (eds.) *Papers from the Eighteenth Regional Meeting Chicago Linguistic Society*. 282–93. Chicago: Chicago Linguistic Society.

Krzyszpień, J. 1980. The Periphrastic Subjunctive with *Magan* in Old English. *Studia Anglica Posnaniensia*. 11.49–64.

Kuno, Susumu. 1976. Gapping: a Functional Analysis. *Linguistic Inquiry* 7.300–318.

1981. The Syntax of Comparative Clauses. In Roberta A. Hendrick, Carrie S. Masek and Mary Frances Miller (eds.) *Papers from the Seventeenth Regional Meeting Chicago Linguistic Society*, 136–55. Chicago: Chicago Linguistic Society.

Kytö, Merja. 1987. Can (Could) vs. May (Might) in Old and Middle English: Testing a Diachronic Corpus. In L. Kahlas-Terkka (ed.) *Neophilologica Fennica, Société*

Néophilologique 100 ans (Mémoires de la Société Néophilologique de Helsinki 45). 205–40. Helsinki: Société Néophilologique.

1991. *Variation and Diachrony, with Early American English in Focus* (Bamberger Beiträge zur englischen Sprachwissenschaft 28). Frankfurt: Peter Lang.

Lakoff, George. 1987. *Women, Fire, and Dangerous Things*. Chicago and London: University of Chicago Press.

Lakoff, George and John Robert Ross. 1972. A Note on Anaphoric Islands and Causatives. *Linguistic Inquiry* 3.121–5.

Lapointe, Steven G. 1980a. A Lexical Analysis of the English Auxiliary Verb System. In Teun Hoekstra, Harry van der Hulst and Michael Moortgat (eds.) *Lexical Grammar*. 215–54. Dordrecht: Foris.

1980b. A Note on Akmajian, Steele and Wasow's Treatment of Certain Verb Complement Types. *Linguistic Inquiry* 11.770–87.

Lass, Roger. 1980. *On Explaining Language Change*. Cambridge University Press.

Leech, G. 1969. *Towards a Semantic Description of English*. London: Longman.

Leonard, S. A. 1962. *The Doctrine of Correctness in English Usage 1700–1800*. New York: Russell and Russell, reprint of 1929 edition.

LeSourd, Philip. 1976. *Got* Insertion. *Linguistic Inquiry* 7.509–16.

Levin, Nancy S.1978. Some Identity-of-sense Deletions Puzzle Me. Do they you? In Donka Farkas, W. M. Jacobsen and K. W. Todrys (eds.) *Papers from the Fourteenth Meeting Chicago Linguistic Society*. 229–40. Chicago: Chicago Linguistic Society.

1980. Main-verb Ellipsis in Spoken English. Ohio State dissertation, and in *Ohio State Working Papers in Linguistics* 24.65–165. Republished with annotations as Levin 1986.

1981. Conditions on Ellipsis of Infinitival *Be*. In David Sankoff and Henrietta Cedergren (eds.) *Variation Omnibus*. 393–401. Carbondale and Edmonton: Linguistic Research Inc.

1986. *Main-verb Ellipsis in Spoken English*. Annotated version of Levin 1980 dissertation. New York and London: Garland.

Levin, S. F. 1958. Negative Contraction: an Old and Middle English Dialect Criterion. *Journal of English and Germanic Philology* 57.492–501.

Levinson, Stephen C. 1983. *Pragmatics*. Cambridge University Press.

Lightfoot, David W. 1979. *Principles of Diachronic Syntax*. Cambridge University Press.

1980. The History of NP Movement. In Teun Hoekstra, Harry van der Hulst and Michael Moortgat (eds.) *Lexical Grammar*. 255–84. Dordrecht: Foris.

1988. Syntactic Change. In Frederick J. Newmeyer (ed.) *Linguistics: the Cambridge Survey*, vol. I: *Linguistic Theory: Foundations*. 303–23. Cambridge University Press.

1991. *How to Set Parameters: Arguments from Language Change*. Cambridge, Mass. and London: MIT Press.

Local, John and Bill Wells. 1983. You Don't Have *to* Resort to Syntax. *York Papers in Linguistics* 10.147–57.

Long, M. 1944. *The English Strong Verb from Chaucer to Caxton*. Menasha, Wisc.: George Banta.

Lyons, John. 1966. Towards a 'Notional' Theory of the 'Parts of Speech'. *Journal of Linguistics* 2.209–36.
1977. *Semantics*. 2 vols. Cambridge University Press.
McCawley, James D. 1971. Tense and Time Reference in English. In Charles Fillmore and D. Terence Langendoen (eds.) *Studies in Linguistic Semantics*. 96–113. New York: Holt, Rinehart, and Winston.
1975. The Category Status of English Modals. *Foundations of Language* 12.597–601.
1986. What Linguists Might Contribute to Dictionary Making if they Could Get their Act Together. In Peter C. Bjarkman and Victor Raskin (eds.) *The Real-world Linguist: Linguistic Applications in the 1980s*. 3–18. Norwood, N.J.: Ablex.
McCawley, Norico. 1976. From OE/ME 'Impersonal' to 'Personal' Constructions: What is a 'Subject-less' S? In Sanford Steever, C. Walker and S. Mufwene (eds.) *Papers from the Parasession on Diachronic Syntax*. 192–204. Chicago: Chicago Linguistic Society.
McDonald, Christine. 1981. Variation in the Use of Modal Verbs with Special Reference to Tyneside English. Newcastle dissertation.
McIntosh, Angus, M. L. Samuels and Michael Benskin. 1986. *A Linguistic Atlas of Late Mediaeval English*. 4 vols. Aberdeen University Press.
Madden, J. F. and F. P. Magoun, Jr. 1964. (4th corrected printing.) *A Grouped Frequency Word-list of Anglo-Saxon Poetry*. Cambridge, Mass.: Department of English, Harvard University.
Maling, Joan. 1983. Transitive Adjectives: a Case of Categorial Reanalysis. In Frank Heny and Barry Richards (eds.) *Linguistic Categories: Auxiliaries and Related Puzzles*, vol. I. 253–89. Dordrecht: Reidel.
Maratsos, Michael P. and Mary Anne Chalkley. 1980. The Internal Language of Children's Syntax: the Ontogenesis and Representation of Syntactic Categories. In Keith E. Nelson (ed.) *Children's Language*, vol. II. 127–214. New York: Gardner Press.
Marchand, Hans. 1938. Remarks about English Negative Sentences. *English Studies* 20.198–204.
Milroy, James and Leslie Milroy. 1985. *Authority in Language*. London: Routledge and Kegan Paul.
Mitchell, Bruce. 1976. Some Problems Involving Old English Periphrases with *Beon/wesan* and the Present Participle. *Neuphilologische Mitteilungen* 77.478–91.
1985. *Old English Syntax*. 2 vols. Oxford: Clarendon Press.
Mittwoch, A. 1988. Aspects of English Aspect: on the Interaction of Perfect, Progressive and Durational Phrases. *Linguistics and Philosophy* 11.203–54.
Mossé, Fernand. 1938. *Histoire de la forme périphrastique 'être + participe présent' en germanique* (Collection linguistique publiée par La Société Linguistique de Paris 42, 43). Paris: Klincksieck.
1957. Refléctions sur la genèse de la 'forme progressive'. *Wiener Beiträge zur englischen Philologie* 65.155–74.
Murray, James. 1873. The Dialect of the Southern Counties of Scotland. *Transactions of the Philological Society for 1870–2*. 1–251.

Mustanoja, T. 1960. *A Middle English Syntax*, Part I: *Parts of Speech* (Mémoires de la Société Néophilologique de Helsinki 23). Helsinki: Société Néophilologique.

Myhill, John. 1988. The Rise of *Be* as an Aspect Marker in Black English Vernacular. *American Speech* 63.304–25.

Nagle, S. J. 1989. *Inferential Change and Syntactic Modality in English* (Bamber Beiträge zur englischen Sprachwissenschaft 23). Frankfurt: Peter Lang.

Napoli, Donna Jo. 1983. Comparative Ellipsis: a Phrase Structure Analysis. *Linguistic Inquiry* 14.675–94.

1985. Verb Phrase Deletion in English: a Base-generated Analysis. *Journal of Linguistics* 21.281–319.

Nehls, D. 1974. *Synchron–diachrone Untersuchungen zur Expanded Form im Englischen*. Munich: Hueber.

Neijt, Anneke. 1980. *Gapping: a Contribution to Sentence Grammar*. 2nd revised edn. Dordrecht: Foris.

Nevalainen, Terttu and Matti Rissanen. 1986. Do you Support the DO-support? Emphatic and Non-emphatic DO in Affirmative Statements in Present-day Spoken English. In Sven Jacobson (ed.) *Papers from the Third Scandinavian Symposium on Syntactic Variation* (Stockholm Studies in English 65). 35–50. Stockholm: Almqvist and Wiksell International.

Nickel, G. 1966. *Die Expanded Form im Altenglischen: Vorkommen, Funktion und Herkunft der Umschreibung 'beon/wesan' + Partizip präsens*. Neumünster: Wachholtz.

1967. An Example of a Syntactic Blend in Old English. *Indogermanische Forschungen* 72. 261–74.

Nummenmaa, Liisa. 1973. *The Uses of So, Al So and As in Early Middle English* (Mémoires de la Société Néophilologique de Helsinki 39). Helsinki: Société Néophilologique.

Ohlander, U. 1941. A Study on the Use of the Infinitive Sign in Middle English. *Studia Neophilologica* 14.58–66.

van Oirsouw, R. 1987. *The Syntax of Coordination*. London: Croom Helm.

Onions, C. T. 1966. *The Oxford Dictionary of English Etymology*. Oxford: Clarendon Press.

Ono, Shigeru. 1958. Some Notes on the Auxiliary *Motan. *Anglica* 3.64–80.

1975. The Old English Verbs of Knowing. *Studies in English Literature* (English number 1975) 33–60.

Ossleton, N. E. 1983. Points of Modern English Syntax LXV, 200, *English Studies* 64.469–72.

Ouhalla, Jamal. 1990. Sentential Negation, Relativised Minimality and the Aspectual Status of Auxiliaries. *The Linguistic Review* 7.183–231.

Palmer, F. R. 1974. *The English Verb*. London: Longman.

1979. *Modality and the English Modals*. London: Longman.

1983. Semantic Explanations for the Syntax of the English Modals. In Frank Heny and Barry Richards (eds.) *Linguistic Categories: Auxiliaries and Related Puzzles*, vol. II. 205–17. Dordrecht: Reidel.

1986. *Mood and Modality*. Cambridge University Press.

1988. *The English Verb*. 2nd edn. London: Longman.

Perkins, Michael R. 1983. *Modal Expressions in English*. London: Francis Pinter.

Peterson, Peter G. 1981. Problems with Constraints on Coordination. *Linguistic Analysis* 8.449–60.

Phillipps, K. C. 1970. *Jane Austen's English*. London: André Deutsch.

Plank, Frans. 1984. The Modals Story Retold (= Review of Lightfoot 1979). *Studies in Language* 8.305–64.

Platzack, Christer. 1987. The Scandinavian Languages and the Null-subject Parameter. *Natural Language and Linguistic Theory* 5.377–401.

Pollard, C. J. 1985. Phrase Structure Grammar without Metarules. *Proceedings of the Fourth West Coast Conference on Formal Linguistics*. Stanford: Stanford Linguistics Department.

Pollard, Carl and Ivan A. Sag. 1987. *Information-Based Syntax and Semantics*, vol. I: *Fundamentals*. Stanford: Center for the Study of Language and Information.

forthcoming. *Information-based Syntax and Semantics*, vol. II: *Topics in Binding and Control*. Stanford: Center for the Study of Language and Information.

Pollock, Jean-Yves. 1989. Verb Movement, Universal Grammar, and the Structure of IP. *Linguistic Inquiry* 20.365–424.

Postal, Paul M. 1966. On So-called 'Pronouns' in English. *Nineteenth Georgetown Monograph on Languages and Linguistics*. Washington: Georgetown University Press.

1969. Anaphoric Islands. In Robert Binnick, Alice Davison, Georgia M. Green and Jerry L. Morgan (eds.) *Papers from the Fifth Regional Meeting of the Chicago Linguistic Society*. 205–39. Chicago: University of Chicago Department of Linguistics

Poussa, Patricia. 1990. A Contact-universals Origin for Periphrastic *Do*, with Special Consideration of OE-Celtic Contact. In S. Adamson, V. Law, N. Vincent and S. Wright (eds.) *Papers from the 5th International Conference on English Historical Linguistics, Cambridge 6–9 April 1987*. 407–34. Amsterdam and Philadelphia: John Benjamins.

Price, H. T. 1910. *A History of Ablaut in the Strong Verbs from Caxton to the End of the Elizabethan Period*. Reprinted at College Park, Maryland by McGrath 1970.

Prokosch, E. 1927. The Old English Weak Preterites without Medial Vowel. *PMLA* 17.331–8.

1939. *A Comparative Germanic Grammar*. Baltimore: Linguistic Society of America.

Pullum, Geoffrey K. 1982. Syncategorematicity and English Infinitival *To*. *Glossa* 16.181–215.

1991. English Nominal Gerund Phrases as Noun Phrases with Verb-phrase Heads. *Linguistics* 29.763–99.

Pullum, Geoffrey K. and Deirdre Wilson. 1977. Autonomous Syntax and the Analysis of Auxiliaries. *Language* 53.741–88.

Quirk, Randolph and A. P. Duckworth. 1961. Co-existing Negative Preterite Forms of *Dare*. In *Language and Society. Essays Presented to A. M. Jensen on his Seventieth Birthday*. 135–40. Copenhagen: Det Berlingske Bogtrykkeri. Reprinted in R. Quirk (ed.) *Essays on the English Language Medieval and Modern*. 114–19. London: Longman, 1968.

Quirk, Randolph, Sidney Greenbaum, Geoffrey Leech and Jan Svartvik. 1985. *A Comprehensive Grammar of the English Language*. London and New York: Longman.

Quirk, Randolph and Jan Svartvik. 1970. Types and Uses of Nonfinite Clause in Chaucer. *English Studies* 51.393–411.

Radford, Andrew. 1988. *Transformational Grammar*. Cambridge University Press.

Rankova, Maria. 1964. On the Development of the Periphrastic Auxiliary *Do* in Modern English. *Annuaire de l'Université de Sofia* 58.509–64.

Rettger, J. F. 1934. *The Development of Ablaut in the Strong Verb of the East Midland Dialects of Middle English*. Language dissertation (Supplement to *Language*) 18. Philadelphia: Linguistic Society of America.

Rissanen, Matti. 1985. Periphrastic *Do* in Affirmative Statements in Early American English. *Journal of English Linguistics* 18.163–83.

Roberts, Ian G. 1985. Agreement Parameters and the Development of English Modal Auxiliaries. *Natural Language and Linguistic Theory* 3.21–58.

1990. Some Notes on VP-fronting and Head Government. In Joan Mascaró and Marina Nespor (eds.) *Grammar in Progress*. 387–396. Dordrecht: Foris.

forthcoming. *Verbs and Diachronic Syntax*. Dordrecht: Kluwer.

Rosch, Eleanor. 1975. Universals and Cultural Specifics in Human Categorization. In Richard W. Brislin, S. Bochner and W. Lonner (eds.) *Cross-cultural Perspectives on Learning*. 177–206. New York: John Wiley.

1977. Human Categorization. In N. Warren (ed.) *Studies in Cross-cultural Psychology*. 1–49. London: Academic Press.

1978. Principles of Categorization. In Eleanor Rosch and Barbara B. Lloyd (eds.) *Cognition and Categorization*. 27–48. Hillsdale N.J.: Erlbaum.

1988. Coherences and Categorization: a Historical View. In F. Kessel (ed.) *The Development of Language and Language Researchers: Essays in Honor of Roger Brown*. 373–92. Hillsdale, N.J.: Erlbaum.

Rosch, Eleanor and C. B. Mervis. 1975. Family Resemblances: Studies in the Internal Structure of Categories. *Cognitive Psychology* 7.573–605.

Rosch, Eleanor, C. B. Mervis, W. D. Gray, D. M. Johnson, and P. Boyes-Braem. 1976. Basic Objects in Natural Categories. *Cognitive Psychology* 8.382–439.

Rosch, Eleanor, C. Simpson and R. S. Miller. 1976. Structural Bases of Typicality Effects. *Journal of Experimental Psychology: Human Perception and Performance* 2.491–502.

Ross, John Robert. 1969. Auxiliaries as Main Verbs. In W. Todd (ed.) *Studies in Philosophical Linguistics*. 77–102. Evanston, Ill.: Great Expectations Press.

Rydén, Mats. 1979. *An Introduction to the Historical Study of English Syntax* (Stockholm Studies in English 51). Uppsala: Almqvist and Wiksell.

Rydén, Mats and Sverker Brorström. 1987. *The **Be/Have** Variation with Intransitives in English with Special Reference to the Late Modern Period* (Stockholm Studies in English 70). Stockholm: Almqvist and Wiksell International.

Sag, Ivan A. 1977. *Deletion and Logical Form*. Bloomington: Indiana University Linguistics Club.

1979. The Nonunity of Anaphora. *Linguistic Inquiry* 10.152–64.

Sag, Ivan A, Gerald Gazdar, Thomas Wasow and Steven Weisler. 1985. Coordination and How to Distinguish Categories. *Natural Language and Linguistic Theory* 3.117–71.

Salkie, R. 1989. Perfect and Pluperfect: What is the Relationship? *Journal of Linguistics* 25.1–34.

Salmon, Vivian. 1965. Sentence Structures in Colloquial Shakespearean English. *Transactions of the Philological Society.* 105–40.

Samuels, M. L. 1972. *Linguistic Evolution.* Cambridge University Press.

Sanders, H. 1915. *Der syntaktische Gebrauch des Infinitivs im Frühmittelenglischen.* Heidelberg: Carl Winter.

Sandved, A. O. 1968. *Studies in the Language of Caxton's Malory.* Oslo: Norwegian Universities Press and New York: Humanities Press.

Scalise, Sergio. 1984. *Generative Morphology.* Dordrecht: Foris.

Schachter, Paul. 1976. A Nontransformational Account of Gerundive Nominals in English. *Linguistic Inquiry* 7.205–41.

1978. English Propredicates. *Linguistic Analysis* 4.187–224.

1983. Explaining Auxiliary Order. In Frank Heny and Barry Richards (eds.) *Linguistic Categories: Auxiliaries and Related Puzzles*, vol. II. 145–204. Dordrecht: Reidel.

Scheffer, J. 1975. *The Progressive in English.* Amsterdam: North-Holland.

Schmidt, A. 1962. *Shakespeare-Lexicon.* Revised and enlarged by G. Sarrazin. 2 vols. Berlin: de Gruyter (originally published 1874–5, 1902).

Schmidt, Fredrik. 1900. *Studies in the Language of Pecock.* Uppsala dissertation Uppsala: Almqvist and Wiksell.

Seebold, Elmar. 1966. Die ae. schwundstufigen Präsentien (Aoristpräsentien) der *ei*-Reihe. *Anglia* 84.1–26.

Seppänen, Aimo. 1979. On the Syntactic Status of the Verb *Be to* in Present-day English. *Anglia* 97.6–26.

Shieber, Stuart M. 1986. *An Introduction to Unification-based Approaches to Grammar* (CSLI Lecture Notes 4). Stanford: Center for the Study of Language and Information.

Simon-Vandenbergen, A. M. 1983. On the Decline of Dynamic *May. Studia Neophilologica* 55.143–5.

Skeat, W. W. 1897. *Chaucerian and other Pieces, being a Supplement to the Complete Works of Geoffrey Chaucer.* London: Oxford University Press.

Söderlind, J. 1951–8. *Verb Syntax in John Dryden's Prose.* 2 vols. (Uppsala Essays and Studies on English Language and Literature 10, 19). Uppsala: Lundequistska.

Solo, H. J. 1977. The Meaning of **Motan. Neuphilologische Mitteilungen* 78.215–32.

Sommerstein, A. R. 1972. On the So-called Definite Article in English. *Linguistic Inquiry* 3.197–209.

Spevack, Marvin. 1968–80. *A Complete and Systematic Concordance to the Works of Shakespeare.* 9 vols. Hildesheim: Olms.

Standop, Ewald. 1957. *Syntax und Semantik der modalen Hilfsverben im Altenglischen:* MAGAN, MOTAN, SCULAN, WILLAN (Beiträge zur englischen Philologie 38). Bochum-Langendreer: Pöppinghaus.

Steele, Susan. 1978. The Category AUX as a Language Universal. In Joseph H. Greenberg (ed.) *Universals of Human Language*, vol. III: *Word Structure.* 7–45. Stanford: Stanford University Press.

Steele, Susan, Adrian Akmajian, Richard Demers, Eloise Jelinek, Chisato Kitagawa, Richard Oerhle and Thomas Wasow. 1981. *An Encyclopedia of AUX: a Study in Cross-linguistic Equivalence* (Linguistic Inquiry Monographs 5). Cambridge, Mass.: MIT Press.

Stein, Dieter. 1986. Syntactic Variation and Change: the Case of *Do* in Questions in Early Modern English. *Folia Linguistica Historica* 7.121–49.

1990. *The Semantics of Syntactic Change: Aspects of the Evolution of 'Do' in English* (Trends in Linguistics 47). Berlin and New York: Mouton de Gruyter.

Stockwell, Robert P., Paul Schachter and Barbara Hall Partee. 1973. *The Major Syntactic Structures of English.* New York: Holt, Rinehart and Winston.

Storms, G. 1961. *Ne say þu hit þin areȝe* PA(T) 204. *English Studies* 42.304–5.

Stowell, Tim. 1989. Subjects, Specifiers and X-bar Theory. In Mark R. Baltin and Anthony S. Kroch (eds.) *Alternative Conceptions of Phrase Structure.* 232–62. Chicago and London: University of Chicago Press.

Stump, G. 1985. *The Semantic Variability of Absolute Constructions* (Synthèse Language Library 25). Dordrecht: Reidel.

Sweet, Henry. 1891–8. *A New English Grammar Logical and Historical.* 2 vols. Oxford: Clarendon Press.

Sweetser, Eve. 1982. Root and Epistemic Modals: Causality in Two Worlds. In M. Macaulay, O. Gensler, C. Brugman, I. Čivkulis, A. Dahlstrom, K. Krile and R. Sturm (eds.) *Proceedings of the Eighth Annual Meeting of the Berkeley Linguistics Society.* 484–507. Berkeley: Berkeley Linguistics Society.

Taglicht, J. 1970. The Genesis of the Conventional Rules for the Use of *Shall* and *Will. English Studies* 51.193–213.

Tatlock, J. S. P. and A. G. Kennedy. 1927. *A Concordance to the Complete Works of Geoffrey Chaucer and to the Romaunt of the Rose.* Washington: Carnegie Institution.

Taylor, John R. 1989. *Linguistic Categorization: Prototypes in Linguistic Theory.* Oxford: Clarendon Press.

Tellier, André. 1962. *Les Verbes Perfecto-présents et les Auxiliares de Mode en Anglais Ancien (VIIIe S.–XVIe S.).* Paris: Klincksieck.

Thráinsson, Höskuldur. 1979. *On Complementation in Icelandic.* New York: Garland.

1986. On Auxiliaries, AUX and VPs in Icelandic. In Lars Hellan and Kirsti Koch Christensen (eds.) *Topics in Scandinavian Syntax.* 235–65. Dordrecht: Reidel.

Tieken-Boon van Ostade, Ingrid. 1987. *The Auxiliary Do in Eighteenth-century English: a Sociohistorical–Linguistic Approach.* Dordrecht: Foris.

1988. *The Origin and Development of Periphrastic Auxiliary 'Do': a Case of Destigmatization* (Dutch Working Papers in English Language and Linguistics 3). Leiden: Rijksuniversiteit te Leiden.

Traugott, Elizabeth Closs. 1972. *A History of English Syntax: a Transformational Approach to the History of English Sentence Structure.* New York: Holt, Rinehart and Winston.

1982. From Propositional to Textual and Expressive Meanings: some Semantic-pragmatic Aspects of Grammaticalization. In W. P. Lehmann and Y. Malkiel (eds.) *Perspectives on Historical Linguistics.* 245–71. Amsterdam: Benjamins.

1989. On the Rise of Epistemic Meanings in English: an Example of Subjectification in Semantic Change. *Language* 65.31–55.

1990. From Less to More Situated in Language: the Unidirectionality of Semantic Change. In S. Adamson, V. Law, N. Vincent and S. Wright (eds.) *Papers from the 5th International Conference on English Historical Linguistics, Cambridge, 6–9 April 1987.* 497–517. Amsterdam and Philadelphia: John Benjamins.

Traugott, Elizabeth Closs and Ekkehard König. 1991. The Semantics–Pragmatics of Grammaticalization Revisited. In Elizabeth Closs Traugott and Bernd Heine (eds.) *Approaches to Grammaticalization*, 2 vols. vol I. 189–219. Amsterdam: Benjamins.

Trudgill, Peter and Jean Hannah. 1982. *International English.* London: Arnold.

Tversky, A. 1977. Features of Similarity. *Psychological Review* 84.327–52.

Uszkoreit, Hans. 1986a. Constraints on Order. *Linguistics* 24.883–906. Also published as report CSLI–86–46, Stanford: Center for the Study of Language and Information.

1986b. *Categorial Unification Grammars* (Report No. CSLI–86–66). Stanford: Center for the Study of Language and Information.

Venezky, Richard L. and Antonette diPaolo Healey. 1980. *A Microfiche Concordance to Old English.* Newark, Del. and Toronto: Pontifical Institute of Mediaeval Studies.

Visser, F. Th. 1946–56. *A Syntax of the English Language of St. Thomas More: the Verb* (Materials for the Study of the Old English Drama, series 2) vols. 19, 24, 26. Louvain: Librairie Universitaire.

1963–73. *An Historical Syntax of the English Language.* 3 parts. Leiden: Brill.

Voglsam, J. 1951. Der Gebrauch des Verbums *to do* im Tagebuch des Samuel Pepys. Innsbruck dissertation.

Wallum, M. K. 1973. The Syntax and Semantics of the English Modal Verbs from the Late Tenth to the Fifteenth Century. Michigan dissertation.

Warner, Anthony R. 1982. *Complementation in Middle English and the Methodology of Historical Syntax.* London: Croom Helm, University Park: Pennsylvania State University Press.

1983. Review of Lightfoot 1979. *Journal of Linguistics.* 19.187–209.

1985. *The Structuring of English Auxiliaries: a Phrase Structure Grammar.* Bloomington: IULC.

1986. Ellipsis Conditions and the Status of the English Copula. *York Papers in Linguistics* 12.153–72.

1987. Two Verbs with the Infinitive in Shakespeare's English. In P. Edwards, V. Newey and A. Thompson (eds.) *KM80: a Birthday Celebration for Kenneth Muir.* 141–2. Liverpool: School of English, University of Liverpool.

1989a. Multiple Heads and Minor Categories in Generalized Phrase Structure Grammar. *Linguistics* 27.179–205.

1989b. The Range of Gapping and the Status of Auxiliaries. *York Papers in Linguistics* 14.297–307.

1990. Reworking the History of English Auxiliaries. In S. Adamson, V. Law, N. Vincent and S. Wright (eds.) *Papers from the 5th International Conference on English Historical Linguistics, Cambridge 6–9 April 1987.* 537–58. Amsterdam and Philadelphia: John Benjamins.

1992a. Elliptical and Impersonal Constructions: Evidence for Auxiliaries in Old English? In F. Colman (ed.) *Evidence for Old English. Edinburgh Studies in the*

English Language, vol. II. 178–210. Edinburgh: John Donald.

1992b. *English Auxiliaries: a Lexical Account in HPSG*. York Research Papers in Linguistics, YLLS/RP 1992–1. York: Department of Language and Linguistic Science, University of York.

Weerman, F. 1989. *The V2 Conspiracy: a Synchronic and a Diachronic Analysis of Verbal Positions in Germanic Languages*. Dordrecht: Foris.

Weida, Gudrun. 1975. *Der Gebrauch von 'Shall/Should' und 'Will/Would' in englischer Prosa am Ende des 16. Jahrhunderts*. Munich dissertation. Augsburg: Blasaditsch.

Wekker, H. Chr. 1976. *The Expression of Future Time in Contemporary British English*. Amsterdam: North-Holland.

Wienke, Helmut. 1930. *Die Sprache Caxtons* (Kölner anglistische Arbeiten 11). Leipzig: Tauschnitz.

Wierzbicka, Anna. 1988. *The Semantics of Grammar*. Amsterdam and Philadelphia: John Benjamins.

Wilson, Sir J. 1915. *Lowland Scotch*. Oxford University Press.

Wright, J. E. 1892. *A Grammar of the Dialect of Windhill*. London: English Dialect Society.

Wülfing, J. E. 1894–1901. *Die Syntax in den Werken Alfreds des Grossen*. 2 vols. Bonn: Hanstein.

Wyld, H. C. 1923. *Studies in English Rhymes from Surrey to Pope*. London: John Murray.

Zagona, Karen. 1988. *Verb Phrase Syntax: a Parametric Study of English and Spanish*. Dordrecht: Kluwer.

Zwicky, Arnold M. 1980. Stranded *to*. *Ohio State Working Papers in Linguistics* 24.166–73.

1985. Heads. *Journal of Linguistics* 21.1–30.

Zwicky, Arnold M. and Nancy Levin. 1980. You don't have *to*. *Linguistic Inquiry* 11.631–6.

Zwicky, Arnold M. and Geoffrey K. Pullum. 1983. Cliticization vs. Inflection: English *n't*. *Language* 59.502–13.

Index of scholars cited

General index